Copyright © 2018 Sam Gambier

All rights reserved. No part of this publication may be reproduced, stored in a retrieval system or transmitted, in any form or by any means without the prior written permission of the author.

This edition published 2018 by Sam Gambier

Terning

Around the world by bike.

Sam Gambier

To my parents

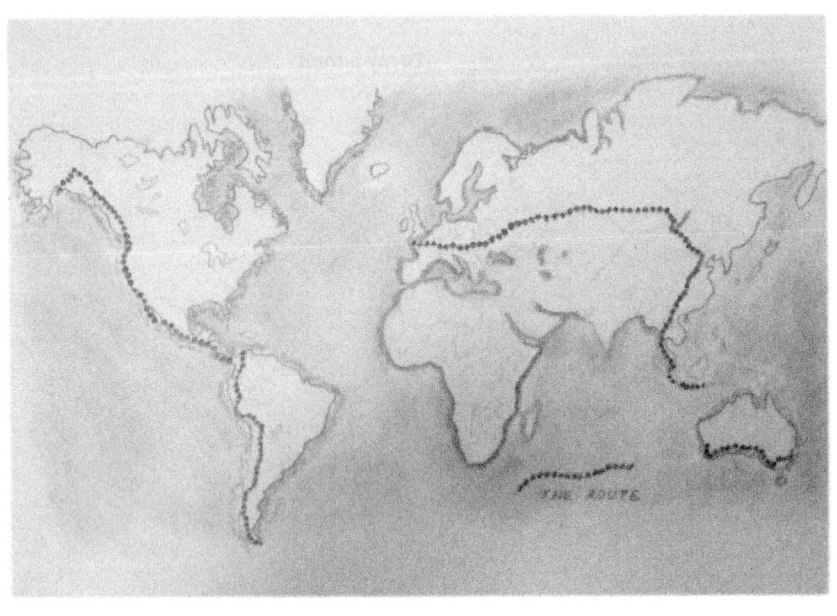

What about the world?

The idea is there now, formed by the lines of roads leaving Europe to the east, and spreading and joining with others across Asia, and beyond. And once the idea is there it will not go away. Once it is thought it cannot be unthought. And then, one day, I say it and it is real. Not just for me, but for others. And it grows. And soon I have a bike, and a tent, and visas, some money. It has become more than an idea.

All my imaginings end with death. It is my death and it terrifies me. It will be a story of proximity, I tell myself. My proximity to home, and my loved ones, and in the end (my mind seems always to skip to the end) my proximity to water, my proximity to a bullet. It is hard to quell my imaginings, and I do not try. For though they almost always end in death, and though I am often stricken with fear as I trace my finger along the map, my imaginings also thrill me. I close the atlas, wondering how I will cross the Gobi, as the road on my map comes to an abrupt halt. I imagine sand dunes. I have never seen a picture of the Gobi. I imagine a train of camels and an open expanse of sun and sky and a vast emptiness. I imagine myself, my proximity to help, a broken bike, no water. My imaginings always end in death.

I have never been clapped for riding a bike before, but as I leave the village square, applause clatters behind me and propels me forward. I cannot change my mind in front of so many people.

I ride through the village, past my primary school, my house, on up the hill until the bay lies beneath me to the west, from the lighthouse to St. Ives. It is the same route I ride to work; a strange way to begin a journey around the world. I try not to think as I follow the road towards Plymouth.

Europe

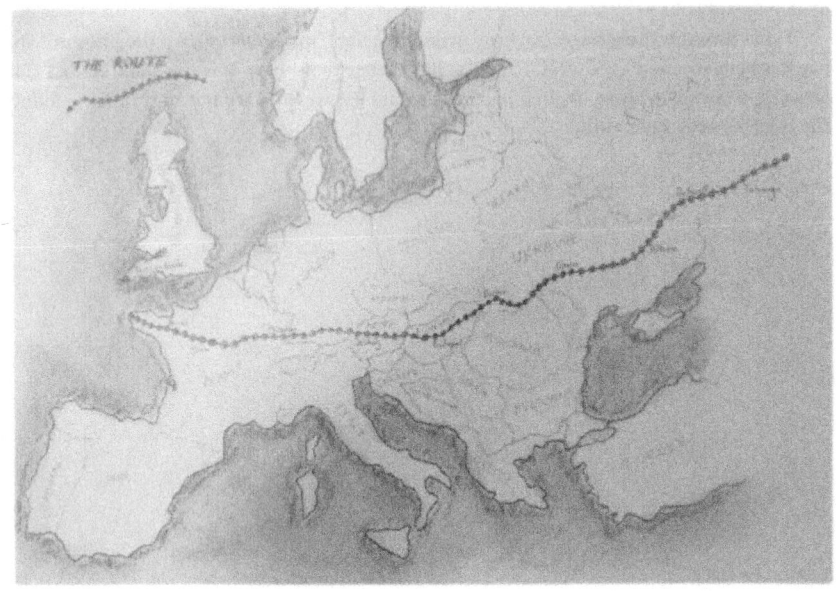

France

22nd March – 1st April, 2009

I sit by a closed campsite, waiting for dark.

I leave my bike, squeeze through a hole in the fence and look around.

Unused in winter, the campsite has fallen into disrepair – overgrown grass and rusted padlocks. A door hangs dead on its hinges. Inside, dried, stale human excrement, wet, piss-damp concrete and a sweet, acrid smell of urine and diarrhoea. The toilet chain clings to a metal lever, unhooked, broken and dry.

It will do, but I'll have to wait. No good, pitching a tent before sunset. Not in view of the village across the lake.

On the far shore, houses are shuttered against the cold, the village almost silent. I do not think about what I am doing. I do not think of tomorrow. I do not think of Rennes, or Germany or Austria. Russia, China, Singapore. Or what will happen from there. I think only about the dying light, and whether the campsite will be safe.

Perhaps, this is how it will be; a life in the shadows of others, waiting until people sleep to hide in dark places, on unused land, in forests, in the dark unseen. While the people who belong sleep in their houses, I, who do not, will be here, unseen and transitory. Perhaps I will harden against the cold that creeps now into my fingers, and the fear in me will lessen or become part of me. I will slip by unnoticed, leaving only a squashed patch of grass, a patch of dirt, broken twigs and crumpled leaves. And in the mornings, I'll be gone. So, now, I tell myself –get used to it. For stupid as it seems, this has been chosen by you. It is the first day in France, for now, don't think too much.

Two figures draw closer. I look up as they pass and smile.

"You are cycling from England?"

I nod. "I'm cycling round the world," The words come out automatically. They sound funny. I have cycled for 2 days – 160 miles. But I smile as I say them and they embolden me somehow – make it more real.

"I love travelling," the man says "But the times I like most are when people invite me to their houses. To their homes. If you want, I live there," and he points across the lake to a row of small houses. "You can stay. We're going for a walk, but we'll meet you there. I'm Jules, by the way. This is Izumi."

"I'm Sam."

As I watch them turn the corner something like joy overwhelms me. The first night. A place to stay. Perhaps, I think silently, this is how it will be.

I push my bike across a small bridge to the front door. I am not used to its weight. My wrists strain against it to stop it falling into the ditch below. It is too heavy. It pulls down on me as I roll it through the door, a tired, dead weight.

We sit at a small table and drink tea. Jules rolls a joint, passes it around. Izumi leaves to pick up her child.

"Will you send me a postcard when you get to Mongolia?" Jules asks, as he fills a galette with cheese and ham.

"*If*," I say. "*If* I get there, of course I will."

I think about how I must look; what I am saying I will do, and what I have done, so far apart.

"You'll make it," he says. "I'm sure you will. 100, well, 99 per cent."

I write his name and address in my journal and in brackets the words, POSTCARD, MONGOLIA.

In the morning, I leave Jules outside the little white house with blue windows. The smoke from his roll-up mixes with frozen breath and disappears in the air, and I say my first goodbye, my first thank you.

...

It is not our quaint English countryside, not the hilly southwest of close horizons, sheltered by trees. The French landscape stretches out until the sky blurs with trees and the edge of my sight. Bare branches, wispy grey, fall black with dusk. There is nowhere to sleep where I would feel safe and I refuse to spend money on a hotel, so I continue. The roads are empty. For an hour, not a car passes. My front light picks out a circle in the night and bright reflective sparks shatter the dark like stars; broken glass and cat's eyes. Above too, the night is clear, and real stars shine, icy bright, and cold. Signs roll past, in and out of the circular light like an old black and white film; *Luceau, Neuvy-le-Roi, Château-Renault, Blois, Lilly-en-Valle.*

These villages and towns huddle against the winter; frost is in the air and the cold burns my fingertips. I calculate that if I cycle all night I can make the 200 miles to Gien on the Loire River. The wheels roll on, steady through the dark and I pass through tiredness; crisp air wakes tears in my eyes and the landscape slips past unseen.

At 3am I stop, exhausted. My light flickers, dims and dies and the glow around me fades until I am standing in the grey village with only my breathing, caught silver in the air, and the scrape of my shoes, loud against the road. Away from the village a tree sticks its naked branches into the sky and a field lies bare under the stars. I have cycled for 15 hours and I am empty. Gien will have to wait until tomorrow. I follow the road out of the village, turn up a dirt track towards the blackened tree and the promise of sleep.

I rest my bike against an overgrown hedge; brambles claw down and frost glistens on the thorns, colourless under the moon. I sit on the cold ground; legs burning still, but knees frozen. I roll out a sleeping bag, take off my shoes and lie between the bike and the track. Over my face, the shadows of spindly branches fall, and the rustle of mice or birds disturbs the silence. I snatch moments of unconsciousness, and wake in panic. I check my passport and money are under my t-shirt and feel in the darkness for the lock, still tied around the bike's wheels. The saddle bag lies, a heavy lump, at the bottom of my sleeping bag and rubs against my calves. All these things. I wish I didn't have to worry about them. I don't know whether it is the fear of their loss or the cold that keeps me awake, but I stare at the empty sky until the darkness stings and I close my eyes.

When dawn comes, the frozen air has seeped into me. The dirt, grey or blue before, is brown and sandy in the new light, and the bramble leaves have moved to green. I do not really know if I have slept, but when I stand up and shake away the stiffness in my legs I feel alive, and safe in the quiet of the new day. I pack the sleeping bag, damp and covered in a film of light brown dust, and push the bike back towards the road, the brighter, eastern part of the sky caught in sunrise fire.

...

It is true that I am happier in the mornings. The day is brighter then and I feel the excitement; that with every turn of the pedals, I am carried to somewhere I have never been before, and in everything I see novelty. My eyes open and I drink it in; the loneliness, the adventure and how small I feel. It terrifies me and fills me with fear and delight, and shooting rushes of excitement, and I think about whether I could love this new life.

I cycle through a village; two straight lines of houses and bungalows without a centre. Now, in the first week of spring, people are in their gardens, cutting down trees and trimming hedges. An old man ploughs his front garden with a hand-held petrol plough; rusted blades chop mechanically through the soil, grown dense and heavy with winter. The man walks backwards, pulling the heavy object as it slices the thawed ground. And in the morning, I love this scene; the sense of utility and energy, how everything is used here; the farmland all around, and people's gardens. The bright air awakens me and I speed through the village, joyful and unslept.

Already though, I know, the afternoons are full of dread. As I think about where I will sleep the shuttered windows turn from quaint, to dull, to hostile and the endless farmland and private property, untenable. I glance in panic, searching for woods and other dark shelter.

...

I get to Gien early. The campsite office is only just opening and the smell of coffee and crackling bacon fills the air. I pay ten Euros, put up my tent and sleep.

When I wake, there is still enough of the day left to cross the Loire, over an old stone bridge, and stock up on food. I buy 2 litres of Coca-Cola and find 500g of chocolate for 1 euro. I eat almost half of it, sandwiched in a baguette.

I make coffee and take out a Lonely Planet guide to Russia. I am too tired for real reading. On the back pages is a map, depicting all the time zones from Alaska in the west across to New Zealand in the bottom right hand corner. I look at how far I have come in 6 days and feel despair. The world is fucking huge. I close the book, vowing never to look at a world map again.

The afternoon of rest is too long. It gives me time to think. I begin to ask myself stupid questions. What am I doing? Am I happy?

Am I happy? I am strong, I tell myself, and strong people can live without happiness for a long time. So no, I am not happy. But, not unhappy either. It is early, and this life feels strange and lonely to me. And this, after only 6 days. To talk about strangeness and loneliness seems absurd. But I cannot help but think of what is to come, and feel, therefore, not the loneliness of 6 days, but of 600. And being so close to home only makes the direction in which I am going more difficult to understand.

Now, if people ask, I will be able to tell them, at least what it is like to start cycling around the world on your own. You will feel a desperate loneliness and a great love for all the people you have known, and a longing to be with those that you love. You will feel very small and very fragile and very vulnerable. If you didn't consider yourself to be dependent upon the company of others, now you will crave it more than anything. And for safety, familiarity and belonging.

...

In Vesoul, after 9 days, I phone home for the first time. My mother's voice sits next to me, inside me almost. What she says I barely hear, but I feel her there, her voice, with the same tones and warmth as ever. I feel myself gag as I try to speak. And I struggle against a crying which seems to rise from my stomach and fall into silence, looking at the floor, as a single tear falls and splashes on the concrete below.

...

'Why?' was always the question before I left. I had so much practice the answer should have been rehearsed, and finely honed. I should be able to captivate my audience with a witty line; something thought-provoking and memorable. And yet, my answer always changed: "I want to know my world." I told them, vaguely. "I want to understand the spaces between people." "For charity," I lied, or "It was the best thing I could think of."

None of these answers really touched the truth. "I want to be interesting." I should have said. "I want you to be interested in me." "I want to have sex with beautiful women, who now I'm scared to talk to, and I think this will make me seem attractive." "I am scared of dying having done nothing. I am dull in my life and I have no work to do. I am untalented, and my looks frustrate me, and my flabby soft body annoys me, and my stupidity makes me rush with boiled up anger. But when I finish this, I will know all about the world and about the people in it, and when I tell girls that I have cycled around the world their knickers will fall off." But I never said anything like this and people looked at me, bored, as I mumbled something about the space between us.

Now that I have started, I don't know *why* – only that I feel that I have begun something that I cannot stop. Something that is too big for me.

...

The countryside around Vesoul reminds me of the Yorkshire Dales; no sheep or drystone walls, but pretty and quiet, away from the industrial hum of car factories, and the sprawling grey mess of the city. I don't know if it is truly reminiscent of the Yorkshire Dales, or anywhere I have been, but I cling to the idea and find comfort in the imagined familiarity.

...

Then the Alsace Mountains come into view. At five miles an hour I climb, twisting my way up the mountain until snow lies, piled up high by the sides of the road, and the melting ice seeps into the tarmac below. From the pass, the road tumbles down to Masevaux. And it is a joyful thing, to descend a mountain on a bicycle.

Germany

1st April – 7th April, 2009

I cross the German border on the 1st of April. On one side France is still sleeping, or waking from hibernation. On the other, people are out walking dogs and cycling, driving expensive cars and living in expensive houses - big wooden frames and glass.

Police drive in convoy. In the first day in Germany, I see more police than I did the entire time I was in France. They move quickly and with purpose. *Polizei*, the word itself is harsh and unsettling, and the way they stick together, gang-like, as if awaiting riots. I wonder what they are all for as I cycle through quiet mountain villages.

The afternoon light dims towards night, and I stop at a small patch of forest. A car park and a wooden hotel stand at its side and footpaths crisscross through the trees. I wait for the path to become clear and push my bike into the undergrowth, the dry cracking of twigs and the light padding of pine needles below. I wait till dark, to put up my tent. Its green melts beautifully into the forest and the way it loses its shape and becomes almost invisible in the dusk puts my mind at rest. I sit on the floor outside, playing with twigs and listening to the hum of insects and the growing gaps between birdsong. I breathe in deeply and feel the fresh, earthy dampness of the forest air. Below people pass, walk dogs or jog; flashes of bright clothing through the trees. I think about the stories I listened to as a child; bandits waiting in the forest to ambush passers-by.

From my vantage point, I can also see the car park through the trees and I watch it slowly empty as the light disappears. I am about to go to sleep when I hear the rumbling of engines below and see another convoy of police enter the car park and come to a standstill. I can still distinguish the green and white lines and make out the word *POLIZEI*, painted in sharp font onto the sides of their vehicles. Perhaps that's what these convoys are for; arresting people who try to camp in forests. It seems there's little else for them to do here, and someone must have seen me. I duck down, waiting for them to get out of their cars, but no-one moves. I wait as the evening draws up through the trees, colours turn to silhouettes and objects in the distance become hazy until eventually I can barely see the tent a couple of feet behind me. Convincing myself that the police have not come for me, I climb back inside my tent and listen to the forest's noise, quieter now with the dark. The sounds come sparse and jarring; long silences broken only by a snapped twig, or the scattering of feet and wings. When I wake in the morning the police have gone.

...

The first rain comes at night. Drops fall into my cooking pot, lightly at first, so that the flame still burns. I stare at the food. Pasta, mushrooms, onions, salt and butter in water, a kind of rubbish soup. Wet food for a wet evening.

At night, the rain on my tent is like the cracking of fire; the taut canvas bursts in explosions and sparks as I lie awake in black flames. In the morning, grey drizzle falls, silent as cinders, and I rise, mud squelching under foot, to brush water from the tent, to load the bike again, and head east.

...

I ride across the south of Germany. The sky is blue and butterflies in love flit in and out of my path, in courting dances. Bright blue and white they cling to each other in the warming air, tumbling in and out of flight. Are they thinking? I wonder. And, is it love that they are feeling? Do they know why they cling to each other and whirl in and out of each other's grip, oblivious to the world around? And do they know how small they are?

And how their wings are like silken paper without substance? Scores of butterflies fill the road, each one devoted to its pair, and the mating ritual, if that is what it is, takes place with an air of delicate violence. Lightly they crash and collide, catch hold of each other and lock in a fleeting embrace only to separate again. One of the butterflies gets caught in my spokes, and is knocked and battered around, too soft and light to die at the initial blow. Then it falls and lies unmoving on the ground. From that moment I begin to notice too, the corpses of other butterflies, caught in the passing traffic, their dusty paper wings flickering with the last efforts of life or tousled by the breeze.

...

I cross a bridge over the motorway, and get the attention of a boy about my age who is listening to music with big headphones.

"*Ich suche einen campingplatz.*" I say to him as he takes the headphones off. I say the words wrong. I don't know if the *ch* should be a k sound or a sh sound, or neither. But the word *campingplatz* seems to be understood, if not for my delivery then because it is almost night and I am carrying a tent.

"*Campingplatz?*" The boy says to himself. "Where are you from?"

"England."

"And you've ridden all the way? From England?"

"Yeah, well apart from the sea." I have already heard enough jokes about not being able to cycle across water on a bike.

"Wow," he says, "that's pretty cool. Where are you going?"

"Well, around the world, maybe – that's the plan. But Austria now – I should get there in a couple of days."

"I wanna do that," he says. "Maybe, I will one day. Is it hard?"

"I don't know, really – I guess I've just started." I ask him about what he does and he talks about his studies a little bit, and playing music in a band.

"Well, anyway man, that's cool," he says. "Good luck! Cool t-shirt by the way – I love the Pixies."

I thank him and leave, marvelling at his English and the way he said 'wanna' and 'cool' and "by the way". I feel invigorated after such a simple conversation and I realise that it is the first time I have spoken to anyone for over a week.

Austria

7th April – 12th April, 2009

I leave the river banks of Salzburg, and wind my way up the mountainsides. Now, in April, the gentle heat of the sun soaks into my back while the mountain breathes; crisp cold air rising from the not yet melted snow. I love the sensation, and I realise as my legs turn hard against the climb, that I am beginning to love this; this journey. I feel my life becoming simple. Rising, moving, sleeping. And the world has changed again. Now, in Austria, the air seems cleaner, and the lines are crisp; rock and snow against deep blue skies, and lakes absorb the world and shine its image back.

I am also discovering hunger. I devour bread and cheap Swiss rolls; I empty packets of peanuts and eat yoghurt half a litre at a time. I count the calories in supermarkets; 1000 calories for a euro is my aim. And always sugar. I live on junk food until I feel the need for fruit. In the evenings I pour packets of powder and pasta and rice into water, stirring and boiling until it becomes the consistency of food. I sometimes find myself staring at livestock and hungering for its flesh.

The road circles pristine lakes and runs through small towns and pretty farmland. Churches nestle in sheltered valleys or teeter impossibly on cliff tops. And the road runs further still to the vertiginous banks of the Danube. I follow the river's curves east, to Vienna.

...

I leave Vienna's city centre and walk back to the campsite, stop at a shop and buy 6 cans of beer, reduced to 25 cents each. It is the first time I have drunk alcohol in three weeks, and I feel myself swimming and thrilled by the drug. I delight in its warm sensation, at the difference in my state of mind. It is an old and constant friend; its effects barely changing, its ability to heighten my mood, to share in my joy and wallow in my misery. I could have chosen this very easily, I think. How it compliments me perfectly, and how after a while it allows nothing but itself; how hard it is to function. How lovely it is to slip into useless drunken slumber, and how my mind now scrawls upon itself half-finished recycled thoughts, and congratulates itself upon their insight. I must drink more I think, and fall asleep.

In the morning, ants have invaded my tent. I have spilt jam on the floor and they feed upon it. I brush them out, tearing unseen limbs. I wonder if in some world smaller than our own, their world, the sound of this tearing is as violent and horrifying as the cracking of bones, and tearing of flesh, and screaming. But it is a time to be brutal. I cannot have a tent full of ants. I crush them with my fingers and lightly rub their legs, and bodies and eyes and brains into a small black paste and flick it into the grass outside. What a tiny act! How easy! These deaths will not trouble me; it is no more than the crushing of an ant. A tiny speck of the universe rubbed out, to turn to something else, barely visible now in the grass outside. And yet I know that for this ant this was everything. That its life and being has all come to an end, and with my fingertips I may as well have crushed the universe and all that it contains. It is over; it is the same, I think. I have killed just now not an ant, but the universe. Fifty universes.

Hungary

12th April – 18th April, 2009

Flat into Hungary, the road falls into disrepair; potholes eat away at the tarmac and its edges crumble into the grass. The check point at the border is deserted; an empty concrete shed sits as if it were on a neglected building site. Someone has sprayed the word *Servus!* on the wall in red, friendly graffiti. There is no natural border; the land flat bright green in front, flat bright green behind. I dig around my bag for the Forints I have carried with me from England.

It grows hot, and my body feels lethargic and heavy. Real food would be good. I'm tired of this powder stuff I pour into water. I see the process like a broken illusion before me; powder to food, and I stop believing in it, and now my body feels sapped of its energy.

Hungary is emptier than other countries, and greener. The west of the country has no smell and the cycling is boring, flat and easy.

After 3 days, I reach Budapest. Dirt, petrol fumes and dust rise in thick clouds and the road fills with traffic; machinery clangs and screeches from building sites. The city is chaotic and ugly in the urban sprawl. By the time I reach the centre there is already too much to forgive the city for; I've seen what it has become and I cannot love it.

At the top of a steep track the campsite is an old converted railway station. A woman watches me struggling up the hill, disappears and comes out with an ice-cold beer. I collapse into a bench, and try to take small sips, aaaaaaaaaaah.

It is 4000 Forints to camp, more than a day's budget, including breakfast, but I will enjoy being in a city.

Budapest is beautiful, even after the sprawl; all carved stone and old, but living and unclean and not like Vienna. A thunderstorm gathers in the sky, clouds like dripping ink ready to burst above the city. But the sound that rumbles is not thunder, but human voices from a nearby square. I walk around the corner. Angry words break over speakers and armed police line the road. A crowd gathers, many holding Hungarian flags with the numbers *1956* scrawled across them in black ink. Some of the flags have huge holes ripped through the centre, like symbolic bullet holes, ripping out the heart of the fabric. Sirens ring through the air and more riot vans screech to a stop; police pour out with Perspex shields and batons. Then the first drops begin to fall, thunder cracks and the rain falls, torrential, in a curtain-like cascade. I leave the gathering crowds and run for cover.

At the campsite I ask a lady about the demonstrations, but she says her English is not good enough to explain what was happening.

...

In the morning, I eat. Bread and jam, cheese, sausages, ham and pancakes. And three cups of thick, black coffee. It is the first time I have eaten real food in weeks. I race out into the city; east through the morning traffic. Cars brush past my panniers and I breathe fast and heavy, exhilarated and alert, with a pounding heart.

Caffeine races through my blood and now the east is here. Budapest becomes a gateway. Behind me is everything I have known, all the static past; the hundreds of thousands of rotations of my wheels, and the path I have followed. The safety of it, I think, all that I have done I have survived without scars and it sits, unmoving, but also gone; unchangeable apart from the distortions of memory. But now I long for the past, and its certainty; for the deep green forests of Germany, with their padded pine needle beds, and police, and the knowledge that nothing came out of the darkness. I feel the hot dry sputtering of lorry fumes breathe into my face and horns rise behind me. I brake hard, dodging in and out of cars and out of the way of motorbikes, and always this sense of being propelled forwards, by something else, hurtling towards the unknown and thrown into the future. The coffee and the sound of horns burn in me, and my mind is unsettled and anxious. All my energy is poured into pushing the bike forward, out towards the east, towards the morning sun, and the traffic is wild, like a sea.

After 22 miles the city lies behind me, and I pull over to sit by the edge of the road and breathe. There is a change in the air, almost imperceptible. If it were not for all the coffee in my veins, would I notice it? There is something hanging off the buildings, like some kind of half invisible veil. Or is it the buildings themselves which are slightly crumbling? Something has changed crossing now into this East of Hungary, but it is difficult to say what it is. Before, the green fields of the west had seemed an extension of Austria; the towns, new and tidy and the change to Forints superficial. Giant new Tescos had dominated the landscape outside even the smallest of towns, packed with the same stuff I could buy back in England.

I stop. For the first time I feel conspicuous. People's skin is darker and more weathered; their clothes thicker, more substantial, more homemade, or simply older, made to last longer, dull earthy colours. Old ladies, with dark crisscrossed brown skin and grey hair and hats, lean out of windows or over garden walls as I pass and I feel a slow wave of stares follow me, until I come to a fork in the road.

A group of children runs towards me, as I take out my map, carrying sticks and an old half flat football. "Whas your name?" They shout at me in turns, laughing delightedly at the words, and staring expectantly for a response.

"My name's Sam." I say.

"Sam?"

"Sam."

They burst into fits of laughter, peals, screaming at themselves and dancing with delight. "Saaaaaaaamm!" they scream, "Saaaaaaaaaaaaaaam!" pointing at their eyes and almost crying with laughter at the absurdity of my name.

"What's your name?" I ask one of the older boys, who has stopped laughing and stands next to me, looking inquisitively at my bike.

"My name is Gergo whas your name?" He replies, joyful and mechanical, unbreathing between the answer and the question. The other boys come back screaming, "*One. Two. Three. Four. Five. Six. Seven. Eight. Nine. Ten.*" I look impressed and they start again, "*One. Two. Three. Four...*"

After several counting renditions, an old lady comes out from her home and speaks sternly and calmly to the boys and they scatter like pigeons, reforming their group again at a safe distance and run away; one of them hits the punctured football with a stick and the thud of it and the peal of laughter flies past us at the fork in the road.

The lady smiles at me and says something to me, pointing at the map. Or maybe she isn't smiling; she has a flat steady face not made for easy smiles, but a calm face that gives the impression it is smiling without the need to actually do so.

"*Tokaj?*" I ask her, and she looks puzzled.

I point to the town on my map, "*Aah, Tokaj,*" she says. "*Tokaj.*" The vowel sounds seem longer than mine, the *j* becomes a *z* almost. She thinks, and points right, down the hill. Further into the east.

...

I camp just a couple of kilometres from the Ukrainian border on a flat patch of forest. Winter's leaves are still brown on the ground, softened by rain and time and voices come from the village, muffled and distant. I sit silently in the clearing, listening to the sounds around me, and placing them before night falls and they lose their shape, mutate. Birdsong has changed, the birds different to those I had heard in Germany, so I have moved through borders other than man's. The light rustle of leaves in the breeze sparks the quick scattering rustle of an animal in the undergrowth; the falling of leaves then, the crack of falling twigs and branches, and then the light patter of rain. Again, as night falls, the drops on taut textile become the crackling sizzling popping sound of fire and the rain warms and burns the darkness.

In the morning, I gather myself and my things. I look at the perfect angular shape my tent has left on the ground; light brown against dark. There is something beautiful and satisfying in the mark I have left; straight lines in a forest, two almost right angles. There are no right angles in nature; they are an expression of man, corners. I think about this patch and if it would catch the attention of someone walking in the woods. It is perfectly balanced; man-made, but unobtrusive. How long will it take to disappear? And will the leaves around it fade into the same pale brown, now in the dryness of dawn? Or will new rain wet these leaves, protected all night so that they too will be one again with the forest floor. I smile, pulling my bike through the leaves and over branches, knowing that no-one will ever come across it. I am no longer cautious about the noise I make; the cracking of sticks and heavy breathing that I fear may betray my presence when finding a place to sleep at night. Now I am almost triumphant. It is like I have tricked the world; another free night in the woods. I feel for an instant like the world is mine. I can sleep where I want, and in this I find some quiet sense of power. I am also beginning to feel close to nature. I know nothing about it. I can identify only a handful of trees from their leaves, and fewer birds from their feathers and calls, but I am beginning to love it. I love the feeling of playing with the soft brown leaves and being there as the woods turn quiet. I love watching ants carry away small scraps of my food, and I follow their path to the entrance of their world. I wonder if their communication is as silent as it appears, or whether, if I reached their level, I would hear the steady hum and drone of busy direction and communication. I wash my hands with wet moss, like a sponge, and breathe in the deep, fresh earthy smell, my hands wet with the night's rain.

Ukraine

18th April – 4th May, 2009

At the border the guards smile and wave me to the front of the queue, past the cars and trucks that glint under the sun. They ask me questions and I tell them about the journey. I stumble though, on the words *transkontinyentalnaya veloexpeditziya*, and when I look up they are staring at me blankly. It is the first time I have been able to try out the Russian I have learnt. It is perfect; they ask me what I have in my bags, and I recite all the things I know in Russian, and leave out all the things I don't.

"Guns? Drugs?" They ask, laughing.

"No."

They ask me where the sausages are from. "We don't want any meat from the UK," they say, and then say something I don't understand which I guess is about foot and mouth.

I speak so little, and so badly, but, for the first time since leaving home, I feel like I can talk to people.

I cross the border with a 3-month visa in my passport, and my first stamp, feeling happy, and open and smiling at everyone and calling out to people "Dobry dyen!" But apart from a few old women, I meet only with blank stares. People's faces turn hard, and cold towards me. The buildings crumble and become dilapidated, but even then, they seem rigid and stern, frightening somehow. The beautiful Cyrillic script that I have dreamt of is everywhere, the harsh angular edges of its font peel off shop fronts and road signs. XYCT says the sign. "Khoost" I mouth the word, practicing a throaty kh sound and stretching out the long ooo. "Khoost"

The road follows the gentle slopes that rise to the Carpathian Mountains and as the sun falls toward the western horizon, I scan the landscape in search for trees or cover. Nothing.

Twenty kilometres later, as I begin to lose hope, I see a sign for a campsite lying, rusty, in an old farm yard. Outside a stable two blonde girls play, chasing each other around in circles, though when they see my bike, they skid to a stop in the dusty ground, and stare at me.

"Is this a campsite?"

They look at each other and laugh, perhaps at my accent, perhaps at the fact that it is obviously not a campsite.

"Can I camp here?" I ask. They laugh again and I am about to give up when a lady, who I take to be their mother, comes out.

"You can sleep over there," she says, pointing across an overgrown field, "by the river."

The two girls walk with me. One of them holds out a stick so that it rattles against my spokes until the other takes the stick away from her and uses it to swipe at the long, wet grass. HHHWWWWPPP. It slices. HHWWWPPP.

When we get to the spot next to the river, light drops have already begun to fall and above us black clouds mark the encroaching thunderstorm. "Zdesh." Says the girl with the stick. Here.

"Is there any water?" I ask the girls and one of them points at the river flowing past our feet and starts laughing. The water is brown, caught up with mud, and all along the bank are cans and bottles, plastic bags, torn and clinging to the trees.

"To drink," I say, and the girls run back towards the stable carrying the empty bottles from my bike.

Ten minutes later they are back with the water. The younger girl holds out her hand. "20 Hryvnia," she says smiling. I give her the money; perhaps her mother has asked her for it, or perhaps this is what campsites are like in the Ukraine. But they run away laughing and whispering to each other; perhaps I've just been robbed by two little girls.

...

My Russian visa has already started ticking and I count the miles I need to cover to reach Mongolia in time. 75, 80 a day and I make it. Just.

I race through small towns in the south-western corner of the Ukraine. The place is wary of me, and I of it; like some invisible distance lies between us, as if I were staring through a pane of glass from outside the world. Men stand outside smoking and drinking in the morning sun and follow me with their stares, as though they too were looking at me through glass, deciding whether to smash it.

It is only when I stop, when I rest my bike against a wall and sit on the floor, that I feel the mood dissipate into something resembling friendliness or at least curiosity. One of the men will rise from the table and come over, offering simple words. "Where are you from? Where are you going?" These are always the first questions, the first words. How to take them? Simple questions, but wonderful and deep too. How many possibilities! "Where are you from? Where are you going?" I offer nothing clever. I answer their questions. "From England. Around the world." Some break into a gentle smile, and some seem astonished, others stare blankly, incredulous, or laugh like I am joking. I have a young face; I might have run away from school.

Again, it is the thought of not knowing where to sleep that disturbs my peace. My life now is very simple; I wake, I eat, I move, I see and hear and smell, and feel the movement in my body and the good it does and I find somewhere to sleep. It is when the thought of the latter overwhelms the simplicity of my experience that I am moved to unease, a nagging feeling of being lost, or alone.

I sleep again, hidden in the forest. Ukraine, ah the Ukraine... tomorrow I will try to sink into her. For I feel very much now as if I had been thrown upon her surface. Full pelt.

...

In Rachiv the small guesthouse I find is full; a group of artists from across the Ukraine have gathered to paint the mountains and eat and drink and speak together. It is Easter and the country is on holiday.

Emma, the host, doesn't let me turn away.

Have you come far? She asks.

From England, I say.

"*Eez Anglee*," she says, her eyes wide open and her face soft and round. "*Mozhesh spat zdesh*," she says. You can sleep here. "*Mozhesh*," she says again, the sound long and kind, "*mozhesh*."

Somehow, she sees my need; for a place, for a temporary home. She asks her daughter to clean out a small study and they organise a makeshift bed.

...

I wake up early. The room is full of gentle yellow light and everything seems to be glowing; a pile of clothes catches the light and specks of dust fall, golden in the air. The smell of coffee comes from the kitchen. The artists are deciding where to go, looking at a map of the national park and discussing where they could drive with the small van that is parked outside. Emma gives me a bowl of soup, and a thick slice of bread. She puts her hand on my shoulder and tells me to eat. "*Kooshai,*" she says, soft and smiling. The soup soaks into the bread and the dough becomes drenched; tiny bubbles of oil run in the water, coiling in the stock and running off the darkened wetted bread dripping back into the bowl. I say thank you for the soup and leave to explore the town.

The track that runs away from the guesthouse is dust dirt brown. A dog barks viciously and runs towards me. I jump away, and it snaps against its short chain, spinning round on its neck; the chain clangs taut and slack as the dog's neck twists hard against its pull and is, again, pulled back, trained to be angry and driven slowly mad.

Rachiv feels like it is gently crumbling; corrugated metal roofs and walls glint in the sun, and the warped wooden walls of houses, like soaked and rotten drift wood, drunk, lean diagonally wise against the roofs. Smoke rises from small fires, through rusty metal chimneys, and old Soviet factories lie decrepit and deceased. Rubbish tumbles out of bins, unemptied for weeks and dogs pick at the waste; tear at plastic bags with their teeth. Two men ask me for money. I refuse, apologise, and they politely turn away.

I follow the river downstream, its gentle rushing current to my left. Cans, bottles, plastic bags, scraps of paper, empty tins lie in the long, unkempt green grass; it doesn't look like any national park I have seen before. I walk into a shop to buy cheese and bread for the next day. A lady stands behind a counter, like an old chemist. Behind her, tins, packets and boxes line the shelves. It seems scanty, poor, rationed; perhaps this was what it was like to buy food in wartime. I wait in line and ask how much it is for cheese; there is one type of cheese; hard and white. I ask for 100g and then, on seeing how little the 100g is, another 200.

As I leave the shop, I see a man, lying face down, drunk on the ground, unconscious. His skin is hardened and sunburnt red; matted hair and unkempt bristly stubble, but shaved a few days ago, not homeless. His clothes seem like they would be stiff to the touch, scuzzy, crisp and dry, that they would stand up on their own. In the heat, the smell of piss rises from the ground. His forehead rests upon his arm, like it had been a decision to sleep here, albeit a hasty, unavoidable one, but a decision, not just falling. I cross the road, stepping around him.

I look at him and remember waking up in an ambulance, 3 years before. *They thought you were dead*, were the first words I remember the paramedic saying to me. The day had started in Trafalgar Square at a Love Music Hate Racism gig, watching Belle and Sebastian and Pete Doherty. I had a bag full of cava and beer and vodka. I remember the warm drunken rush, passing around a bottle to strangers, talking and feeling generous and happy. Then I remember the ambulance, the brightness of its lights, and the unfamiliar firm, padded mattress beneath me. They had picked me up in an area of South London I had never been to before, lying face down on a busy street. *They didn't want to check if you were breathing* the paramedic had said. *You could have had a knife, or you could have been violent.* I sat in the waiting room for an hour, before telling them I wanted to leave and walking home.

Anonymous is how I had felt then; a drunk, a stupid drunk in the middle of the pavement in London, in a neighbourhood I had never been to, and would never go to again. What was I doing? Had I simply missed my stop, or was I looking for something? Blank. I felt stupid. I felt like I had wasted the time of the paramedics and the doctors, and deep inside I knew that what I had done was dangerous; for hours I wasn't there, or at least I could remember no conscious thought or ownership of my body. Why didn't I just walk into the road or fall into a train track? Some underlying sense of survival must have kicked in, but I could have done anything. I was anonymous though; lost in a huge city, to fade back into it, and I was allowed to forget the incident, or at least hide it, not speak about it.

Rachiv, I think, looking at the man. Rachiv is too small. Here this man must be known. As his spit dribbles onto the pavement and his piss soaks into the ground, and his neck grows even more sunburnt, the people must think: There he is, there's what's his name, again; pissed. His poor kids, poor what's her name, at home; drunk again. I feel sorry for the man on the ground; here he will not be able to forget, and in the small town I know the best way to relieve the shame will be later, with another bottle of vodka.

A funeral procession runs past; a military tank rolls slowly down the road at a slow walking pace. Flowers are strewn over the dark army green; delicate, straggly and weak. In front of the tank a priest walks, his stride slow and rhythmic as though being paced by some silent internal music. Little girls wear dresses and seem to be constantly straining themselves against the will to walk faster. Just behind the tank, leading the small crowd, an old woman in black is being helped to keep pace. She wears a heavy black headscarf and light thin wisps of silver-grey hair escape, falling bright over worn out skin. I turn away and the procession begins to sing; something aching and beautiful fills the sad and sun soaked streets.

I sit looking over the cemetery from a distance. Men with shaven heads cross themselves, their necks bowing in front of a big, twisted cross with ornately corniced edges. They wear suits. Most of the men in the town wear suits in fact, not just those in the funeral procession. Old suits, shabby, strange looking suits. Blue suits, polyester suits, rough old woollen suits from decades past, or from no time. The men have hardened faces and a dormant ingrained sadness; something permanent, not simply called for in this hour of visiting the dead. They cross themselves and kneel before the graves.

A man, in a grey t-shirt, too big for him, crosses the road. I prepare myself to refuse him money, to refuse him bread and cheese. I feel my hand sweat, gripping the plastic bag. He rocks slightly, steadying himself against the spin of the world and his eyes stare out from deep within him. His face, bordered by short grey hair, is deeply lined, and a kind smile with closed lips spreads across roughened skin. Two big ears make the face seem boy-like, as if he hasn't yet grown into them. He holds out a cigarette and asks for a light. I fumble around in my pockets, holding the small thin plastic bag containing the cheese in one hand, and bring out a cheap yellow lighter.

He lights his cigarette and grins. Slowly, he lifts his hands to my face, holds them there an instant, covering my ears almost, the smoke gently rising from the cigarette, and he kisses my cheek. I feel the wetness of his lips, the scratch of stubble lingers on my skin for an instant, and I smell the sweet strong scent of vodka on his breath.

"*Kak tebya zavoot?*" the words slow and separated, purposeful; *Kak. Tebya. Zavoot.* Clear drunk words. It feels good to be asked my name, before being asked where I'm from.

"*Meenya zavoot Sam,*" I tell him.

"*Meenya zavoot Ivan,*" says Ivan.

I follow him up the steep, muddy path to his house; a huge metal skip rusts in the ground and old chicken wire twists and gets lost in the grass. Old boards, corrugated iron, and rusted metal stakes form fences between the gardens and the tiny houses. And always, as if spewed up by the earth all over Rachiv, cans and bags and bottles lie, half submerged, in the wet and muddy ground.

White sheets and clothes hang on metal wires and string, blown and tossed around in the breeze. As we pass, an elderly neighbour sees Ivan and shakes her head. From her garden comes the warbling, squabbling sound of chickens.

"This is my friend," Ivan tells her. "From England. We're going to my house to drink vodka and smoke cigars."

Ivan crosses himself as we walk up the hill, and crosses himself again as he looks down towards the river. He breaths in the fresh air, and it seems like something rises within him; something rapturous. Tears appear in his eyes, and he crosses himself again. "My land," he says, proud, as though the cans and the bottles and the rubbish across the valley remain, by him, unseen.

He leads me further still, up the path; the wooden shacks around grow more dilapidated still.

"I have another bottle of vodka at home," he tells me. "And cigars."

Ivan stops a girl walking past him, and puts his arm around her shoulder. "This is my daughter," he tells me. "*Eto moya doch.*"

The girl releases herself from his embrace, and continues walking down the path towards town. When we reach the house, Ivan's wife is waiting in the garden. She is bigger than him, and stronger, and soberer. *Ivan,* she says, angry and he cowers and the joy goes from him. For the first time he seems to become conscious of his drunkenness and uncomfortable. He begins to speak, but his words are half-hearted and feeble. With a barrage of angry words his wife sends him inside the house; his head falls, and he follows like a chastised child. She waves me away, and, as I walk back down the hill, the argument begins; her strong voice and his weak one. And quickly, then, his silence.

Back at Emma's guesthouse, I am invited to eat again; spiced pork ribs in a beautiful herby sauce. After a month of eating food from packets, I feel the richness and the freshness of the food like a tonic; full of warmth and happiness. We talk around the dinner table, into the evening and for a moment, I feel like I belong.

The next day I say goodbye to the family and the artists. They wish me luck, and as I leave I feel something for the first time. Like I have left a part of myself there, and I am carrying a small piece of them with me.

...

I ride up the valley from Rachiv, over the Carpathian Mountains. The last vestige of winter, white snow browning and muddy at the edges, clings to the crevices and the north facing slopes, eating away at itself. Ice melts and undercuts overhangs, and collapses in a slow and warming suicide.

...

I am in a kitchen speaking with Katia and Anna. They both speak good English. And from that moment it is always Anna. She smiles, and her eyes shine bright when we talk, and sometimes she looks down, and there is sadness in her eyes. And maybe it's the sadness that I like the most. She puts her hand on my thigh, without shyness, leaves it there. Rests it there, and squeezes gently.

"So you haven't been out, in all this time?" she asks, her hand now on my knee.

"I've been camping, mainly. In forests. Kind of boring. Well, not boring, just a different kind of, you know."

She still has her hand on my knee when she looks at me and says, "Tonight, you will drink."

Katia casts her a look. "She has a boyfriend in Holland," she says. To me. But she is looking straight at Anna as she says it.

Anna glances back at her. "I haven't seen him for six months." She says, but she takes her hand away from my knee slowly, and if there was ever any doubt that the touch meant something, it is gone now. And maybe there is no touch that means nothing; no act, no word or smile.

"I would love to travel like you," she says. "But it's so difficult for us; not just the money, but the visa, the permits, everything. It's like they say, Ukrainian – second class."

I would marry her, I catch myself thinking. Just so she could move, I would marry her. And the conversation moves on.

"Don't you miss your boyfriend?" I ask. It is a stupid question. I don't know why I've asked it – to show that I have listened, that I've heard and understood.

"I used to miss him," she says "but now it's dying. There's nothing – soon there will be nothing."

I wonder whether she would have used the same verb in Ukrainian. Dying. A thing, a time, a life between two people, dying. It seems beautiful and sad. "Anyway," she says, "he's probably fucking other girls." And the word hangs there in her soft foreign accent, *Fucking*. Out of all the words it is those that stay the longest, and won't go away, it's like you can see them painted on the air. *Fucking other girls*.

The girls clear away the plates: the pickled vegetables, cold meats, and salads that had covered the table. In the kitchen I hear them exchanging muted words, hurried and strained.

"We're going out," says Anna, returning. "We're going to call our friends. They'll meet us at the bar."

I am wearing shorts. I go to change. I still look stupid; I have no clothes for going out.

When we arrive, the bar is dark and full of smoke, and noisy with the sound of laughter and raised, drunken voices. Their friends are all boys. They order vodka and six shot glasses. The bottle comes, ice cold, a thick and freezing sheen around the glass. Anna saves me a place next to her on a wooden bench. Katia sits at the other end of the table.

One of the boys raises the first glass, and makes a toast, welcoming me to the Ukraine, to Kolomiya. Everyone drinks; the freezing vodka smooth and tasteless sliding down my throat, sinking into my stomach and spreading into my blood in thrills. Everyone reaches for the food in the middle of the table; crackers and salami, and I follow. After the third shot, I begin to feel comfortable. Each time the glasses are raised someone makes a short speech, which Anna translates, whispering or speaking softly in my ear. Each time she turns to me, her hand rests on my shoulder for a moment longer than it did before. "He's talking about his sister and, oh, I can't explain it properly in English, but it's really funny." I feel her hand on my knee and I lean in towards her, and put mine over hers. Is that worse? Is it me then? The knee and the thigh and the shoulder, maybe this was just friendly, but it is me who touches her hand first and now our fingers, lightly interlock. Another bottle is brought to the table. But now the alcohol has awakened in me, more than lust, the search for oblivion, that familiar fall to unthinkingness that I crave at the taste of alcohol. I feel myself growing indestructible, laughing and joining in with the conversation, and the shots of vodka flow easily. I go to order another bottle, but Anna stops me. "No. Tonight, you don't spend any money." My head swims, I am losing myself. First Katia says goodbye and leaves, and then we are stood outside saying goodbye to everyone else, Anna holding my hand.

On the way home we stop to help a hedgehog out of a ditch. "Yorzhik." Anna whispers softly, as if she were talking to a kitten. "Go on yorzhik."

I am drunk. Only the cold night air keeps me standing as Anna turns to me and puts her arms around my neck and kisses me. It is a long, drunken kiss. She bites lightly on my lip, and then she starts to gnaw my chin. There is a moment of clarity, when I stare into the black sky, with a girl gnawing at my chin, at my neck, like a bear, and I ask myself what I'm doing. It is too late now. I am too drunk to make decisions and even though I'm sure the biting thing is weird we turn and go back to the guesthouse.

I am so drunk that I take us into the wrong room. It is empty though, and I close the door. I run to the bathroom, but as I pull down my trousers I piss for a second into my boxers and over the toilet seat before steadying myself. For a second I panic, thinking what to do. I scrunch up the boxers, throw them in the bin and wipe the toilet seat clean; I wash myself and pull up my trousers, and walk back into the room as if I hadn't just pissed myself. Anna is lying on the bed. I'm too drunk, I tell myself and I feel myself falling, and then there is only black.

I wake up naked, holding her, my face nestled into her back. Lightly, without thinking I brush the nape of her neck with my lips. I feel cigarettes and vodka, dry and bitter in my mouth; repulsive and stale. I get up and stagger to the bathroom, throw water on my face, and brush my teeth. My eyes are bloodshot and I grimace at myself from the mirror.

When I lie down, Anna turns to me, "You're fresh," she says. "I'm not. Wait." She gets up to go to the bathroom.

...

Outside it is brighter than the day before and she walks beside me. I still feel slightly drunk, and my stomach turns and my head hurts, and the taste of vodka has returned to my mouth and my saliva has become a thick, dry paste. Anna is wearing sunglasses; her hair is combed in a neat fringe, tied back in a ponytail. She doesn't look like someone who has been out last night. I glance at her for a moment, over the loaded bike between us.

"Do you want to stay?" she asks me, looking up. I can only just see her eyes through the dark brown lenses.

"I have to keep going. My visa."

"Ah. Your visa," she says.

I don't know what to say. I feel embarrassed and ashamed of myself. We walk for a while in silence, the sun catches the old white buildings of Kolomiya and makes them shine.

"Have you been good?" she says, after a while. "I mean, do I have to worry?"

"No. You don't have to worry."

"Well, thank you," she says, and she kisses my cheek. But not like last time. This time it's a sadder kiss; everything about it is different. I don't know what it's for; I don't know whether I should remember it or not. I leave. It is difficult to move the bike. I don't turn back. I feel a number of emotions all at once, but most of all I feel shame.

...

What if? I think. I think of diseases. Infections. Viruses. Sex is something dirty. From the moment it was talked about in my life, it has been accompanied by warnings. I remember being taught to be scared of blood when I was a child in school. You do not touch it; it carries disease. Disease that can kill you. Sex, I have been taught, is like rubbing together two open wounds. There is fear in sex; fear of blood, and spit, and cum. What if? I think. And I think of a child, unwanted. And I think about a jealous boyfriend, driving across Europe, chasing me. On my blog there is a link to my satellite tracker so that my friends can follow my progress. I press the button as I set up camp and a marker appears on Google Earth. I imagine Anna's boyfriend tracking me down, driving from

Holland, murdering me in my sleep. Stupid. I have not missed what excessive alcohol consumption does to my mind. Yesterday, everything seemed like one, so unified and comfortable. I felt so close to people and hadn't worried about myself, about what I looked like, what I said, what I did. Everything had held together; one big whole, and I had been a part of that whole. Now, everything seems to be falling apart, and I feel the pangs of guilt like stabbing pains. Stupid. I want only to get through the day, to reach Chernovitsi and sleep. The hills of south-western Ukraine drag on torturously, up and down, never getting anywhere. My head feels like it would explode no matter how much water I drank, and I feel my body shaking. As I push the pedals round, slow and churning, images of the night before flash through my mind, and again, embarrassment and shame.

Slowly my head begins to clear; my vodka addled blood runs clear, and I feel sweat run from my pores and imagine that it is cleansing me, throwing out the bad intoxicating substance that is making me feel sick. I count down the kilometres to Chernivitsi, 45, 38, 30, almost there. I feel a change in the bike; it becomes softer, and sinks. For a second I don't realise what has happened. I glance at the milometer; it is the first puncture, after 2235 miles.

I lean the bike against a concrete wall. I unload it, remove the wheel and take out a small metal shard with my fingers. I patch the inner tube, run it around the rim of the wheel and hook it over the tyre bead, flipping the last taut stretch over with a lever and run my hand, again, around the rim to check that it is fitted, that it will not pinch and burst. I am inflating the tyre when a man, wearing camouflage trousers, a camouflage jacket and hat, opens the gate in the wall and comes towards me.

"Everything good?" he asks.

"Everything good."

His name is Yuri. "Come in!" he says. "We can drink vodka." He speaks Russian for me, slowly.

"No," I say smiling. "I can't. I drank too much last night."

"Aaah. Where are you from? Where are you going?"

"I'm from England. I'm cycling round the world."

He repeats the words to himself. *Eez Anglee. Mire.* "Would you like a cigarette? No? No, you're a sportsman."

"Not a sportsman," I say "just travelling."

I am resolving to leave when another man opens the gate and comes outside. "I'm Igor," he says. "Yuri is my friend. Come in – we have food and coffee and marijuana."

I push my bike into Igor's yard. Wooden pallets lean against the walls and beams lie stacked up neatly on the ground; criss-crossed under corrugated iron to protect them from rain. The house is still under construction; the bricks, not yet pointed, have visible layers - changes in style, suggesting sudden bursts in energy, or periods of saving for materials. Each window is different and a big red metal roof, sits on top, waiting for the walls to reach it.

Yuri and Igor lead me inside to a small kitchen; the floor is still bare concrete; a tall fridge stands by the wall and Igor fills a metal kettle and places it on the stove. A pan is simmering gently and Igor removes it from the heat. "Fish soup," he says.

Igor pours sweet, black coffee; the table fills with cold cuts of meat, sliced cucumbers, salami, bread, beetroot and horseradish salad and cakes. Yuri lays plates down on the table, "Eat!" he says. "*Kooshai*"

I dip bread in soup, chew the fresh flesh of fish, picking out fine translucent bones, and lay them on the edge of my bowl. "It's delicious!"

The men pour themselves more vodka, in two small glasses. I refuse more food, trying to be polite, and Igor takes a generous helping of everything and puts it on my plate. It really is delicious; full and filling food; beautiful, salty cold beef and the deep strong flavour of horseradish burns my mouth.

They have only finished one room; the bedroom already has a carpet, and a piano stands against the wall. "My daughter plays," Igor tells me. And the unfinished house of bare concrete walls is warm and already a home; Igor smiles and glows with pride and we sit and talk again. We talk about our homes and our jobs and our families and Igor takes out a framed black and white photograph and points to his grandfather.

"I was a soldier too," he says, "a UN soldier in Lebanon."

"That must have been a hard job, hard work. *Tyazhyorlaya rabota.*"

"Hard? No. We smoked, we drank, in the evenings we walked into town – I wasn't there long. I loved Lebanon."

Yuri fills a small pipe, pours vodka, again, into the two small glasses, and Igor continues to speak. "I'd love to travel more, but it's always the same. It's difficult for Ukrainians to get visas. I went to Europe once." He uses the word Europe, *Yevropa,* as if we were sitting somewhere outside of the continent, not Europe, not Asia, no place.

"I liked Spain," he tells me. "I liked the life there; the heat, the food, the wine. I felt free in Spain, people let me be. In Germany the police checked my papers all the time, always stopping me – like I was dirty." He points to himself with a grin, "Polish face."

Igor pours more coffee, and Yuri lights the pipe; the pungent sweet smell of cannabis rises in thick, coiling smoke.

"What about your favourite country?" I ask.

"*Ukraina.*" They say. Both of them at once, laughing. An easy question.

Igor's wife and daughter come home; his wife does not seem surprised to see me or concerned by the almost empty bottle of vodka on the table at 4 in the afternoon. She smiles at me warmly and carries a bag into the bedroom.

His daughter, who is eight, plays the piano for me. She plays, tentative at first, her fingers slowly working over the keys, until her left hand finds a rhythm and the room fills with gentle, practiced music. When she finishes Igor holds her tightly and kisses her cheek; he has tears in his eyes and he is beaming. He asks me if I want to stay the night.

"Thank you," I say. "But I have to keep going. Thank you so much. *Spaseeba Bolshoi.*"

It is true that I have to make progress. But I don't think that's the reason I refuse the offer. It has been two perfect hours; all my thoughts have turned to the present, I have lost reflection, and my mind that has tortured itself all day seems at peace again. I have loved sitting here in the kitchen, feeling the warmth of a family home and time has felt like liquid, something free and flowing and not fought against. But now I want to leave the experience as something wonderful; I am scared of touching it; I am scared of waking up with a hangover; shaking, and awkwardly saying goodbye; I am scared of losing the memory. I am scared of damaging this thing, these two kind hours of hospitality and deep generosity. As I cycle the last 15 miles to Chernovitsi, I feel myself bursting with all the kindness people have poured into me in such a short time.

...

I ride long days from dawn's first light to the dying glow of the sun, when all the forest is shadows of itself and the world is quiet and still. I ride long days and push on, across central Ukraine, until I reach Uman.

The city's face is crumbling and cold. Tree roots rupture the pavements and dirt settles, embedded in the cracks, until it looks like it has been this way forever.

The city is full of grand old disintegrating buildings. Statues are left with missing fingers and chipped faces, standing above poor fountains; bottle caps and crisp packets glint like worthless coins under the surface of grim, milky water. I stand, looking up at a concrete man, a rough flat patch in the middle of his face, and I wonder where his nose is; lost or turned to dust.

The city is made of sharp grey concrete bus stops, tower blocks, and pot-holed roads, the noise of buses and cars. Sunlight splatters the ground with blinding specks of white light. And underneath the city, even in the early afternoon, violence simmers in the heat. It is in the stares of men, in their clothes and in their shouts, their spitting, and the squealing of the traffic and the sharp lines and the way the city crumbles, and falls apart; shedding pieces from its skin like someone unloved, or loved poorly and ill-treated.

I push the mahogany door of a cheap pension and it swings, slow and heavy, on its hinges.

"You can't stay here," says the maid. She wears a starched white apron that gives her corners. "Not with a bicycle. It's not allowed."

I push my bike back out into the city, and walk away from the centre down a quiet tree-lined street. The second cheap hotel stands, its windows boarded up, covered in graffiti. Smashed glass and rusty metal wire lie on the floor, eaten up by brambles and vines where a garden used to be. I sit on the wall, facing the derelict building, thinking about what to do next.

I look down at my bike. Some people name their bikes. I see cold metal and wheels. A chain. Dead material things. Hard. Something too expensive to lose. Something I depend upon, that carries me, but hangs around me too. I look back up the road, towards the pension and down again. I do not see a name.

I am looking at my map, at the roads trailing east out of the city, when I feel the presence of someone near me. I turn around to see a woman carrying two plastic bags, and staring at me. Her hair is dark black and dishevelled and her make-up has run slightly under her eyes. She is drunk. "It's closed," she says, and I look behind me, again, at the wrecked and boarded building.

"Do you know another cheap hotel?" I ask her, and she mentions the one I have tried before; the maid with pointy corners and the face which has already formed in my memory as a face with hard edges, whether it truly was or not.

"They won't let me in." I say. "Not with a bike."

She looks at me for a moment; her eyes glazed over. "I have a house," she says. "It's a student house. For a little bit of money, you can stay there for a night."

The woman's name is Vicky. We walk down the street until we reach a group of small houses and turn off the road onto a dry, dirt track. My bike dips into smoothened holes in the road, the earth compressed and hard. We walk past people's yards; chickens run around in mud, pecking at grain. There is a squabbling fight between them and amidst the flurry of feathers a chicken is pushed into a corner, its white wings beat against the wire. The hen snaps back angrily and the other chickens retreat; a feather gets caught momentarily in one of the holes, and is loosened by the breeze and floats down, rests, upon the dirty ground. By one of the single storey houses, a goat is tied with a piece of rope to a metal ring sunk into the wall. It stands chewing over the ground, bare and with only the odd sinewy blade of grass in a perfect semi-circle, denoting the animals reach within the world.

We walk further through the houses. An old woman holds a bucket underneath an old metal pump. Her arm slowly moves the creaking handle, up and down, and the water surges out in rhythmic, gushing torrents. The sound of the city is heard, only faintly now, through the trees and the group of houses feel like a small, old village; a place from another time, hidden by trees among the tower blocks and concrete streets, forgotten.

Vicky opens the front door and leads me into the kitchen: a gas pipe feeds an old brown stove, and covered buckets rest by the fridge. She shows me the sitting room; for 50 *Hryvnia* I can sleep on the floor. It is not cheap; she has the glazed eyes and shaking hands of an alcoholic, and the need for money of an alcoholic too. But she is not unkind; there is a warmness in her, and I trust her. I decide to trust her.

The girls come home a little later; we drink coffee around a table which looks like something that should be in a caravan. Yuliya, Lesya, Olena and Oksana. They are, apart from Oksana, English students, and they speak well, if tentatively. They sit, away from me, and make small, cold conversation. They are guarded and wary of me – I note the way they throw quick glances between themselves and I worry that I have intruded. They don't know who I am, why I am here.

"Why don't you take something out the fridge?" Vicki says to Yuliya and she gets up, slowly, almost against her will. The other girls go to help her, light the stove, bring the pan to the boil, and soon the table is full; soup, and bread; salads of eggs, salami, gherkins and mayonnaise; fish stuffed with vegetables and spices; stuffed cold pancakes; mashed potato and meat and home-pickled vegetables; courgettes, cucumbers, peppers and tomatoes. I try to eat a pickled tomato with a fork and it grows heavy and bursts over my plate and its juices run down my fingers. "*Konyechno,*" I say, and I feel my cheeks burn. "Of course." The girls laugh. I look up and they are smiling at me; something has changed between us; the room feels suddenly kinder, more comfortable; something tense that had hung in the air has burst.

"Do you want some vodka?" Vicky asks me. "*Khoteesh?*"

"A little," I say. "*Choot choot.*" But the girls flash me panicked looks or warning looks. Yuliya, shakes her head in a minute unseen gesture, with just her eyes almost, as Vicki turns her back and dips a jug into a huge vat of homemade vodka. It is too late; I cannot refuse. I take small, careful sips.

The girls clear the table and we go outside into the village in the middle of the city with its sound of farm animals. Oksana brings out a bottle of something red that she calls *Vincheek.* She has made it with her brother and the word *vincheek* makes the other girls laugh. It tastes sweet and strong and homemade. She makes the first toast to her grandfather, who has recently died, and tears come to her eyes, and the next three glasses she fills to the brim.

The shadow of tall buildings blocks the sun now to the east, and the heat of the afternoon grows pleasant and cool. The girls speak of their hopes for the future; of travel and work abroad, and they speak of their expectations; wives, teachers, civil servants.

As we clear away the glasses, and get ready to go out Yuliya turns to me, suddenly serious. "You should be careful," she says, and she lowers her voice to a whisper. "Vicky. She's not an honest woman."

"You mean she'll steal?"

"No. Not steal. Just be careful."

I am still running these words over in my mind (Careful how? Careful of what?) when we reach Sofiyevski park.

A guard stops us. "Where's your alcohol?"

Yuliya looks at him. "We don't have any."

"Then what are you doing in a park?"

"Walking," she tells him.

The guard looks doubtful as he lets us pass. "Walking!" he says to himself and then something else that I don't understand.

The park lies like some beautiful rich soul of the city in the crumbling grey mass of Uman. Its slopes and leaves turn the warm air cool and the violence I saw earlier in people's faces disappears. Paths wind in and out of the thick undergrowth, and trees rise, not tearing the ground, but gently heaving the shifting soil and moving it aside. The whole place seems intoxicated with some beautiful, tranquil sadness; the way people slow and their gaze grows calm and lingering.

We stop at a lake; gentle swarms of lily pads float on the surface, and ripple away as two swans swim towards us. A long, white neck stretches out and an orange beak shakes in the green water, sends shining droplets flying in all directions as the beak tangles itself amongst the reeds.

Oksana asks me if I carry a knife.

"No," I say laughing. "No, I don't." I look to the other girls to help me with the second conditional, frustrated at my Russian. "Tell her that if I carried a knife, I'd probably be the one to get stabbed with it."

Yuliya translates and Oksana looks at me, her eyes narrow. "You should carry a gun," she says and lifts her hand up into the air like a pistol, and makes the sound of a bullet being fired. "Puuffv!"

"I hate Russians," she says. Her face is pretty and doesn't grow less pretty for what she is saying. Her eyes flash at me, sad and serious. "Russians are criminals. Here in Uman, criminals. Russians, Ukrainians; criminals. You should carry a gun."

"I don't think that's a good idea."

She looks at me straight, already knowing the answer to her question. "Where do you sleep at night?"

I hesitate, "In the forest. Mostly."

"You will die," she says, and the others try to hush her. "If you sleep in the forest in the Ukraine, you will be killed by bandits, in Russia; eaten by wolves."

I laugh at her, and she shakes her head. "It's not funny," she says. "The world is full of liars and cheats and thieves. Don't trust people. Nobody."

The others try to disagree, to dissuade her from prognosticating my violent, gory death, but she is already revelling in it. "Don't listen to them," she says. "They are filling your ears with *lapsha*." With pasta. With rubbish. "They are filling your ears with rubbish. The world is not a good place."

Yuliya looks at me, and smiles. "You'll be okay," she says. "People will be nice."

The words are meant to comfort me, but I can't help but love Oksana's more; how her eyes light up as she predicts my death and how she scorns the world playfully, as she speaks about its evil.

The sky swells purple above the trees and without us noticing the light fade it is suddenly dark. We walk back along the lake, and through the trees, past boulders, and a small white marble statue of an angel, now shining in the dark. Oksana points at the rubbish in a pond and moans about thieves and liars and people who drop litter in parks.

Then she turns to me: "Can we call you Samcheek?"

"Yeah, let us call you Samcheek," the other girls say laughing, and I feel my cheeks burn under the darkened sky, and hope that they don't see my face grow red. I feel lucky to be walking with these four girls; here, where I have never been before and at this time that has never been and never will be again. It is night in Uman. Six hours ago, I arrived here on my bike and knew no-one, and now, I am here, walking through a park and talking with these girls. It is a small thing, this, but if it is so small, why does it seem to fill me? Why am I not thinking of where I am going or what I have done or anything else? Why, for this instant, am I only here?

In the morning, the girls wake me up with ice-cold beer, and we sit on the floor in Oksana's room before they go to university and we quietly say goodbye. I feel, for the first time as I clip into pedals and head out east again, truly sad to go, to leave something behind.

...

I ride through the Ukraine amazed. I revel in the openness of the people and feel delighted and surprised by it every day. Children chase me up hills, and quiz me and share their sweets, and old men invite me for a breakfast beer as the children walk to school eating ice cream in the summerlike heat. The kindnesses are so many, so generous and so deeply felt that I feel myself beginning to love the country. It is the most foreign place that I have visited so far, and yet it is the place where I have felt most at home. There is just one thing that separates us; they are still and I am moving.

For all the sadness I feel, when I say goodbye, there is something that propels me forward; that feeling in the morning; that today I will go further east than ever before, and I will do it myself, under my own power. Today I will see things I've never seen before, and where I will be, no-one can tell. I shake off the happiness of meetings, I hold it in me, I ride quick. I feel the sting of burning muscles and the fresh air courses through me as I glide down the long sloping hills of central Ukraine.

One day, I come to the sea where there should be no sea. I look at it disbelieving; a long bridge, supported by huge boulders, stretches across an ocean. I do not know where I am. There is supposed to be no sea, and I worry that I have taken some drastically wrong turn to find myself here. It is a while before I realise that it is a reservoir. The expanse of water stretches out; its horizon meeting only sky and waves roll gently in and crash, white upon the boulders and the bridge. It is open like the sea, and I breathe it in with my eyes. I may not see such a vast expanse of water until Lake Baikal, that long blue finger that stretches down towards Mongolia, visible on my world atlas. My legs feel hollow and weak at the thought of somewhere so far away, but I am beginning to believe that I can make it. For now, I race across the bridge, across the tiny ocean, hurtling ever further east.

...

I leave Kremenchuk behind on the road to Poltava. The sides of the road are forested by deep evergreen pine trees and dirt tracks run into the woods, away from the road. It will be easy to find somewhere to camp. I stop at a gas station to buy Coca-Cola: it has become a ritual, that when I camp in the forest I buy myself a treat; an ice-cream, a bottle of Coke, or some chocolate. When I leave the shop, a security guard is stood over my bike, playing with the gears, clicking them in and out of place. In his uniform, he looks like a policeman; a black shirt and heavy black boots laced up tightly around his shins. Held by a holster at his hip a pistol juts out prominently – I am still not used to seeing guns, and I feel my heart quicken as he turns and stands above me. He has a skin head; a dark, thin face and his chin is covered in harsh, black stubble. He speaks in a sneer.

"Where are you going?"

"Poltava."

"Now?"

"Yes," I lie. It would be a bad idea to tell him that I am just about to sneak off into the woods to find somewhere to camp.

"It's too far," he says. "It's too late."

I point to my lights and tell him it will be okay.

"Do you have dollars?" he asks. I pretend not to understand. "*Dolares*," he repeats. "*Dolares, dolares.*" He is almost shouting now.

I shake my head. He takes out a wallet and from it extracts a crisp twenty dollar bill, which he snaps taut in front of me, as though demonstrating its strength. "Dollars," he says again, smiling, betraying a silver tooth. "Give me dollars. Twenty."

I shake my head, apologetically. "*OO meenya nyet, izvinitye.*" I haven't got. I'm sorry. He stares down at me, and points at the protruding bulge from a wallet under my t-shirt in which I keep my money, debit cards, passport and things I cannot lose. "*Moi passport.*" I say.

He says nothing more as I get onto the bike, clicking the levers back into place so that the gears won't jam. As I leave he shouts to me; "Be careful. There are lots of bad people around here. *Ochen plokhiye lyudi*" Very bad people he says, and as I look back he is smiling.

I cycle away. The long straight road drags on, until a curve pulls me out of sight of the gas station. I cycle a further 10 km, praying for the forest not to run out as dusk sets in and the sky grows dark. I pull off the road, down a dirt track. After a kilometre I stop, look around, and see that I am on my own. Only now do I hear birdsong and notice the new quiet under my breathing. I look up and see the birds, in the last bursts of chaotic activity, bringing home the last scrapes of whatever it is they have found, before the night draws in and the forest becomes black and silent. I pull my bike over fallen trees and drag it through brambles, until I can no longer see the track. In the fading light I put up the tent, trying to forget Oksana's words; bandits in forests! It's 2009, I tell myself - bandits don't live in forests!

...

On the other side of Poltava a pack of stray dogs chases me out of a small village. I stop the bike and shout at them and they scatter, slinking off to nose around rubbish or skulk into the shade. I ride further up the hill, the road now gravel and dirt, and hear the sudden scratch of chasing claws behind me. I shout at the dog, try to outrun it, spinning my legs as hard as I can against the slope, but it snaps at me and tears its teeth into my skin, drawing blood, and I kick out at it, hard, and send it whimpering. When I look, it is not as bad as I thought; a pair of scratches and a slight tearing in the skin. I wash it with water, and carry on. Do I need to worry about rabies? I'm not sure. I know nothing about the disease. I decide to ignore it.

...

The road towards the Russian border passes through small villages. Wooden houses, straighter than the ones I had seen in Rachiv, stand neat like pictures, along the narrow road. A horse pulled plough trudges around a small field of corn and black and white cows lie, basking in the sun. It feels so Russian! The slow, gentle pace of life makes me think of the Cossacks in Sholokov's books; those long, rich passages about bringing in the harvest, pretty girls and rural life, before the violence comes. It's still here, I think. And I feel sure that across the border this feeling of being in a place of books and films will come only more alive; Raskolnikov's tenement blocks far away now, to the north, and his exile, along the road that I will take, and somewhere in the vast landscapes to come, I feel sure to hear the echoes of Tarkovsky's men, moaning about their existence, and gazing at the sky.

Clockwise from top left: Camping in France - Snow in Alsace – a lake near Prien – Budapest – Igor – Ivan, Rachiv - Austria -frozen slopes in Germany

Russia

4th May – 4th July, 2009

At the border, Ukrainian trucks are parked by the side of the road; the faces of their drivers suggest they have been there for days. The guards stamp my visa without too many questions, I cross into Russia and the sky grows huge. Again, I feel something invisible move; the air changes, grows tense. The world is different, and I feel it; something hollow and sick creeps into my stomach. The road doubles in width and cars drive past faster and closer.

I stop in Borisovka to get some money out; the building is bigger than banks in Ukraine. Everything is bigger, faster, newer. I do not see the Russia I have read in books. A group of men walk past; skinheads wearing leather jackets, jeans and leather boots. They lead with their arms out, ready to swing. I look down, avoiding eye contact until they have passed.

I leave the town, barely breathing. I felt these things in the first days of the Ukraine; this unease, and fear. At the beginning, everything seemed hard and unwelcoming; the faces and the scowls. But now I leave with the country inside me, warm and beating still. It is just another change to get used to. I pedal, concentrating on the traffic.

A car drives slowly behind me. I feel its engine whirr as it drives at my side; a battered red Lada, with blacked out windows, blaring out Russian rap. I look down, straight along the road, before I glance up again; they have wound down the windows; it is the skinheads from the town before. One of them lifts a rifle and points it out the window, the barrel resting on the glass. I see his face grin at me and he raises the gun, points it at my face.

My legs still rotate, stuck somehow in motion. I don't think to brake. My bike rolls, steady with the car, and I look at the gun, the black hollow of the barrel, the way it trembles up and down with the surface of the road, and I stare, unable to tear my eyes away. I do not think; nothing occurs to me. Only, I feel my body drain. And I see the men grin at my terror, and I hear their laughter as the wheels spin hot, and they leave me without breath. Has it all just been a joke? A Russian joke? My first Great Russian Joke? I cannot stop – I don't get off the bike, clip out of pedals or put my feet upon the floor until I reach Belgorod, fifty kilometres later.

....

I ride for days, smaller than I've ever been, through this part of Russia – it is like someone has taken the edges of the landscape and pulled it out so the hills become never ending gentle slopes and the horizons seem ever to expand. The steppe is farmed for endless miles and tractors look like toys, tracing fine black lines in the yellow fields. I look for forests, for places to camp, and find none.

I look for cheap hotels then: concrete soviet boxes that cost 350 roubles a night, leaving me 150 for food. The hotels are overstaffed, yet nothing works. The paperwork takes 30 minutes to complete, before I am handed the keys by a receptionist. I have to state my name, address, passport details, visa details, the purpose of my visit, where I was before, and where I will be next, filling the registration slips for the local police and then for the hotel. The forms are stamped and copied, often by hand, and I have to sign them again. Someone else takes me to my room, and cleaners sit in the corridors drinking tea. Often a security guard stands outside the doors. The hot water is cold, and the taps leak, dripping rusty water. The sink is cracked and light bulbs flicker.

I go to the post-office to look for internet and find four women talking to each other, waiting for non-existent customers and telling me the computers don't work, and that there isn't a public phone. I am asked for money continuously, not just by beggars, but by drunks, and the prices in the shops are higher than those at home. Old men stare at the shelves in confusion, picking things up and putting them down, before taking a miserable handful of something they can barely afford, and paying for it begrudgingly at the till. It seems that something has gone wrong. Outside in the streets, the world seems hard; men seem hard, and boys too as they drive cars, ride motorbikes and smoke like men. Factories rot, and lie deserted, and small shops' shelves are dusty and bare. No-one smiles and no-one says hello. The Russia of which I have dreamed, nowhere to be seen.

...

When I camp in forests everything is directed outwards. My thoughts turn out towards the light shining through the trees, the feeling of sticks and rotting leaves beneath. I listen to the sounds of the wind rushing through the forest like a great wave, and the scattering animals, the birdsong which fades with the light, and the flies and mosquitos which whine around me. I listen out for the sound of human voices, and footsteps, a distant car engine, a slammed door, predators. I look for hidden spaces camouflaged by thick undergrowth; for rotten trees or branches that could fall in the night, and clues in the forest that betray a human presence; a worn path, the bending of grass, fragments of litter; scraps of paper, foil, or an old tin can, and judge, by its state of disintegration, the length of time it has been there and whether the forest is safe. I sit outside my tent in the fading light until I cannot see my hand, held close in front of my eyes. I grow accustomed to the sounds of night; the heavier nocturnal animals; foxes and badgers. I learn to distinguish their footsteps and the way that twigs snap under them, the way they freeze at my scent, or at the unfamiliar shape of my tent looming in the darkness, and the way they scatter. I sleep and dream, not falling into myself, nor into my memories, but with relation to the immediate world outside; a gust of wind, or the howl of a distant animal, and when the thin light of morning invades my tent, so too my dreams grow bright and rouse me before sunrise.

In a hotel room my thoughts turn in towards myself. Electric light bounces around the bare walls as I read. I look down at my stomach. Small flabby rolls gather, white and pasty. My nipples are puffy and I have pointy out breasts I cannot get rid of. I am meant to be a fat person, I think, there is nothing I can do. But since I started this journey, and forgot about veganism, I have rediscovered my sweet tooth. Now my gut sags with ice-cream-chocolate-pancake-eating, beer-Coke-drinking fat, and it makes my thoughts turn viciously in at myself.

Why am I cycling around the world? It all comes down to sex, I think. I have an-inflated opinion of myself, and for a mate I look for someone more beautiful than myself. So it is no more than a mating dance. My cycle round the world and subsequent attempts at writing and further education, my displays of interest in culture and language will be no more than a transparent trick, designed for the proliferation of my genes, the swelling of my ego. The thought seems ugly, not part of me. Untrue. There is something more that drives me. Something more immediate. Without ulterior motive. More honest. I lie back on the bed and stare at the ceiling. The bare light bulb flickers, dims golden, and shines bright again.

...

In the morning I collect my things, unchain my bike, and leave. A tail wind catches me and for the first time in days I fly, effortless and giant above the open world. The sun's heat falls, gentle on my back, and the air is fresh and clean. Clouds gather then, swell and burst. Huge drops of rain fall cold upon my face, and soak my arms, and my t-shirt sticks, heavy and cold against my skin. For a month, a tiny circle of drought has followed me across Europe, it has only rained at night. Now, as the rain soaks into the ground, its scent hits me; beautiful, bitter and earthy sweet. The smell of damp leaves and wet grass fills me and I am struck by the lushness of the smell as though for the first time. It is as if, back in Cornwall, I had become accustomed and blind to its scent, as one who spends years in a smoke-filled room.

...

Outside Talovaya the land is flat. So flat, that, as Gerna sat outside his dacha, I must have appeared as a speck on the horizon; tiny and black under the vast blue sky, and edging slowly closer.

When I reach him he is waving at me, wildly. "*Ot kooda ty?*" he shouts.

"*EEZ ANGLEE.*" I scream.

He waves for me to stop and a smile spreads wide across his face. The behaviour seems eccentric after days of people looking at me through sullen, sunken eyes. The grey soviet buildings, the bureaucracy and size of Russia all seem to contrive to weigh the people down. But here is this man, bursting it seems and joyful, waving for me to stop. I look at him and see one of the kindest faces I can ever remember seeing. I stop. I have to stop. I know, I feel, I have to.

The *dacha* is the first building I have seen for miles. Its wooden walls sit alone, under a metal roof, and around it the spring trees are in blossom. A small turquoise bench sits in front of a neat wooden fence; beyond it, the landscape is almost empty, only long green grass for as far as I can see and the small clusters of trees, nestling between the earth and sky. In the emptiness, I see the man is happy.

He stops me from speaking, tells me to sit down, rest, and he runs inside. The bench sags slightly under my weight and I look around the garden; dandelions scattered in the bright green grass and an empty glass rests on a tree stump.

Gerna comes out with a bottle of ice cold sparkling water. The liquid fizzes in my mouth and down into my stomach, "Drink it all!" he says, "*Vsyor*" and smiles at me – his eyes are watery and shining. They see right through me, not past me, but into me; it is one of those rare times in my life when I feel that someone is looking at me, really looking.

He hands me an egg.

"Eat!" he says.

I thank him, and I go to gently tap it on the arm of the bench to break the shell and peel it away. He stops me, takes the eggs back and makes a small hole with a knife; it is raw.

"Like a drink," he says.

"Like a drink?" I say.

"It's good! Good for energy! Good for life!"

I lean back and suck the slimy liquid through the hole; the richness of the yolk breaks and runs into my mouth and the strange coagulate goo of the white slides down my throat. I gasp; I have swallowed it in one and feel the lightness of the empty eggshell in my hand, grateful that I don't have to do it again.

Gerna beams at me. "I'll get some vodka. To take away the taste."

Gerna sits on the bench next to me, and I show him a small map of the world with a thin black line, traced from Roscoff, through France and Germany, Austria, Hungary and the Ukraine, lingering slightly before the border of Russia, where I haven't yet drawn the last two weeks of the journey. He looks at me, his eyes wide open in amazement. There is something boy-like in him; the way his mouth curves in a smile, and the roundness of his face.

"All of this?" he says, "On a bike?"

I nod and laugh at his amazement, and revel in the fact that someone gets it. Gets the idea straight away. Understands that there is no real why, that it cannot be put into words, that it is just ridiculous, that it is just itself and all the hard parts, and the easy parts and the boring parts and the exciting parts, and it makes me grin. For the first time I feel slightly proud of what I have done.

He follows my finger as I trace it across Russia and down through China, demonstrating the route. My hand hovers over Singapore for a moment, unsure of where to go next, before I close the book. "And then, I'm not sure," I say.

He takes an old mobile out of his pocket, "I'm going to phone a friend," he says smiling. "I want you to meet him."

Soon Nikolai's car appears from the opposite direction I had come in; a small black whirring shape, which eventually pulls to a stop outside the dacha.

A table is brought out and Gerna cuts salami, bread, cucumber and *salo*, cold white pig fat, and lays the food out on little plates. Then he cuts an orange, gives us each a piece and pours three glasses of vodka.

I wait for the long toasts that I became accustomed to in the Ukraine.

"*Davai,*" the men shout "EEEE- UP!" and we pour the drinks back, bite into the sweet orange, and laugh; everything is perfect. Again. "EEEE-UP!" and I bite into salami and bread. "EEEE-UP!" and now we eat the cucumber with a sprinkling of salt, and again, "EEEE-UP!" the hard, fatty *salo* and the bread. I feel the pig fat melt, and its salty fatty flavour fills my mouth.

When Gerna's son-in-law arrives I am slightly drunk, and the two men are joking and laughing like boys. Gerna shows me around his dacha. He shows me the wooden beehives and the well. He lets me winch up the bucket, and appears joyful and surprised that it is full of water. We pour it into a tank where he has constructed a small outside tap and basin, and we wash our faces. He takes me to the vegetable patch and runs his hands through the thick, black soil, lifting it then, and letting it sift finely through his fingers. Everything he does, and everything he looks upon is lent his quiet and childlike joy. He is proud of the well, and the beehives and the sink and his home. And everything around seems to shine with his pride and with his love and joy and as I look at all these simple things I feel myself shining too.

He tells me to bring my bike and things inside. I stop in the entrance, staring at a picture of Pushkin hanging on the wall. I am in Russia! I feel it; if this is all that happens, if everything from here is bad, it has been worth it. I am stood in Gerna's *dacha* looking at a picture of Pushkin on the wall and I am happy. I feel nothing, but a deep and overwhelming happiness.

Above us we watch the blackening sky. Igor, Gerna's son-in-law, takes nets out of the car and hands me a pair of old leather boots to put on and some wooden stakes to carry. We are going fishing. We walk through the long grass, to two small lakes, half hidden from the road. We drive the stakes into the ground and set to work untangling the net. Igor walks around to the opposite shore and Gerna ties a weight to the end of some string, which he tries to throw to the other side. Nikolai and I stand watching, and I take a swig of cognac from the bottle he offers me. The first two attempts fail and we drag the net back through the water to try again. On the third attempt the weight lands with a thud on the bank. The nets are set.

Another black shape is heard on the horizon and as it comes closer Gerna motions for me to duck. We hide in the long grass as the black silhouette of the car turns to the shape of a *militsiya* vehicle and passes without seeing us. It is only then that I realise we are poaching. We set another two nets.

In the water, huge clouds wrestle; black as ink and tumbling grey, and on its slick surface a leafless tree gets caught in the last yellow light of the sun. In ringlets, heavy drops disturb the water's calm and thunder breaks again. All around, as though it comes, bubbling through the soil, the sweet damp scent of rain rises.

We collect buckets, boots, the bottle of cognac, and Gerna looks up to the sky, at the rain falling down and the drops, running cold down our faces. "*Horosho*," he smiles. "It's good."

"Do you want to sleep?" Gerna asks me. The sun has gone down and the colours have all faded into different shades of blue and grey. I nod my head and he takes me, past the picture of Pushkin and shows me to my room. I lie down on the bed fully clothed, the bulge of my passport and money under my T-shirt as I sleep when in a forest.

"You can't sleep like that," says Gerna, and I lift the wallet out through the neck, pulling on the piece of string, and hand it to him in the half light. He looks at me and smiles at the small show of trust, but gives it back to me, places it under my pillow.

"*Spokonoi noch*," he says. "Good night."

I struggle to sleep and my breathing becomes shallow and asthmatic. I feel my throat closing in and try to remain calm as my breaths become shorter. I curl up on my side, wheezing, and rasping noisily in the dark. When Gerna comes in his face looks panicked, shining in the light of a lantern.

"Are you okay?" he asks and I nod my head.

"Normal," I say, struggling to get the words out between painful breaths, "*Nor...mal.. no*" though it isn't. It's been years since I've been this asthmatic. I wonder if it is a change in diet, if the transition from veganism to *salo* has been too quick.

"Can I do something?"

I point over to the door where my bike is. "Bag!" I say "*Soom... ka!*" and he bring the bag to me and I take out an inhaler, breathing in the spray which tastes like medicine and dust. "*Spaceeba. Izvineetye.*"

Gerna stays there for a moment as my breathing settles, and soon I am in a deep, vodka laden sleep. I am woken by the early morning light, grey through the window, and by the movement coming from the room next to me.

"Good morning!" says Gerna as I walk outside.

"Good morning!"

"Are you okay? Did you sleep well?" I nod, cupping my hands to the bucket he hands me and splashing my face with the cold water.

"I was worried about you," He says handing me a cup of black, syrupy sweet coffee.

"I'm fine. Thank you. I'm sorry."

We wait until Nikolai and Igor get up and trudge across the field, the long grass wet with rain. As we pull the nets up, I see why the fishing is illegal. The big net isn't fair in such a small lake, and small pike twist and flip against the air, caught in the holes, and only entangling themselves further with every movement of their struggle. We empty the fish into buckets and they snap at each other violently and become asphyxiated.

Gerna makes a huge saucepan of soup with the fish and the flesh falls easily from the bones. A bird begins to sing in a rhythmic clicking, whistling and trilling, and I ask Gerna what it is.

"It's a *solovei.*" he says. A nightingale. "Do you want to stay another day?"

"Yes. I do. But I can't."

As I am leaving, Gerna gives me a small bag of food and a 100 rouble note. I thank him for the food, and try to refuse the money, but he pushes it into my hand. He waves now, not as before, but standing still, though his face still shines with kindness.

"Goodbye," I say. "Thank you." Again, I turn to a black spot and fade into the horizon, past the clusters of trees under the Russian sky.

...

I follow the same road for 4 days. I watch the miles roll by; 3508, 3509, 3510. I try not to count, though the steppe is nothing but empty farmland, upturned fields and never-ending waves of wheat, and my eyes forever dart back to the milometer. 3512, 3513.

The days are long; I wake at dawn when the birds begin to sing, and cycle for hours on end, stopping to eat, to drink, and cycle again until the shadows stretch out, long across the fields and pull me towards sleep. Distance is greater than I have ever known it before; it takes 14 hours to cycle 100 miles, and Russia stretches out before me, unending. It seems like it is growing as I move, like some great expanding universe within itself. And yet, in the days, when I look back on them, there is nothing. Already the memory is vague and eventless; the blurred grass at the side of the road and the white ticking lines; this village, that village, a cup of coffee, a break to piss, to read a book, an empty shop. Even at the end of the day the memory of what I've done is not whole; why do I no longer feel the monotony of the passing miles, and the hours of endless nothing? Why have I lost already the truth about my journey, to pick out only what I remember as events? I feel the day's length only in my legs, and the happy exhaustion as I lie down to sleep.

...

Soon loneliness sinks into me again. I long for closeness with someone. In the endless hours on the road I daydream. The daydreams are always different, but there is often a girl I do not know who talks to me. "I see from the tan," she says, "which is darker on the outside of your right leg, your right arm, that you have been travelling east for a long time. Since the beginning of summer." The daydream starts like this – with Sherlock Holmes' like intuition she sees what I am doing, and I don't have to talk. Even in my dreams I am shy. But there, people reach into me, and see inside me, and give a shape to something without form, something that I myself cannot describe, in waking hours or in dreams. There are so many hours of nothing with nothing to do but think: I remember the faces of primary school friends and the smells of a beach from my infancy; the feeling of snow sending my hands stinging red; I remember a worksheet and a supply teacher; a drunken conversation; the feedback from a university lecturer; dropping an ice-cream; a rocking horse; scooping the head of beer with my fingers; skiving school; good sex; bad sex; failure; the chattering of teeth; drug come-ups; come-downs; a joint smoked at a gig; a cricket ball smashing a window, the way it hangs in the air before crashing down, and the screaming; a hand held; a foot lovingly resting at my back, but then the way she stands up and walks to the door, and the foot is not a loving foot, not even a foot, but the strap of a bag and she is standing there saying, "you know I don't, don't you", and me saying, "yes," I know, "I knew," and a partial eclipse, and running inside and sitting in the kitchen eating crumpets, and my mouth dry, and she's saying, "he's not my boyfriend, but...", and I sit there silent, holding a half-eaten crumpet in my hand, and sitting, and sitting, and the pages of a world atlas, the red lines of imagined roads, and the road past my primary school, my home, the ocean from St. Ives to Godrevy lighthouse, and the list surges endlessly on and I wonder whether, if I cycled like this forever, there would come a time at which I'd have remembered everything I'd ever done and everyone I'd met. Now, I realise, the road slopes downwards, and on the right a man stands by a car, waves for me to stop.

He asks me for a knife – he needs it to start the car. He is a huge man, with grey hair, and a strong round face. He wears a leather jacket and his hands are twice the size of mine, and perhaps it is the realisation that he could kill me easily enough with his hands which convinces me to reach inside my panniers in search for a suitable tool. His name is Victor. I hand him a small sharp kitchen knife and it takes him less than 30 seconds to start the car; the engine rumbles into life.

"Come and stay at my *dacha*," he says, handing me back the knife. "We can eat and drink. You can sleep! Put your bike in the back of the car."

"I can't," I say. "I need to cycle!"

I try to explain how important it is that I ride every metre on a bike, no cheating – it has to be like that. Cycling round the world getting lifts in cars and holding onto lorries instead of climbing up hills isn't cycling round the world – the whole thing would be broken if I didn't pedal the whole way.

"Is it Guinness?" he asks.

"Guinness?"

"Guinness. Records. Sports."

"Not exactly," I say. "But I need to cycle."

Victor seems perplexed, but he climbs inside his car, and I follow the white Lada for 25 miles, at a pace which feels excruciatingly slow for him and impossibly fast for me. I dig into the pedals, my legs burn, and my breathing is loud and constant through my mouth as I chase the car ahead which seems to be crawling. I struggle up hills, my legs spinning, as he waits at the top, and without a moment's pause the car pulls away again. We arrive at his *dacha* in 90 minutes and I am exhausted.

It is not like Gerna's *dacha*. It has electricity and wallpaper, curtains hanging from the windows, and a fully-fitted kitchen. He shows me to the shower and for the first time in more than a week hot water cascades over me. I scrub myself with soap, under my nails, and even the black oil from my chain that has become ingrained in the fine lines of my hands, frees its hold and gushes away down the plughole.

When I open the bathroom door, the steam shrinks, as though taking an inward breath, before billowing out into the colder air. Victor has laid the table and covered it with plates; borsht, cold meats and salads. We eat the food, and every time I empty my plate he fills it again.

"This is excellent," I smile at him. "Really, excellent food. Thank you!"

"In Russia we understand our food," he tells me. "We grow it, and harvest it, we rear it and kill it. It brings us closer to what we are eating. And besides, the shops are too expensive, so we have no choice. I have chickens here, but pigs too in a field."

"Was this your pig?" I ask him, pointing at the plate.

"*Konechna,*" he says. "Of course."

We drink black coffee, and Victor asks if I would like some vodka. Do not get drunk again, I tell myself. Tomorrow is a long day; I need to make it to Saratov on the banks of the Volga. I need to cycle an average of over 80 miles a day to make it to Mongolia before my visa expires. "I'll have a tiny bit; tiny, tiny." And I draw my fingers together to show him what tiny means.

He brings out a shot glass and a half pint glass, which is for water, and lays them on the table; the hard sound of glass on laminated wood clinks short, without an echo. He pours into the small glass and I tell him to stop before the vodka gets half way. He then pours into the half-pint glass without stopping; the cold, clear liquid settles just below the brim, a millimetre, no more than two.

"*Davai!*" he says, almost shouting, and I pour the vodka back, feeling its warmth slide down my throat and sending small shivers down my back. I put the glass down and look up to see Victor finishing the glass as one might down a pint of beer. He puts the glass back down on the table without flinching and I look at him in shock.

"Don't worry!" he says, laughing at me. "For me, that's all."

I take a cigarette from him and we are smoking when his friends come to the door. There are three Russian men and me and I realise now that not drinking vodka is not an option. We drink shot after shot, and as we do I feel myself becoming closer to them and my terrible Russian stops being a barrier, and the men sing songs loud and late into the night.

Victor speaks about his time in the army. "In Russia we hate fascism," he says drawing in smoke from his cigarette in a long deep breath, and it swims into his lungs. "We fight fascism, we kick it out. I've been in Yemen, Cuba and Afghanistan. In Afghanistan I was shot." He lifts up his shirt to reveal two scars, one on his stomach, and another, the exit wound, on his back. "Since then I've been a pensioner," he says laughing. "Eating, smoking, drinking!"

We go out into the yard with an air rifle. The evening sky is clear and deep dark blue, and Victor takes a small can and puts it on a fence, 5 metres away. He hands me the gun and I take it reluctantly. I aim, knowing I am going to miss. The trigger is harder, stiffer to pull back than I imagined and I fire; the bullet pings as it pierces the can and knocks it to the ground. I am elated. I never want to fire a gun again, it was my first and last shot, and Victor and his friends shout and clap and I am carried back inside like a drunken hero. Victor leaves for a moment and comes back with a brown and orange ribbon.

"This is a *georgovskaya lentichka*. It is for Russian heroes." He is about to hand it to me when he has a better idea. He takes it and ties it to my handlebars. "It will be lucky," he says.

...

In the morning I leave early, drowning the oncoming hangover with a litre of water and returning to the same long road. I battle all day against a headwind, and a lingering headache. The bridge across the Volga is long and wide and I am battered by a side wind. As trucks pass me I fight against being sucked into the path of cars behind. I cannot face the city and barely stop to look at the huge body of water that tumbles below like a sea. Why is everything in Russia so big? Again, I find nowhere to camp; fields stretch open without places to hide. I roll north following the banks of the river, now miles to my west. Slowly, and without hope, I scan the landscape for patches of trees, or scrub, or any kind of shelter. After 120 miles I am exhausted, and pull into a motel. I am spending too much.

There is a photograph of Putin on the wall. He looks over the reception with something that is not quite a smile on his lips, staring through the glass of the frame. I find myself mistrusting a populace that has so much faith in its leader, that adulates him and raises him up. I wonder if there are houses or hotels in England with pictures of Tony Blair looking over the living room or reception and hope that there are not.

The woman at the desk looks at me distrustfully when I ask her for a room. She takes my passport flicking over each page in turn and scrutinizing it.

"250 roubles." She says without looking at me, sliding the keys across the surface.

"*Spaseeba.*" I say.

"*Porzhalusta,*" she says, in a sarcastic, weary tone.

...

The next day, I cycle the remaining 6km into Marx and sit on the ground outside a supermarket eating a cheap Swiss roll and an expensive dusty apple. I hear the word travelling, *putyeshestviye,* and look up to see a boy my age, with crazy black hair and a goatee, and a woman with slightly red hair, who appears to be his mother, walking towards me.

"Are you travelling?" asks the woman. "You can come to our house for some real breakfast."

I gather myself, brushing the dust from my shorts, and we walk through the streets of Marx, soaked now in the early morning sunlight of mid-May, until we come to an old block of flats. The yellow paint peels off the walls, failed in its attempt to warm the cold and brutal architecture. We enter the block of flats and I lean my bike against the bare metal staircase.

"Don't leave it there. It's not safe. We should take it upstairs."

I begin taking off the panniers, but have only removed the front two when the boy with the crazy hair stops me, lifts up the bike and carries it up four flights of stairs. I stand and watch, astonished. I struggle to lift it over curbs; its dead weight as heavy as a man.

"Gerna's in the army," the woman says, offering an explanation. "Oh, I didn't say – I'm Sveta."

I follow her up the stairs. Gerna has left my bike by the door, and he sits in the kitchen breathing steadily as if the effort of carrying it up four floors were no exertion at all. We sit down at the kitchen table and the smell of soup, rich chicken stock and potatoes, fills the air. A young girl stands by the door, watching us shyly.

"This is Valentina," Sveta tells me. "She has come to stay with us. Valentina – this is Sam – he has cycled all the way from England. Come and say hello."

"*Privyet. Kak dyela?*" she says quietly, and I tell her that I'm fine, that I'm good.

Sveta fusses over us, me and her son, filling bowls with hot soup, and pouring tea. She holds Gerna's shoulders and rubs his hair as if he were a young boy.

"Gerna is only back for the weekend," she says. "Then he has to go back to the army." She looks at him proud and beaming, and he looks back at her like she is paying him too much attention.

We sit around the table talking. The family is from Turkmenistan. Sveta is an artist and a teacher, and Valentina has come to live with her for two weeks to learn how to paint.

"Why don't you stay? Gerna can show you around town and you can meet his friends."

I have to stay. I never know when these meetings will come to an end, and I will be left on my own in cold, vast Russia, with nothing but a bike and a road. How could I say I had really been here, if I refused these offers of kindness? I agree happily, soaking up the last of the soup with crusty homemade bread, and we walk through the town to the river.

His friends wear System of a Down and Korn hoodies and smoke roll ups. We spend the day fishing on the banks of the Volga, and leave potatoes, wrapped in tin foil, to bake on the cinders of a camp fire. The boys try out their English swear words on me: "You fucking bastard mother fucker!" It's the only English they know.

Patrick, who runs around the bank collecting sticks for the fire and throwing stones into the water, wearing only an army jacket and a pair of grey underpants, screams at no-one in particular and falls into fits of laughter. "You fucking bastard mother fucker! Russian bitches, yeah!"

We open a brown plastic bottle of beer; ice-cold and delicious in the sun, and we unwrap the potatoes and eat them, dry and crispy, the taste of smoke from the burning wood. Patrick asks me if I want to box, and I decline. Gerna agrees that it would be a bad idea and gets up himself. The two boys circle each other, their fists held up high, and duck out of the way of punches. Patrick strikes Gerna, hard on the jaw, and he stumbles back two paces, trying not to fall. The game is over.

Later we walk through the dark streets of Marx, dimly lit by the odd yellow streetlamp, the road now a bare earth track. We come to the house of Gerna's friend; an old German wooden house, it appears as something out of a film set, too rickety to be standing. Inside the boys are smoking, and tiny fish hang to dry on lengths of metal wire. Patrick gives me a fish and I take it, biting off the head, chewing the bones and its dried out salty flesh; it is like all the flavour of a fish has been condensed and dried out and packed into its tiny body. I don't know if I like it, but he offers me another one and I take it.

Back at the flat we drink green tea, and Valentina interviews me for the local newspaper. I struggle to express myself, but she is patient with me and writes down my answers. "It's not a sport," she repeats back to me. "You just want to travel the world and learn new things?" I nod. I wish I could say something better.

The next morning Sveta takes me to an exhibition of paintings. There are paintings of landscapes and portraits, and works of abstract art.

"Which one is your favourite?" she asks me.

I take her to the painting; a picture of a saint in the style of the Orthodox Church. It is not something I would normally be drawn towards, but it glows in the room, and is so painstakingly detailed and exudes a sense of calm. It is the only painting there which seems alive. "This one," I say.

"Really?" she seems surprised. "This one is mine."

We are outside when Sveta says, "I'm going to take you to see *Otyetz* Andrei." Father Andrei.

The church is a simple white building. I feel stupid going inside, like I shouldn't be there. I cross myself as she does, not wanting to upset her, but feeling hypocritical and uncomfortable. She leaves me for a moment in the silent hall, and goes to the back room. When she emerges, she is followed by *Otyetz Andrei*. He is different from any priest I have seen before; he has a thin face, and his eyes shine at me clearly from above a huge black beard. His skin is pale, almost translucent, as if this, the inside world, were his; a man who rarely walks outside. He talks to me kindly, first about what I am doing and then asks my religion. I tell him I have none, that I do not go to church. I do not tell him that I do not believe in God.

I don't understand all that he says to me; much less than half. After a while, I stop trying to concentrate on what he is saying and let the words flow over me. Just the sound of them, and his voice, quiet and soothing. In that moment, I feel like I am becoming part of him, absorbed into his energy, his hypnotic words. There seems an aura, a real and tangible presence emanating from him. And as I look at him, I feel something that I have felt only once in my life before; a feeling of magic when standing in front of someone who believes so much; all thought seems to leave me, all analysis. I am there and I feel this man's presence within me and it fills me with calm, and I feel shivers run down my body. As I leave I cannot speak; I feel my body changed.

Before I leave, Sveta gives me a necklace; a black leather cord with a small silver idol of Saint Nikolai. He is a saint for travellers, she says. He will protect me.

Gerna rides with me to the main road, and points me in the direction of Samara, and I say goodbye. So often, upon leaving people who have shown me great kindness, I feel an exaggerated sense of loneliness; like the warmth of their act only serves to make colder the sense of being alone. I feel their spirit fall away from me, and again become slightly frightened of the world. Now, I ride away from Marx, along the flat road with a breeze at my back, and I feel their warmth still in me. Was it a conjuring trick? Had I fallen, induced into some kind of psychological spell? Or was it because I couldn't follow the words, that I had felt the sense of them more deeply and without prejudice? I laugh at myself with my logical brain. I feel, I cannot help but notice it, protected.

...

"*Ich sprecke kein Deutsch,*" a drunk man bawls at me, the tone of his voice like spitting. His eyes are deep bloodshot red, and he laughs at what he considers to be his own joke and takes a few difficult steps over to my table, puts a filthy hand on my shoulder, and a stale stench of vodka suffocates the air. "*Ich sprecke kein Deutsch*" he shouts now for the rest of the customers in the café, looking around for laughs.

"*Ya ne nemyetski*" I tell him, "*Ya anglichanin.*" hoping that, if it is Germans he has a problem with, he might leave me alone.

He stares down at me, with that gaze of a drunk that seems to come from very far away, some sunken world. He steadies himself on my table and breathes down on me. "*Ich sprecke kein Deutsch,*" he says again, taking out a crumpled-up cigarette from his pocket and a blue transparent lighter. He flicks the flint twice, struggling to line up the lighter and the end of the cigarette, but the spark fails to ignite. He lifts himself up, and takes in a panorama of the room, but everyone is looking down, avoiding eye contact. He tries the lighter again, and again it fails to light and he drops the lighter to the floor, whether on purpose or not I do not know, and stamps on it, splintering the plastic, and the smell of lighter fluid sifts up through the air like petrol or poppers or glue.

"Give me some money!" he says, again bearing over me.

"What?"

"Give me some money! *Dyengi! Dyengi!*" he says, rubbing his fingers together.

"*Oo meenya nyet.*" I say firmly, and walk out leaving the café full of people silently looking after me.

I close the door behind me, gather my bike and turn the pedals, stiffly, clicking from a high gear into a low one until, when I reach the road the pedals turn with ease. "*Ich sprecke kein Deutsch!*" the man shouts at me, staring at me with the bloodshot eyes, and I leave Pugachev behind singing The Smiths. The grids of dirty wooden houses and garages and run-down shops slide past as I sing "I'll probably never see you again! I'll probably never see you again! I'll probably never see you agaaaaain. And if the people stare let the people stare. Ooooh, I really don't know and I really don't caaare!"

I stop on the outskirts of the town to fill up with water and food because I didn't eat at the café. The roads are still dirt, and a pair of small houses sit sadly, as though outcast by the stinking town of Pugachev. A small boy, about four years old, comes up to me and stares – he is wearing dirty trousers, no shirt and, in his arms, he holds a ball.

He stands and stares for a while before speaking. "Where's your house?" he asks. It is a reasonable question.

I point to where the sun is setting in the west. "It's that way. You have to go on a plane for about 4 hours. It's far away."

"My house is far away too," says the boy. "You have to go down this road and over a bridge and, ah... *daleko, daleko!*"

...

In Samara I find a cheap hotel and decide to stay two nights. The room has a small balcony which appears to be slowly falling into the courtyard below. The railing has broken loose from the wall on one side and the floor slopes slightly downwards.

I go to a supermarket and walk slowly up and down the fluorescent aisles. I pick up a 200g pack of walnuts and look at the price; 950 Roubles. £20. Two days' budget. I put it down, and search for cheaper food. I leave the supermarket with eggs, bread, beer and cigarettes and get change from a 200 rouble note.

Back in the hotel, I light my stove and fry the bread dipped in egg, remembering childhood camping holidays. I eat the eggy bread with the cold beer, but it seems like something is missing. Ketchup? Perhaps, even with ketchup it would not be the same as it was when I was a child. What am I doing? If I am trying to rekindle some childhood memory, it doesn't work. Before, eggy-bread had been a magic food, we asked for it the night before, me and my brother, and watched as my dad dipped slices in a gloopy, eggy mess, and it sizzled brown, over a red camping stove. I loved everything about it; the tube from the gas tank, and the smell of matches, and the piles of spongy bread on plastic plates. Now I look at it, chew it with anticlimactic disgust; it is just egg and bread, it doesn't taste the same. But the beer is magic; refreshing and strong and cheap, and now in my solitude, safe in my hotel room, I welcome the inebriation. As the light fades outside I smoke a cigarette, leaning over the balcony, not daring to step on it. I look at my watch and decide to run outside and buy 2 more bottles of beer before the shop closes.

I drink quickly now; the three litres of beer that are left seem limitless and tomorrow I won't be cycling. Outside, the sound of fairground rides rings in sickly sweet chimes, like some Soviet-Newquay-on-sea. Inside, I am happy. I flick the end of a cigarette over the balcony where it lands, in the dank dark liquid filled by other cigarette butts turning the water ash black. I light another cigarette; though now the taste is bitter and the smoke that I had first welcomed greedily into my lungs feels like poison. I tap the end, and the ash falls in a big clump; only a tiny fragment of burnt paper falls so slowly to the ground that it could be as light as air; I watch as it comes to rest and soaks up the dirty water, a dark and sodden speck.

The cold liquid courses through me. I take the world map out, draw a thick black line from the Ukrainian border, where I had left it, to the banks of the River Volga. Russia takes up most of the map it seems. I count the three shining instances of kindness, but the vastness of the place seems to swallow them up; the sadness and the dull landscape is what I think of. The general air of harshness that I encounter everywhere; I have come in search of Tolstoy and Dostoyevsky and Tarkovsky, but there is as much a chance of finding them here, as finding Hardy in a Tesco Extra. Better not to have expectations I think, opening the last bottle and flicking between the channels of Russian TV; abrasive news, chat shows, game shows, singing contests, the same as everywhere else.

...

I leave Samara, following the busy, fuel-choked roads the city spits out to the east. Rain has turned the dust along the roadside to mud and *marshrutka* buses screech to jarring halts and spray dirty water into the air as people pour out the sliding doors into the middle of the road. The city fades away reluctantly; seedy motels, stalls selling *kvass* and mechanics' workshops cling to the roadside, trying to scrape something from the passing traffic, until at last the city is gone and fields lie on both sides; silver birch forests and pine at their farthest reaches, and the road rolls on. I ride out to the east. The days are long again. I cycle until I find somewhere to camp. Wake, and ride again.

...

It is dark when I hear the screaming voice of a man. Inside my tent I am suddenly awake. There shouldn't be human voices in this forest, miles away from the nearest town. And yet the voice is undoubtedly human as again it bellows. I hear the slamming of a car door, and though I have dragged my bike for over 100m, deep into the forest over logs until it was hidden from the road, I lie there frozen, listening to the forest outside; my heart thuds beneath me, audible, and I stifle my breathing. For an agonising length of time there is silence. Just go to sleep, I think; it is just a car broken down, you cannot be seen. Anna's boyfriend? Stupid. Just go to sleep. I listen to the never silent forest; the rustle of leaves or the call of nocturnal birds. I am exhausted, but I cannot go to sleep. I climb slowly out of my sleeping bag; the rustling of the material amplified in the quiet. Sssssh. I pull on a pair of shorts with a quick intake of breath. In the dark, I brush around the floor for my shoes; I want to be outside, where at least I can see the outline of the trees, where at least I can run.

I hear footprints coming closer. Purposeful, heavy footprints, the cracking of twigs. I freeze and the footsteps continue circling my tent. I bite my sleeping bag to stifle my breathing, I feel the warmth of my breath and the material turn damp, then wet. I have no fight or flight instinct, I realise in that moment. I am frozen, stuck still. The footprints are human. I am certain of it. After three months of sleeping in forests I have heard nothing like them. With a final crunch of leaves they come to a stop outside. I'm dead, I think. There is someone outside who wants to kill me. There is a gun or an axe, or some other heavy object. I am dead. And yet I do not move, still I am frozen to the spot. It has not been worth it, if it ends here. Please, that I don't die here. I need to move. I need to move now. And in an instant, I grab the zip, open it and run into the forest, where I lie, half naked on the floor.

There is no moon. Light barely reaches the forest floor, and even when my eyes can make out the slight line between the black trees and the dull black purple sky, I can see nothing else. Not my tent. Not a man. Or an axe. But I am convinced there is someone there.

"*Ya nye znayu shto khoteesh...*" I say to the darkness. "I don't know what you want," I say. "But take it."

I wait for movement, for the darkness to speak back. For the man to move towards me. I am ready to run. I will stay like this all night, I think. I am awake and will not sleep. But then the forest explodes in a fit of movement. The heavy footsteps move too quickly for a human, and stop too suddenly and without a sound; somehow in the darkness I see the glint of two small eyes. From behind me heavier footsteps tread through the forest, loud and unafraid. I pick myself up, noticing the cold for the first time, and crawl back into the tent. Don't worry, I tell myself, it's just a wolf, or a couple of wolves. There's no-one here. The footsteps of the mammals beat away, fading into the distance along the forest floor, and I no longer feel afraid of them. But I have learnt something about myself; that when I think that I might die I do not run or prepare myself to fight, but lie down, frozen with fear, and wait for it to come.

...

A police check point breaks the monotony of the road, and a policeman holds his arm up: STOP.

"Stravstvootye." I say, smiling, but not too much.

The policeman stares at me for an instant. "Passport," he says flatly, and holds out his hand.

I lift up my T-shirt to reach inside the wallet hanging from my neck and hand it over to him. He flicks through it, like it is an alien object. He lingers slightly over my photo, and then flicks through the rest of the pages without finding the Russian visa; either he does not know what he is looking for or he is looking for nothing at all.

"Can you give me Euros?"

"*Nyet.*"

"*Dollar?*"

"*Nyet*"

"*Roublei?*"

"*Nyet.*"

"Where are you going?"

"I'm going to Mongolia."

He looks at me for a second and hands me back the passport. "You can't cycle on the road. You must go on the side."

I look at the crumbling, muddy bank along the side of the road, full of big stones, and impossible to cycle along. "*Zdyesh?*" I ask him, pointing to it. "Here?"

He looks at me and screams, high-pitched, into my face. "DAAAAAA!"

I get off the road and push my bike awkwardly along the rocky ground until I am out of sight. Climbing back onto the bike, I laugh to myself remembering the policeman who screams at Withnail or I: "Get in the back of the van!" They have the same voice.

...

After 4200 miles, the Urals come into view; a shadowy hazy green on the horizon. They seem to have been beaten into the ground, worn down by time, or stretched out flat like everything else I have seen in Russia. Still, they are thick with old forests and, though scarred by logging in places, there are plenty of places to camp.

I pull my bike across the forest floor. Brambles scratch at my legs, already a crisscross of dark dried blood, from forests before. I lift the bike over a fallen tree trunk and push away the leaves to find a tiny clearing, sheltered all around. A gentle golden light, flickers, now green; as the summer leaves absorb it and breathe it out, there is a constant humming glow. The way I unpack my things is set now, in an almost ritualistic formula. I untie the straps and release the bungees in the same order without thinking. The tent poles, I extend and lie out on the floor, unroll the fabric of the tent.

I have come closer to the village than I had thought. The sound of a dog's bark causes me to look up, and now I hear the villagers calling to each other. As I listen, I could be hearing the sounds of a village two hundred years ago, and I imagine I have fallen back in time. Chickens cluck and the lowing of cows reaches my ears, but through the undergrowth I see nothing. In the distance, I hear an axe; its dead thud, chopping into wood, and again the lowing of cows further in the distance, and a bell. Birds sing lightly and the gentle hum of insects that has filled this forest for thousands of years buzzes under everything. I sit, imagining myself a time traveller, listening to the sounds of rural life from centuries before, until a chainsaw breaks the spell.

The next day I come to a small sign by the side of the road. Its concrete base covered with moss roots it in the vegetation below and a strange kind of Russian modernist spike hits a small punch into the air. Азия says the sign. Tears come to my eyes for the first time since Vesoul. Asia! I have crossed an entire continent.

Asia

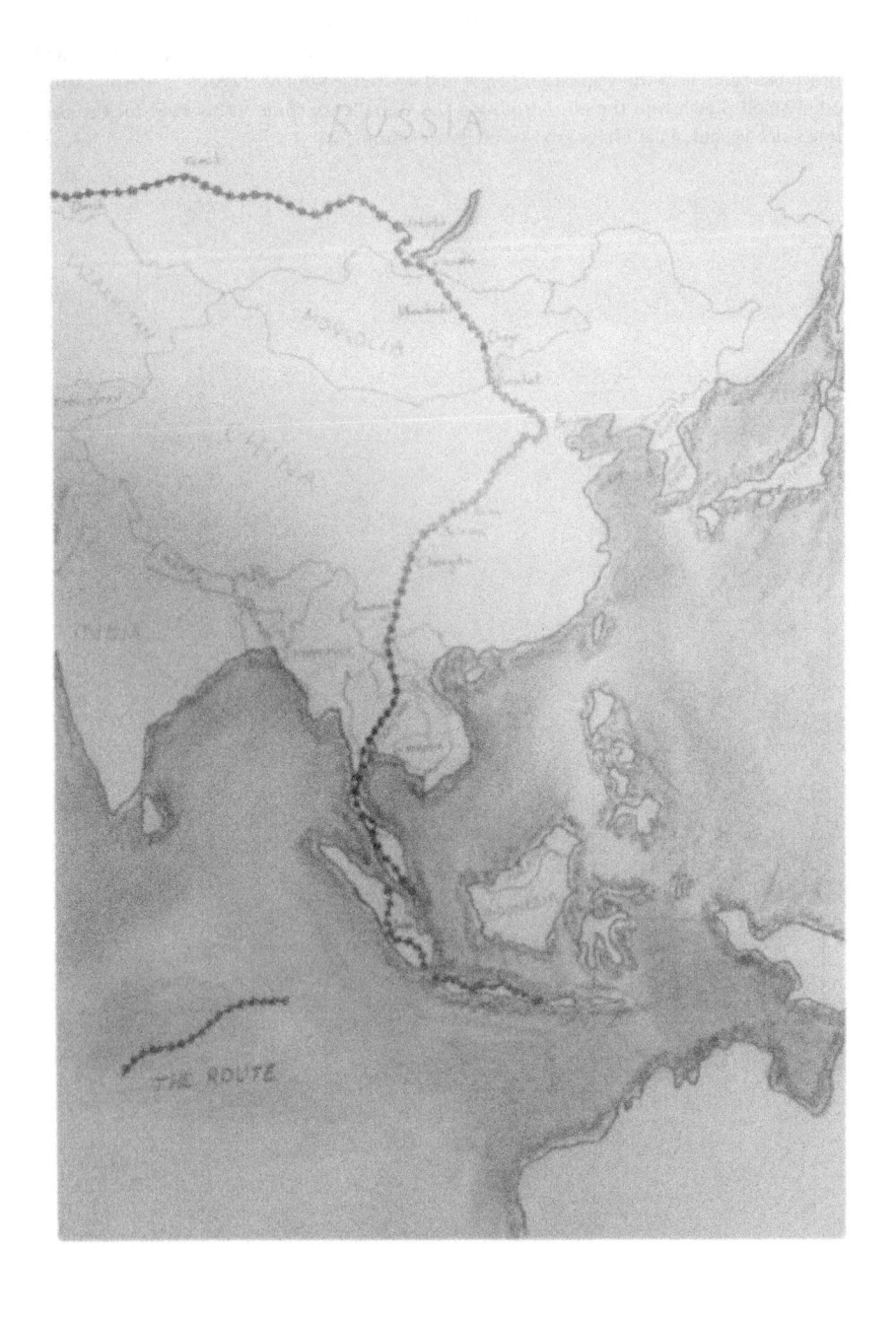

The rusty spade strikes down into the hard soil and stone. I stamp on it, placing my full weight on the thin edges of the blade and the splintered, wooden handle, rebounds in my blistered hand. I look around for other tools; a pick axe, a fork, and see none. I clear the few loose stones, without satisfaction, and strike again.

Andrei has invited me to stay the night in his mother's flat, but now I see them talking, she looks at me, unsure. I overhear her saying something about money, and I plunge the spade down into the earth again, again, again. Now the hole is two foot deep, the sides are straight and smooth. Andrei comes over with a wooden post, drives it down with a mallet, but it goes no further, and we fill in the hole with loose soil compacting it with our feet, until the post barely moves when we push it. It'll do.

"Is your mother okay?" I ask him.

"She's fine. She has gone home to cook."

I begin digging another hole and Andrei returns to untangling barbed wire. We are putting a fence around their allotment to stop people stealing potatoes and tomatoes and cucumbers. Or to make it easier to steal those things from someone else.

On all four sides, Soviet tower blocks leer over the allotments. Is it possible that this is where Russia's sadness comes from? From the buildings? The way they encroach on people's lives, look down on you, their domineering presence, squashing people into small, dark boxes, one on top of the other. They are everywhere; cheap and perfectly useful, they cram into small towns and make them pointlessly claustrophobic, the steppe, the taiga, stretching all around for thousands of empty miles. They seem to be built to rid people of their privacy; the thin walls, and echoing staircases.

The allotments sit, in the shadow of these buildings, each no more than ten strides across, bordered by wire and wood, laid out like a giant chess board. It is the 27th May, and though the hour is approaching ten, there is a bustle of activity. The sound of digging and sawing fills the air, and sometimes the light, sharp snip of a broken stem, the thud of heavy soil falling into a wheelbarrow, or the splicing of an axe through wood. The ground is well thawed, and the late spring evening teems with insects and birds. The sky still light, people make use of the too short summer; sowing, weeding, pruning, lopping, readying themselves for winter, before summer has begun.

It is almost midnight when we pack up; the barbed wire is taut, hooked to new nails, along two sides of the allotment, and we gather the tools into a small shed and padlock the door. The last light fades to grey and street lamps ignite our path. Men with skin heads stare after us as we round the corner; I catch the outline of leather jackets, and big black boots, but their gaze is challenging and I know not to meet it. We are silent as we reach the door of the tenement.

The metal door is unlocked; it clanks open on its heavy hinges; screeches open, screeches shut. The sound of the door slamming echoes up the stairs and bounces off the bare damp concrete. The place is dark and cold; water drips from a leak in the roof and soaks into the dank floor. The electric murmur of televisions, behind doors, betrays what, at first, I took to be silence.

Andrei takes out a pair of keys and turns them until the lock clicks, and the reinforced door swings open. Somewhere above us another door slams shut and its hollow echo falls down several floors, followed by the sound of heavy booted footsteps. We step inside and Andrei bolts the door behind him. He turns to me and smiles. "Thanks for your help," he says.

His mother is standing at the door to the kitchen. She is a round woman, with broad shoulders and wrists as thick as the fence posts we have been driving into the ground since late afternoon. But now she smiles at me, as Andrei tells her what we have done, and the homely scent of sizzling fat and cabbage fills the kitchen.

Outside, the booted footsteps stop. A rattling cough and the sound of spit slaps against concrete and rebounds off the walls outside. Difficult to kick down, these metal doors, but all the breathing, shouting, spitting noise of the neighbours, rattles outside the flat, amplified and close. Again, the door screeches open, screeches shut, and the flat feels warm again.

I go into the kitchen. Huge glass jars line the shelves, full of pickled vegetables; tomatoes, onions and cucumbers. The jars remind me of the Darwin wing at the Natural History Museum in London; fish, reptiles and mammals floating in formaldehyde. In these big Russian jars, vegetables swim like sea creatures: sea cucumbers, and red sea anemones, and small transparent jellyfish; all lifeless, half-floating, and vinegary.

Andrei appears at the door. "Come with me; I want to show you something."

I follow him to his bedroom. A streetlamp outside casts the shadow of metal bars onto a bed-sheet which hangs across the window. A map of Russia takes up an entire wall. There are lines drawn all over the map from Andrei's travels, spreading from Shadrinsk like spiders' legs, up to Moscow, down to Kazakhstan, and even up to the Arctic. But it is not this that Andrei wants to show me.

"*Ya khoodozhnik*" he says. "I am an artist."

While we were working in the garden I had barely taken in Andrei's appearance, but now I look at him. His hair is cut short and a pair of angular glasses shades his eyes. He is wearing open-toed sandals, black and purple lycra shorts, and a red, netted shirt through which it is difficult not to notice his nipples. How have I not noticed until now that the man is dressed like a maniac?

"What kind of art?" I ask him.

His eyes glint as he takes down a painting from the wall. It has a golden frame and depicts a lake, trees and mountains. The colour of the lake is bright blue, like unmixed acrylic paint. The trees are flat green and the sky is a slightly lighter shade of the same blue. It is a childish painting. The trees look like paintings of a painting. A painting of what a tree should look like; symmetrical and flat, and the opaque surface of the lake is matt and unreflective; it is only by piecing all the elements together that I realise that it is a lake. I am at a loss for what to say. It seems that the goal is realism, but I am unsure. I feel Andrei looking at me; I need to say something.

"It's good," is all I manage.

"I have more," he says, "not here; they're at an exhibition. But I have the photos."

We look through the photos. The paintings are almost identical. I wonder if I am missing something. All of the paintings have lakes, or rivers in the same unmoving blue; the trees the same dappled brush strokes without layers. In some of the photos Andrei is stood next to them in an ill-fitting suit, the same rectangular glasses.

"We are a community of artists in Kurgan," he says, showing me a newspaper cutting of himself in the suit, standing and staring, dead-on camera, with an enigmatic half-smile, like a great artist showing off his work. "We paint and we make important work together."

He seems so utterly convinced that I wonder if this is the art: his character; a man pushing 30, living with his mother, and knocking out frame after frame of the same landscape, looking at me now with pride and sincerity, wearing a net t-shirt and lycra shorts, putting on exhibitions of odd, dead things in dark wood and golden frames. I feel a sudden pang of guilt; stood next to this man who has given me a place to stay and welcomed me into his home, and me there, silent and mocking. But he is strange and slightly maniacal, and it takes many minutes before we leave the topic of his painting and leave his room to eat.

We sit at the table and eat fatty, doughy food and pickled vegetables.

"I've been showing Sam my paintings," Andrei tells his mother, and she looks at him out of her small eyes, sadly. There is something tender in her, and she doesn't say anything else on the topic. Instead we talk about their family. They are from Magadanskaya Oblast, Russia's last province on the other side of Siberia, a claw held out towards Japan. The talk is tired and sad, and I love the Russian sadness and the slow, heavy tones. Andrei's mother has light blue eyes that are now soft in the light as she talks to me. She is of an age in Russia when women find themselves without a husband; widows to vodka, and cigarettes, and a heavy fat-filled diet. She refers to her late husband, not by his name, but as Andrei's father, though mainly she speaks of her mother and the big family she left in Magadan.

As we are clearing the table Andrei speaks to me: "Tomorrow, we can go to Kurgan, you can meet my friend and stay in his flat. We'll see the exhibition."

"I can't," I say. "There's no road back from Kurgan and I can't go to Kazakhstan without a visa. I'm sorry, I haven't got time."

"But you have to go to Kurgan. You can see more of my paintings!" he says, looking at me intently.

His mother shouts from the kitchen, "He can't," she says. "Didn't you hear the boy? He hasn't got time. Hasn't got a visa."

Later, she calls me over to the sofa on which she is sat. I pull up a chair and look over her shoulder at an old black and white photograph of a family gathering in Magadan. Behind the glass, stand about fifty people, looking out from a time when people looked somehow different; different hair and clothes and faces. The people stand in long neat rows, stiff and still, as though they were being painted and all conscious that the taking of a photo was a serious event.

This is me, she points. This slim beautiful girl, with the long dark hair tied back, looking softly towards the camera. This girl with a sad smile, and slim strong hands held together. This is my father, this stern man, with dark eyes and square shoulders. And this, she points, is my mother. This woman here, with broad shoulders and thick wrists, and a worn out, tender gaze.

I say thank you when I leave. "You are very kind people," I say – the words do not seem stupid. "Thank you for being so kind. I will always remember it."

There is something about this language, which I cannot speak, that forces me to gush, to speak with a heightened emotion, which I would not employ in my native tongue. But it is true, I think as I leave; I will always remember their kindness.

...

I ride long days, from long dark shadow to long dark shadow, 200km, day after day, across the flat and never changing landscape.

At night, I pull my bike into the forest and immediately find myself in the middle of a cloud of mosquitos. They swarm so thickly that when I breathe through my mouth I inhale them; I feel them tickle in my throat, and though I feel discomfort, I am also glad that I have killed one. I close my mouth, but now they only tickle my nostrils as I breathe them in, and they lodge under the internal skin beneath my eye, which is worse. Others cling to my legs, or attach themselves to my back, out of reach, and pierce my skin through the t-shirt. They are too many to stop, their fine needle-like snouts search for blood vessels under my skin and their abdomens swell red, with blood that's no longer mine. I squash them, in small red blotches against my skin, but there are always more, and though the itch no longer irritates my skin as it did before, I hate them with all my soul. They circle my face, and eyes, and bite my ankles and wrists, and will not listen to my screams, or flee as I swipe at them with my arms. It is endless attrition warfare; I squash them only for more to take their place, and they suck my blood in such small amounts that the fighting will go on forever. It does not help that I rage at them, but I have taken to torture. I no longer squash them quickly. When I can, I hold them between my fingertips, pulling off their legs one by one and then their wings, their searching proboscises, before I rub them into my skin, a dark grey mush. Do they know? Does this infuriate them more? It is monstrous, I know; I am worse than them. It is vengeful and pointless violence. And it serves no purpose, there being too many, too many clouds of them. But why do I take such joy in it?

Sweat trickles down my neck and arms to dry later as salt and dusty lines. I stink; my armpits are old like stale onions, my groin like vinegar. I feel sure that the rest of me smells just as bad, but I have become accustomed to these, less hidden scents. My hair is matted and dirty; it is not unusual for me to find a small twig, or a dead insect in it. It is 8 days since I showered; my hands are calloused and fresh blisters appear on the insides of my knuckles. I sometimes wince from the pain of saddle sores and have to cycle standing until I dare to sit again. The insides of my groin are red, with rubbing sores, and threaten to open, and my legs are crisscrossed with scratches and cuts, and are covered in dried out crusty blood. A tick has buried its head under my skin, and I search around for a pair of tweezers to remove it. I look at my hands ingrained with dirt, and feel the dampness in everything I am wearing from days of drizzle and rain. But I feel okay; I am moving; tomorrow will be different to today, and I am approaching Omsk, and rest. I picture myself, clean and walking around the city's streets, visiting the Dostoyevsky museum, eating and drinking. I take the tweezers to the tick's body, hold tight by its head, not further up near its belly so as not to squeeze the contents of it stomach back into my bloodstream and pull gently; the neck snaps, its head still half-buried in my skin. Again, I hold the tweezers, and this time, it comes out clean and painless, and I flick the head to the forest floor. It has barely left a hole.

...

The jeep rounds my tent again. Headlights shine through the branches and glint off wet leaves. I kneel down in the wet undergrowth, damp moss against my skin, and the scratch of something sharp. I breathe in slow and silent, conscious of every movement; too scared to move, to crack a twig, to send shivers down the leaves. I pray the lights don't find me, don't find my tent. The whine of a mosquito passes my ear and sweat trickles a line down my neck, tickling my skin, and stinging fresh scratches. The jeep drives past again, at walking pace. A torch shines through the trees towards me – they know I'm here. They must have seen me ride across the open farmland to this small patch of woods, between the fields, and clamber in. Please, fucking Christ, don't get out your car!

It was a last resort, this patch of woods, an hour or two west of Omsk, only empty flat farmland all around. But someone has seen me, and wants to find me. Why do they want to find me? I don't know what they want. Would they simply kick me off their land, or would there be a lesson? Between me and the torch, lies about 30 foot of forest. If it were light they would see me. Again, the lights circle, searching in the dark, there is no mistake that they are searching. I crouch, dead still, resisting even the temptation to follow the lights with my eyes until, at last, they leave. The jeep bumps down along the tracks and out of sight. I tread still as quietly as I can, pull up the zip of my tent and, as it rips open the silence, crawl inside. It is hours before I dare close my eyes, waiting for them to return, and all night I lie half-awake, listening in my sleep. I leave before dawn, while the sky is orange and pink.

...

I am sleepless and unwell, and I stop at a café for breakfast and a coffee. The waitress comes over; it is too early for food, I can have a coffee, she tells me and seems to blame me for the trouble I've caused in asking her to make it. Stale vodka lingers in the air, even after she has turned and walked away.

Omsk looms on the horizon. The sight of the city makes me swallow with dread. Across a wasteland, concrete chimneys bleed a thick white smoke into the sky; long grey miles, thick with industrial dirt. I feel disappointment rise within me. More than that, anger.

Soviet tower blocks crowd the roads, each one the same sad form, there to make life dull. I feel like this country is chewing me up, as if to cross it has become a battle. And now Omsk; just another Russian city, a sprawling, filthy mess; an industrial wasteland, a shithole; tired and worn out. I rage against it; there is nothing here, and I have forgotten even what I was looking for. I am too tired of Russia, but I want to rest, for my humour to return.

The cheap and filthy hotels are full. The one room I find costs 3500 roubles, £70, more money than I can spend in a week. The centre is cloying and sickly sweet; tacky funfair rides, and designer clothes shops in the tiny centre of the urban sprawl; everything about it angers me. As I leave the city without looking around, I can find only one positive: I am half-way through Russia, it is half done.

...

I ride the long days across Siberia and I see the taiga as it truly is; thick evergreen forest, blanketing rolling hills and enveloping mountains in the hazy, blue-green distance. It is an unfathomable place, of impossible distances, and here am I, rolling through it.

Tiny villages of crooked wooden houses perch on hillsides. Logs pile high against the walls, ready to warm a terrible winter. Though now the sun's heat swells over Siberia, and I ride into its depths.

Then the day becomes too hot for itself. The sky opens and soon the road is flooded; brown muddy water soaks my legs and I push on through the torrents until I find a truckers' motel.

I walk into the bar, the water falling off me, dripping off my hair and running down my face, boots squelching, and my clothes stiff cold and damp. Before I can ask the waitress about a room, two men call me over to their table. In Russia it is bad luck, or perhaps just bad manners, to leave an empty bottle on the table, and Victor and Evgeny sit, with 2 bottles of vodka resting on the floor. I walk over and they call for another.

"And *shaslik!*" Victor says.

"Yes, *shashlik.*" Evgeny calls after the waitress in agreement.

"We saw you two days ago." Evgeny says, now turning towards me. He does not seem drunk; his gaze is straight, and though perhaps his posture is more relaxed than it might usually be, he does not look like a man who has drunk a bottle of vodka. "It was...Victor, Victor where was it we saw him?"

"Two days ago," Victor shakes himself awake for another round, rouses himself from stupor. He takes a glass of water and empties it. "It was, I don't know where, two days ago... Omutinskoye? No, too far."

"We stopped for the rain too. Still, it's worse on a bicycle."

The waitress brings over another bottle, another glass, and Evgeny fills them without asking, slides them across the table. "Are you going to Vladivostok?"

"No. I want to, but I don't have time on my visa." The truth is now I don't want to, I am ready to leave Russia, or ready for a change, but it is the stock answer and it comes out, the way practised answers do in an unfamiliar language. "I'm going to Mongolia, then China, to Singapore."

"*Davai!*" says Evgeny raising his cup. In all the times drinking in Russia I have never heard anyone say *nastarovye*.

"*Davai!*" I say and the ice-cold liquid warms the cold dampness of my body, and I forget about drying and taking a shower.

Victor and Evgeny are truck drivers on the long slow road from Moscow to Irkutsk. I ask them what they are transporting and do not understand the answer.

"Will you continue tomorrow?" I ask them, and Victor shakes his head.

"Not anymore – tomorrow's a holiday" he laughs, pointing to the bottles of vodka on the floor. "Ten years ago, fine. But today – there are too many police."

The waitress comes over, the *shaslik* kebabs sizzling, freshly barbequed meat. The last time I ate meat was at Victor's house and it is fatty and succulent, and a perfect accompaniment to vodka. Perhaps my gaze wanders after the waitress for an instant, because Evgeny is suddenly laughing at me.

"Do you want a girl?" he asks.

"What?"

"A girl. *Devotchka*," and he looks at me meaningfully. "We'll pay."

"No," I look at him as he pours another three glasses, emptying the bottle. "I'm okay, thank you."

"*Davai*," and we drink. "Why don't you want one? Are you gay?"

"No. I'm not gay. I don't want to pay..."

"Don't worry, we'll pay. No? Why not?"

I'm losing arguments, "I'm tired," I say and the men laugh at me.

"Don't worry – you won't have to do anything," says Evgeny, and lies back further in his chair, bringing his hands behind his head and laughing. "Still no? Okay, well, if you don't want to. You'll have to try the *banya* here, at least."

A few hours later it is almost dark. The sky spits fine mist tiredly as though it too is worn out with all the rain, and we sit outside smoking in the cold air, brushing away mosquitos. "I hate the summer," says Victor, squashing one on his arm.

"Winter's worse."

"Yes, winter's worse."

The waitress comes out and walks with me to the *banya*. Steam rises inside the sauna and she hands me a towel, and stops there for an instant. "You can put your clothes there. There's cold water here." She walks back up along the path to the bar, and I hear the jeers from the truck drivers. The steam soaks into my pores; it is cold outside, but warm in here, I think, pouring cold water over my head and watching it rise as steam. It is cold outside, but warm in here, and I sit, vodka heavy in steam.

...

I am used to watching the black shapes that appear on the horizon form cars, trucks and motorbikes. Though one day, I see a shape that I do not recognise; too thin and slow for a motorbike, too small to be a car. I ride another two kilometres before I distinguish the turning legs and loaded panniers of a touring cyclist.

We slow to a stop and the cyclist on the other side waits for a lorry to pass and crosses the road. I ask the same questions I have been asked for the last three months; Where are you going? Where have you come from?

The cyclist's name is Sierd. He started his journey in Ulaanbaatar, the capital of Mongolia and is cycling a route of 6000km to Moscow. He is clean shaven, and his bike looks clean and well organized. I stand next to him with a straggly half beard and unwashed clothes, plastic bags hanging off my panniers.

I ask him about Mongolia.

"Hard. Difficult," he says. "I cried with pain, from the shaking in the road. They are the worst roads, honestly, the worst roads in the world. Not even roads. When I got to the Russian border I lay down and kissed the tarmac."

"And the food?"

"Goat," he says. "But not good goat – they don't barbecue it. Everything is boiled. But it's different – not like here. You'll be okay. You look strong."

Perhaps he means I look dirty, but as we wish each other luck and say goodbye I feel happy to know that there is someone else sharing the road with me, and the meeting gives me strength.

...

I ride towards lake Baikal and for a week it rains. Each morning I roll up my tent and pull my bike from the forest, wetter and colder than before. The bike rattles over the broken road at four miles an hour; mud and rough cobble stones. Puddles rise, opaque brown, disguising deep, jarring potholes and the bike slams hard each time. Still the wheels don't buckle, the spokes don't snap. The bike rolls on. I am beginning to think that it's invincible.

Inside damp gloves, my calloused hands are wrinkled and dirt runs down my legs, like oil slicks on water. The cold snap has seen the mosquito population plummet, but although they no longer swarm in thick clouds, I still feel the itch of bites all over my back. My tent, and clothes and sleeping bag are all somewhere between damp and soaking; the rain and the colder temperatures continue without respite. I climb the long shallow drag through the forest, and my legs rotate in a monotonous burn.

At the top of the climb, two trucks loaded with thick felled trees rest their overheated engines and lumberjacks stand around, smoking or chewing tree resin.

Dima is the driver of one of the trucks. His smile reveals a missing front tooth and a cracked one, but it is a friendly smile, which doesn't hold anything back; a smile that bares itself, honest and flawed.

"Where do you sleep?" he asks.

I usually lie, if only to avoid the warnings of *banditos*, but now it seems pointless. "Here," I say. "In the forest."

"Follow us."

The trucks' engines sputter into life and roar the way old engines do, coughing out black fumes. I roll down the hill behind the vehicle and as we reach the bottom I spin my pedals into the climb and struggle up the hill. They are waiting for me a few kilometres later at a muddy turn off, down the road.

"We can put your bike on the truck," Dima says. "You can start again from here tomorrow."

I loosen the bags and load them into the cab; we tie the bike on top of the trunks, and the truck bounces down the rough muddy track to Alzamai.

At the entrance to the town, a policeman pulls us over and demands to see a logging licence. He steps back from the van, looks up. One of the lumberjacks is sat on top, but he doesn't seem to care. Instead he looks at me, and points. "Him?"

"A tourist."

"What's he doing here?"

"He's staying at my house."

The policeman turns to me, "Passport."

I hand it across, and watch as it is passed down through the window. The policeman flicks aimlessly through the pages, and passes it back with a scowl.

"*Nash moosor,*" Dima says to me as we are leaving. Our rubbish.

We get to the timber yard and climb out. The men drive two sharp claws into each end of the trunks, and the chains are pulled out taut. One of the lumberjacks stands on the log as it rises, swinging into the air. Then, the claws are pulled loose and the process is repeated until the truck is empty. It is late now; the clouds darken and puddles glimmer with the faint yellow glow of street lamps.

Dima smiles again, his big gapped grin, "Come on!" he says. "Let's go home."

Children ride on old bikes or run beside us as we walk. They ask Dima questions about the stranger he has brought to town and I hear them echo his answers, calling to their friends in excited tones. "*Eez Anglee. Eez Anglee.*" they scream. They seem less concerned that I have arrived on a bicycle; it is enough for them that there is someone here from England, from a foreign country, far away to the west, far away from Alzamai.

I love that name. Alzamai. This town, so far from anything, in the middle of Asia, in the thick vast forest, down dirt mud tracks. The buildings are small and wooden with corrugated roofs. Cranes lift timber onto trains bound for Europe or China. The streets are muddy and the shops' shelves bare. Everywhere hangs a kind of dead, industrial tiredness. Or perhaps it is the kind of energy that a place acquires when it is only there for one thing; for felling trees, and cutting wood, and putting it on trains. But still, *Alzamai.* There is magic in that name.

When we arrive at his house I see the reason for Dima's smile. His wife Olga is pretty, and his young daughter teeters around on the floor, half walking. She falls, clambers up again; lifting herself up with the chair legs.

I kneel down to greet her. "*Kak tebya zavoot?*" I ask.

She tells me her name, but I don't catch it, and her parents look so proudly at her for answering, I don't ask them to repeat.

Olga cooks fish and potatoes, and their friends arrive with a bottle of beer. Vladya brings milk from her cow and we sit eating and drinking beer, then milk from small glasses.

Dima brings out an acoustic guitar and after dinner we play and sing together; Russian songs, and Nirvana songs. Everyone joins in and we sit in the middle of Asia, singing "*I need an easy friend, I dooo, with an ear to lend, I doooo, but she has a clue, I doooo...*" I have never been so far away from home, but it is just like home; a small group of friends gathered around a guitar.

Before bed, they heat the *banya* for me, and I stand in a wooden room in the middle of the night, as the steam pulls out sweat and dirt and the rush of cold water wakes me up.

Dima leaves early in the morning, and I walk with Olga and her daughter down the rough worn tracks of Alazamai. I say goodbye, and thank them, and slip out of their lives.

...

The road turns south, and the weather grows cold. Truck drivers tell me there is snow ahead, and when I ask them about the road they look at me and shake their heads.

"It'll be impossible for you!" they say, their arms shoot up vertically into the sky, portraying the incline of the hills. The taiga stretches on, the vertical slopes never come and soon I reach the shores of Lake Baikal.

Does it matter that I am alone? That only I see the water's edge catch fire and turn to black? That as I plunge into the water, no-one else feels its icy chill? Mountains line the eastern horizon. The breath of water rasps against the shore.

I turn and walk away from the deepest lake in the world, to buy freshly smoked fish in the village, golden, oily and sweet. I sleep long deep sleep in a hostel, though when I awake I am tired and ill.

I am dying of rabies. I am sure of it. Since reading about the symptoms of the disease I have developed at least half of them. I ride in a cold-sweat and a persistent painful headache throbs; my legs feel weak, my muscles stiff, and I shake. The descents along Baikal's shores bring no relief. I have read about the disease; not just the symptoms, but the period of incubation; up to 60 days. It is now 2 months since I was bitten in the Ukraine, and I am struck with panic.

It is just my own imaginings, I tell myself. Just my own stupid thoughts. But in the morning the symptoms persist. And the next day, and the next. Terrible headaches, exhaustion, sweating, weakness, nausea; I fear that I am going to die, and I write in my journal. In case I do.

I will be so elated if I am alive and well in a week's time. I write. *I do not deserve to be. I have been careless with my life a great many times. This instance being just one example.*

It will not be me, of course – because I cannot get rabies, or cancer, or aids or any other fatal disease, because I cannot die.

If these symptoms are not imagined however, I am so terribly sorry to anyone who cares. So silly if my stupidity costs me my life. Such a strange way to die. Rabies – who'd have thought it?

I round the southern shores of Lake Baikal, and I do not die, but I do not forget the fear either. I want to die at home, I think. Old. In bed. A cup of Earl Grey tea in my hand. The road splits in two. Left to Vladivostok, and the Russian far-east, and the road I take, south towards Mongolia.

...

The faces have changed now, in Buryatia province; darker, smoother, more rounded. I reach Ulan Ude, the last city before Mongolia. The city sprawls now, not with heartless tower blocks, but closely packed wooden houses that hug the river banks.

On the road into the centre, a motorbike overtakes me and its rider lifts his visor to talk. Mikhail has returned from Mongolia, the dust still in his wheels, and is going home, to Vladivostok. He takes me to his friend Anatole's house, in the eastern suburbs of the city. Actually, their friendship consists of Anatole having once repaired Mikhail's motorbike, but we are welcomed like old friends, and eat *pozy*, small dumplings filled with meat, and drink vodka until a black hole swallows up my memory and I wake up on the sofa.

Mikhail leaves early in the morning, and Anatole drives me into the city. I spend the day writing to friends and family and falling in love in cafés, until I phone Anatole, and ask him to pick me up.

He arrives on a motorbike, wearing leathers and a helmet and, at first, I do not recognise the man who welcomed me into his home. He takes off his helmet and hands me a spare.

"I've never been on a bike like this," I tell him. "I'm not sure what to do."

"It's easy," he says. "You just follow."

Anatole takes the plastic bag that I am carrying, and though I see no reason not to hold it in my hand, he lifts up the seat and puts it in the compartment below. I step over the bike, behind him, and gingerly hang my feet down until they rest on two metal bars. My shoes are soft, and I feel the bars' shape press through the soles. My t-shirt, worn and sun-bleached, feels flimsy next to Anatole's thick leather padding. I put my hands behind me, reaching for the small handle at the back of the seat.

"Around me," he says, and I move my hands around his stomach, and the bike moves smoothly away from the pavement. Soon, the old historic buildings of the centre are behind us, and the road is busy with traffic and people walking in the late afternoon. It is a strange sensation to move so quickly after so long on a bicycle, but I concentrate on following his body, leaning with it, as we round the corners, and I begin to trust in the movement.

The road widens; two packed lanes of traffic run together through the city. Anatole pulls my arms to indicate I should hold on tighter still, and my stomach hits the back of my spine. The motorbike lurches forwards with a sickening roar and seems to leave my internal organs somewhere behind. In the middle of the city, we tear away from cars and leave them hurtling behind so fast they could be going backwards. I cling to Anatole's stomach and press my body against the force of air and keep my head in line with his as we undertake and overtake cars and dodge potholes in the road. With each swift lean to the side my insides jump. Still deep within the city, I look for a sign that Anatole might want to live, and find it only in the way we swerve out of oncoming traffic. We slow slightly as two roads conjoin, only to tear away again. I feel naked in the t-shirt I am wearing; too afraid to loosen my grip for a second. I cannot help but imagine my tattered body, flung from the bike, and breaking, snapping on the road, lying as scattered limbs, across a very many metres, and how my head would rattle along the floor, encased in this light shell of a helmet.

We slow down and I dare to peak around Anatole's head; in front a pedestrian crossing slides precipitously until we are on it and screaming away. The speedometer dial swings now to 170km per hour and I put my head again locked in line with the helmet in front. I feel the wind batter my bare arms, and the rush of noise engulfs us; I pray only for it to be over.

We reach Anatole's street, and though it seems that we have slowed to a pace at which I could jump off without causing injury, I see the needle still lingering between 60 and 80 on the dial. Finally, the motorbike comes to a halt, and I jump off, desperate to find the unmoving floor. My body feels lighter, less solid, as if some part of me had in fact left the fragile shell of my body, and lay behind us on the road.

I want to scream at Anatole. "170 km per hour in a city! A fucking city! With people and potholes and crossings and a hundred and seventy kilometres an hour!" but I can't find the words and he is a stranger so instead I look at him and sputter out loose words:

"That. Most. Scary. Thing. Life." I feel like the blood has drained from my body, and I feel exhilarated and overjoyed to be standing there.

Later in the flat Anatole asks me if I want to go out, to the river. "No." I reply instantly. "Thank you, but no. I'm really tired."

"We can take the car," he tells me laughing at the terror in my face.

"Well, okay - that would be good. Actually, I'd love to."

Dasha, his girlfriend, comes over and we pack a picnic into the car: fish, ham, watermelon, grapes and cherries. We drive slowly towards the river. The grassy banks lie, like a half-forgotten wasteland, just within the city limits, and the odd car is parked quietly on small crests of land. People fish or barbecue meat in the last bright fragments of the day, and we find a quiet spot to roll out a blanket, eat and talk. Later, we swim in the river. I feel the warm squelch of mud rising through the gaps in my toes, and the current lick my skin clean. The hard, sharp stones that lie beneath the mud dig lightly into my soles and I push off, and float.

My body carried downstream, and as Anatole says we should go back, I bury my face into the river's surface, my eyes closed against its murky depth, and fight sideways against the current, until I reach the bank. Again, my feet sink into mud, but the reeds respond to my grip. Their strength pulls me up and we climb out of the river and walk back.

It is the beginning of summer; the sun's heat is balmy, late into the night, and the long grass teems with life. And I love these still, slow moving things.

In the morning I say goodbye. And thank you. And leave Ulan Ude.

...

It is the end of Russia. The road has wound south, leaving the taiga to the north. Now bare steppe and mountain range, the world is wild. It is no longer the Russia I have known; only the language stays the same, bears the country's melancholic sadness in its lilts and tones.

In crossing half its breadth, Russia has not grown any more familiar to me, and the tiny line that I have woven proves not even to scratch the great, enigmatic surface. I feel sadness exude from the earth; a prisoner, trapped not in a cell, but in the vastness of its reach.

In Kyakhta, I look down from a land-locked cliff to Mongolia, hazy and unreal. Excitement catches in my belly as I approach the border. The hot July wind tumbles north and rolls across the steppe; from the Gobi in the south, it carries those fine grains of sand upon its breath, and lets them fall across the shifting face of an ever-moving world.

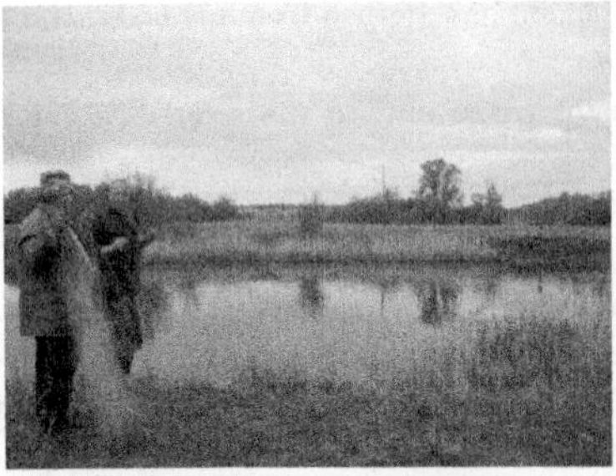
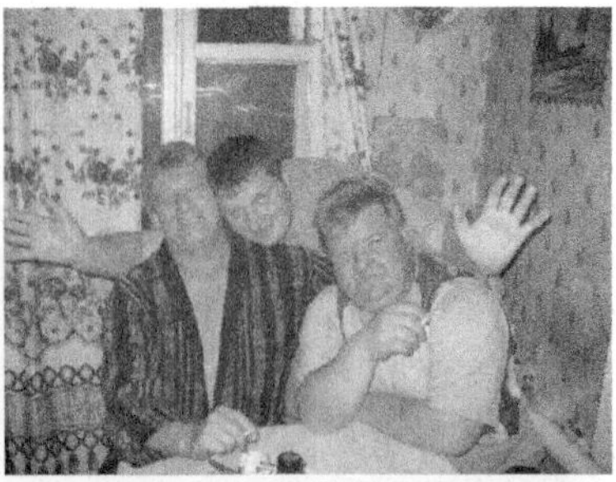
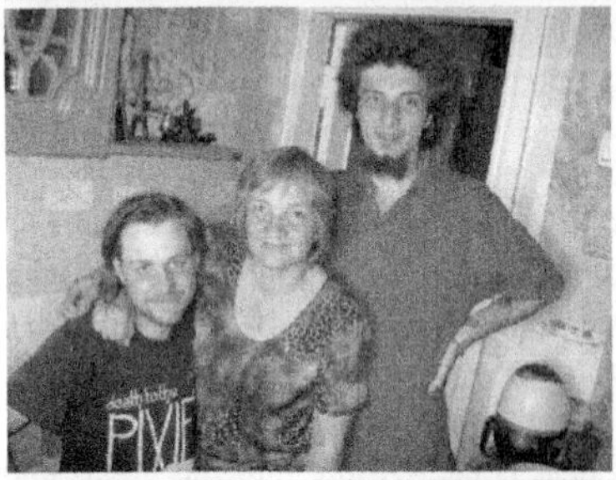
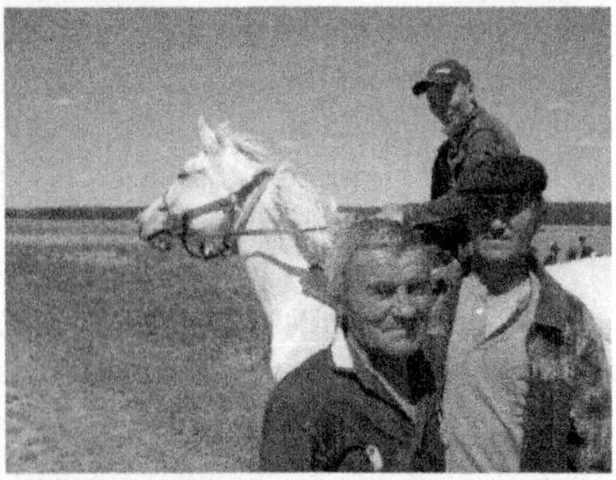
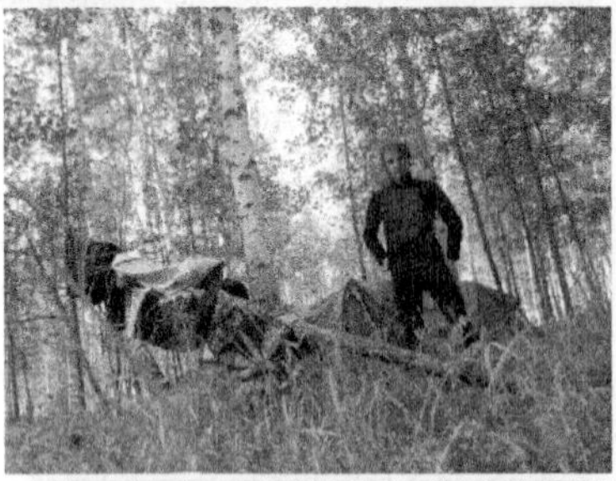
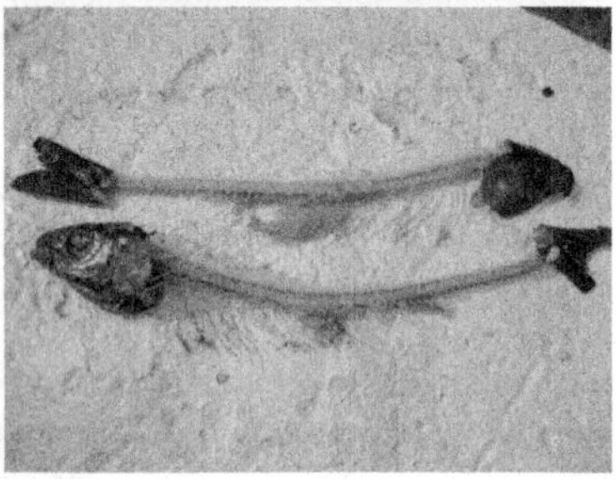
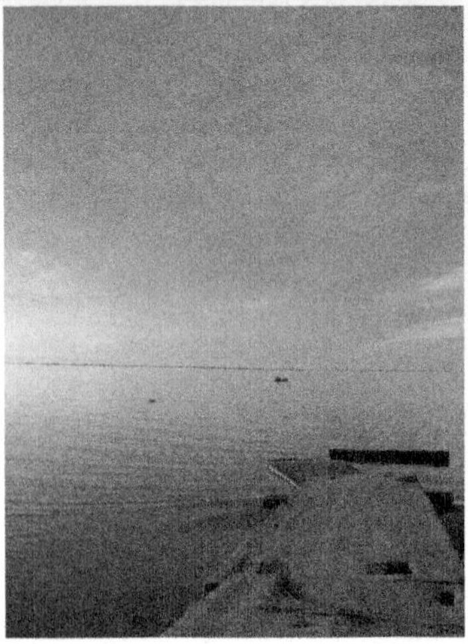
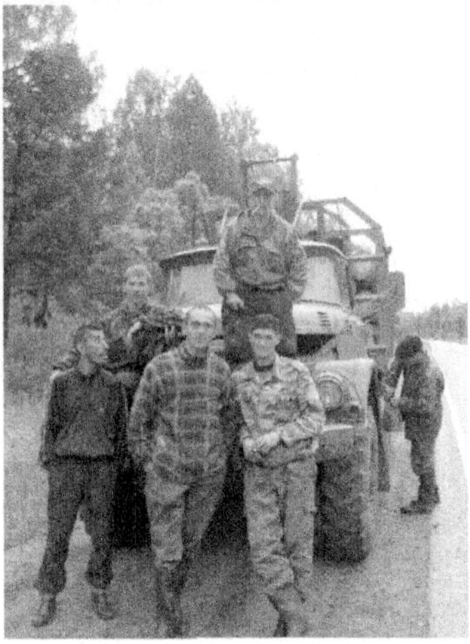

Clockwise from top left: Fishing at Gerna's *dacha* – Victor's *dacha* – In Siberia – Smoked fish, Lake Baikal – Dima and lumberjacks, Alzamai – Lake Baikal – Camping in the forest, Siberia – Gerna and Svetlana, Marx.

Mongolia

4th July – 29th July, 2009

Now the land is fenceless. The grass fades from the deep, rich green under the sky's blue edge to the yellowing sparse reality I see closer to my eyes. This new land belongs to no-one; not even the herdsmen who live from it, grazing their goats and horses on the brittle pastures, and moving across the vast and empty slopes, their nomadic livestock in tow. *Gers* nestle in shallow mountain valleys, and as I stand, gazing out at the empty world, I feel, for the first time, fearless.

...

Shadows fall short and black in the heat of the sun. And I catch my breath, truly happy to be moving and on my own. I marvel at how the world has suddenly changed; the wide-open landscape, speckled white by *Gers*, brown, oval faces, men on horseback, and those fragments of new conversation; throaty and song-like.

I stop to talk to a family by the side of the road. Russian no longer works, as I was told it might, even with the older members of the family, but the girl tells me in English that they are travelling to the capital, to Ulaanbaatar.

The father looks at the water bottle clipped into my bike. I have carried it from England for several months, as some pointless vestige of home, and now algae, or something green, is growing on the plastic.

The man coughs out a sentence and the girl turns to me, translates. "He says you shouldn't drink rain water."

He opens the boot and refills the bottle with cold, fresh water from the huge vats they are carrying. The mother takes out a pack of Kit-Kats and hands them round.

"Would you like some tea?"

She pours the thick, grey liquid into a cup; it is smooth and swills around like cream. I sip it. If I do not think of it as tea it could be pleasant; the first taste is salt, an undertone of bitter herby tea, and then the oiliness of something like butter lingers on my lips. I drink it enjoying how the chocolate melts and tastes sweeter with the salt.

Further down the road, a group of farmers stop me; they pick themselves out of the trees' shade and gather around me with small gifts of bread, pâté and sweets. I understand nothing that they say, but they crowd in on me, playing with the bike, testing its weight and the pressure of the tyres, clicking the gear levers. They take my helmet and pass it around themselves, trying it on, and open and close my panniers. In all these gestures there is nothing which resembles threat, no hint of violence, or robbery; only it seems, curiosity.

I thank them for the food, and ride on south.

...

There is nowhere to hide. No small huddle of trees to obscure a tent's silhouette, nor any sudden contour in the land to block the glow of a camping stove, but it feels so safe and free I do not care. I am not so bold to camp by the side of the road though. As the sun begins to fall, and my shadow stretches, long towards the hills, I follow a track for a couple of miles until I reach the grassy crest of a small hill, and lay my things behind it.

I stop what I am doing and leave a tent pole, slackly curving in the air. Five camels walk past, in front of me, black against the sun. As their unfamiliar shapes cross my path, and the dry yellow grass shines, now golden, in the evening light, I think to myself, how wonderfully like a child I have become. I feel such joy at everything I see; it is like nothing else - the way they move, these camels and the empty world, and the setting sun. I see these things as one sees something for the first time, with the eyes of a new born child, when sight itself is magic. I am lucky to have this feeling, when each day brings new encounters and wakes me from complacency. I had been so close to losing it in Russia. I remember how I mocked Andrei's strangeness whilst eating his food, and feel suddenly ashamed.

In the morning I unzip the tent and a perfect crescent frame of blue and green is formed. On the horizon, hundreds of sheep and goats form a long line on the crest of a hill, like some ramshackle army of woolly Celts, ready, at the order, to charge. I sit drinking strong, black coffee and watch the advance. The army skirts around me, followed by a herdsman, who waves at me from a distance, before I pack and resolve to leave.

...

Trees stand in pained postures of stunted growth; torn and leafless branches form awkward silhouettes; short, ragged and barbed. Before I reach Darkhan all but the hardiest of plants have given up and the soil has turned to sand.

I see three bikes leaning outside a red-brick café and go inside. I have heard about them on the road; a French couple, and a German. "They are just a couple of days in front of you! If you peddle fast you'll catch them."

They too, have heard I was behind them on the road, and are unsurprised when I walk through the door, making the chains hanging across it rattle and chime. "You must be the English guy! We were expecting you sooner – someone told us you were cycling 250km a day." The mouth to mouth form of communication along the road passes information around inefficiently, like Chinese whispers.

Jan has cycled here from Germany and plans to return through the wilder western reaches of Mongolia, back home a different route. Emilie and Arnaud have cycled around Patagonia, Madagascar and are riding now from Lake Baikal into Mongolia.

"We've just eaten," Arnaud tells me, "but eat something if you want – we're in no hurry."

With four bikes we take turns to bear the brunt of the wind, climbing the steady hills, edging ever closer to the capital. When a sign for Ulaanbaatar reads 20km we turn off the road and push our bikes up a steep incline to find a secluded spot.

The experience of camping changes now, as we share our food and pass around a bottle of cold beer and speak without fear of being discovered. Or perhaps it is only me who notices the calm - they have spent the last ten days together and perhaps, before he joined them, Jan had not been so disturbed by the night's unquiet noise. I do not speak about the fear I have felt when camping on my own; perhaps it is irrational, my expectation of attack, my conversion of the forests sounds to anthropocentric steps. Still, we look around and judge the open landscape, decide not to light a fire. We would easily be seen. On the road you meet enough people in daylight hours; there is no need to call for curious visitors during the night.

As the light fades to silver, we climb the stubbly earth to a ridge overlooking the city to the east. It is ablaze; amongst the bare deserted slopes the lights are mesmeric, roads swarm in blurry yellow lines and the city appears to buzz and move.

We sit on the hill looking down. "Well, from here," Arnaud says, "it looks like a very beautiful city."

...

It is not. The next day we follow the road towards what, now in daylight, heaves with dust and noise.

Minibuses jostle for position on the road, spilling out passengers as boys hang out the windows screaming their destinations into the heat. The road breaks into pieces of cracked concrete and we follow the traffic onto the dirt, as a market overflows. Open drains, their covers stolen, sit in the middle of the road – wide rectangular abysses, lying in wait. In the dry heat, dust and fumes stick to sweat, and the noise is a deafening roar. By the sides of the road, goats tied to rusty pick-up trucks are being inspected. No longer do the old nomadic rules apply; five goats for a horse, and one and a half horses for a camel. Now it is cash, and pick-up trucks, TVs and mobile phones. I follow Jan's wheel. Around us, *Gers* line the wide, open valley of the city, like a temporary shanty town, caught up in the new glass and concrete buildings that rise up from the ground. Huge, dusty billboards cling to the sides of buildings; half torn streams of Cyrillic script with its letters doubled to fit, uncomfortably, into the ancient language.

We reach the open square that is the centre of the city. The few polished government buildings that gather around give the impression that we could be anywhere; so why does it feel like we have arrived in Mongolia? A name, perhaps, just that.

...

I apply for a tourist visa at the Chinese embassy. I hand over a reservation for a return flight I do not intend to get on and the details of a hotel I do not intend to stay in. Chinese embassies can be dubious about granting cyclists visas so I decide not to mention it, jump through hoops. The visa, they tell me, will be ready in 10 days.

I kill time. I walk aimlessly around the city. I learn that almost every car in Ulaanbaatar is a taxi. You have only to hold out your arm and within a matter of seconds a driver, with the need for some extra cash, will pull over and take you wherever you want to go. I don't know where I want to go.

One day I find myself at a Gandantegchinlen monastery. Its name translates as *The great place of complete joy*. There is a charge to enter. I scrape my feet through the dusty courtyards. Stray dogs slink, black under the sun. The golden paint is chipped, and much of the stonework reveals itself to be cheap concrete imitation. One of the temples is a shop, and the monks manning it seem reluctant to be there at all. The only person I see who may be near complete joy is a young child running amongst a kit of pigeons, causing it to burst into black, flapping havoc in the sky.

Cities are easy. I wake in the morning, and drink coffee. I read. I go out and eat. I wander, half lost and eat again. I stave off alcohol until the afternoon. The longer I stay, the harder it becomes to leave, to think of leaving. Outside the hostel, men scavenge through the bins. In the mornings they lie on the floor, drunk, until they rise again, to beg, scavenge, and drink. The difference between my current way of life and theirs is minimal. With greater comfort, I too am rotting. It is the longest I have spent in one place since I left, waiting for a visa and a new wheel from home. I decide to leave, pack my things, to return in a few days.

...

Now, the dust of the city is gone. And the sheep for sale by the side of the road. And the goats tied to rusty pick-up trucks. So too the chimneys' smoke, the crowded bus stops and the windowless breeze block walls. The cacophony of squealing brakes and lisping voices, of traffic whistles and loud abrasive horns, sounds only now as a memory; a vague recollection, no longer in my ears, but somewhere in the faded distance.

Above the dryness of the empty steppe, the heat of the air swells and grows humid. The light, spattering rain from the gathering clouds promises downpour, and soon enough I am trundling over the earth, away from the road, in search of a place to camp.

Fat drops darken the ground and the sandy earth drinks, thirstily. I find a place to camp on a gentle slope. Far across the weeping valley, a cluster of *Gers*, white against the green, huddles against the rain, so distant that I see the horses gallop, before I hear the sound of hooves.

I wait in my tent for the rain to pass – the same green yellow walls; the spread of books, and clothes, and maps across the floor, the dried-out mud; the dampened smell of everywhere I've been all mixed to make the scent I know so well that now I barely notice it; as one's own childhood home smells of nothing.

Only several hours later does the sun make its presence felt; light, warming rays shine bright through translucent walls. The new light is accompanied by a beautiful, mourning voice, singing outside my tent. Its tones ache gently through the walls, without sudden turns or staccato beats. It is simply an announcement; I am here.

As I open the zip the singing stops. Outside there is a boy my age; his horse waits patiently a few yards away. He wears a long deep yellow robe, tied with a red cloth sash around his waist. He walks slowly towards me and I invite him to sit down.

His name is Mungo, he tells me. He is a *malchin*, a herdsman. We sit around my phrasebook, pointing. He is married, has two brothers, and he lives with his parents, across the valley. I take out a packet of sweets I bought in Ulaanbaatar, and offer him one. We speak in gestures and smiles, little else, and he plays, fascinated, with various parts of my bike. He points inside the tent, asking for permission to have a look. He moves the zip, tentatively up and down. Has he seen a zip before? His eyes are like mine when I saw the camels. We sit a while longer, outside eating apples, and he leaves saying goodbye, and we both say thank you.

Later, I am making coffee on my stove, the percolator bubbling and hissing out steam, when a sound startles me. I look up to see a horse galloping towards me, full pelt, heading straight for my tent. At the last moment, the horse rears up on its hind legs and shudders to a halt. Another *malchin* jumps down from the saddle. He is older, fatter, but smiles as he takes my hand and shakes it firmly with apparent friendliness. Again, I share fruit and chocolate; I offer him a cigarette and he takes one, holding it out for me to light. I pour the bitter black coffee into two cups and watch as he winces at its taste.

Again, we flick through the phrasebook. I point at the words as my pronunciation renders meaningless everything I say. He tells me that he lives alone and, pointing to the clouds, still dark in the sky, he invites me to spend the night in his *Ger*. I am excited, curious to look inside these homes like no other I have seen, and I hurry to say yes.

He asks me for some money to buy *airag*, fermented mare's milk, and I root around in my pocket for spare notes. I give him 5000 tögrög, about £1.50, and he smiles and puts his thumbs up. It is agreed.

It is only as he begins to rip tent pegs from the ground that I notice he is drunk. I call for him to stop and collect the pegs that he has thrown across the floor. It is time, perhaps, to be on my guard, but not yet cause for panic. He sits, smoking a cigarette, and watches as I lift my panniers out, set them on the ground, roll the tent into its bag, and begin to load the bike. We are almost ready.

It is now that he changes. He pushes my bike to the ground and kicks my helmet, motioning to hit me. His eyes have grown hard and violent and he grinds his teeth, swinging his fists and I jump out of his way. For a moment I stand, perplexed at this change of behaviour. In an instant he has turned and we stand, staring at each other in silence. Then he smiles, steps over the bike and comes towards me slowly. I am ready to duck. To run. I am not ready to fight. But he hugs me, tightly, drunkenly, and I feel the wetness of his lips upon my cheek. I smile at him, and return to pick up my bike, resolved to leave. Again, he pushes it to the floor, and grinds his teeth.

I duck down to pick up my helmet and put it on. When I look up he has taken out his horse whip, and it comes crashing down over my head, with a snap.

"Bayta," I say, "Goodbye." I am pleading, I realise. He grinds his teeth.

It is time to leave. To do anything to leave. I pick up my bike and push it against him as he tries to force it to the ground, and now I stare at him with anger.

"Go home," I say in English. I spit out the words. I am scared. Again, he swings his fists. He pushes the bike over, but immediately repents, and smiling, with his thumbs up, comes to hug me. This time I back away. It is like watching a man hovering between two worlds, each one of them insane.

Again, I watch him clamber onto his horse. It takes him four drunken attempts, but eventually he manages it, and I watch with great relief as he trots away, towards his *Ger*, with my 5000 tögrög in his pocket.

He has covered just a few metres when he turns and, again, gallops towards me. He lashes wildly with the whip as I dive out of his path. He no longer seems drunk, but masterful and confident in his skills as a horseman and he spins around, swinging again for my scrambling body. Perhaps half a minute of this pantomime ensues before his former character resurfaces. Smiling again, he motions toward his *Ger* and indicates through gesture that I am welcome as his guest.

"Bayta" I say. Goodbye.

He stays there, stuck fast on the saddle, staring. I load the panniers onto my bike and cycle away, as fast as I can.

He is not following me. I am almost certain. But for the next 15 miles I check, glancing behind at every sound, at every panicked thought. I am surging with adrenaline, my heart beats, pounding into my chest and I feel it in my throat. When I eventually find somewhere to sleep, far from the road, I am intoxicated with fear. I bury myself in the grass and look down again at the road, in search of my pursuer, but the road is empty, and I try to imagine him, safely in his Ger, at the bottom of a bottle of *airag*.

I wake to find my legs stinging and red. In the rush to get away, or in the violent struggle over the bike, camping fuel spilt over my sleeping bag. Now my legs are covered in chemical burns; they will fester, and erupt in blisters the size of my fingers before I make it back to Ulaanbaatar.

...

When I leave the city, it is with the splitting vodka headache to which I have become accustomed, though I carry no alcohol with me. It is too hard to start each day in pain. And I cannot let my judgement be impaired; there are times, even at night, when I should be on my guard. And besides, I rarely feel the call for it when I am moving. It is enough, this nature, this movement, to fill me. So apart from the light and unrequited yearnings for an ice-cold beer at the end of the day, my abstention is not thought about, and welcome.

On the second day, the sky turns to black; so dark that it appears as a premature night. Thunder echoes across the mountains, and crackles. It will be okay, I think. A drizzle, a shower, and it will pass. But from across an open plain, where horses and other animals graze, those who know this land and sky better than I, are calling me over to shelter.

It takes me less than twenty minutes to pull my bike across the softer ground and erect my tent, but by the time I finish, my arms are stung red and the hailstones have grown to the size of peas. There is a rush of activity to round up the animals, and people wave at me from the *Ger*. I run through the hailstorm and duck through the doorway, into shelter.

Inside the noise changes. The barrage of sleet and hail and freezing wind, turns to a hollow popping, as hailstones slap the canvas roof. A fire gently roars, young children gurgle. The pain in my arms grows numb.

Two posts rise in the middle of the tent. Between them a small stove is fuelled with dried horse dung and smoke rises through a metal chimney in the roof. Earthy orange rugs hang from the walls, and deep red blankets make the tent seem warmer than it is, and muffle the storm outside. Seats, which will later become beds, line the circumference of the walls, and though only a sheet of plastic lies between us and the earth, I had not expected to find such a cosy home, inside the frame of trestle wood and felt.

I take a seat to the left of the stove with the men. To my left sit the older men, and to my right, the children. Across from us the women sit, they too in age ascending order. I count – there are twelve of us; the two other *Gers* now empty as the family groups together, to shelter from the storm. Still there are men outside, taking care of the animals. A woman opposite me breast feeds her baby, and the others clean or occupy themselves with the stove and the younger children. The place is full of laughter; children run around, and I am thrown quick glances, smiles and giggles. Some of the younger children stop in front of me and stare, until they are told to do otherwise and run back to their mother, rub their faces into her leg and clamber with their arms grasping at warm, familiar flesh and folds of fabric. I am handed a bowl; something like soup and rice pudding with specks of carrots, and goat.

"*Bayalalaa*," I say, smiling too much to show my appreciation. "Thank you." But then again, I am a silent visitor, an outsider. 'Yes', 'no', 'thank you'; enough to survive, but with little joy.

We watch the changing weather through the open door; the swelling black of the sky and flashes of blue light. It is wonderful to watch the mountains in this way, framed like a moving picture, and then watch them disappear as the rain falls so heavily that all outside is lost, and the frame gives way to a pelting curtain of hail. The rain and hail are so heavy that they come through the ceiling and up through the walls, and we have to pail the water out with buckets. Still, the baby does not cry. Attached to its mother's breast, it seems oblivious to the violent storm and the rush to save the *Ger*.

Soon, the mountains come back into view; the cold glimmer on their peaks betrays the setting sun, and water drips from the door frame, draining from the roof. Before I say goodnight, we drink a cup of *airag*; it is thick and milky sour, and I feel the bits of churned milk in my mouth long after I have swallowed the liquid.

Outside, the hail has churned up the earth so that the never farmed land appears ploughed. The horses are whinnying in protestation at the sky; their hides glisten with melted ice. My tent is covered in mud; half buried in walls of earth and hail, but the inside is miraculously dry. I lie back and sleep more deeply than I have before, protected by the surrounding *Gers*, and thankful that they saw my need and the violence of the storm, before it broke.

...

It takes me half an hour to pull my bike up the dry river bed, dragging it through soft sand. There is still long grass, like dunes on each side and I follow the river's twists and turns until I am out of sight of the road. In the sand there are strange things. Dried dung, camel or horse. Bones. A goat's skull. Stories.

Still, the flow of water is seen in the river bed, its smoothened sand. It would be a bad idea to camp on the bed itself. The sky is threatening; flash floods are in the air.

Overhead a cloud stretches across the sky, leaving only a tiny crack of light on the western horizon, now red with the setting sun. I watch as the cloud swells with electricity. Way out in the distance the sky flashes blue, and I watch the thunderstorm sweep across the land, exalted. There is a moment when I think it will never come, that I will watch the storm from a distance under a dry sky, but soon the drops fall on my tent, and the flashing light and thunder are simultaneous. I am inside the storm, but I lie quietly watching the walls shudder in the wind, flash bright and then to black.

The morning is bright and dry again. I pack, and ride on, south.

...

The town of Choyr lies on the edge of the Gobi Desert like a shipwreck. Its half-deserted blocks are worn grey with the wind and its rectangular grid-like form, eloquent as a scratch on a toilet door, says Russia was here. Now life churns over, resentfully. Cars sputter and sandy unsurfaced streets lie rubbish strewn and desolate, but it is the last real town for days. I stop and sit in a dark café eating *khuusur*, minced goat in crispy batter, and *buuz*, minced goat in a soft, soggy dumpling. Perhaps it is only flour Mongolians take from the passing trains. At midday, I am the only customer the radio plays to, through small, tinny speakers, *If you're going to San Francisco,* it sings in long, drawling tones. I am. But I do not like the reminder. I had forgotten the world's enormity. San Francisco. I am going the wrong way.

I sit for a while, reluctant to leave, until two drunks enter and try to prise me away from my watch in return for a glass of Coke. It is a cheap watch, but worth more to me now, than the glass they place before me. I thank them, but leave the bar only with a 2 litre bottle of frozen water. As I walk out again into the 40-degree heat, I feel like I am taking the best part of Choyr with me.

A kilometre later the road runs out, left hanging in the air, corroded by flash floods or desert winds. It has been broken and whoever has been charged with its repair has given up, or has turned to other things. I face the desert. I have reached the Gobi. Now, I just have to cross it.

...

Though the road has disappeared, a myriad of tracks crisscrosses the desert's surface, and to my right a constant black line to China marks the trans-Mongolian railway. I will keep it always in my sight, I think, and my bones begin to rattle over the corrugated ground.

The track leads only to a mine. It ends at a fence, not even a gate, and I ride on the bare hard sand, around the perimeter until I come to the train track. I lift my bike over the rails on to the other side. There are no tracks here, but the sand is compact and I follow the rails southeast. I have lost time going only sideways, but it is water that I think about. I am carrying 20 litres; enough to reach Sainshand, but not if I have to cycle sideways, zigzagging my way across the sand. My thermometer reads 42 degrees, and I turn towards the shade of a tunnel under the train track. Brown, opaque water gathers in the shadows. My approaching footsteps cause a horse to bolt into the distance. For a moment I feel bad, but I need the shade more than it needs the muddy water and for a moment I sink into it and look around. Animal excrement and torn lengths of barbed wire. It is not a place to sleep. I force myself to get up and carry on.

After an hour I see a track in the distance and I walk towards it, pulling my bike over the sand which has become too soft to ride on. As the sand becomes firm, I clamber onto my bike again. For a while the harder surface provides relief, but then I grow tired of the jolting, up down motion, and the pace which feels slower than walking. The railway is a distant line on the horizon when I see a single *Ger* and decide to stop.

Two young boys run over to where I am sat on the floor, gathering the strength to mount my tent. They are seven, perhaps, seven and eight. I wave to their father who has watched them from the *Ger*, and the boys talk at me without noticing that I do not understand.

They want to help me put my tent up, and I am surprised when their help proves useful. They pull the material taut and hammer pegs into the ground with stones, threading them through the loops. Eight years of moving a heavy felt tent and livestock around the desert has made them handy. They are already tough. The boy who I take to be youngest is covered in hard white lumps; insect bites, or scars from pox. The tent is up and they help me with my things, running around and passing me my bags. It is an event. Around there is nothing; the landscape bereft of anything that appears able to support life and the horizon constant and flat, dull and sandy grey. The father calls the boys home and I sit and cook. I pour a tin of Heinz baked beans I have carried with me from home into a pan, and fry a slice of half stale bread in oil. I look around. The surroundings make the familiar food seem strange.

I wait until night. I cannot read. There is too much to see. Too much nothing.
...
The next day I wake at 5.30, as the sky grows light, and leave.

The tracks follow a spider's web of different directions. It is impossible to know which one to choose. A road that seems to start well soon deteriorates into deep soft sand or bog. Others spin away from the train tracks and turn north. I abandon them, scared to cycle for days only to return again to Choyr. Or worse, to ride into the Gobi's depths, get lost and die. The thought seems suddenly real. I haven't seen the tracks for hours, and my only navigation tools are a 1:1,000,000 map and a compass.

I ride directly east until I find another track. Its corrugated bumps are a torment, but I follow it slowly south, south east. I ride for an hour and stop; I check the compass, scan the horizon in search of the train tracks, give up and ride again. The ridges dissolve into deep sand then, the wheels sink and I fall. For a moment, I lie in the sand; the heat of the sun heavy above and in the sand's soft scratch. I pick myself up, I carry on. I am tired, and stupid for wanting to do this.

Barbed wire catches under my wheels and the tire hisses empty. There is no shade to shelter in and I sit on the floor, pulling out the wire and replacing the inner tube. The water I am carrying is as hot as everything else, but it is also disappearing. If I get stuck here, it would last two days, three at most. The only thing I can do is keep moving.

Hours later, I come across another *Ger*. A group of men are sat outside and I ask the way to Sainshand. They point, simultaneously, in different directions, and I look around, hopeless. Eight tracks run, first parallel, but then fork away from each other. I pick the middle one and again after a mile it is lost in deep sand. I ride over the desert sand and stones, to another track. I follow, until it too is lost in sand and search for another. Give up. Head south east. I am beginning to hate this place.

After 16 hours I have ridden 43 miles. I stop, exhausted. There is nowhere to hide, but no-one to hide from either, and I drag my drained body and a heavy bike across the sand, a stone's throw from the track. I stop myself crying and set up camp.

As the sun's heat mellows so too does my mood. I no longer feel hatred towards this place, but terror. I am in awe of it. And I am glad to be on my own. It is empty, and would be less so if I had company. There is no-one for many, many miles and with this realisation comes a sense of freedom I have not felt before. Though I do nothing with the freedom. I sit down and watch the tiny stones in the ground glow golden, cast long shadows, and I sleep.

...

After four days I reach Sainshand, with 2 litres of water to spare. My hands are in agony. It is as though I have been tied to a pneumatic drill for days, but I am caught up with joy and relief as I roll into the town on a smooth concrete road. I find a place to sleep called 'Od hotel'. The owner stands, laughing at me as I mime 'sleeping' and 'one night' – he replies in English.

"If you don't want a Mongolian to share a room with you, you can buy two beds and have the room to yourself."

I haven't got a problem with Mongolians, I tell him. But for 5000 tögrög, the space would be nice. He tells me that a group of Germans passed through on bicycles a week before, on their way to Ulaanbaatar – it is a common choice of torture it seems.

I eat twice, I shower, I phone home, and all these things are wonderful. Later, I watch from my window as a sand storm sweeps through the town. Gusts of sand swirl around the main square in opaque waves.

...

Leaving the town is hard. I move now with an outpouring of foul language; a constant torrent of swearing, spoken out loud and sometimes screamed. I mumble under my breath, "I fucking hate this fucking cunt place. Fucking cunt. Fucking cunt," over and over again. The words soothe me. I have never sworn so much in my life before, but the words are needed, and somehow provide relief. Later, another puncture. Thorns this time. And the wind blows a hot gust of sand, whipping it across my face. "Fuck Off!" I scream. And then again, louder "Fuck off!" Over and over again as the sand whips harder, "Fuck off!" And then it becomes uncontrollable and it breaks into a "Fuck oh oh oh oh oh," and a heaving, dry sobbing.

...

I make progress. Slowly, the miles tick over, and convince me of the fact. I ride all day, from early morning till sunset. And I stop and sit, and feel the silence and the stillness of the desert seep into my body.

I hate this place. I have found my Winston's rats and it is here. If I ever cross this desert again, it will be on a train. Even as I think this though, I realise it is not a bad hatred; it is a struggle, a realisation of my size, my weakness and my strength. Even as the sun falls, I struggle to recall the agonies of the day; I feel only the cooling of the night, and the stillness. What a gift it is to forget. It is how we carry on – remembering that there was pain, but not feeling its surge. I laugh at my recent rages, they seem petty; already the desert cannot be as bad as it truly is.

...

I have reached the last bottle of water when I see *Gers* in the distance and ride towards them, dry-mouthed. I do not dare take a sip in case there is no water to spare. The last two villages on my map have not appeared, nor have I seen them. The wrong track then. Two days of the wrong tracks. I am welcomed inside by a man who speaks Russian. He offers me a place to stay, but I refuse. I want to keep moving, every daylit hour of every day until I leave this place.

"Some water would be great, if you have it."

He goes outside to a plastic barrel and scoops the water up with a plastic jug, filling my bottles. The water tastes of goat and old milk and camel. I am deeply grateful that the man is here, and that he has shared his foul-tasting water, but even now I wonder at his life, and the lives of all the people in this desert. It seems an existence of scraping. It makes everywhere else I have seen seem plentiful and rich, and I feel frightened and amazed that people can live here.

He smiles at me as I leave. "You're almost there. It's 130km to Zamyn Uud and the border."

...

I wake to find that the wheel has deflated slowly overnight, and search around in the half-light with my fingers looking for a barb or thorn. After it is mended, I pick up my things and leave. It is not long before obscenity falls from my mouth again. The jolting of the road has sunk into my body; my fingers tingle with pins and needles and my knees ache.

When at last I make out the shape of Zamyn Uud and realise that the horizon I am looking at belongs to China, I break down and cry with real tears for the first time since I left home. I let myself. I take off my glasses and rub my eyes, and taste the salty wetness of tears with my tongue. I cry with relief and exhaustion and joy, but bitterness as well. I am still angry at the desert and the pains in my hands and the blisters covering my skin. But mostly I cry with relief. I have made it.

...

The town cannot keep the desert out. Gers huddle like fat white penguins around the border's trade. Beautiful structures that for centuries have moved across Asia, as far as Eastern Europe, stand still. Stained the deep rusty brown of the desert sand, the ground clings to them, or they sit hooked to it.

Perhaps it is a sensible move, to an easier life. No longer dependent on the land which seems only to scorn, now each day there will be water and food. But it seems no more than a miserable transport hub; there is no other reason for its existence than the artificial border and the railway tracks. Sand piles up in banks at the side of the road, and rubbish lies, uncollected. The few miserable examples of livestock are tied to posts; straggly bare and thin, they have given up even bleating.

Only a kilometre away, China lies to the south. But surely, it makes no difference. This last week in Mongolia has impressed upon me a picture of a treacherous and uncompromising landscape; a place where the environment dictates the actions of people and not the other way around. It must be impossible to live differently, I think, and picture a similar town, on the other side of the border, a miserable speck on the desert. There is nothing to sustain anything else.

I am not allowed to cross the border on a bike, nor enter China on foot. Whether it is a law handed down from Beijing, over-zealous officialdom, or simply some quiet agreement between the border guards and those who provide transport for the short journey, I do not know. But I do not argue with the guards, and turn back to look for a jeep to carry me across the short distance. The continuous line of which I have dreamed is broken. I have pulled and pushed and dragged my bike across the bare back of the Gobi, only to be told that I cannot ride the few hundred metres on tarmac into China.

Clockwise from top left: Camping near Ulaanbaatar with Jan, Emilie and Arnaud – The first sight of camels, Mongolia – Crossing the Gobi – Nearing China, Gobi – Tent putter uppers – Camping on the steppe – Skull, Gobi Desert.

China

29th July – 11th October, 2009

It is a shock to find Erenhot, alive and bustling, on the other side of the border. People ride on rickshaws, loaded with rice and corn, and fresh vegetables shine brightly. Everywhere, in bright new plastic, indecipherable Chinese characters promise things I can only guess at, and the language is no longer throaty, but singsong, bellowed and loud.

The central square is as big as the square in Ulaanbaatar; a wide-open expanse of smooth polished stone, and beneath, a small park. Pathways lead through deep green grass and trees, past water fountains and artificial lakes. A small wooden bridge crosses an artificial stream, and from it, I look to the small red rectangle of fabric with yellow stars on it, hanging above the square and dancing in the heat of a Gobi breeze.

It is a town to show off. Built quickly, it stands on the border, peering over at Zamyn Uud, and says to the northern plain: *This is China. If we wish, we will have water fountains and lakes in the middle of the desert. In the shade of our walls you will forget the desert's heat and the sand that whips, and thirst and hunger too. This is China; look what we can do!*

I wander the streets enraptured, barely noticing that, above the orange haze, the sky has turned to black. The air falls thick with the sweet smell of sugar and roasting peanuts, the scent of meat and spitting fat, of chilli that catches in the back of the throat and hot pepper that draws water from my eyes. Fresh sticky rice lends its earthy sweetness to the mix, and cumin, and star-anise, and the burnt charcoal smoke of barbeques swims in the evening air. Everywhere there is an intoxicating clamour of activity; a frenetic excitement fills the streets. People shout through megaphones to sell their wares, or wander the streets, looking for trade. They sell cold beer and cigarettes. Photographs and plastic toys. DVDs and magazines. Clothes, underwear and socks. They sell polaroid photographs and fair rides. Yo-yos, flashing lights. They sell bowls of noodles, sticks of meat, spicy fried chicken and sickly-sweet juice. It is impossible not to get sucked in.

The heat of the Gobi serves no longer to lull the body into lethargy, but to spark a fire instead; to chase after all of capitalism's joys, and run from its discontents.

I sit on a stone wall, ripping meat off a metal stick with my teeth, feeling its crispy fat and the heat of chilli on my tongue. It has been so long since I ate food that tasted of anything so good.

Gamba and Zerhka, the Mongolians who helped me cross the border, and with whom I am sharing a room, are sat at the hotel, drinking.

"Beer?" Zerhka, asks me.

"How much are they?"

"2 kuài!" he says smiling. "Cheap. Everything in China, cheap!"

I take a beer from the fridge and the cigarette he offers me. The boys have come here to buy things to take back to Mongolia and sell. Zerhka is an engineering student, and he is learning Chinese and English. Gamba is his friend and speaks to me in gestures, most of them obscene. We walk out into the streets, towards the square, and we buy more beer from a street vendor. Gamba looks at me in disgust as I eat another kebab dipped in chilli and spices.

"We're Mongolians!" Zerkha tells me. "We don't eat chilli!"

I am happy sitting in the square and watching the people walk past, but Gamba wants to go to a bar; a 'Mongolian Club'. He stands in front of me miming a stripper, takes off a pretend bra. I look at him, for a moment, puzzled.

"There are girls at the bar." Zerhka says, and Gamba finishes his mime with a decisive gesture; *even their knickers!*

I follow them to drink in company, and because they tell me it's free. It is not what I expected. Bigger, cleaner; the stage looks like a production set, or a fashion show catwalk. We sit around a table with a big group of their friends, but next to us a couple of middle-age Mongolian ladies sit, staring at the lights on stage. I order three beers. They are 25 yuan each, and I think about how much happier I would be outside. Another of their friends speaks English and we shout over the music, barely catching what the other is saying, until the girls appear on stage. It is a dance, more than a strip-tease, rehearsed and repeated over and over until all surprise or accident has been squeezed out of it and the performance has been rendered sterile. At the end of it the two girls are naked, and for a moment they stand in front of us, before walking off stage. I have never felt less excited to see a girl naked in my life.

As we walk back, the streets are quiet. No-one is around, but the ghost of activity is still present, like the crowds have left something behind; something that buzzes, under the streetlamps. Girls stand in what look like café entrances. The glow of pink lights behind them catches the silhouettes of short dresses, tiny bodies and light brown skin. Gamba is gesticulating again, and this time I do not need Zerhka to translate. He is saying we should share a girl, for 100 yuan, and he slaps his palms together leaving no doubt about what we would do to her. I look at Gamba' s face, fat and sweaty in the light. I am sober after the prohibitive prices of beer, and it is easy to say no.

...

I am surprised, the next day, to find the desert still there. Beyond Erenhot's reaches the landscape is just the same; a sandy, rocky wasteland, stretching as far as I can see under the deep blue sky. Only now, I ride above it, lifted by a smooth tarmac road, and the expanse slips by with such ease I can almost forget where I am. I am no longer connected to the desert, and for this I do not feel sorry; it no longer rattles my bones, or scares me with its size. On this side of the border the flat emptiness of the Gobi lies always interrupted by telephone wires and electrical wires, power stations, factories and fences. Though the heat grows strong and the wind whips sand into the air, cars and trucks pass and rob the desert of its silence. And a single black line steals from its vastness, and provides safe passage. All that remains is its ugliness. Its lifelessness. I ride on south.

...

First, short, brown blades of grass appear, grow greener, then tall. Then, the cob walled huts of small villages begin to dot the landscape and flocks of sheep, first small and sparse, grow in frequency and size. Shepherds sit under the shade of small twisted trees, and there are leaves; brittle olive green. Then the neat green lines of arable farming, and the ploughing of land. A fine drizzle spatters my face, light and cold, from a greying sky, and at the sight of each new living thing I feel excitement and happiness; immersed once more into all that makes life rich. It is as if I had been under water for far too long, and only now, bursting out from under its surface, am I able to draw breath.

...

In the middle of nowhere, I find a café and a cheap truck-driver hotel. The bed costs 10 yuan. I am to share with three Chinese truckers, and every so often the door, hanging slightly off its hinges, is pushed open by chickens seeking refuge from the rain. I watch them fill the room with their feathers and bustling movements, but I do not bother getting up.

When the sky clears, I shoo the chickens outside and follow them into the fenceless yard. They peck at the dusty earth. Occasionally, I watch them venture from the patch of land they have made their own, with their shit and straw and scratching feet, down a shallow slope where the grass is slightly longer, before returning again to eat. They peck, mindlessly, at the earth.

Someone in the restaurant orders chicken. The waiter comes out and walks amongst the birds, and they scatter, without urgency or fear as he bends to pick one up. It is easy enough, and soon the chicken dangles, pre-emptively lifeless, in his hand. He walks back across the yard, unmindful now of the chickens, and they scramble to avoid his steps. He kneels on the floor and takes a knife from his apron. There is a moment of quiet it seems, but perhaps it is only a catch in my breath. The chicken is silent as he bends its neck towards the sky. And silent as the knife cuts a precise slit down its throat. The man holds the chicken still, as the blood runs down in a slow steady stream to the ground and the other chickens gather, pecking at the dust and lifting the blood in strands. For several minutes the blood trickles out of the wound and the chicken's body convulses. The slit is made deeper, the artery is cut perhaps, and the blood rushes quicker, in pronounced, pulsing beats. The dying chicken clucks; the sound breaking in its open throat. And as the blood runs dry, the chicken falls limp and dies. Still, on the ground, the chickens peck and stab at the blood, and lift it up, fresh and warm, before it dries or soaks into the ground.

Two hours later the process is repeated, and again the chickens gather to peck at the blood and dust. I look at the fenceless patch of earth, and the open, unguarded world and wonder at the stupidity of chickens, eating grain and blood, and waiting there to die.

...

In the morning, I am woken by the movements of the truckers, just as their snoring disturbed the night. For hours I have lain with a blanket over my head, trying to align my breathing with the uneven thunderous noise. The swing of the door on its hinges, the passing trucks, the desert wind, and all the comings and goings of the night have kept me awake. Now, outside, the sound of spitting and the early crispness of the air seep under the open door. When I look up the other beds are empty, and I pull on my shoes to walk across the bare concrete floor. The chickens have returned to pecking and scratching; yesterday's traumas, if they were ever seen as such, forgotten.

I inspect my bike, before I load it. It has felt strange over these last two days on tarmac; noiseless, something slight, but I have noticed it all the same. The wheel is buckled, and I take out the spoke key to true it. It is frustrating work; though the wheel now spins with only a slight curve, no longer that pronounced wobble, the tension in the spokes is too inconstant. I do not know what is wrong, and worse, I have attracted a crowd to witness my incompetence. One of the Chinese truckers takes the wheel, spins it; straight. Straight enough. He puts his thumbs up; it'll do. But now another man steps forward and is pointing at something else; the hub. Fuck! I think. Nothing more. There is a tear in the alloy, ripping around the hub for about a quarter of its circumference. The extra weight and rough terrain of the desert have taken their toll. It explains why the wheel was so hard to true, but it is unfixable. Welding will not help, nor gaffa tape, nor anything else I have at my disposal. Though I have passed through the southern reaches of the Gobi, there is little chance of finding a new wheel here. I look at my map; it is about 650km to Beijing.

As I leave, the truck drivers are protesting, drawing their fingers across their necks, *You will die,* they say. But the wheel holds, and I pedal the bike gently south, checking every now and then that the crack has not got worse.

...

On the smooth roads, the hub's condition does not deteriorate and the world grows greener still. The rain falls heavy in the morning, though I no longer smell it. It is not a place for subtle scents. The road teems with traffic. Truck after truck after truck. And the sky has changed; it is oppressive now, and humid; without edges. The earth and the sky are no longer separate, one breathes into the other, and everything has become hazy, that polluted Chinese grey. My skin is wet with sweat, and the people walk slow, trudging under a heavy sky. And there is more noise than I have ever known. Horns are louder, and incessant. People shout. There is no silence. The towns become bigger, more difficult to navigate, and I look, helpless, at the road signs and try to guess what they might mean.

I push my bike through a market place in Huai 'an. Motorbikes with trailers, piled high with boxes push through the narrow lanes. A woman sits by a cart of apples and a kitchen scale, hollering. And the homely smell of garlic and chilli fills the streets with pungent steam. Carts and trucks sit, sheltered from a hazy sun by red umbrellas, and on the floor a girl sits, picking up scorpions from a washing-up bowl with chop sticks, placing them in a small plastic bottle as they squirm in her grip. The insects are still alive, but many have lost their stings or limbs in the struggle to escape. People push their bicycles, loaded heavy from the market; woven baskets and carrier bags. By the side of the road men dig a trench. It is work that in Europe would be done with heavy machinery, but they break into the hardened ground, with pickaxes and spades. Their bare backs twist and shine with sweat.

I am no longer invisible, as I was in the desert. And no longer free. When I sit down to eat, or drink, or read I attract attention. Children stare at me or hide, behind their mothers' skirts. Girls point at my nose and laugh. People take photographs of themselves with me; of themselves with my white face. In the small towns it seems like the sight of a lǎowài is rare, and the people gather to see how I eat, how I drink and how I look lost when they talk. They are curious and friendly, and they smile, and the men offer cigarettes.

I remember speaking to two Japanese travellers in Ulaanbaatar. "China is a smoker's paradise!" they told me, and it is true. Every time a stranger, a man, approaches me, I am offered a cigarette. They hold them out before nǐ hǎo. If I refuse they look shocked and, I begin to suspect, offended. Now I take even the cigarettes I do not want, and smoke as they poke and prod my bike and talk about me in words I can't understand. People smoke in restaurants, on buses, in internet cafés and bars, in hotel rooms, before a meal, after a meal, during a meal, riding bikes, carrying food, carrying children. It is a smoker's paradise. It crosses my mind that a government that enforces a 1-child-only law and still struggles with a growing population may not be inclined to tax this deadly drug.

...

There is a knock at my hotel door. The police walk in.
"Do you know Chinese language?"
"Nope. Sorry."
"Where are you from?"
"England."
"Where are you going?"
"Beijing."
"Passport."

They are friendly enough. They take photos of my passport, and leave. They tell me nothing more.

...
I cycle along the flat floor of the valley. Workers move slowly through small rice fields, irrigated by the passing river. Their backs curve, bent at the hip and heads disappear between the lush green blades. They lift their arms and heads up again, throwing strangling weeds into a basket, growing heavy.

On the outskirts of Beijing the mountains turn to cliffs and tumble down towards the city. Lush undergrowth, thick dark green, exhales into the air, into the fumes from passing trucks. The edges of the cliff fall steeply away, and I stare down into ravines to see only the thick wet smog of the Chinese sky, flatly covering everything.

Trucks overtake on hairpin bends and blind summits and brakes hiss and squeal. The gradient now precipitous, I glance back at my wheel, praying it will hold these last few miles, as the road sweeps into a tunnel, the end of which I see as a dull grey light before the road turns to black and disappears from beneath my wheels.

Roads sweep above me in huge circles, packed with trucks and tunnelling through the mountain, rising far above the valley floor. It seems impossible, the way these highways sweep through and down the cliff sides, defying all doubt.

As the land grows flatter so the city's sprawl begins; the sixth ring road, the fifth ring road. Now the road I ride along is seven lanes wide, with one for bikes alone. Scooters fly past, and I follow the wide flat highway towards the city centre. Fourth ring road, the sign says in English. I no longer stand out, my white face and my big white nose. I see people take an occasional second glance, but it seems that it's the bags and strange appearance of my bike which draw attention; foreigners are nothing new.

"Hey!"

I turn around to see a Chinese guy riding a yellow Giant bike. "Hey!"

"Where are you going?" his accent is North American.

"Ummm... I'm going around the world. I've just come down from Russia."

"I was in Russia!" he says. "I just got back from there. I rode Saint Petersburg to Vladivostok."

"Wow!" I change gears and ride at his side. "I heard about you. People told me there was a Chinese guy ahead of me."

"I'm not Chinese, I'm Canadian."

"Oh," I say. "I'm sorry."

"No, I'm just kidding. Well, I am Canadian now, but I'm originally Chinese."

We speed up to overtake a rickshaw, weighed down by an enormous tower of cardboard boxes and sputtering exhaust fumes into the air. A scooter beeps as it passes, and a young child stares at us, standing between the legs of the scooter's rider.

"So, how was Russia?" I ask him.

"Big, flat. You know, you were there."

"Did it change much? I only got to Ulan Ude."

He thinks for a moment, "No. It's pretty much the same for thousands of kilometres after that. There were some nice meadows around Chita though."

"And what about the people?"

"They were okay. The women were nice. But the *men!*" and he pulls a face to say uuggh!

"What's your name?" I ask him.

"I'm Song!" he says, and smiles at me. "Some people call me Mad Dog Song!" I laugh at what I presume is some kind of joke or reference I don't understand.

We ride under another bridge, past a park. An ice-cream truck stands by the gate. "Listen," says Song. "I have to go to a Spanish lesson right now, but here's my number. Call me. I'll show you around Beijing."

I take his number, putting it in my pocket and keep following the road, swept along by the constant torrent of cyclists and rickshaw riders, and scooters, propelled towards the city. The second ring road. The road is still wide and flat, a huge angular valley, and buildings rise, ten or fifteen storeys, into the sky. It is not the city I had expected. After the bustling provincial cities I have passed, Beijing appears like some sterile idea of New York. But one to which a giant hand has been taken; squashed, flattened, crushed and spread out like biscuit dough.

Then I hear Song's voice behind me, "I was so mean," he says. "I'm sorry, I was so mean."

"What?"

"Follow me!" he says. "You can stay in my flat."

"Thanks, that would be really cool. But I need to find a bike shop. My wheel's broken."

"Follow me!"

Song takes me to a bike shop. And he talks to the shop assistants.

"Don't worry," he says. "They'll sort it out. By the way, they know a guy who wants to cycle to Xi'an. I don't know if you'd be interested, but you could meet him. It would help you see a different side of China."

"Yeah." A change, some company would be good. "Yeah, I'd like to. Thanks."

I leave the bike shop with a new chain, new wheel, new brakes and no-one will let me pay for anything. "It's a gift," says Song.

"From who?"

"From us," and he sees my face and stops me. "Don't worry about it."

...

The next day we go to meet Ren Hong Chang, the boy they were speaking about in the shop. He is planning to cycle to Tibet, but he wants to ride with me to Xi'an. He speaks no English, but with Song as a translator we agree a day on which to leave. Song has a friend coming to stay at his flat so I thank him, and decide to stay in a youth hostel for the remaining four nights of my stay in Beijing.

As we are leaving Song turns to me. "Can I ask you a personal question?"

I nod, but I feel myself flush red with anticipation, "Yeah, sure."

"Ren wants to know if you like girls."

"Umm... yeah, sure. I like girls."

"No. But, he wants to know, if, when you're travelling, you want girls. He's thought of everything. He wants you to have a good time."

I am too slow to catch his meaning. "If I want girls?"

"Yeah, like, you know? You're travelling, and you get lonely, and maybe you want to get a girl for the night. He wanted me to ask you."

"Oh. No. I don't want girls. Thanks. Not like that. Tell him no."

...

At the hostel I meet Leo, a Finnish backpacker, and we go out into the city centre. There is a gig on at a small bar by the Forbidden City. As we approach it, we hear the band sound checking; the opening chords of *God Save The Queen*. It has been so long since I heard live music; the distortion of the chords, the volume, seems misplaced in Beijing. We are a short walk from Tiananmen Square, and that strange portrait of Chairman Mao; a painting which appears as a photo, and gives nothing away. The sound reminds me of teenage band practices; when what we did was caught between inept talents and dreams.

Still, after so long, the sound of those chords excites me: the wall of amps piled up on one side of a smoky room; the scuzzy, stickiness of the floor, and the smell of stale beer and sweat poorly masked by the smell of cigarettes. We drink ginger wine, waiting for the bands to start. It is sickly sweet, insipid, and we drink it quickly so that we can move on to beer. The sound check comes to an end. The bar fills with Chinese kids and their indie haircuts, the sounds of punk and rock 'n roll.

The band begins. They play their own songs, and a small crowd jumps around, moshing in front of the stage, screaming out the words. The next band comes on. A girl in square red glasses takes to the stage and sings cute electro pop. The last band play Chinese hip-hop, and we go outside to escape the heat of bodies.

The beer is not working; it is too watery. But it has dulled my taste buds just enough to return to the ginger wine and we sit outside swigging from the bottle. The lead guitarist of the first band comes over and I offer him a cigarette. "That was really good," I tell him. "I liked it."

He turns to me smiling. "Thanks, man." He is wearing a black shirt with white stars on it and his long black hair is plastered wet against his face with sweat.

We sit on the floor, surrounded by empty bottles of Tsingtao. Across the road, leafy trees stretch their arms over the walls, as if trying to escape from the confines of their entrapment. In the light, their branches loom strange dull oranges and purple.

"I fuckin' hate this country," the guitarist is saying. "I can't fuckin' watch youtube. Ah, ah, it's fucking fucked man."

We sit talking about British and American bands they like while he strums chords on his unplugged electric guitar. "I fuckin'," he begins almost every sentence in this way. "I fuckin'. If I go out on the fuckin' street and say 'Fuck this! I don't like this fuckin' shit!' they arrest me. I hate this fuckin' fucked up country man."

The rest of the band comes over and we sit, screaming Libertines songs over the wall of the Forbidden City, rapturous and drunk, in the orange haze of Beijing, and the warm, sticky night. I remember vaguely that I am going to meet Ren Hong at 8 o'clock in the morning, that I'm not supposed to be out this late, and that I wasn't supposed to drink. I should never have taken money out before going to the bar.

We walk across Tiananmen Square, now quiet, but for the odd couple walking home, and we laugh about the Chinese punk who couldn't speak without swearing.

"I shouldn't have got drunk," I say. "I've got to be up in 5 hours." But when I turn to look at Leo he is no longer by my side.

I look across the square, stupidly, before looking down at my feet. Leo's face gazes up at me, stunned, his head below ground level, peering out through an open man hole.

"Shit! Are you okay?"

He says nothing, too shaken by the fall it seems, but nods. I offer him my hand and he pulls himself up and out of the drain.

"That's crazy," I say. "I didn't see that at all! There's no tape or anything. Are you alright?"

He puts his hand to the back of his head, still without talking, and when he brings it round to look at it, it is wet and dark with blood. I look at the back of his head, caught by the metal frame around the open man hole, a steady flow of blood trickles down his neck.

I stop a passer-by, half-drunk and shouting 'ambulance' until I realise the word has no meaning. I point to Leo's bleeding head, but still the passer-by only looks and stares at us. "Nee-naw, nee-naw!" I say, feeling silly as I say it, until another girl stops and takes out her phone.

The paramedics inspect the cut and, when they see he isn't dying, demand cash before we get in the ambulance. I take out a 100 ¥ note and he writes me a receipt as we pull away. They are cleaning the wound, and telling us that he'll need stitches when we get to the gates of the hospital. They need another 150 yuan to go through.

I walk around the hospital corridors, sobered by the fluorescent lights, and the cleanliness, but still out of place. It is the cleanest place I have seen for months; healthcare which most Chinese people could not afford. The doctor comes out.

"How much have you had to drink?"

"A lot. I don't know, too much."

"Not you."

"Oh, him," I say. "Less than me, I think. Is he okay?"

"He needs stitches."

"But his head? He isn't concussed? Have you checked?" I'm still too drunk to feel stupid asking a doctor if she's checked for concussion. I should have fallen down that hole.

"He's fine. We're going to stitch him up, but we need 350 yuan first – you can pay at the front desk."

I pay, emptying my wallet, and wait. An hour later, we walk, Leo sober, and me not quite, back through the empty streets to the hostel. The sky grows light with dawn. I am supposed to be leaving in two and a half hours.

...

I have barely closed my eyes when something jolts me awake. I look up to see the face of Ren Hong Chang; bright and beaming and childlike, and ready for our adventure. I half fall out of bed. My lips are stuck together, and my teeth feel strange. My eyes sting, bloodshot, and I ramble an apology, shaking. I don't know if I feel worse for sleeplessness or drink.

I don't want to go, but I cannot let Ren down on the first day. Leo's bandaged head emerges from under the sheets. He pulls hospital receipts from his pockets, makes additions, and gives me a handful of money, crawling back to bed.

"Thanks man," he says "Good luck!" before pulling the sheets over his head, against the daylight's glare.

Outside the hostel, Ren is waiting. The rush of traffic and the sticky air make me feel sick, but I clamber on the bike and sweat in the humidity and car fumes, following the wheel of Ren Hong Chang. I am glad to be leaving the city; to know soon I'll feel clean again.

We watch Beijing dissolve. The long wide streets, which remind me of an American city I have never been to, turn to highways, ring-roads. Office blocks and tower blocks, sterile and shiny new, disintegrate into shacks and concrete dwellings as the city refuses to die. Rickshaws are piled higher than before, their contents dirtier, and people spit more; hacking and coughing and covering the floor in oozing, slimy phlegm. It is as if tuberculosis had never been heard of. On the industrial edge of Beijing, grey chimneys strike smoke into the sky. In the dust-thick air though, it is hard to see where one substance begins and the other ends.

A green swamp breaks the city. Men in conical hats walk, bent and lethargic, as though weeding paddy fields, but the bags on their backs, fill slowly not with weeds, but rubbish; glass bottles, plastic and cans. A long grey concrete bridge runs over the swamp-like ground, stringing pieces of the city together. On the other side a line of trucks stands stationary, spewing out fumes, thick black specks of fuel, as though the engines were running on coal.

At last the shacks and buildings and factories give in. The mountains rise and we look back to the open plain of Beijing, and the centre of the Chinese world.

...

Ren Hong Chang speaks no English, but he has brought a small orange electronic translator, which he passes to me now, smiling a boyish smile. How old is he? Later I will ask, take the time to type the words into the machine.

"Let's eat!" says the machine. It copes well with simple things.

We find a restaurant. The wet concrete floor is covered in fish heads and chicken bones that have been discarded, the smells from the kitchen - garlic, ginger and chicken fat – mix with the smells from outside – piss and shit. In no place that I've been does the smell of beautiful food, come so closely followed by the stench of shit. Ren offers me a cigarette, which I refuse – I cannot face smoking before I ride, and I feel the taste of it will bring back the sickness I felt upon waking.

A plate comes out sizzling; a whole chicken chopped into bite-size pieces; head and legs and feet and all; spicy and salty-sweet. The first taste is delicious; crispy fat and salt, and the warming heat of chillies. Then our mouths sting with salt and MSG. But we are hungry and eat even the feet. Chang chews at the chicken's head, before throwing it on the floor. We look at each other across the table, order another beer, and Chang asks me what I thought of the food. "Good. But Salty." I type. "Very salty."

He nods slowly in agreement; the food has lulled us into sleepiness. He calls the cook over and shows him the screen, laughing at him. He reads the message to himself and says out-loud: "Salty, very salty," in an accent that would render the words meaningless, if I had not just written them myself.

...

Mist rises from artificial lakes, hugs the mountainsides like bearded moss, and curls like smoke.

Chinese tourists row in kayaks; fluorescent orange life-jackets reflect in the green water, and screams and squeals reach the man-made shores. Families on day-trips from Beijing get out of black Buicks and Audis, to take photographs and drink Coca-Cola. Pot-bellied men stand with their t-shirts rolled up, exposing their rounded guts, chain smoking and watching their children. They have turned the mountains into a theme park. A wooden bridge, built with plastic rusticity, leads the way to a waterfall and a queue to have your photo taken in front of it. Billboards advertise restaurants, people pour out from coaches and horses carry children over concrete footbridges.

Ren turns to me with one of his new stock phrases. "Take a photo!"

We stop and take photos by the lake, by the bridge, under the cliff, by a restaurant; three or four each time. It is getting dark.

"Wǒmen zǒu!"

Ren laughs at my pronunciation, but he repeats the words, shouting and raising his arm out like a Thundercat. "Wǒmen zǒu!"

...

I sleep in the same room as Ren. There is no space. The wordless communication is constant; endless smiles, endless gestures, effortful.

In the bathroom I crouch down over the floor, shitting into a dirty porcelain hole. I lift the bucket of cold water over myself, and he is in the next room, through the thin door.

We are tired. The road, and the climb through the mountains has worn us out. But we cannot rest.

Ren sits smoking on the corner of the bed. I hate the smell that fills the room, that sticks to me. The air in the room is still, and unclean.

"Let's go outside," I say. Motioning the door, miming walking with my fingers.

He stares at me blankly and hands me the translation machine.

In the dark, we walk the pebbly shore of the river. Above us the cliff is sheer; its shape dark and domineering; the water rushes white in the moonlight. We have arrived too late to see where we are. When we go back into the room the smell is still there, and the room too full of bodies.

...

The next day we cross into Hebei province and the theme park comes to an abrupt and startling halt. We find a room in a village.

Around the stone buildings, mountains rise. From their roots, thick green with vegetation, they stretch to the bare and rocky peaks which kiss the sky, now – for the first time in China – a crisp and clear light blue. Stone walls run between thin dirt lanes, and the roofs are bobbly and crooked, piled up with tiles. The houses huddle close together. People's yards are muddy with the squelch of trotters and the scavenging of hens, and trees twist their way through the stonework and provide the animals shade.

There is a knock on the door and Ren passes me the electronic translator. *"We go to find the house of miserableness and orphan."*

We are led by the man who has rented us a room, down the hard dirt tracks. Sunflowers peer over the walls, under the August sun. And old men sit outside their houses on plastic crates, doing nothing. It is as though something has been removed from the scene; a book, a cigarette, a cup of tea, or conversation. They watch us pass without a greeting, and return to staring blankly at the world. In the village square children play table-tennis on a concrete table. We are led down another track. A pig snorts, snuffling around a sty. Its black hide grey with mud; dark and wet around its flanks, lighter further up, where the mud is flaky and dry.

I do not need Ren to tell me we've arrived. Even in the falling down village the house is noticeable for its state of disrepair. Chickens clamber wildly along the garden walls. There is something mutinous in the way that they have left the ground and run amok, without fear of repercussion, flapping up to the lower branches of the trees, and strutting arrogantly. It is a yard without a controlling hand. Scant bundles of corn hang from the exterior beams; the roof sags. The windows are paneless, and their frames worn down to paper-like bare wood. Bundles of kindling clutter the yard, with baskets, weeds and stone. And a single black shoe sits on the windowsill, the same mud grey as the pig's dry back. We walk through an empty hole in the wall, gaping black, and doorless.

From the bare earthen floor comes the stench of piss, and wood smoke, chicken shit; and then, from the corner, the acrid, cloying smell of straw soaked in animal urine, the smell of rats. It is dark. Perhaps this is why it is the smell I notice first. But as my eyes become accustomed to the light, I see that we are in a small room of useless, dirty things. Empty cardboard boxes and plastic buckets climb the walls, piled high and without order. Light grey ash spills out from under a cooking pot, blown around the room, and the walls are black with soot and smoke as if damaged by fire. There are bin bags full of rubbish, and old crates, and faded sheets of newspaper line the walls; rows of characters, soaking up the smoke. I hear a crunch beneath my feet and look down to see that I am treading broken glass into the floor, it glints the colour green against the earth. In the pot, the water is cloudy, and dirty. Bits float inside it, and now I smell something like vomit. There is a sudden movement and a chicken breaks free of the cardboard boxes, bringing one tumbling to the floor. It escapes through the hole in the wall. I'm not sure what we are doing here.

We walk through another hole in the wall. An old lady is sat perfectly still, moaning. Her legs hang off the side of a bed, not quite touching the floor. Why didn't we hear her before? The sound is constant, and her lips quiver and contort with the cadence of her moans. There is nothing sad or anguished in the sound she makes; she is creating her own company, perhaps. It takes several moments for me to notice she is blind. Her eyes stare straight ahead and she does not register our presence. The neighbour who has brought us here shouts something in her ear, and Ren turns to me. "Take a photo."

I pass the camera, unwillingly, to him, and its flash lights up the woman's face; for a second the moaning stops. She is startled. Ren takes my camera around the rest of the house, like he is collecting evidence. The smoke-stained walls and ceiling flash and grow dark again; he photographs the boxes and the animal shit, the dirty cooking stove. I don't know what he plans to use these photos for, or what results he hopes to gain. We leave the old woman silently clinging to the door frame, staring at the chickens without seeing them. And as we walk away her moaning begins again.

I am still unsure about the purpose of our visit as we walk back through the village, past the men still sitting on their buckets and crates. Did Ren simply want to show me something far away from the shiny glass buildings of Beijing? Or does he think that by showing photos of these houses of miserableness and orphan to people in the city, he can somehow reduce their number? When we leave the next day, Ren gives the neighbour a 50¥ note and instructions that I don't understand, and we leave the village.

...

The road rises out of the valleys and we look down from the mountain pass. The snaking road below is toy-like; tiny figures and horses toil on the valley floor. While cycling usually disappears, an ephemeral and traceless act, now we see our day behind us; there and concrete, the road we have ridden, the winding hair-pin bends. The ancient towers of the Great Wall dot the mountain ridges above like giant castellations, though the main body of the wall is no longer visible, crumbled into dust, consumed by time, or pillaged for its stone.

In the mountains the air is fresh and cool. Only as we descend and pass through tiny villages do I choke on the stench of warm and rising shit from communal toilets, and cover my mouth with my hand, against the tasting of it. Sometimes sweetcorn lies by the side of the road or covering petrol station forecourts, drying in the sun; the husks, in separate piles, turn to the brittle brown of paper. At intervals, the air grows thick with spice and sizzling oil. We stop for food, spooning chilli oil over the fresh, thick noodles and stirring it into the broth. Further down the road, in a perfect red rectangle, a million peppercorns lie drying on the road. Ren picks up a bunch from the hot tarmac and hands me a single tiny red ball. I bite into it and the fresh and fiery juice bursts in my mouth, numbing my tongue and lips; the flavour fills my mouth and my lips tingle for hours.

...

The hotel is much cleaner than the bare concrete rooms we usually patronise, and, at 26¥, only slightly more expensive. The beds have sheets that have been washed and real mattresses; there is a lock on the door and a TV, bright unmarked paint on the walls. For the first time in a week, there is hot water and a shower. We wash, go out to eat and when we come back Ren hands me the orange translator. *"The service here is massaged."*

We walk downstairs. Through a glass door, the silhouettes of men appear, engulfed in steam. They walk around slowly, from a sauna to a Jacuzzi, a cold pool, naked or wrapped in identical white towels. They sit smoking and drinking bottles of beer. The white tiles echo with the loud gabble of conversation, shouting and half drunk. The ethereal alcoholic fumes of *báijiǔ*, slink into the steam. I feel strange being in a room full of Chinese men. I stand out. A man sees me and wraps his towels around his waist, suddenly embarrassed of his nakedness.

We do not join the men in the Jacuzzi. Instead, I follow Ren to a smaller room full of girls wearing short shorts and tight white t-shirts. We pay 22¥ for half an hour's foot massage and I sit back, deep into the chair. The girls giggle and exchange glances, half-shy in front of me. The men around are laughing and making jokes; the content of which, I can only guess at. The girl rubs deeply into my calves and I feel the tension ease from my muscles. Her hands awake nothing in me but a sense of relaxation. It is with curiosity then, that I realise, this is the first time someone else has touched my skin for months.

Back in the room, there is a knock on the door. Two girls enter. Two whores. There is a moment, upon entering the room, when they glance at each other, deciding which one will stand in front of which bed. It is likely they have been told of my presence; that a *lǎowài* would be waiting for them, but I see the surprise in them still. They pick us, without it seems, much thought. Like a factory worker might choose a workstation or a field hand might ponder, only momentarily, before deciding from which row of crops to begin the day's work. It is perhaps of little consequence; one place on a conveyor belt, one side of the field, is much the same as another. And it is much the same for the field or the conveyor belt, the hands which uproot its weeds or harvest its crops, the hands which take the half-made product, lay it down again. The girls are dressed in much the same way; I do not register what they look like, do not look at them properly, feel myself turning away. I am not thinking. The image of them will only form in my mind after they have left. Small breasts, the shorts, more like knickers, the made-up faces, already cloudy as I see them, I cannot hold on to their features. They are dressed to say fuck me. Their eyes, it seems, are somewhere else, not in this room.

I do not have time to think this. I do not run its details consequentially through my mind, but I see an image of a green wall. It is my first memory, embedded in shame and secrecy. It is a memory from school. I am five. I know it is my first real memory, because for more than 15 years I tell nobody about it. It is true that I may well have memories from before then, but these are shared memories, they have been talked about with other people, retold, reconfigured; they are not entirely mine. They are mixed with the false memory of photos or the distortions of retelling; they do not belong to me.

My memory is this. I am five. It is playtime. I need the toilet, but for some reason, I do not want to ask the teacher if I can go inside. Instead, I run away from the other children and, behind the Elliot hut, out of sight from the teacher on duty, piss against the wall. The urine runs down the dull green surface, darkens it, and collects in a small puddle at my feet, running down towards me, following the contours of the tarmac. I turn to my left. I know it is my left, even if I did not then, as I see the high granite wall that runs around the playground, and the trees that rise above it on the other side. I see a child staring at me, and the child runs to tell the teacher, and I am summoned inside. I feel scared; I have never been in trouble at school before. The classroom is huge. Even huger now, that I am on my own, at a table with the teacher. I have never been there before without other children, and I feel uncomfortable. I want to hide.

"Why did you do it? Why didn't you ask me to go inside?" the teacher asks me. Her face looks angry. I have only ever seen her face passive, or smiling towards me, before. I do not know the answer.

"It was a bad thing to do," she says. "You mustn't do it again. Do you want me to send you to the headmaster, so you can tell him what you've done?" I shake my head, I say sorry, and she lets me go.

I tell no-one about it when I get home. For years, until I am a teenager, the memory is accompanied always with a shooting pain; I feel the guilt rise within me. It is not until I am much older, when I have more serious things about which to be guilty, that I see the episode as small and unimportant; but it has already become a part of me, and I cannot forget it.

What if this becomes a memory? I think. This hotel room, and these two girls? Is it a memory that will be easy to forget, or one which will torment me? I am sat on the bed in silence, in the middle of China. It would be so easy to leave behind, an untold story. Perhaps our acts scar, only if we are watched. Perhaps, I could leave this memory behind, buried in some distant Chinese town, to which I will never again return. I wonder if our deeds are redeemable, if they become a constant part of us, mounting up, and tallied, even as our body's cells die and are re-born. Are we forgiven for these silent deeds, for straying from our own ethics? Surely, this would be easy to hide, to forget. I could lock it in some distant quarter of my memory, and never speak of it again. Or perhaps, I will find that there is nothing to be guilty about; that in it is only pleasure.

And what of these two girls, not yet twenty? Will they always be whores, even years after they stop selling themselves? Or with time will they make different lives, for these days to be forgotten? Perhaps, shame is not the same for them, or for other people. Maybe it isn't a physical thing that rises and surges through the body, that lies in stagnant permanence ready for the call of memory to rush. Maybe other people have learnt to banish guilt from unimportant acts; to regenerate, forgive, or merely not create the sin.

One of the girls begins to take her top off, and I glance at Ren, blankly, I think, as the girl's eyes widen and she bites her bottom lip, like she's studied mating behaviour, to make this over quick. Her hand rests on the bottom of the bed. And Ren tells them to leave. There has been a mistake. It isn't what we wanted.

I watch the girls leave, the door closing lightly behind. We laugh it off, opening another beer – he has done what I had asked in Beijing. I am glad, and I thank him for it; he has spared me future thoughts. But, silently, I am left wondering about a different turn of events.

...

We leave the city of Taiyuan behind. The road fills with trucks. You can chew the air; the flavour of burnt coal. The roads heave with the turning of engines, and the trucks stand still, each one piled high with coal under dirty fabric covers, or tarpaulin pulled taut. It would be a dull exercise to count the trucks, but as I see them stretch into the distance, I take note of the kilometre mark. We ride past them, bumper to bumper, for 22 kilometres. They are squat, solid trucks, old and dirty, perhaps 10 metres long, and each leaves no more than half a metre between the other. I make the calculations as we ride; more than 2000 trucks, carrying nothing, it seems, but coal. The drivers abandon their vehicles, the engines at a standstill. It seems we are at some tiny point of a vast and broken machine. How long will they have to wait? And how many more times across China is this scene being repeated? Vendors walk up and down the jam, selling cold drinks and snacks; it seems this is a daily occurrence. It has become the livelihood of some to feed these drivers.

We reach the Yellow River. Ren is excited; he turns to me and shouts, *"Huang he!"* In Chinese the river's name sounds like 'wanker' and I stifle a laugh. It carves through the cliffs, and leaves a grey, silt shore on its outer curve. A steel railway bridge holds its heavy weight above the water, jammed into the stone. The line of trucks is behind us, still unmoving, but in the distance we can see the huge chimneys, of what I think is a power station, spitting out smoke in heavy breaths, a constant burning day and night. The air is no longer air. It is hard to breathe, and tastes like smoke and bitter fumes. People sit by the side of the road selling cold drinks, and sweets and packets of chickens' feet, to anyone who passes. They wear white masks across their mouths, though the edges have turned to black. Still, closer to us, more chimneys, and the shoots and ramps and grindings of a concrete factory. We have passed mountains that have been severed in half; huge right angles cut out of them; there is something here that will not stop. But, in the dirt, it is hard to think of this; better just to breathe, and feel the cold icy syrup of Coca-Cola quench your thirst. Now we face the river, my face black from the air; the black mixes with my sweat and seethes into my pores.

"Beautiful," says Ren. He is talking about the river. But more perhaps, he is talking about the idea of the river. It is difficult to make out where the water and air and the land begin. They grow together in one seething mass of grey. It is like watching something dead.

"Very beautiful!" says Ren, again. But I cannot respond. It is enough to try and smile for photos, and to imagine what the place would look like if I could see the sky.

...

It looks like they are fighting. We have come to this village to ask if we can camp in the surrounding fields, and now we stand, outsiders, by a small stone house. The man is shouting at Ren, and a crowd of villagers has gathered to watch. Ren shouts back, and though I understand nothing, I know that they are angry. As the shouting grows louder, other people join in, pointing and gesticulating wildly, and I urge Ren to turn around and go. We are outnumbered here, and we have clearly upset the villagers with our request. I lean in to touch his shoulder, to motion that we should leave, but he holds his hand up for me to wait. Finally, the argument comes to an end and Ren turns back to me. At last, I think. We can give up. We can find some other quiet spot, or stay in a cheap hotel. But he is smiling. *"Hǎo!"* he says. *"Hěn hǎo!* Very good!" We can camp in one of the fields.

The man still seems angry as he gives us water, and walks with us up a lane to show us where we can sleep, but he smiles as we say goodbye, and I am left with the impression that it is just the way he talks.

We set up two tents and build a small fire on a granite slab of rock. Down below us, in the village, the silence is interrupted only by the barking of dogs, and an occasional shout in the darkness. We take the plastic bags of food we have brought from the last village, and pick at them with chopsticks; they are still warm as the night chill of the mountain air descends and the logs on the fire turn to gently glowing cinders.

It is well past midnight when I hear the zip on my tent. It is Ren. He says nothing, but he is shivering with cold. He wants to sleep next to me. With the panniers it is a squeeze, and I find my face pushed up against the tent wall, with Ren snoring on his back by my side. At three or four I give up on sleep and carry my sleeping bag outside. It is cold, but my sleeping bag is designed for the cold. Before long, I am woken by the dawn. Ren too, is shuffling inside my tent.

As I wait for coffee to boil, I take the translator and write to him. "*I'm worried. You don't have the proper equipment. I'm worried that if you go to Tibet you will freeze.*"

He reads the message, apparently translated into Mandarin, and laughs. "Very good!" he says. "Very good."

...

I say goodbye to Ren in Xi'an. It is his hometown. He has decided not to continue his journey to Tibet. Another time, he says. Yesterday, I watched him writing. His fingers danced, as he made the tiny pen strokes on the paper; each symbol, beautifully formed, and meaningless to me. We have shared our time, but our space too. Perhaps, I have become difficult to live with. My time and space have been my own for too long; too long to make me easy company. The first thing that I feel, heading south from the city, is relief; I stop when I want, and no longer have to smile for photos, or anyone at all. With every person I meet, I am new. I realise that I have always struggled with repeated meetings, always felt awkward and unsure. I doubt the first impression that I make; or, if I am confident I've made a good impression, I worry that it will crumble, that as people get to know me they will see my faults. Perhaps, I am better at these constant hellos and goodbyes. Perhaps lone travellers are running from something. Perhaps, it is the lack of something for which they search. In France, in that first week, I had missed my friends and family more desperately than at any time since. I wonder what is wrong with me, that I can live without these ties.

...

The knock on my door comes at ten. The streetlamp's haze fills the room, through the thin grey curtains, so there is no need to turn the light on as I let the policemen in.

Black leather shoes step inside, stand still. A light, flicking movement then - scuffing the dust on the concrete floor. A tiny grey cloud. Then still.

"We are policemen," says one of the men, standing in the shoes.

"Yes." I say, and I am shown a badge.

"Do you speak Chinese?"

"No," I say, returning to sit on the bed. "I'm sorry."

"That's okay. But you have to move. This hotel is not allowed to accept foreigners."

I look around at my things, strewn across the floor, and look at my watch. "It's very late," I say. "I really don't want to move. Could I just stay for one night? I'm leaving tomorrow."

The policemen consider. "Where are you going?"

"I'm going to Chengdu. I'll leave in the morning, I promise. The hotel never told me."

"Okay, okay." The policeman cuts off my protestations. "We need to copy your passport. But for one night, you can stay."

As they leave, I wonder if it was only Hong and his ID card which had saved me from these night time visits from the police. The last time they knocked on my door was before Beijing. It is better to stay in the countryside, I think. Where the people do not have telephones with which to report my presence.

At 3am I am woken by torrential rain. It is dark outside now, the streetlamp extinguished, and I fumble around for my watch, change the alarm from six to seven thirty. When I wake again it is light, still the sound of rain gushes in great torrents outside my window. I drag myself up; I do not dislike the rain in itself, but I hate the filth and grit that fly from the unsurfaced roads, that scrape between brake-pads, grate on the chain, seep into tubing, and make the bike fall apart. But it is not rain. A dull grey haze glows in the sky. I look out the window, down a concrete alley, and see that a stream is rushing past my window. Why then, did I only notice it in the dark, when my sight was impaired and I invented rain? I gather my things, as I said I would, and leave.

It is a new month. The 1st September, 2009. The sixth month. At home it is the tail end of summer, but I am slipping further south where such distinctions between seasons do not exist. It is a quiet day, and the road rolls along a river valley, climbing the contours of the banks and sliding down again. Trucks carry piglets in cages and motorbikes sag under the weight of entire families. Still, those perfect rectangles of sweetcorn and peppercorns lie, drying on the floor. Is this where the pepper on our tables begins, on a road in Shaanxi province, raked over by an old lady? I am thinking about this, and the trains carrying Dima's trees to China, when I notice that a car is following me.

Eventually, the car overtakes, but drives only a few hundred metres before pulling over and waiting. Three men get out. Policemen. Two in uniform, the other in plainclothes, and it is he who does the talking.

"Do you speak any Chinese?"

"No. I'm sorry."

"Where you?"

"England."

"No," he seems to get frustrated. "Where *you?*" and he spins his arms around to mime cycling.

"Ah, I'm going to Chengdu."

The rest of the conversation is carried out in Mandarin. He seems to be saying that I shouldn't pass, but I don't know why. He speaks loudly, as though trying to get across the message through volume alone.

"*Wǒ tīngbudǒng,*" I plead, I don't understand. I take out a map so that he can explain what he is saying to me. The only other way to Chengdu, is hundreds of extra miles I work out, as the policeman searches to find where we are. Eventually he points at Xi' Xian, the next town. Then at himself. I should meet him there.

"Ok!" I half shout at him, using his tactics to make myself understood. "I see you in Xi'xian"

I get on the bike and the car follows. The inclines become steeper, and after an hour or so the police tire of travelling so slowly. One of them winds down the window and shouts to me. "I'm hungry," he says and he waves for me to stop. A small pick-up truck is commandeered, and my bike is loaded onto it and I am shown into the back seat of the car. What concerns me is not that I am sat in a police car, that I don't understand why, cannot ask and do not know what will happen. I'm worried only that they're breaking my line. My continuous line of which I've dreamt. They're breaking it, again.

The policeman hands me something called *France Bread*. It is a perfectly round ball of crustless bread, and I take it gratefully, hoping that it means, *don't worry.*

The police station is the newest building in town. We walk up the white stairs, through the glass doors to a small white office. A girl stands in the middle of the room; my age, slightly older. A policeman that I haven't seen before sits behind a desk, smoking and drinking tea behind small piles of paper. The plain-clothed officer, who has escorted me, takes a seat behind me.

The girl shakes my hand, and indicates that I too, should take a seat. "Very nice to meet you," she says.

"Very nice to meet you too. I think."

For a moment there is silence. I sit, waiting.

The girl looks at me. She too, has felt the silence, and reassures me. "I've come to help the police with their questions."

"Good."

The officer, rests his cigarettes on a heavy, glass ash tray and speaks, to the girl really, though he is looking at me.

"Xi'xian is a forbidden zone," the girl translates. "Foreigners are not allowed here freely. If you come here, we will think you are a spy."

"Oh." It seems pointless to protest at this stage.

It seems a strange point at which to halt the proceedings, but again the policeman returns to his paperwork, and I am left wondering whether I ought to say something. I turn to the girl and make small talk. I tell her about my travels, and she tells me that she is an English teacher. That she teaches eleven to fourteen-year olds. She has always lived in Xi'Xian.

"Do you have to do this often?" I ask.

"Often?"

"Do you have to come here a lot? To help foreigners."

Her face is puzzled. "I'm sorry," she says "I don't understand."

I feel my faith in her abilities to get me out of this situation ebb away. I don't know if it's a good idea to raise my fears. "I think you may be a very good English teacher,"

"Thank you," she replies, over the comma in my sentence.

"but if you don't understand me, I think we might have some problems here."

"Yes, yes," she says enthusiastically, without even a trace of understanding what I have said, and the questioning begins.

"Where are you from?" The first question is easy. And the second. And the third.

After an hour we have spoken about my work, my home, my family, my time in China, the places I have visited, and what I am doing next. I begin to wonder if she is translating the questions put to me at all, or merely inventing some bland conversation that falls within her linguistic capabilities. Can this be all they are asking me, a suspected spy? Or perhaps, more likely, it is this; I am not a suspected spy, they are simply following procedure with half-hearted small talk, filling out forms, until I can go. A spy from the west, I think, would surely look Chinese, speak Mandarin, and not arrive on a bicycle.

At the end of the interview she looks at me, serious, translating the policeman's words. "You have to get out of here immediately!"

"Okay." I don't know whether to get up.

"Also, there is a 500 yuan fine."

I look shocked. It is almost exactly the amount of money I am carrying for the week, before I reach Chengdu, and a cash machine. Apparently, I look shocked and poor enough that they let me off the fine. "But you have to pay more attention next time."

"Pay attention to what?" I ask. "There are no signs - even the policemen in the next town didn't know about this."

"Okay - but just pay more attention."

It is not a time for arguing. It is a time for thanking them, apologising, and leaving. My bike is waiting outside, but I am unable to ride it. "You will be escorted to the bus station," the girl says. "Good luck! It was nice to meet you."

I watch the landscape roll past without the effort of turning pedals. From here, this higher vantage point, the world looks different; I can see further. I sit back, occasionally looking behind to check my bike hasn't been blown off the roof. The other passengers watch me in silence until it becomes clear that I am doing nothing but sitting, just like them. After half an hour, the bus stops, and I am told I can get off.

...

The bus drops me outside a row of houses; a restaurant, shops, signs I can't understand. A girl smiles at me and I go over to ask about a hotel. I take out my guide book and point to the symbols on the back pages; *I'm looking for a cheap hotel*. I'm not even trying in this language. The songs, and phrases Ren taught me are slipping already from my mind. I use only the numbers one to a hundred, how much is it, and pointing. I have learnt to count to ten on one hand, *liù*, the outstretched little finger and thumb of six to the closed fist of *shí*. But it is joyless and practical, a way to decide how much money I will hand over, and what I will get for it.

The girl looks at the words, reads the English, *"A cheap hotel"* and walks me to a pair of wooden doors, in silence; it seems that, in China, I am never far from an affordable bed.

Empty buckets stand neglected, paint peels off the walls, and the communal toilets make me gag. The room is quiet though, and the bed has a real, if dirty, mattress. For days I have slept on beds as hard as tables, twisting and turning in the night. It is 20 yuan, £2. Perhaps the police will visit me again, but I settle down to read.

When I hear the knock on the door, I ready myself to argue. To complain about these hotels that don't even know the regulations and these constant denouncements, but when I open the door it is not the police, but the girl who had shown me the room. An older man stands behind her.

"This is my uncle," she says. "We would like to invite you down for some conversation."

I am amazed. She had walked with me to the room, without saying anything at all, but now speaks to me in a perfectly clear accent. Relieved that it is not the police, I follow them downstairs.

We sit and talk. School. Family. The usual. The girl's name is Easter. Of course, it is not really, but it is the English name she has chosen at school, and strangely I barely notice it. Easter. Why not?

I tell the family about my trip, but perhaps they don't believe me. They've just seen me arrive into town on a bus.

"Did you know that foreigners aren't allowed in the next town?" I ask her.

"Yes," she says. "I heard about it."

I don't ask her why. There's something nagging at me, a sense that I have to be careful about what I say. I would rather not know than cause problems, and I turn to small talk once again.

"What do you want to do when you're older?"

"I don't know," she says. "I want to travel. I want to go to Europe. That's why I'm learning English."

"You will," I say. I'm sure of it. "If you want to do it, you will."

"Do you want to eat something?" She asks me. "We can go to the market."

It feels good to be outside. The town is bigger than I had thought. It teems with people on scooters and the sounds of shouting and horns. Tens of food stalls line the square; scorpions, whole baby crabs, frogs, noodles, rice, stuffed bread rolls and dozens of other things. You could eat for a year, every day, at this market, and each time try something new. It is no less chaotic, no less exciting than Erenhot, on my first day in China, but I am somehow dead to it. Tired and hungry. But used to it, too. I need to wake up again, I tell myself. I need to become alive.

"Do you like spicy food?" Easter asks, and I nod. The first thing that I learnt in Chinese was *Wǒ ài làjiāo*, I love chilli. If I don't say it in restaurants, the food is tempered; diluted to what they think I will like, to a *lǎowài's* taste.

Easter pays for my meal. I carry it away in a clear plastic bag; shrimps, swimming in oil and sizzling with spice. She walks me back to my room, says goodbye, and again, I am alone.

...

The road traces a line through the mountains. It hugs the valleys and winds up impossible slopes. It is an old road, falling into disrepair. The only smooth surfaces are found in the kilometre markers which appear only sporadically. The rest of the track is sticky mud, and rocks; my wheels spin and sink into the ground, and rocks jut out on hazardous descents. Above me, vast concrete pillars support the new highways. Giant cranes lift huge blocks of concrete, bigger than houses, into place. Men look like ants; they hang off pillars by ropes, impossibly high, or sit on top of the concrete structures, their legs dangling over the edge, over a thousand-foot drop. And the new road begins, straddling a great, wide valley, breaking the sky. Corners are cut out of the mountains, and holes are driven through them. It seems that I can sit and watch China moving; creating and destroying at impossible speeds.

The leaves have grown thicker; greener, wider, rubbery. I notice them now - they are tropical plants. The air breathes like a jungle; hot and sticky wet. And I feel the world changing again as I slowly pedal south and the heat grows into me, the wetness of the air, the warmer nights. Now, the road reaches a confluence in the river, and it tumbles down the mountain in tight hairpin bends; mud sliding and the whole track full of dirt and brown puddles.

Where the two rivers meet, a town fills the steep banks, and I look down towards it. Grey buildings sink their long, spindly foundations into the cliff, towering over the precipitous edge. It is nerve-racking simply to watch. From here they look like shells of buildings; no windows, only gaunt black holes like empty eye-sockets. It could be a ghost town, but already I see it buzzes with traffic and people and noise. A bridge clenches two thin arms onto each bank, and I hurtle towards it, glad to see tarmac.

I cycle through the streets. Away from the river, the roads run in spirals; just when I think I am leaving the town, I return to it again. I try to leave, down a different road, but fail. And as I see the grey sky deaden towards night, I give up. I will find a way out tomorrow.

Later, I sit on the bridge and the river crashes down beneath me, so far away it is barely audible. I take out a book and the satellite tracker to send a message home. When I look up, I have an audience.

A girl hides behind her mother; the sight of me has made her cry, and I hear her whimper against reassurance. Old men are leaning on their rickshaws, smoking; their rickety vehicles pulled to a halt. And others are looking over my shoulder at the book I am reading.

"*Nǐhǎo*," I say.

There is no reply, from anyone, so I smile again, look at them. It is easy to stare at people when they are staring at you. The man behind me is pointing at my book; at the strange letters. He leans over and touches the pages and I hand it to him. He holds it upside down and passes it around the group; they are laughing at the words, at the funny meaningless symbols. There are perhaps twenty people crowded around me now.

They hand me back the book, and a man points at my nose. *It's so big,* he says with his hands stretching them out wide, and the others who have gathered to look at me laugh in agreement. He puts his thumbs up "*Hǎo!*" he says, it's good. So, he likes my enormous nose, and the rest of the crowd, now covering half of the bridge make gestures with their hands, fingers in round circles; my big round eyes. The crowd grows still, so that now those that are stopping, stop simply because they see a crowd, they push forward to the front to see what the fuss is about. I smile, prepare to leave, to push through the crowd. I wonder if they will follow me.

I have arrived so slowly. The road through Europe. The slow disintegration of the west. The fading desert, and now the breath of the tropics exhales from the south. The mud track has twisted gently through the mountains to this town, but I was not ready for it. As I walk through the streets, I feel as if I could have landed from space. I cannot describe why. There is something in the energy of the town; the way the children turn and run, or hide from me, the stares and the shouts of lǎowài running after me down the narrow alleyways so that people poke their heads out to have a look. "*Lǎowài!*" the people shout, "*Lǎowài!*" and within a few moments the whole street is aware of my presence. The windows fill with faces and the street watches me walk past.

My heart races. I feel my hairs prickle with the strangeness of where I am and I smoke three cigarettes in quick succession. They make me feel terrible; a dull headache and a bitter dry taste, but my mind no longer races at this place, and I settle, return to the pension, smile as I pass the fruit sellers, sitting by the door. I smile as I feel them, following me with stares. The room is welcome, and quiet and bare. I lock the door. A single light bulb swings slightly and flickers; I must have knocked it. I steady the wire, and the light settles on an enormous spider. Much bigger than my hand, its body is fat and furry, and, like everything else in this town, it is staring at me. I will not sleep while it is alive. I lunge at it, and it scuttles away, behind a broken wardrobe in the corner of the room. It's more scared of me, I tell myself. It will stay there until I am gone. But all night I am awoken by my imaginings; its light and furry feet, the way it scuttles, and its touch across my face.

...

I cycle south along a cobblestone road. The fields are full; crops are being harvested, and neat conical bundles sit drying in the sun. Old men walk, their backs bent against the weight of woven baskets. Goats scatter; their clanging bells ring in cacophonous song. And women beat their cows with sticks, as they stray from the narrow road.

I watch the daily chores; the hours' walk up hillsides and the hours' walk back down. Sometimes, I slip by unnoticed, through this China where time stands still. I barely look into these lives. There is some invisible, impenetrable barrier. Though I am close, I am not here; too caught up in the jarring struggle against the cobblestone road to imagine these other lives; what is left at the end of the day. The conversations around television sets, in the old, and mud-brick walls. I am more than an outsider, I am unseen. But as my arms tingle with the constant drilling of the road, I feel glad to be looking at untold tales and the daily movements of people's lives. Occasionally, someone looks up and I catch them by surprise.

In a village, a girl lifts her face from behind a wooden fence. She meets my gaze, and with her eyes shining into mine, she says in disbelief, *"Wàiguórén!"* Foreigner! A trail is set.

A wave of similar cries follows me down the road. *"Wàiguórén!" "Wàiguórén!" "Wàiguórén!"* I am still not used to my face. I never realised it was that different, or imagined how it could dominate my experience; how people would look at me with undiluted curiosity, and wonder at the strangeness of my features.

The road climbs further; now the cliffs fall away and the mud crumbles. I cross a make shift bridge; a single warped wooden board lies across a small abyss. Later I stop and look down from the road. Beneath, the clouds rise like smoke, concealing the valley floor. At first, I do not realise that the road is overhanging, nor do I realise how high the road has climbed. As the cloud shifts, I feel sick with vertigo, and a shooting tingle stabs me from my toes, as I imagine jumping. I push the bike from the edge, walking with hollow legs, and roll towards Kunming.

...

It is the 60th anniversary of the founding of the People's Republic of China. I am in Kunming and I walk the streets alone. Red flags, on which the number 60 has been printed in bold yellow numbers, shiver outside restaurants and shops: KFCs and McDonalds; Prada and Rolex; Luis Vuitton and Versace; Zara and Mango; Carrefour and Wal-Mart.

A huge screen in the central shopping area transmits a live feed from Beijing; 250,000 people in Tiananmen Square. Each regiment moves in perfect synchronicity, each man the same height as his neighbour, and truly it seems that they march as one. As one body. The ranks, the thousands of bodies, have surpassed homogeny and now they stare straight ahead and the smoothness in their movement seems mechanical and unreal, as the images of armies, tanks and missiles marching through Beijing are beamed to us in Kunming, 2000 miles away.

People put down their shopping bags to watch the giant screens. And then they grow bored and carry on shopping. New people stop, put down their shopping, stare at the screen, grow bored, carry on, put down the shopping, stare at the screen, grow bored. How stupid I was to scorn and scoff and laugh at the communist banners, draped around great global emblems of capitalism, as if they had symbolised some great failure. There is no contradiction. No one is losing. The people have rice. And clothes. And televisions. And the people are happy. Here in the square, everyone is dressed in different clothes, different colours, hair dye, bags, and shoes. They are free to express their individuality with the things that they buy.

It is not just rice that is cheaper. And not just rice to be bought. Rice cookers, cheaper. And ovens, cheaper. Air conditioning units. And televisions. Heaters. PCs. Laptops. Mobile phones. Designer clothes. And cars. There is everything to keep people working. So if it's communism or McDonalds, army uniforms or hipster jeans, what difference does it make? They have won, they have won; the walking pigs have won.

...

On the 6th of October I cross the Tropic of Cancer. The monument looks like a bus station; grey steps and looping concrete arches, painted yellow and green.

I have started taking anti-malarial tablets and my skin burns red, even under the misty, overcast sky. It feels like the heat of the sun has swollen again. Though I cannot see it, I feel it in the sweat that runs off my skin, and in the way the clouds are a blinding haze, towards the burning south.

There is the smell of shit. And, from the forested mountain slopes, comes the smell of rotten fruit. I had not thought that the tropical heat would bring with it such decay.

The road weaves through jungle, and I follow the long hot climbs towards the border and China's end.

Clockwise from top-left: Chickens in the Gobi – A cracked hub – Pingyao – In the mountains, leaving Beijing – stopping for beers in China – Ren Hong Chang, Beijing

Clockwise from top-left: near Taiyuan – Easter's family – A town in Sichuan – Climbing on the way to Xi'an – Peppercorns drying on the road – Traffic in Chengdu

Laos

11th October – 22nd October, 2009

I was right to bring money into Laos. The buildings which cluster around the Chinese border are wooden and the building with a sign saying 'bank' on it is closed today. The bank too, is just an old shack; some wooden stakes, and an old bare wooden door; you could rob it with a claw hammer, though I doubt there's much inside.

The money-changers carry leather bags, stuffed full of notes, millions and millions of kip. I count twice, three times. I check the unfamiliar notes; the new script and its curls, and look for a number that makes sense to me on the 50,000 kip note.

...

In Laos the road cuts a smooth black line through the mountains, though few people, it seems, own cars and the route lies quiet for hours at a time. I come to the crest of a hill and stop for breath. I watch my sweat as it falls and splashes on the tarmac, and reach for a bottle of water.

In front of me, on the otherwise deserted road, there is a woman. Cloth holds a baby, tight to her back, and she wears a long, brown skirt, heavy and swaying, slow, with her slow heavy walk. She has small bare feet; dark-brown, burnt by the sun, on top, pale, where her soles meet the ground. She is standing on the verge of the road; the blades of grass, bent and crushed, beneath her. I watch her lean across the stream, still flowing quick, in this, October, the last month of the rainy season. She stretches her arm out across the water and snaps a leaf from a banana tree. There is a moment where she seems about to fall, but she rocks back, pushing herself, and steps to the other side. The shadows fall now, black almost, upon the burning road, and for a moment I do not move. The woman holds the thick, broken stem to her shoulder, and as I watch I can almost feel its torn, rough surface, wet now with the snapping of it, and the thick cold sap that runs white, and drips onto her hand. The leaf is let to bend behind her, a darkness falls; a perfect shape of shade behind her to shelter the baby's head.

I watch her walk on. And I know that she too, as a baby, had been sheltered in this way; and her mother, and her mother before her. I know from the simplicity of it, and from its thoughtless beauty, because the sun is not new and banana leaves are old.

I breathe in the hot air, deep, step into pedals again. The promise of a country that has escaped the perils of a growth too quick, rolls beneath my wheels.

...

I follow route 13 towards Luang Prabang. Thatched roofs nestle in the steep valleys, flowers grow, bright colours under the sun, and children play in deep puddles on the road. It seems the country is sleeping. Villagers line up to collect water, and young women wash themselves behind walls made of sticks by the road. They scoop up the cold water in buckets and it glistens golden as they step out of the makeshift walls. They wrap themselves, and the cloth sticks wet to skin. I ride up the steep mountainsides looking for shade, and find none.

...

I walk through Luang Prabang's night market. Cheap, wooden restaurants line a candle lit street; a silent market full of handicrafts. There is a small wine bar, and though it is 40,000 kip for a glass, it is more than six months since I've drunk wine that wasn't Chinese, and the taste is smooth and full, and I saviour it slowly, promising that I will leave after just one.

I am joined by an English woman, and we order another glass. "Enjoy it here," she says. "The import tax in Thailand makes wine way too expensive."

Adelle works for the WHO in Bangkok, and she has come to Luang Prabang for a conference.

"I used to work in marketing," she tells me, "but then I thought, if I'm going to persuade people to do something, I might as well persuade them to do something good, like quit smoking, or look after themselves."

I agree. I don't light a cigarette. It is nice to talk quietly, without effort.

A Swiss man joins us, and I am finishing the third glass when the conversation turns to drugs, to opium.

"It's easy here, it's everywhere," he says, and I feel myself grow anxious and excited in spite of my intentions before I arrived. I am easy to persuade, or perhaps it is me that does the persuading. Adelle leaves, wishing us goodnight, and we pay the bill.

I climb into a tuc-tuc. 'O?' asks the driver, a boy no older than eighteen, and I nod. 100,000 kip for a wrap. I hand him over the two notes, but when I hold out my hand he is showing me the notes again; a 50,000 and a 5,000. It is a simple trick, a slight of hand, but I am too slow with wine, or too unsuspecting, to notice it. I apologise for my mistake and hand over a 50,000 in return for the 5,000 he says I had given him and he hands me back a wrap. I hold its solid weight in my hand, squeezing it gently before putting it in my pocket. Thick black goo, wrapped in cling film.

There is a 12 o'clock curfew in the city. The bars close, the streets are empty, and police walk around, escorting people back to their hotel rooms, or worse. There is one option for those not yet ready to sleep; a bowling alley on the edge of town, and we take a ride, free it seems with our purchase, and the small forgotten swindle.

The place is full of backpackers, who wouldn't be there if it were not the only option; we go into the toilets, unfold the wrap. We have no cigarette paper so instead tear the film in half. It is stained a thick dark brown. Its taste is bitter, like a poison. If it were anything else I would spit it out onto the floor without thinking, but I suck it, chewing over the plastic until it is clear and wet with my saliva, and the opium sits heavy in my stomach. I keep it down for as long as I can, and sit outside, waiting. The lights are bright here, and the constant clatter of bowling balls on wood and drunken shouting makes me wish I were somewhere else. Then I feel a rush, an urge to be sick. I walk back quickly to the toilet, and vomit; liquid red and acid. But it has sat there long enough, and when I walk outside a feeling of uncaring bliss takes me away from the dirty bright lights; it doesn't matter where I am. I do not equate the feeling with happiness, but I am no longer in the mood for equating anything with anything. If I were thinking, it would thrill me not to care about the other people here, to have no need to talk to them. And I feel myself sinking.

I am sat outside, laid back deep into some rough corner, when I feel the freshness of the predawn air; it convinces me that I am dirty and sweaty, and have barely been conscious all night, and persuades me to sleep. My movements are slow as I walk back through the deserted streets. I sneak quietly into the guesthouse, turning the key, and cursing it for clattering in the silence, and collapse onto the bed, as the city outside comes to life.

When I wake, it is impossible to think about going outside without imagining disaster. Impossible to think about opening a book without the pages slicing through skin. Or look at the pencil on the side without envisaging its tip piercing something's eye.

Impossible to think about cutting something without the image of severed fingers and blood. Of walking outside without being robbed, or attacked.

I bring my hand to my chest to touch the necklace I was given by Svetlana. The tiny icon of Saint Nikolai. The movement has become almost instinctive. A comfort. The way I rub the flat metal figure between my fingers, its predictable texture. I have worn it ever since I left Marx. But it is gone. I bring my hand to my neck, but the leather is not there, and the icon will not be found. The loss of the necklace makes me panic.

I am struck by the notion that the worst has not yet happened. That we live our lives not knowing whether we will have to suffer something unimaginably awful. The world is full of terror, I think, and one day it will find me. There are too many awful things and there is too much time. For a moment, I wish I could stay in this room forever. I bury my head in the sheets and close my eyes, but when I open them again the world is still there, with all the unknown horror of the future. I wipe sweat from my eyes and look around; the air stagnant, and still.

In the corner of the room there is a bottle of water and I clamber across the floor. The liquid is the wrong shape, doesn't fit in my throat; it is painful to swallow, but I am dehydrated and I need it. I put the bottle down gag, and run to the sink; the water bursts out of me in torrents. It is my own fault. I will waste the day. I'm stupid. Stupid. Stupid. And I never, never learn.

...

I leave Luang Prabang, south towards Thailand. A jagged mountain sticks into the air. Its peaks are like vicious spikes, and with them it has pierced a cloud, and the grey mass of water droplets is impaled. It is a picture of doom.

I ride through the hot days; there is no time to cleanse, and I make it to Thailand, in time to catch up with an old friend.

Thailand

22nd October – 14th December, 2009

"I don't know where you find good in this world."
Silence.
"I mean, what I'm doing, is it good?"
"You're helping people," John says.
"*I'm* not helping people. People give some money to a good cause 'cos I'm doing this thing. And maybe that's good. But *I'm* not helping."
"But you're learning."
"I'm getting confused."
"Maybe that's learning."
"It doesn't help."

We are sat by the river in Nong Khai, outside a pub. Inside, an old white man slaps a young Thai girl's ass, squeezes it in one palm. "Look at that ass," he says. To his friends, but loud enough for the whole bar to hear. "Look at that beautiful ass."

"You see? I don't even know if that's wrong anymore."
"You know."
John looks at me. I'm being childish.
"I'm sorry," I say. "I'm lost."

We cycle along the Mekong river. Laos lies to the north; the river bank, heavy and green. We leave our bikes outside Salakeawkoo Sculpture park.

"It's just," I begin. It is good to see a real friend. "I thought this journey would be purifying. I know that sounds silly."

John doesn't say anything. We walk between the huge concrete sculptures; snakes' heads, Buddhas and other things. John knows about them, I do not.

"You know when we were at school?" I ask. "I feel like we used to believe in something, you know? Now I'm just grey."
"You mean, you're getting old?"
"I mean, I'm getting worse."
"Same thing," says John.
"Same same," I say, for no reason. I look over at my friend. "Not for you, though."

I want to thank him for coming all this way. For bringing a new wheel for me. For being here. But I don't. Not properly.

"Let's go for a drink."

At the pub I play a prostitute at pool, and lose. The next day, we take the train to Bangkok. We visit the palace and the river. Walk around Khao San Road over and over again.

We get drunk and go to play pool. The girls at the bar are working. The place is seedy – it makes John feel uncomfortable and I wonder why it doesn't do the same to me. It should. I know it should; a year ago it would have.

The night before John's flight leaves we go out drinking. John gets a couple of hours sleep and I stay up till 5 or 6, sat at a table outside in the street, more drunk, until the minibus picks me up and we go to the airport. On the bus I say something hurtful, but I am too drunk, and I immediately forget what it is. When I say goodbye to John, I feel like I have let him down. But John is good. I am cloudy. I am losing myself, I think.

I take the train back north, to where I have left my bike, and begin to ride, back down towards Bangkok.

...

After the long flat plains of northern Thailand, sprawling grey nowhere towns and straight roads the ground erupts into jungle.

A struggle against a steep climb and weeks of inactivity, flat roads and cigarettes, leads me to a clearing in the forest. A few tents stand in the middle of Khao Yai national park, and I put mine up too. Monkeys swing from the trees above, sending leaves shivering as they leap, and branches shake as they fight over the fruits of a raid. A man across the clearing sends a monkey scampering up a tree trunk, a packet of crisps, held tightly in its jaw.

I leave the clearing. Follow a path into the jungle. The path grows thin, the undergrowth thick, I get lost and have to turn back. I scan the floor and follow, half unsure, the bent twigs and broken stems of plants; the lightly trodden floor.

The jungle hums and whistles with noise. Birdsong and insects. I step, heavy. There are snakes and tigers in this forest. If they are near, I want them to hear me coming. I want them to scatter and slither, to run from my noise and scent. The scent of guns and traps.

The air is hot, the leaves drip wet, and again I lose my way. For hours, I see nothing but trees and plants. Animal tracks crisscross the path; the fine lines of claws and padded paws, printed in the mud. If there were no path, I realise, I would not find my way out. Not for days. Or weeks. Or ever. There is nothing around, but trees. No landmark visible beyond a hundred yards, and the sun's rays splash, intermittent and uncertain, through the leaves.

I stop at a stream. A thick band of termites traipses across the makeshift bridge; a fallen branch and rocks. I stop. The noise that fills the air overwhelms me; the constant ringing of insect calls and birds and the steady hum of life trudging and slithering and flapping all around. The millions of lives in this tiny spot. Before we thrived, this was what the world was like. A teeming, living place.

Hours later, I make it back to the campsite. A group of Thai kids invite me over to their tent, and we drink whisky and tell ghost stories until the jungle around is black.

...

I meet Mook in a bar and he tells me about a journey he made by bicycle to Beijing, in 2008.

"For the Olympics?" I ask.

"For the Olympics."

"What about London?" I ask. I'm half joking.

"Yes," he says. "Yes, London. I'm planning it now. I'm planning the visas. The route. I don't know which way to go."

We talk about China, and the possible routes, and pitfalls; things we know about, and things we know nothing about, and before we say goodbye we agree to ride to Bangkok together, tomorrow.

"My friend, Boonlert, comes too," says Mook.

...

The three of us ride, along canals and quiet roads, into the city, until there are no quiet roads. Only the heaving four-lane arteries that strike into the urban sprawl, and we dig hard into pedals to get through quick.

"Tell me when you get to Indonesia," says Mook as we say goodbye. "I'd like to see it. Maybe we could ride together."

...

My days on the Khao San Road are the same. I wake up with a hangover and prepare to leave the next day. I go outside though the sun hurts my head, and I walk to the 7eleven. I stop myself from picking up beer and reach for an ice-cold bottle of water, and an ice-cream; breakfast. Outside people are already drinking, or still drinking. It's difficult to tell. I go back to my room, pack and try to read.

Again, I am in a world where nobody knows me. Where I know nobody. It is this, the joy of travelling, and the fear. I can reinvent myself one hundred times, and leave. I can be talkative or quiet, I can have opinions, or none. I can care nothing for the world or I can listen and be serious. But perhaps I am not capable of all these things; perhaps, I am always trapped inside myself, and this idea of reinvention is a myth. What can be said truthfully, is that I do not have any will to go and meet people without first having a drink. Or courage; for if there were no will, I would not begin.

Towards the afternoon, I grow tired of my own company, and I wander the streets. The same stalls selling t-shirts and bags, hair braids, banana pancakes, pad-Thai. It is easy, and mind-numbing – a constant circling; I should go home, but I go to a bar, meet new people, and then it is morning. And I am not well enough to leave the city on a bike.

On the final day, I lock myself in my room; books, bottles of water and food. The bike rests against the wall, in the corner of the room. It is the same object that I left England with; metal frame, wires and plastic tubes. The paintwork is scratched here and there. The wheels are new. The tyres are worn and the brakes are soft. Under the frame, there is a patch of bare metal where the handle bars have scratched away the paint. It is covered in small scars, and though it carries on, resilient, this journey is beginning to take its toll.

On my skin, the scratches and burns and bites have faded, without even a scar. I look no different to when I left. Inside though, I wonder, whether I am being hollowed out. Whether beneath my surface, some digression has carried me away from myself; rotting, ugly and vile, like a picture in an attic.

I am jealous of my bike, it seems more honest. I wonder what I would look like, if each deed made its mark.

I leave shattered, ride through the streets of Bangkok. It is good to move; it is the only time I know who I am, and what I am doing.

...

Outside Bangkok the roads are perfect; smooth tarmac and flat. But for the heat, and the soreness in my throat from too many cigarettes, the cycling is easy. As the road slips by, I begin to feel better. Cleaner.

For the first time in 8 months I see the sea, flat and blue to the east. I stop to eat cheap squid and prawns, garlic, chilli and rice. A palm tree curves a frame over the beach and cuts through the sky like a cheap postcard, its shadow falling across the white sand.

I think of Choyr, that town of white half-empty tower blocks, on the edge of the Gobi desert. That tiny rectangle of flats with nothing else around. Still they live there, in late November. It will be cold. Minus forty cold. I think about Dima, and his little girl, his wife. And Gerna, and Marx. How their lives have carried on. I am moving, they have stayed. But Gerna will have returned to the army. Dima's daughter will have grown. Cold, in Alzamai. It will be a long winter. Longer for the little girl; forever for her. I do not think about whether they remember me; it barely seems to matter. But they are here in me.

I stop in Hua Hin. The room is the cheapest I could find. A sign on the door says "DON'T TAKE LADY (OR ANYONE) INSIDE!" There is no room for anything but me. I can touch both walls with my hands, and I lie down and sweat. A fan rattles and pushes hot air around the windowless box, until I feel the need to go out.

I walk along the street. I eat quails' eggs, par-boiled and deep fried in crispy batter with chilli sauce, papaya salad and baked fish and Coca-Cola, poured into a plastic bag and handed to me with a straw. I walk down a different street, back to the hotel. Girls sit outside in groups. They wear black and red dresses, and say *massage* in a way that makes certain the word does not mean just a massage. I walk past, and they return to waiting. There are too many girls; waiting seems to be most of what they do. I lie down in the box, the fan whirring. I go outside, check that my bike is still chained up. It is dark now. Music comes from the centre of town. I lock the door, I am better inside. In the morning I move on.

...

The sun casts its last burning rays onto a beach in northern Phuket, and I scan the shore again, and see no-one. My tent is hidden in the trees, a few miles from the nearest town, and I take out my stove for the first time in weeks. I have nothing with me, but a packet of rice, salt and dried chillies. I swim in the sea, body surfing at low tide and then sit in the shade until it gets dark. At 8.30 I fall asleep.

The next day, I do the same. It is free. Then my rice runs out, and my water. It is time to leave. But I would stay here on this beach, eating rice and swimming and reading. I crave no company, and do not long to be better than I am. I watch the whole day; the way the sun rises behind me, and sets in front. The tide sweeps old twisted bits of wood and bones, up almost to my tent, and sweeps them out again. I watch the long shadows, and the short; the hot, bright peak of day. And if I stayed for longer I would see the rains come, and go.

I pack up my things. I am thinner. I am hungry. I long for something fatty. But I have somehow helped myself, I have snapped myself back. I have remembered what I am doing, and in some way, I see I am not bad. Is it only solitude in closed doors that drives me into myself and darkens my mood? It is the same again as before; the hunger, the feeling of sand, and the rotting vegetation, the broken shells and snapping of sticks, that have made me look out.

I ride with something in my legs now, more drive. I feel joy at the ice cold water, and my hot sweaty skin, and in the people's smiles, and the noise of markets; the tastes that fill the air. I follow the road south. I have crossed the country from the Gulf of Thailand to the Andaman Sea, and I move, still south, towards the burning line of the equator. I am excited simply to be riding a bike. It has been some time. Before I reach Malaysia, I turn off towards the island, Ko Lanta.

...

The cigarette papers Hutyee takes from his pocket are crinkled: yellowed by the sun, or as though dipped in tea, the way treasure maps are aged by children. He smooths the tiny rectangle with long fingers and stretches the yellow paper taut, folds it into a small rectangular valley. The tobacco he takes from a plastic bag is dry; brittle strands that will crackle in flame, burn in the throat. He pushes the strands down and they bend to his will, without spring. He folds the paper, rolling with two hands and licks the gum moist.

As Hutyee lights the cigarette, the thin strands ignite in flame. He coughs in fits, bringing his hand to his throat, pinching and pulling at the flesh in an attempt to sooth the pain, but it does not help.

Smoke, smattered with the tiny specks of light that dance through the trees, traces an outline of Hutyee's face. He closes a practised eye against its sting, and smiles at me; a smile with teeth, white against dark brown skin.

"So I think lie," he continues, "I think maybe lie, maybe no. But there my boat. Longtail boat. Smashed on rock, like she say. I think, cannot, cannot. I look out: many, many wave - maybe two metre, maybe three metre."

He puts down his cigarette and begins tying a thin nylon string around a small fluorescent plastic fish. Around the mouth of the fish there is a perfect circle of small, silver spikes.

"I run back to see children. Waves getting bigger, bigger all the time - more and more. We go back - bit away. I think, here we okay; okay."

He looks out towards the sea: blinding bright now to the west, but deep, blue and calm in the shadow of the rocks.

"You come too far," he says, falling back into our previous conversation "too far." And he laughs, and picks up his cigarette, sucks until the tip glows red. His throat now used to the smoke, he breathes in deep and slow.

"In Ko Lanta only littelnun die. Only little. Khao Lak many, many. Six. Zero. Zero. Zero."

We take the little plastic fish, now tied to a line, and a bucket, knife and oars, and walk down towards the sea. Hutyee's new boat is a rowing boat, and we drag it scraping along the sand, and into the water. I love that moment, when the boat stops being heavy; when it becomes light, and floats.

He turns the oars slowly and I watch for movement; for the lines to be pulled taut, the bait to be taken. And he reels the squid in. I watch their final efforts to warn off predators; violent spurts of jet black ink. They soak my hands and arms as I unhook their bodies and drop them into the bucket. And there they die slowly; one on top of the other. They do not die like fish – the way fish snap violently against a murderous air – but shoot ink impotently over their fellow dying, and stain the bucket black.

We circle the bay again; now the bucket is half-full, and the sky to the west is red. Hutyee turns the boat towards the setting sun, lays down his things and prays. I sit looking at the shore. The beach empties slowly. The bars fill. It is five years since the tsunami destroyed this coastline.

I look back. Hutyee is sitting upright again.

"Muslim," he says. "Do you believe in God?"

"No," I say. "I don't know."

We decide to circle the bay one more time. But we catch three squid in quick succession. Then four. Five. They seem to be throwing themselves at the hooks. Now both lines pull at the same time, and it is as much as I can do to unhook the bodies and cast the line again while Hutyee pulls the oars and twists the boat back around. We catch more in fifteen minutes than in all the hours of the afternoon, before again the sea turns quiet and we decide to return to shore.

"You will come to eat with us?" he asks.

I nod my head. But as I begin to speak I feel the first urge to vomit, and the dizziness of heatstroke. The thought of the squid makes me feel worse, and I stagger away to be sick, drink water and sleep.

Clockwise from top-left – Crossing the river in Luang Prabang, Laos - Children playing in puddles, Laos – My wonderful friend, John - Squid fishing – Market in Ayutthaya, Thailand - Hutyee Boat -Ayutthaya – Sunset, Ko Lanta – Mook and Boonlert

Malaysia

December 14th 2009 – January 3rd 2010

The Thai border guard stamps my passport and I cycle towards the check point on the Malaysian side. A policeman waves me through.

"Passport?" I ask him. "Visa?"

"No need." He tells me in English. "British passport – no visa."

I cycle into the twelfth country, without so much as a stamp in my passport. It has been the easiest border crossing since I left the European Union.

...

I reach Georgetown on the island of Penang on the 15th December. It will be Christmas in ten days, but it does not feel that way. It is too hot, and the only decorations are in shopping malls. I walk through the old town, and stop at a Tandoori chicken restaurant.

A man, sat at the next table, speaks to me. "Hello."

"Hi."

"Have you been here before?"

I shake my head, "I've just arrived."

"It's good. It's the best Tandoori restaurant here."

"Good. I miss Indian food."

"Where are you from, England?"

"Uh-huh. And you?"

"I'm from here. Well, I'm Chinese I guess, but I was born here. My name's Lim, by the way."

"Sam."

"Nice to meet you. Do you mind if I join you?"

I don't mind. Lim takes a seat opposite mine, and the food comes; fragrant, yellow chicken, crisp and sizzling on two red plastic trays. We eat and talk.

Lim tells me about his great-grandfather, who migrated to Malaysia in 1880. His father had given the land to his eldest brother. There was not enough land, not enough rice, to feed everyone. In the early part of the twentieth century he had married a woman from Thailand. He was too poor to take a Chinese wife.

"So, I'm a mix," he says.

"I think everyone's a mix."

Lim tells me about the different types of schools in Malaysia. "My parents never sent me to a Chinese school. They weren't very good at the time. But maybe that's why I speak Cantonese like a foreigner. I cannot read it."

"But you speak it, and good English, and Malay."

"And Mandarin," he says. "You kind of have to here, as a Chinese person. And at university. I studied psychology and counselling, but I'm not a very good counsellor. I take the problems home with me. Now I work as an English teacher – Malaysia is short of English teachers and I get a 5% increase in my salary."

"And you have family?"

He shakes his head, "My wife passed away. She died in a car accident."

When the waiter comes, Lim speaks to him in Malay. "Do you want to go for a drink?" he asks me.

"Sure, yeah. I just need to pay."

"No, you don't," says Lim. "I just did it for you."

We walk past shops selling saris and Bollywood DVDs. Small TVs blast out music into the street, and people sit outside their stalls. "I don't know where you want to go? I don't drive."

"That's okay," I say. "We can find somewhere close."

We go into a brightly lit alley way. Stalls serve fresh fruit juice, nasi goreng, sweet desserts and Chinese food. Lim buys me a beer and himself a Milo. "My doctor says I can't drink," he says, by way of explanation and we sip our drinks in silence for a moment.

"I was the driver," he says. "I fell asleep. There was a lorry that had broken down. You know on the passenger side they are 60% more likely..."

"Yes, it's more dangerous."

"You know," he says. "Malaysia is very safe. Not like South Thailand. Or Indonesia. Pakistan. The Middle East. The Muslims are good here. They are used to other cultures. We used to have problems with black African men. They sold fake dollars to local people – they brought it in plain, white paper – then you wash it and there are dollars underneath, but fake. They made Malaysian girls fall in love with them and they used them to smuggle drugs. There are Malaysian girls in China now, Thailand, Singapore, waiting..." he ties an imaginary noose around his neck, lets an imaginary trap door open, and dies an imaginary death.

The waiter brings us a plate of small sweets; something like Turkish delight, and tiny jellied tropical fruit.

"I haven't been able to drive since. My elder brother - his wife died in a car accident. He was the driver too. But after six years he forgave himself – he married again. I can't remarry. His was an arranged marriage. It's different with a love marriage."

"Some people are different" I say. "I don't think it's wrong or right to forgive yourself. Especially when it's not your fault."

"It was my fault. I killed her."

"Yes, but.."

"I fell asleep."

"Well then, yes" I say, "I guess it was your fault." I look at him; he smiles and I laugh.

We speak about Hindi being a very beautiful language, and Lim talks about the Indian caste system, about China. His family. "From one man," he says "from my great grandfather, just him. He had four younger brothers but they died almost straight away. Cholera, malaria – tropical diseases, I don't know. We don't have those diseases in China. So it was just him. From just one man, there are now 340 members of the family. I'm the odd one out," he says. "My line stops here."

We talk about the Chinese leaving food because it represents lifespan – if you eat all your food it is like your last meal. "Old people would rather fight than eat the last spoonful."

"And you?" I ask.

"No, that's just for superstitious people. Even when I was at school people had stopped believing that.

"I went to an all-boys school," he says. "But some girls managed to get in. My wife did. It started when we were fourteen. We went to university and then we got married. My wife had two miscarriages. She had a weak womb."

Lim orders some more sweet coconut jellies, and cakes.

"We had quarrelled the night before," he says. "I hadn't slept well. She was asleep as well. She died in her sleep."

He tells me about his nieces and nephews in Australia. "They don't speak Chinese; they learn French at school, but they forget everything so then they only have one – Australian English. Chinese people in Malaysia now have three – English, Malay, and Mandarin."

"And sometimes four, like you."

"Sometimes five," he says. "Do you want another drink?"

I shake my head.

"You know, my friends have told me that they killed people too, driving. But they didn't love them. Maybe if you kill someone you love it takes a long time to forgive yourself. Maybe never."

Lim points to a man who is walking with two women. "You know, Muslims can have four wives here, if they can afford it. If they can support them. The wife cannot say no. She cannot object. Now they can buy them from Vietnam. Vietnamese girls are considered very beautiful and for their families it's better than prostitution."

Lim looks at me, and it seems he is waiting for me to say something.

"Sometimes couples quarrel."

"I know," he says. And we take the empty glasses back, put them on the counter, and say goodbye.

...

I leave Georgetown the next day. Rain falls. Light in the morning. The sky grey with cloud, heavy and hot. And then the sky fills with thunder, and rain falls down in sheets and strikes up from the floor. All day the constant slicing sound of my wheels cuts through water. My waterproof shoes are less waterproof than they were nine months ago and by the end of the day my feet are wrinkled and spongy; cold, in the heat of the day, as if I had been for a nine-hour swim.

I huddle under a tarpaulin shelter, by the side of the road. A plastic plate of *pesambur sotong* on a plastic table; crispy fried tofu and a sweet spicy sauce, shredded cucumber, spinach and peanuts. And a metal tray of barbecued meat and satay sauce; the rainy day is forgotten.

I walk around the small town, in search of an internet café. A single cardboard cut-out of a snowman on the door, reminds me that it's December, and I sit down at a whirring slow computer.

There is an email. *Greetings from Kuala Lumpur.* I don't know anyone in Kuala Lumpur.

Hi Sam,

How are you doing? You won't know me but I have heard about your travels from your Mum who tells me you are in Alor Star at the moment. You are very welcome to stay with us in our small apartment when you get to KL. We are spending Christmas day with my family so if you fancy a roast turkey meal, please spend it with us.

Best wishes

Tiggy

I had resigned myself to Christmas on my own, but the next morning, as the rain begins to fall, I can think of little more wonderful, than roast turkey on Christmas day.

...

Tiggy and Martin welcome me into their home more warmly than I could ever have imagined and we spend the evenings going for lovely meals with their friends and meeting their family. We spend an evening at a quiet bar, drinking cold beer and talking into the night. They make me feel like part of their family, and I cherish the few days I spend with them.

On Christmas day we drive over to Tiggy's brother's house. Three generations sit around a huge table; a turkey and all the trimmings. Crackers and wine and conversation and even pigs in blankets. The house is full of laughter; children run in and out, and after dinner, the older men sit around a table, drinking whisky. It is a real Christmas, and as the day slips happily by, I do not forget that I am lucky.

...

The next day, I go to the Indonesian embassy to apply for a tourist visa.
"Where's your entry stamp?" The lady hands the passport back to me.
"Sorry?"
"I can't find your entry stamp. For Malaysia."
"They said I didn't need one."
The woman looks at me through the glass. "They?"
"At the border. They said British passports don't need a visa. A stamp."
The woman takes my passport and returns several minutes later.
"I'm sorry," she says. "We can't issue an Indonesian visa without an entry stamp for Malaysia."

...

Although I know they have a hundred better things they could be doing, Tiggy and Martin drive me across town to the immigration office, where a lady spends about twenty minutes telling Tiggy that she can't do anything. It is too late. There should be a stamp. But they can't give me one now. They can't do anything now.

"Do you know what will happen at the border?" I ask.

Tiggy translates the question, and the answer comes back. "She doesn't know. It will probably be fine."

...

On the 27th of December I say goodbye and ride out of Kuala Lumpur and south, until I reach the town of Seremban.

I wheel my bike around the dusty streets looking for somewhere to sleep. Though I still feel the warmth of the Christmas spent with Tiggy and Martin, and I think of them now as friends, I look at the crumbling doorway and swallow, remembering again, I'm on my own.

Above the open door, the word *HOTEL* is scrawled in faded red paint. I lean my bike against the wall and step inside.

Men line a dark staircase. It is the smell that tells me they are men, before my eyes grow accustomed to the light; the smell of old sweat and stale breath in the stifling heat. I look up now and see that they are waiting outside a closed door and that the queue falls down the staircase so that each step is taken. They wait in silence.

Only one man turns and looks at me.

"You're looking for a room," he says; it is not a question. "This is not the place for you."

Above him, the door opens and a girl in a black night dress stands; behind her, rose coloured light. I look at her face and her slight silhouette, the line of black lace on her thigh, before I turn to walk outside and her image is burnt in the sun.

...

I stay in Johor, another border town, using up the last of a soon to be useless currency. A woman holds out an empty McDonalds' cup, in what I take to be some kind of obvious symbolism, though looking around at all the rubbish on the street, it might just have been the easiest thing to find. I walk past the beggar, go inside, and eat a burger, though there are a hundred nicer things I could eat, and a hundred better ways I could spend my money.

It is a dirty town. There is dirt in the street and foul smells that smoulder in the heat. My room, shared with Malay and Indian men, who do not look at me when I enter, looks out over a flat roof. On the roof there is rubbish; rats scurry around a half-naked manikin, and a stench rises from the debris.

I lie down to sleep. Tomorrow I will enter Singapore, but the thought runs through my head: what if the man sleeping next to me has snuck a kilo of something into my bags and turned me into a smuggler? What if he plans to follow me, to let me run the risk, let me carry the drugs, and I am caught? Well, then I'll be put to death. I'll be hung or electrocuted or injected with poison or whatever it is they do, and my body will be limp and lifeless, my memories gone. And if there is any outrage, Dead is what I'll be. Like countless other desperate souls. Because sure it reduces crime, and drug use, and deters, and prevents and because, and because, and because. And all of these becauses, but I'll be dead. And the journey half-finished. And innocent me. And what then, if later the man is caught, if he admits to his crime, and his past crimes? The revelation is inconsequential. I am dead. Hung. Shot. Whatever. Nothing will bring me back to life.

The thoughts seem crazed in the morning, but still I check my bags. I reach the long bridge, the end of mainland Asia. I have cycled as far south as I can. With all the thoughts of the death penalty I have forgotten that I do not have a Malaysian entry stamp. I am called into the office.

"You are an illegal immigrant in my country," the border guard tells me. "That's how serious this is."

"I tried.."

"Now you listen to me."

"Can I explain?"

He looks at me. "It doesn't matter what you explain. You are illegal. You have entered the country illegally."

"I tried to ask for a stamp. They waved me through."

"It is your responsibility! It is not up to us. It is your responsibility to make sure you have a stamp."

"But every border is different – I didn't know what to do. I went to immigration services in Kuala Lumpur and they told me they couldn't help. They told me not to worry."

"You should have come to us."

"I did."

"I am giving you a warning," he says.

"Right." I do not know what the warning entails, and I do not ask. He shows me out of the office, and I cycle to the next check-point.

Singapore

3rd January – 7th January 2010

"Welcome to Singapore."

"Thank you."

The border guards search my bags, cosmetically. They open them, but it seems almost, that they do not want to disturb me. They feel around the shape of my luggage, hand me a paper slip, and wave me through. The slip says in big red capital letters WARNING. DEATH FOR DRUG TRAFFICKERS UNDER SINGAPORE LAW. It sends a shiver into me and I cycle into the next country.

I walk, bored, around the shopping malls, and half-bored around the streets, and I wait for my visa, and the boat.

Indonesia

7th January – 2nd March, 2010

At first the river mouth is like another sea. Soon though, the banks draw in, and we are winding through the thick brown water, jungle on each side. Below the deck is cool, air-conditioned; people sit in lines, waiting – the view outside obscured by muddy windows. They wait, as if we were on a plane, the only purpose to arrive. Perhaps they do not care for the world outside, or they have seen the passing river, the jungle too many times for it to hold any interest.

I walk up on deck and feel the hot air brush first my face and then my body, as though I have dipped myself into it – a deep dry pool of heat; pleasant at first, later I am glad only of the gentle breeze caused by the movement of the boat. But I cannot miss this. We travel deeper into the jungle; flat for as far as I can see; the deep green cover of trees. No trace of human beings. Perhaps there are animals calling; tropical birds, orangutans, but all I hear is the boat's engine, the sound of wood slicing through water, and its ruptured surface splashing on the stern.

Since I boarded the boat I have been an object of fascination. My skin again; my nose and eyes. Now, as I stare out at the water, fascinated by the new landscape, a boy is looking at me. I smile at him, "*Apa kabar?*" I say. How are you? But he does not reply; transfixed, he keeps on staring. A member of the crew comes to join me, and the boy says something to him.

"He likes looking at you," the crewman says.

I smile and say nothing. There is nothing I can think of which makes any sense at all.

Towards the middle of the afternoon, the boat pulls up at a harbour. Although harbour is perhaps a misleading word. This is more like a makeshift raft. It floats on the water, tied to huge bunches of sticks that protrude from the water at varying angles. Everything seems to be tied together with string. And platforms rest, haphazardly on the water; it seems they are flat and strong by chance rather than by design. I feel the bounce of rubber tyres colliding. The boat's engines rev in reverse, and the harbour, which looks like it has spent the whole day sleeping under slack tarpaulin roofs, bursts to life. Sacks of rice are thrown down to the wooden platform; two goats with their legs tied together; bags and boxes, a scooter, and finally my bike. The pier rocks gently on the water and sinks slightly with every new weight. I load my bike, say thank you, and ride into Sumatera.

The ticket I bought said Pekambaru, so I ask for directions to the centre of town. The woman looks surprised. It's far, she says with her arms outstretched, but she points me to the south.

It is only when I'm soaked by rain and have ridden 100km that I realise she might have been right. There have been no signs, no distances, no villages or towns; just the deep green of jungle and plantations, and the odd wooden hut. Still when I ask for Pekambaru, people point me further south.

I am happy when, as night is falling, the smoke and chimneys of what I take to be the city come into view. A boy rides past me on a motorbike.

"Pekambaru?" I say, pointing towards the town.

"No," he says in English. "This is Perawang."

"Oh, is it far to Pekambaru?"

"Yes. But don't worry, you can stay at my house."

The boy's name is Ichenk. I ride after him, and as we reach the town centre, the streets fill with the buzzing hum of scooters, and voices. People smile and wave as we pass. It is like no place I have been before; there is a different energy. Some new noise perhaps, the smells of different food, or the sounds of new music. I don't know what it is, but it is new, rebirth.

Ichenk takes me to his house. There is a bed, no tables or chairs. A television sits in the corner. I wash, dipping a cup into a barrel of cold water and pour it over me.

We meet Ichenk's friends at a restaurant. The table fills with food. A huge bowl of rice, fresh and steaming, and numerous other dishes; buffalo rendang, squid stuffed with egg, curried lamb and fish, steamed bok choi, chicken wings, and something wrapped in a leaf which nobody touches.

"This is Padang cuisine," Ichenck tells me, "You can take whatever you want."

In the morning, Ichenck takes me to his temple before he goes to work in a palm oil factory. We walk through a maze of streets. Ichenck seems to know everyone, they wave, say hello. "*Selamat pagi!*" Good morning! We walk past a primary school, and Ichenck stops to talk to the teacher. Children squat together outside a school brushing their teeth and spitting white foamy liquid into the drains. They drink water from little plastic cups, gulping it down without breathing. As we leave, I hear the sound of twenty tiny mouths, panting and gasping for air.

Everybody shakes my hand in the same way. It is a firm, but gentle, touching of hands, and then they bring their hand back and touch it to their chest; it seems like they are taking some part of you into them. And everybody looks at me, smiles, and I feel welcome in this place, on this island. We climb up to the top of the temple, and look out over the town at a huge factory.

"Is that where you work?" I ask him.

"No, that's the paper factory. It's the third biggest in Asia."

It's amazing there are any trees left in Sumatera, but I don't say anything. How can I? It is paper for me, palm oil for me, much more than the people here.

Ichenk takes me to drink *teh telur*. It is black tea with whisked egg white and sugar and we drink the warm, delicious liquid, the morning already hot, before I say thank you and goodbye.

...

The sun beats down, but in the afternoon, it will rain. At 2 o'clock or 3 o'clock, every day, in torrents. Now it is the time for the sky to grow hot, and the clouds to grow heavy and black.

A man on a scooter overtakes me.

"Where are you going?" he asks in English.

"Pekambaru."

He slows to my pace. "Me too," he says. "I'm going to an English class. Every week I go."

I ride for a while in silence; the rumbling of his engine at my side. We pass small huts, cafés; each displays a dusty line of glass bottles in the window, growing warm in the sun, to advertise their trade.

"Let me buy you a drink," he says. We pull over at one of the huts.

"Is here OK?" he asks and I nod; it seems a strange question. It is a hut like all the others. From the shelf that it displays to the road, it seems to offer nothing but warm dusty bottles of Ice-tea, but it is no more impoverished than any of the other hut windows.

The waitress wears too much make-up for a waitress, for her age. We sit inside. There are four women. I drink from the bottle, rub the dust off, and see that it comes away in sticky clumps. The Ice-tea, is warmer than I had thought; warmer than the air, I think, like it has held the heat not only of today but of yesterday, and the day before. Higher-latent-heat-capacity, I think, remembering a distant conversation.

The waitress with the lip-stick sits in front of me. Her teeth stick out of her mouth, too big for it. She talks to me directly and the man translates.

"Do you like fucking?" he says.

"What?"

"Do you like fucking?"

I am taken aback. I feel if I say yes, I could get mixed up in something I don't want. Tangled up. I could get into trouble. But to say 'no'? It seems it is not an option though perhaps it would be the best.

"I guess," I say in the end.

She says something else and I turn towards the man.

"Do you want to fuck now? She says she will serve you very well. 200,000 rupiahs."

"No, I don't want to fuck now." I say.

Though when the man translates the woman opens her legs and speaks looking straight at me, and though I don't need him to translate, he does.

"She says she is ready."

The other three women are stood, watching us. Laughing I think, at my discomfort. We leave. The man pays 10,000 rupiah for the two drinks, and says to me, quietly, as though in confidence, "These are not the best girls. Around here, there are some very interesting girls. Do you want me to take you to a different place?"

"No, thank you." I say. I feel 200,000 rupiah richer, 40 ice-teas. 40 bottles of Coca-Cola. As the man says goodbye and speeds away, girls from a hut on the other side of the road wave for me to stop. They are laughing when I wave back, and I leave them to their waiting.

Still the day grows warmer, the clouds gather. I ride for miles past the thinly disguised brothels, the impoverished lines of dusty bottles on windowsills. It is nearing two o'clock when I stop again. The café has the same row of bottles on display, but children run around outside. When I stop, they run up to me. "Hello mister, hello mister."

"Selamat pagi," I say, though we have left the morning behind. They laugh at my mistake. What's afternoon? *Malam?* No. *Siang.* "Selamat siang," I say as I approach the window. I point to a bottle of Coca-Cola. 4,000 rupiah.

I take out my map and an old woman, the children's grandmother perhaps, points to where we are. The children stop playing to stare at me. They ask me questions, only a very few of which I understand. "*Mau ke mana?*" they say. "Where do you want to go?"

"Bali," I say, and through a combination of mimes and lines on maps I try to explain to them what I am doing.

The grandmother says something to the children. "Leave! Go out! Play!" I imagine, because that is what they do. I wave my hand to try and say not to worry, they weren't bothering me, but from behind her a girl comes out; older, my age, a woman then. I am still not used to being the same age as people I would call women. Her hair is wet, a towel is wrapped around her, and she is carrying a baby; the baby too has just been bathed. Where do all these children come from? There are no men; there is no hint that a man lives here; no air of man. It is a woman's home. The girl stands there for a moment, before handing the baby to another woman, and the grandmother looks at me. I have looked at the girl in the towel too long.

The grandmother looks at me and points at the girl. She rests her head on her hands in a gesture. Would I like to go to sleep with the girl?

"No, I wouldn't"

Not *sleep*, now say the woman's hands. She points at a wrist where there is no watch. 15 minutes, she says, 20 minutes of sleeping. Not long.

I say no again, and the girl in the towel disappears behind a wooden wall. She moves quickly. I think I see relief on her face, she smiles at me. I hear the shouts of the children outside that for a moment I had silenced. I thank the woman for the Coke and take two worn 2,000 rupiah notes out of my pocket; damp with sweat, and yesterday's rain. As I leave some of the children gather in the window and say goodbye. They are laughing, they have nothing to worry about; four boys and a girl in a wooden house of women. The girl has not long been walking; she wears a small pink dress, and gold earrings; there is such laughter in the house between the children that I do not wonder how much time she has.

...

Everywhere in Sumatera, I see people waiting; it is their job to wait. Taxi-drivers, rickshaw riders, fruit-sellers and cooks. They wait and wait until it is time to do something. There are too many people for not enough jobs and they jostle and fight, amicably it appears, for trade. With some arrangement between themselves, people could work for a quarter of the time for the same amount of money. There is an hour's work in the day perhaps, but still they sit, and wait, from sun-rise to sun set.

A woman sits with her child next to a huge pile of *duku*. There are ten more stalls selling the same fruit; small, white, the size of a lychee, and the flesh like lychee too. Only, it is firmer, and divided into segments, like a tiny white satsuma, its skin pale and soft like suede.

The other stalls have no customers – it is a quiet road. And yet they sit and wait. Do nothing else. There are no books; I don't know if this is because books cost money, or because there is no will to read, no expectation. So the rest of the fruit-sellers sit, and wait, with their children and families, sheltering from the sun, under the tarpaulin's shade.

The woman hands me a huge plastic bag of *duku*. Her baby plays with my hair, and I leave her again, to her waiting, ride on along the road.

...

I pull up at a juice bar, in Solok, to ask for directions; for a cheap place to stay. One of the girls, Desy, the owner, speaks English.

"Would you like a drink?" She asks. "It's free for you."

I do not have to remind myself that this small generosity is miraculous. I am in the poorest country I have visited and yet I cannot remember the last time I paid for a meal, paid for a bed. It is an overwhelming place, and I am still unused to the hospitality; it embarrasses me, how I have been treated, with such open kindness and a generosity, which I know is ill-afforded.

One of the girls looks at me in shy smiles as she blends fruits and adds sugar. Her name is Lina, she says, and soon my Indonesian runs out. She whispers to Desy and they laugh.

"She wants to do making love with you," Desy says.

"What?"

"She wants to do making love with you."

"Now?"

Lina says something to Desy again. "Why don't you stay? You can sleep with the boys who work here. At their house, I mean."

I walk with Lina, away from the stalls selling juice, fruit, vegetables and DVDs. We cross a small concrete bridge over an open drain, and a dirt track leads to a small courtyard. A boy is standing outside the door.

"My brother," Lina says. I am learning that she calls all boys, all men, who are a similar age to her, her brother. I shake the boy's hand, his name is Danus, and he shows me inside. There is one small room for four people, and now me. A small wardrobe stands in the corner to hold four people's clothes, a couple of mattresses lie on the floor, and a TV sits by the wall.

Lina shows me to a concrete sink and a concrete wash board outside. She takes hold of my t-shirt, it is damp with sweat, but she squeezes it without signs of repulsion, as though she already knows me. She points at herself, and mimes washing and I laugh. I'll do my own washing, I say. But thank you.

She sits, watching me scrub my clothes with soap. I scrub harder, more thoroughly than usual, knowing that she is watching. I feel sure that she is laughing at my incompetence, but she does not offer to help again.

She helps me hang the wet clothes, and our eyes get caught together through the swaying material; they lock and we smile like children. It is a funny, wordless world we have between us. It is easier to be bold, perhaps. She takes my socks from the pile and squeezes them before she hangs them up. Drops of water run from them; look, you do not even know how to wring your clothes. I was right, says her look, you needed my help. I feel half-married.

On the way back, Lina takes my hand without speaking; she looks at me and smiles. I wonder if she is playing with me; I squeeze her hand gently, and I feel the light press of her fingers squeeze back. She lets go just before we reach the juice bar.

It is dark when they close. Shisha pipes are stacked away, glasses cleaned, blenders, knives washed, ice put away. It is a world where alcohol is not consumed in public, and yet it has to be replaced; it is not a world without vice. On the surface though, the vice is harmless; sugary fruit juice and sweet cigarettes; the occasional glimpse of gambling.

"Jalan jalan!" Lina says, and I climb on the back of her scooter. I do not know the translation for jalan jalan, but in every place I have stayed in Sumatera, I have found myself on the back of a scooter whizzing around the streets, on the motorbike equivalent of going for a stroll. Jalan-jalaning, if it is a verb.

The scooter slides away and we ride, going nowhere. She takes my hand and puts it on the outside of her thigh, and I rest it there, flat, do the same with the other hand. We are not going fast enough for it to be necessary to hold her. I do not move my hands, apply no pressure, but there is nothing in my mind, other than this; I am touching her, she asked me to, we both know that it serves no purpose. I lean into her; our bodies fit. Or does she lean back towards me? She waves at people she knows, "My brother," she says. "My sister."

The next day, we are on our own in Danus' house, Danus' room. She closes the door behind her and for a moment I am blinded by the bright, equatorial light turning, quick to black. Then I see the outline of her face, I feel her lips brush mine. Now, in the light, I can see her eyes and I look at her; that wasn't a proper kiss. She kisses me again.

She turns to me and smiles. This is it. We are going to do making love, here in this room. The door is locked, there is nothing else in my mind. Her face grows more beautiful the closer I get to it; a deep face with smooth curved lines, warm skin. She unhooks a big white sheet. We are going to do making love I think, again. She throws it over her head, and for a moment disappears. Strange making love, perhaps, with her under this sheet. I feel nerves gather up inside me, I don't know what to do. Her head appears again; the sheet is a hijab. Its white lace hides her hair, delicate and shining against her brown skin. She laughs at my confusion. "Surau," she says, and kneels down to pray.

Before dawn we wake to ride up into the mountains. We are visiting Yuli's family who live by a lake. Desy and Yuli on one bike, myself and Lina on the other. It is the only cold part of the day, this hour before dawn; silver and wet, the rain from yesterday's torrents still glistens on the road. It is the hour of escape from the constant heat, though I rarely see it; it is an hour when it is comfortable to sleep, when sweat does not run in the body's creases.

As we leave town the world turns grey with the sun, and then deep greens and rich colours, the world coming to life. The road leaves Solok, sweeping up into the mountains, twisting in turns. Altitude comes quickly on a motorbike, and without the effort of cycling it is cold again. Lina takes my arms and I wrap them around her. We overtake a lorry; the engine struggles to move us fast enough and we swerve out of the way of an oncoming bus; horns blaze after us as we climb through the morning mist and I cling to her tightly. She takes one of her hands off the handlebar and places it over mine; it rests only for a moment as we overtake a lorry on the inside of a hairpin bend. I have no control of our movements; my body leans with hers, round corners and blind past traffic, and I look to my left to see the mountain slope tumbling away through the mist.

The house is a small concrete box; flowers grow outside in pots, and a small flower bed, made from wood and walls of sticks, is speckled with tiny green shoots. There is no furniture in the room. I cannot remember seeing a chair in a Sumatran home; perhaps it is an unnecessary expense, or perhaps it is more comfortable to sit on the floor, strange to pay money and change old and comforting habits. We sit cross-legged on the floor and Yuli's family bring us coffee; it is sweet with condensed milk and the ground grains of coffee gather at the bottom of the glass.

"What is it?" I ask Desy. They have been talking heatedly together and now they gather around a scrap of paper. One of the women is writing something.

"It's a recipe."

"Ah," I am surprised that it has caused so much commotion.

"Not a normal recipe," she says. "You know the old woman opposite our stall?"

I shake my head. I haven't noticed her.

"Well, you'll see when we go back. She is not a good woman."

"What did she do?" I ask.

"She used to sell fruits and vegetables. Just fruits and vegetables. But she is greedy. When she saw that people were buying fruit juice she stole the idea and started selling fruit juice too."

"Oh."

"But not just that," Desy says. "She's a wicked woman. I think she has put, how do you say it? A curse. I think she has put a curse on me, on the business, to make it go bad."

"And the recipe?" I ask.

"The recipe is to stop the curse. Yuli's aunty is a witch. A good witch, and she knows how to help us."

When we return to Solok, I see the woman's stall for the first time, though I do not see the woman. It looks like a simple fruit stall, but there are a few glasses and a blender on a rickety table next to it. Other than witchcraft, it appears that Desy has little to fear.

I spend a final day in Solok, drinking juice, talking to people. I sit with Lina over an Indonesian dictionary, pointing at words.

"Do you want to come to Bali?" I ask her. She nods and smiles the way someone nods and smiles in agreement about going to the moon. But for a moment it is a quiet fantasy.

She points over to a group of boys. "My brother," she says.

Again, the glasses are cleaned and put away, the shutters are pulled down. Tomorrow I will leave.

"Touring," says Lina. "Jalan jalan," and we climb onto the bike.

This time we drive away from the town. It is a single-track road and we have it to ourselves. For the first time in days there is quiet, and the fields have turned to empty black holes in the night. There is only the rumbling of the scooter engine, and it slows to a crawl. We are going nowhere, just here to this darkened corner, away from other eyes. The scooter is still moving when she turns around and kisses me. It is an awkward kiss; it is difficult to kiss on a moving scooter. I kiss her nose I think; the scooter jolts with the bumps in the road.

Lina has stopped the engine of the scooter and has turned around to face me when I see her eyes lit-up by headlamps. I turn around to see only a single headlamp, another scooter, tearing towards us down the darkened lane. I think nothing of it, but when I turn around I see that Lina is frightened. Or if not frightened, she does not take the scooter, as I do, to be there by chance. We climb back onto the scooter and pull away. We move faster now than before, but the other scooter catches us, we are heavier with two.

The man shouts something; it is the first angry sound I have heard for days. Lina says nothing, stares straight ahead. She revs the motor, pulls back with her hand, but we are slower, and the man blocks our way, driving us towards a blackened ditch. We come to a halt. The man reaches over and with a quick movement takes the key from the ignition. Now there is only the light from one scooter, the sound of one motor, and his shouting. He leans into her as he shouts and now she shouts back. The argument is heated. I do not understand a single word, but I feel my heart beating. Hard in my chest, in my stomach, I am sure the sound of my heart is drowning out the other sounds; the shouting and the turning of the engine. Lina snatches the keys from his hand, and again we speed away. The road is slippery and wet. We swerve across the road, fly over a tiny bridge and I cling on to her as we turn the corner, the spray soaking our legs. Rain spits now from the sky. It is a pointless flight. With two bodies on the scooter we have no chance, and again the other scooter blocks our path and we end up in the verge, the wheels sink into the mud. They are shouting again. 'If he tries to kill her,' I think 'I'm going to have to die.' Because

I've just kissed her, and I am, perhaps, a little bit in love. Isn't that what love is? Sacrifice? Imagining rescuing the loved one from harm? But I have never come so close. They can hear my heart, I am sure of it. They can hear the way it hammers and thuds, rapid like a mouse's heartbeat. But I know that I will do it. I know I will stop him from doing anything to her. I watch his movements, ready to jump. I feel my feet tingle, my whole body tense. I am not in a dream. Those dreams of not being able to run away, not being able to move, to fight. Here I have to do it. At the first sign, I have to do it. I do not think of anything else. They hear my heart. Can they see my fists clench? I do not remember I cannot fight. Their shouting voices rise again. We are in the dark now; only the distant lights of the town across the fields betray our faces. Lina turns to me.

"Money," she says.

"Money? How much?" She shrugs her shoulders.

I pull out a pair of wet notes from my pocket. It is too dark to see their value. She hands the money to him, and he says words to her face, like spitting. We are silent on the way home. I hold onto the bar behind me at the back of the bike. When we reach the town, our arms are wet and glistening with rain.

"Sorry," she says.

"Are you okay?" I ask. She nods. She looks at me. It was a silly idea. Any ideas I had were silly. And hers too, if she had ideas. Tomorrow I will say goodbye to everyone. I will leave Solok early in the morning, before the sun reaches its burning, high point in the sky and we tread on all our shadow with two feet.

...

No-one ever tells you that heartache is in your belly. Or that it is less like an ache, and more like an empty hole which makes you feel sick. I ride away from Solok, and Sumatera, that once had filled me with new and wonderful shock, seems dead and dull; the food is tasteless, and I do not hear the sounds. For the first time in Sumatera no-one wants to talk, to invite me for drinks, or ask me to stay at their home. Something in my face has changed perhaps.

I ride to the next town and find a cheap hotel.

...

At 4am I give up on sleep, push open the door to the bathroom. Its hinges have been replaced by string; the wood rotten, a piece of it lies on the floor. A snapped toothbrush lies amongst empty plastic wrappers of used soap, over the rusting drain. Cigarette butts soak up a cold brown water, and disintegrate slowly. I feel the dirt of everyone who has ever stayed in this room; it is in the water and in the cracks of broken tiles, in the mould scaling the walls. It is the dirt of men, I am sure. Women do not sleep here; other than perhaps those bought. In the Sumatran lowlands it is too hot to sleep. I wait for that hour of escape, when my body will no longer stick to dirty sheets. I am exhausted and awake, and I have tumbled for hours in the restless night.

I scoop cold water from the barrel and pour it over my feet, over my head and neck. For a moment my mosquito bites cease to sting, or sting blissfully, intense. A cockroach skulks away from the splashing water, languid and tired. It seems it barely wants to save itself; not the desperate struggle of a fish, or a bird, to save a life that is beautiful and needed, but the heavy-footed sidestepping of death of something that lives in a toilet.

I leave the cockroach and I lie, wet on the dirty mattress, but the cool doesn't come. A mosquito lands on my foot. I flick it away, pull myself up again and snatch at it with my fist. I squeeze as hard as I can to kill it, to make sure that it dies, and open my hand to drop it to the floor. It flies away unharmed in a miraculous show of strength or ability in contortion, though it is a recurring miracle and I have lost my sense of wonder. I want my blood back, but the mosquito whines around me, invisible.

The heat eases slowly, but it is too late. 4.30am. The muezzins are awake. The predawn call to prayer floods into my room as if the masjid were next door and now, more than ever, it seems a room profane. The smells of past sins ache under the noise. I cover my face with a thin, dirty pillow, but it barely muffles the sound.

This daily commitment to rise before the sun would demand too much of me. I would waver with doubt; at four o'clock I would convince myself that there were no God and fall again to sleep.

...

It does not take long for me to get caught up in the wonder of the world again. In Sumatera, where people feel so close, where they infect you with their openness, joy is quick to return. I cannot fall in love in three days, I realise. The feelings subside; the emptiness in my stomach has gone.

In Saralampun, Guntur is parking his minivan when he calls me over. He saw me on the road, while he was taking people from the next town. I have not eaten since morning, and have ridden all day. I am starving, I would say, if I had not seen people who looked as if they truly were.

We sit in his home on a sofa. I do not mention my hunger. We smoke clove cigarette after clove cigarette; it distracts from my yearning for food, but does not take it away.

"I love English," he is saying. "I used to speak a lot when I worked in the factory. The owner couldn't speak Indonesian so I found a good position."

"Why don't you work there anymore?" I ask.

He shrugs. "It was sold," he says. "All the workers were told to leave."

"And now you drive the van?"

"Every day. But just one ride. There's no more work than that."

"Is it enough money?" I ask. It is a stupid question.

"It's more than most," he says. "The average wage in Indonesia is 1,000,000 rupiah a month."

I nod. The numbers are too big here, and I am too unaccustomed to the currency, for the statistic to have an immediate effect. 1,000,000 a month. 250,000 a week. And between a family of five. Less than 10,000 rupiah per person per day. I have been cycling on 150,000 rupiah a day and I have been given food, beds, water. I have been *given* everything I need, too many times. I am not blind; I can see when people are poor. Can see that I am rich. But the numbers make me feel guilty and sick. We smoke another cigarette.

"My children will be home from school soon. My daughter, Fany; she speaks excellent English – much better than me."

The children come home with Guntur's wife; the tiny house is full of excitement at my unexpected arrival. The children rush around me. And I speak with Fanny about our families, our favourite hobbies, but then, her dreams. She is twelve. She is bright and kind and open and she has dreams. She wants to travel, to live abroad, to work hard. She is the eldest of three; I hope for her. But when each 10,000 rupiah is needed to buy rice, and it would take forever for the 10,000 rupiah notes to add up to a plane ticket, I have to hide my adult scepticism. If it were not this way the world would implode; you are here, born poor, and unluckily born bright. I was born there. Our lives are of different monetary values; my hours worth more than yours. Our freedoms are different. My passport has a different worth to yours; entitles me to more. If things remain the same, it seems like you are stuck.

We take a photo with my camera, of all of us on the sofa. The family do not own a camera so we go into town to make a print.

"It's okay," I say. "I'd like to pay." But Guntur refuses, waves my hand away.

Fitsasriat, Guntur's wife has prepared food. It is probably more special than I realise. Guntur and I eat first. The children watch us. There is a huge bowl of rice, and crispy fried chicken, vegetables, and a spicy green chilli sauce. I take a whole leg of chicken. I have not counted the pieces. I scoop rice up with my fingers. It awakens my hunger. I will try to fill up on rice, I tell myself. And I take another spoon full; it is hot and sticky on my hands as I lift them to my mouth, flicking with my thumb.

"You were hungry," Guntur says, and I nod.

"It's beautiful food," I say. "Thank you."

We sleep, all six of us on the floor. I ate too much, I am thinking. I ate too much. The guilt will stay with me for a long time. I ate too much. I didn't think. It is a guilt like thieving – I would feel less guilty had I stole. I ate too much.

...

The boat from Sumatera to Java takes less than an hour and I spend the first night on the island in a military barracks, after mistranslating the word for hotel or pension. The next morning, I rise early and ride towards the capital.

...

As if only to demonstrate to humans that they have perfected a method of flight that so easily distinguishes their species from others, sparking an instant recognition even in those for whom birds are of no interest at all, swallows dip perilously into the heavily trafficked road. Just as this same flight, diving and gliding over English cricket grounds, betrays no experience of an African Savannah, so too here, the marks are borne silently of the colder climes from which were sought escape.

I follow the birds' flight as they swoop high into the sky. From where they are now, it is possible to see the whole of Jakarta; stretching out across a vast and simmering plain; 43 miles from the city's centre to its western most reaches, and sprawling again, without end, to Bogor, 40 miles to its south.

From here they see a blue sky. And the point at which it's surrendered. They see a thick smog rise; yellow, then grey, then pink. Dirt. Dust. Noise. They see the very few rich and the very many poor. Even at this height it is easy to tell the difference. They see the rivers, sewers, puddles, drains; blood, spit, bile and piss; and they begin their swift descent.

They see the trucks and the truck stops and the truck stop whores and the truck stop rooms for prayer. They see the child beggars, old beggars, legless, armless, eyeless beggars; boxes, cups, tins, hands. On rickshaws eaten by rust, and driven by tired limbs, they see the men and their wares; men carrying chopped wood, used tyres, empty bottles, live ducks, dead chickens, stagnant disease. Car accidents, bike accidents, industrial accidents, sexual intercourse accidents.

The swallows fly low enough now to choke on the dust and exhaust fumes and breathe in the smell of shit.

They see a girl sleeping on the road. She is three.

Or maybe four.

What can be said for certain is that her torso is the same height, almost exactly, as the curb around which she is wrapped; her head resting in her arms, feet pointed to the road. Except for the dirt on them, they are the same kind of tiny feet that are put into tiny shoes without laces or real soles. Perhaps she is not yet three.

Banks, factories, slums. Swallowed towns. Cracked roads. They see the ice-cutters, steel-cutters, ambiguously employed; smiles, scowls, shouts and stares. The scorching sun, the smacking rain, the dirty air; the fried food vendors, fresh fruit vendors, dirty old rubbish vendors; hoots, horns, whistles, the calls-to-prayer.

They see, and they are just above their heads now, the human-chickens scratching in the rubbish, and the human-chicken-children learning how to scratch in the rubbish; knee high in shit and searching; for plastic bags, plastic bottles, for old metal tins and cans. They follow a tourist on a bicycle. They see the barbed wire, smashed glass, loving thoughts, sinful acts, hard words, tired lives, broken dreams of Jakarta stretch beneath them as a young man walks through the middle of it all, with tangled hair and blackened skin, stark bollock naked, with cuts on his feet and a smile on his face. The smile may suggest to onlookers that he has recently fallen into a modern-day garden of Eden and is currently enjoying the pleasantries of his stroll through the brave new wonders of it all. Behind him, though quite some way behind him, for we are still a long way back in the queue for the poor people who want to become rich, glass tower valleys glint in the sun. And their glint, and their promise, might remind the swallows, though they will of course not speak of this on English cricket grounds, of the shine, in the desert, of water that never comes.

...

When I arrive, the house seems like a palace. A driver opens the gate for me; the family is out. Inside the air is cool. I sit on a sofa and a maid, or a nanny, brings me tea, shows me to my room. It is quiet; the noise from the busy neighbourhood unheard through the double glazing. I cannot remember the last time I lay on a bed so soft and I sit in semi-shock. It takes a little while for me to realise that the house is not a palace; that it is merely very comfortable. But I am sat in a country where most families live in one or two small rooms.

When Andi, Alastair's wife, comes home we sit in the living room and talk, while the two young girls play, and later that evening Alastair comes back from work. He is an accountant in the city; a huge city, cramped and pushed together, where tiny, wooden stalls huddle and ply their trade beneath great glass towers, and boys wait with their scooters outside expensive shopping malls, offering rides for next to nothing.

I feel welcome here, am made to feel welcome. Here as much as anywhere I have been. They are strangers, friends of friends, and they give me all I need and more. We visit their friends and we eat together. It is the same as all the times in Sumatera people took me into their homes; only here, I sleep deeply, in the quiet and cool of my own room, and I am not awoken by the snores and heat of other bodies, rolling on the floor. It is a reminder that different lives exist here, and that these people are no less kind, no less generous than anybody else.

After three days, I say goodbye and thank you to Alastair and Andi and go to meet Mook and Boonlert, who have caught a plane from Ayutthaya, to begin our cycle together through Java, to Bali.

...

We sit in a cafe in Bandung, West Java. Fat rain beats on the plastic sheets, and drips, cold and heavy, onto power-cut-blackened streets. A chicken leg snaps against a burning fat and, though long dead, it spits; a posthumous revenge - onions' sting and chillies' heat, the poisoned gills of crabs. We sit looking up at the black, wet sky, and down at the dirty floor. Across, the constant traffic whines, and coughs unhealthy noise. The chicken fat bursts, and snaps again; smoke rises, thick with fumes; billowing, unwet, and twisting through the rain.

We squash the rice together with our fingers and thumbs, dip it in *sambal*, and lift the small handful, steaming hot and hot. *Pedas. Panas.* We tear the chicken legs apart, one-handed. Right-handed. But it burns and sizzles at each touch, and scorched fingers fly away. Back to rice. Sambal. The crunch of raw cabbage. Of cucumber. We wait for the chicken to cool.

A smile breaks across Boonlert's face, as I glance across the table. Over the tea, rice, chicken - the bowls of water for the washing of hands. "Same same Jakarta" he says, shaking his head through a puzzled laugh. He throws his hands away, "Same same."

He is right. We have cycled for three days from Jakarta. The map assures us we have left - the neat yellow patches of cities clearly defined against the white, open promise of countryside between. But the days have been gridlocked: a lawless hot road, blocked by trucks and a heavy rising dust; by motorbikes and people; rickshaws, horses and carts.

Now though, I look over at Mook, and feel sure he has been smiling the whole time. A picture of contentment, curiosity and hopefulness, as ever. A happy Thai face. In spite of things. Tomorrow, says his face, the city will break.

...

On the fourth day riding together, the buildings come to an end. The afternoon rains begin to fall and we wind up the green steaming slopes of the mountains, until we get to a fork in the road.

"Which way do you want to go?"

"I don't mind," says Mook. "You decide."

"Well, we have two options," I say, opening the map. "We can follow this road up the mountain to Gunung Merapi, or we can go this way, to Yogyakarta."

"And in Yogyakarta, what can we do?" asks Mook.

"I'm not sure; it's an old city." The word city seems to have a bad effect on the two men. Boonlert is shaking his head.

"Yogyakarta, Jakarta," he says, testing the similarity in the sounds. "Jakarta, Yogyakarta. Same same."

We take the road left, towards the volcano. We find a guide to walk us to the summit and at 7pm we try to sleep, ready to wake at midnight.

...

It is something I rarely see, this midnight equatorial world. The small village is sleeping as we trudge our heavy boots through the lanes. An animal moves, the baying of a horse. The lane comes to an end and the concrete turns to dirt. The thin light of the moon is no longer enough to illuminate our way and we take out torches. The path is well trodden, but, in the dark, we would have struggled to follow it without a guide. For hours the world is only the small circle of light at our feet; the long, thin blades of grass, insects hopping out of the way and the grey of volcanic rock. Soon the walk becomes a clambering. The air grows cold, and our misty breath sinks in heavy clouds through the beam of light.

As we approach the summit, dark and hidden in the night's still sky, the rock begins to feel hot under our hands. It is a strange sensation - the chill of 4am at 10,000 feet and this rising heat escaping through the volcano as an odourless gas. I mistake it at first for the burning of my limbs, the warming effect of exertion, the night's thin air. It is only when I stop and place my palms upon the mountain, that I realise it is breathing, and that it feels alive. We are not the first to reach the summit; the sky, growing light, picks out the silhouettes of other walkers. Already I can see the black rocky crags of the crater and the sulphuric clouds of gas.

A little before six, the sun rises. Clouds, a perfect white, are thick below. It feels as if it is just this. Two rocky peaks and a sky growing blue. Eyes watering in a cold, crisp air, and the sense that something very simple and very beautiful and quite miraculous is taking place. It is hard to imagine that this happens every day. Something this extraordinary. The sun going up. Going down. And everything below forgotten. And remembered, all at once.

...

The road to Bali leads us past rice paddies, over mountain ranges and through busy, dirty cities. We are three. We are self-sufficient. We do not need help. We do not look lost. For all the comfort their company brings, I feel I am missing something. How different my time in Java would be if I were alone, I do not know, but it feels like things are no longer left to chance.

Before, I could look back on all my experiences, like an infinitesimal line of consequences, spiralling down to the most minute feeling, event or decision. If I had not at that instant felt a pang of hunger, I would not have stopped at that stall, I would not have met him, he would not have invited me to his home, I would not have met his daughter, I would not have visited her school, I would not have been advised to take that road, and so on and so on forever. Had my wheel not ran over that tiny metal spike, I would not have had to stop, would not have spent the day drinking with Igor, arriving late to the next town. It is not too much to imagine that I would not be here with Mook and Boonlert. Would not have met Mook at the bar, at that hour in that place. Where would I be? It is impossible to think that I am here as a consequence of a thousand different turns, and that a different decision at each turn could have made a different story. Is there one, I wonder, that would have led to death? A different choice. A different road.

When three people have a plan, it is much less likely that events turn them from their path. A tire might puncture, the wrong path might be taken, but with two people to help our problems can be solved internally. There is little temptation to go out alone. There is no space to feel lonely, and little need to seek different company. It becomes almost a battle between ourselves and the land which we are crossing. A team, working together to go somewhere. But in Indonesia the world had worked with me, helped me. I remember that first night in France, when I believed I would have to grow tough. Had I really believed that I would have to learn to fight, to grow distant from the world, in order to survive? I have crossed almost two continents, and everything I've learnt has shown that the opposite is true.

The sun rises over Gunung Bromo and the clouds ignite like golden silk, heavy in the vast crater. I turn back and join my companions.

...

"Thank you," I say as the girl hands me the change. I turn around and walk straight into a wooden beam, the sound of wood thuds against my skull.

Mook and Boonlert break into peals of laughter. They are doing it on purpose, I'm sure, to get the girl's attention. Mook is miming something about clouds and heads being stuck in them.

"He wants an Indonesian wife!" he calls to her.

The girl looks confused. Or maybe scared.

"*Kamu bisa Bahasa Ingriss?*" I ask, and she shakes her head. No English.

I point at Mook, "*Dia...*" and I draw a line across my forehead; he is crazy.

It is like this every time we stop near a pretty girl. Even if I fail to head butt something the two grown men giggle like school children and plot how they are going to embarrass me.

The girl takes a machete to the huge green husk of a coconut. The way she slices through the fruit makes me wince. It looks like a botched beheading. With several swings, she splices a little further, until the blade reaches soft flesh and cold, sweet liquid drips out. She scoops the flesh out with a spoon and lets it swim, jelly-like in the liquid, before handing us the coconuts with straws.

We are on the northern coast of Java, two days from Bali and the end of our journey together. The sun beats heavy; you can feel it in your bones. Tiny silver fish dry in finely strung nets. Rowing boats rest on rocky shores, and I am glad to share it; to look over at Mook and Boonlert and taste the cool sweetness of coconut water together. It is a strange way to end my journey in Asia, halfway across an archipelago, but I have bought my ticket to Australia and arranged to stay with family. And my mum will be flying to Perth.

Clockwise from top-left: Mook and Boonlert, Java – On top of Gunung Merapi – With Tiggy and Martin and Tiggy's parents – On the road to Pekambaru – The Strait Times

Clockwise from top-left: With Ichenck's friends – Padang food – Guntur's family – Borobudur – Selling duku – Children outside the juice bar, Solok

Australasia

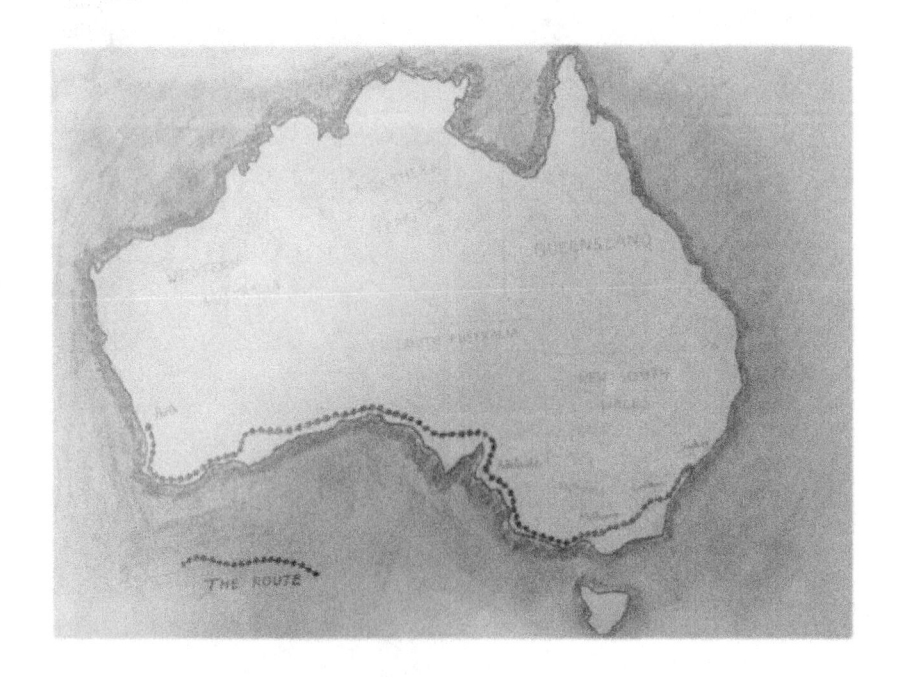

Australia

2nd March – 24th May, 2010

The air is dry in Australia. It is the end of summer. Night falls. The world seems strange during the thirty-kilometre ride from the airport to my Aunt Debbie's house. The city is too neat, too clean. Everything is square and organized; there are traffic lights which people stop at, and bike lanes, and clean new cars. It does not feel like home the way I expected it might.

There is the light of the moon now, above the dusk. I reach Debbie's bungalow, she hugs me, and there is nothing more to think about.

...

I spend ten days doing nice things with family: going for picnics in the park; watching films at an outdoor cinema; eating out in restaurants and visiting cousins' homes. When they go to work, I visit art galleries or ride out to the blue and blinding sea. I get used to drinking tap water again, to not seeing whole families piled on motorbikes, to not being looked at as a curiosity. The day before my mum arrives, fine specks of rain fall and break the long summer drought, and a week later we say our goodbyes. My mum has hired a van and we fill it with enough food to get to the other side of the Nullarbor Plain.

As we leave the city behind, my mum driving somewhere on ahead, south past the grey barren roadsides and the tangled, wiry bush, fragments of conversations come back to me. "It's a good job your mum's come out; you couldn't cross the Nullarbor alone." "You've gotta be careful – it's not like anywhere else." "Australia's the most dangerous country in the world, there's more poison here than anywhere else."

I know that hundreds of people have crossed the Nullarbor on bike, on foot, alone. I love my mum, but perhaps now I want to prove something. A support vehicle, I realise. I am riding with a support vehicle. It seems ridiculous and stupid. I wonder if it will take something away from the journey.

I ride, no longer worried about where I will sleep, no longer concerned about food or water. In Perth I have grown fat. And now this lazy way to ride. There have been times on the journey when I have longed to see my mum, but now that she is here, the ride seems somehow compromised, diluted.

...

As dusk falls, my milometer clicks to a hundred miles, and I see my mum standing outside the van. I pull into the layby, the light falling fast, the trees just silhouettes of anything at all. I reach the van. My mum looks terrified.

"Get inside, quickly."

We climb inside the van, close the doors and sit down.

"There's a prisoner on the loose," she says. "There were signs all along the road, 'Beware Prisoners'."

I don't know what to say. My mum makes food on the stove and we drink tea. In the darkness that lies outside we can make out, only slightly, the black, gnarled shapes of trees against the dimming blue of the sky.

"Where did you see the signs?" I ask.

"Here. For the last 10 miles or so. There must be a prison nearby or something."

"But why would they put signs out?" I ask her.

She puts the plates on the table. "I don't know. To warn us. Maybe we shouldn't stay here. Do you want to drive on? We could come back tomorrow, and you could start again."

"No," I try to be reassuring. "If he's escaped, he won't want to cause anyone trouble; he'd want to hide."

"Do you think so?"

"Yeah. The signs were probably there for people to phone the police if they see him." I do not think about the strange use of the word 'beware' – as if he were a guard dog. "He'll just want to hide."

It seems my mum is convinced. We turn off the lights and she falls asleep. I don't. I peep through the curtains at five-minute intervals, exhausted from the ride and yet terribly awake.

The prisoner does not appear. I do not even hear the playful noise of things outside through the glass windows of the van. But every time I snap the curtain shut, I think about what kind of prisoner he is. I have already imagined a man. Is he the kind of prisoner to break into vehicles violently? Would he use us for escape? As hostages? Or would he lie low, not risking his cover by attacking tourists? Maybe he would see the van as a trap with which to entice him, and consequently stay away. Or maybe he is a psychopathic killer with nothing to lose.

It is almost black outside now; only the silver light of stars. I look out and think, what a strange way it would be for my trip to end. Murdered with my mum, in a campervan, in Australia of all places. The dangerous country of poison, that I couldn't cross alone, the place not like anywhere else. Not like anywhere else because this is where I die? And then I fall asleep.

We wake, unmurdered, and have breakfast. After a few miles I see one of the signs, though in the new, brighter light they have changed their stance. They now read, 'BEWARE POISONS' and go on to inform dog owners that poisoned baits of meat have been placed in the area to kill foxes.

...

The next evening is more restful. And the next. And the next. It is fun to travel with my mum. I remember she is easy company, and forgiving and kind to talk to, that she is the kindest person I know. There are a few challenges now: the dull stretches of empty nothing; the weather, which has turned bleak, and a constant headwind. But there are no problems. The days roll by, predictable. The landscape stays the same. It is not a real desert. It is thorny, and wiry; full of dead, stinking kangaroos that make me wretch, and flies that swarm around our faces when we stop. They collect in the corners of our eyes, looking for moisture. It is a sad place, nothing more. I'm sorry to have brought my mum here. There are other places better than this.

I pull over to let a road train past. I have grown to hate these trucks which demand the whole road. I am growing to hate most things about Australia. There is nothing here, but there is no emptiness either. No space, no quiet, no time to think. The road is smooth, and easy, and full of old couples driving campervans from one side of the plain to the other. There are gaps of perhaps one hundred miles between gas stations that sell ice-creams for $5. Though I no longer have to care for myself, I am tired.

One day we pull up at a closed gas station. To have somewhere to stop, some mark, on an otherwise featureless landscape.

An Aboriginal man sits against a wall, under an advert for Victoria Bitter, old and peeling in the sun. Everything about the man is heavy: matt-black skin and waves of excess flesh; thick dull hair and eyes cast down as though some invisible yet cumbersome weight pulls forever on his gaze.

From the highway, then, a road train roars, and crows scatter black in the pale blue sky, circle and return, as scavengers, to the road. They pick at the bits of kangaroo that are still of use; intestine perhaps, or lung. And the dead animal rots and putrefies the air with a stench so thick you can taste it when you breathe.

Above the man, nailed over a window, a plywood sheet crumbles - the word 'CLOSED' scrawled across it in big black letters. And then, in smaller ones, 'NO FUEL. NO WATER. NO NOTHING.'

Flies buzz around him, and around us too. They crawl over skin and settle in the corners of our eyes, only the man doesn't bother flicking them away.

A caravan pulls in, slows, surveys the scene. A closed pub. A boarded-up roadhouse. Two sad old petrol pumps, their metal stripped of paint. A fat black man sat nowhere. And us. Tourists tricked into visiting this desolate, horrible place. The caravan pulls away without stopping, and soon we follow.

...

I say goodbye to my mum in Port Augusta. It is the strangest goodbye yet. She cries. I do not.

I do not know why I feel so numb at these times. Since my adolescence, I barely cry. As a boy I was moved too easily to tears. Even during the first few years of secondary school. It was not normal. I cried about nothing and everything, and I forced myself to stop. It brought unwanted attention, cutting remarks. But now I cannot cry, even when I want to.

If it were me taking the plane, my mum would be thinking of me as it took off. I do not know what I think about; pasta, cooking, myself. It is half past six when I look at my watch and realise she must be in flight. We love our parents, but it is not the same love. Or, perhaps I cannot say we; perhaps it is not general. I have never known a love so selfless as that of my parents. It makes me feel worse that I was numb as we said goodbye. There is a part of me that wanted her to leave, that wanted to be alone again, not in life, but in this journey. I have realised that I am supposed to do it alone. It should not be easy, and what happens next should not be known, as it was when my mum was there at the end of every day, waiting for me, in a van.

...

I am on my own for the first time in two months. It is like leaving home for the first time. No longer will everything be provided for me; there will be no constant love that I can feel. But also, I cannot deny it, it is liberating.

I turn the pedals for the first time knowing it is only this. That this, my bike and me, is enough to do almost anything I want. Without support or company I remember the joy; that exhilarating fear pounding in my chest. There is no one to save me, no-one I know, and each turn leads to a different place.

Again, my eyes open as the afternoons draw on; the earth becomes my bed. I look for tracks to lead me away from the road, forests in the distance, clumps of trees, or bridges, a deserted hill; somewhere to hide from the world. There was a time when the whole world lived like this; trudging across an ownerless land, searching for food, and resting in places safe from beasts or human competition. Even in Australia, before the great invasion, people followed songlines, ancient oral maps, and had to sleep somewhere unknown. But now it is less usual. The world has changed, obstructs such a life: houses, and towns, and privatised land; fences of wood and barbed wire; rules and prohibitions. There is mistrust towards people who move; gipsies and wandering hoards of travellers. And why should we trust them, these people who move from one place to another, belonging to nowhere and owing nothing to anywhere? What laws do they answer to when they are gone? It is easier to convict a thief who is your neighbour than one that has long since departed with your goods. The world has grown static; or rather the migrations are to the cities, and they are made by train, by bus or car. And there is an end to the migrations; a better static life. Good sleeping places are difficult to find. I look in the cracks between places, for forgotten land.

I turn off the road, away from the city, down corrugated gravel tracks. The sun is setting, I need somewhere to sleep, but there is nowhere. On each side barbed wire fences, battered gates, and signs: No Trespassing. There is farmland for as far as I can see. Then a quarry; the still clunking, metallic sounds of work. I could sneak in after they leave, and set off before dawn. No, a stupid thought. I feel tiredness setting in. Far away, the clean crisp sheets of home are not my sheets, my bed, my home.

With each hill crest comes the same repeated scene and it seems quite certain there will be no place to sleep. Stars begin to show in the eastern part of the sky. And then it comes, the sound at first, before the hazy flat horizon. I had not realised I was so close to the sea. My legs spin with new hope, and I race towards it with the last of my energy. If there is nowhere now, I'll have to stop and sleep beside the road.

The track slips down towards the sea. A couple of cars are parked, empty at the track's end, and I pull my bike down a footpath. Gorse covers the cliff and I drag my bike through the undergrowth, until I find a barer, flatter patch of land.

There is no place amongst the rocks to pitch a tent, but I roll out a sleeping bag and look up at the stars. Only the whites of the waves are visible now below, and I stare up at the sky with that strange spinning sense of being upside down that I always get when I look up at the stars. I am never sure if I am looking up or down or sideways. I am lying down, but I feel the sudden need to cling on to something. Every time I concentrate on a star, more come into view, and more, and more; too many to count, and each a burning sun. I imagine someone else, far away, unseen, lying on their back on a different planet, and looking out towards me.

The sky is still dark when I wake. And long thin blades of grass reach high above my head, as if they had grown through me as I'd slept. First through the blurry, unfocused lens of sleep, and then with a perfect clarity, I watch as the sun's first rays catch the dancing, yellow blades, but seem to illuminate nothing else. I am not me; I have fallen down into this place of roots, and blades of grass, this place where insects, snakes, and spiders crawl, my head upon the earth, where tiny mammals have scurried in the night, and my head upon the earth, looking up at blades of grass, and for that moment I am not me, I've fallen.

...

I ride into the village of Tatanoola, and see the pub, the children's playground and the patch of ground opposite, where I've been told people can camp.

"Oi! Come over here!" Voices call to me from outside the pub. Perhaps camping here is a bad idea.

"Come over! I'll buy you a beer."

I cycle over. There's an hour of daylight left, I can pitch the tent later. I rest my bike outside the pub, and take a seat.

"What you doin' mate?"

"I was just going to camp there, someone told me you can camp."

"Yeah, but I mean, what the fuck are you doing with all that shit on your bike?"

"Oh," I say, I haven't assimilated the Australian fondness for swearing. "I'm cycling round the world."

"But how the fuck did you get to Australia?"

"On a plane," I say quietly. I don't mention either that I have crossed half of the country with my mum. "But from France to Singapore, I cycled."

"Frog," he shouts to his friend. "Frog, get him a beer. That's fucking crazy, mate. Do you want a shotty? Matt, give him a shotty."

I walk over to a car parked by the table. The door hangs open, and I crouch inside. I am tired after the long ride, and the smoke fills my head and limbs. I need to leave soon, or I'll be incapable of pitching a tent. I take another shotty. It's been months since I smoked weed, and my body feels slow and heavy.

I come back to the table. The beers have arrived. The conversation is about wanking off dogs, or prostitutes, or both, and I sit there drinking, trying to clear my head. I shouldn't have smoked that weed. I need to sleep.

I finish the beer, preparing to make my excuses, but I'm still too stoned for the words to come out. What do I say? Thanks for the beer? Cheers? I'm going to go and sleep in that field over there? My voice sounds stupid, even in my head. They've invited me over and all I can say is nothing. Someone puts another beer in front of me.

"Thanks," is all I manage, and I try to focus on the conversation again. All I get is fragments.

"Yeah, that's not what you want," someone is saying. "You want one of those fat girls, who's like 'I just like it any old way.'"

I'm struggling to stay awake. It's darker now – I'm not sure how many times I have made the walk to the car, but each time it grows longer, my legs heavier, and the words to say no don't come. Easier to say, sure, yeah, thanks. Perhaps it will level me out, another cone another beer. And I shake myself awake.

"Sam," someone says. "Mate, you can't put up a tent. Come with us, you can stay at Fish's place."

I push my bike, walking with them through the dark, until we get to Fish's house. I can do no more than stay awake and wonder whether they regret inviting this dull tired boy for a beer and a pipe. I ask where the toilet is. Maybe, if I just splashed water over my face, I could wake up and talk.

"Go and piss in the garden, mate. Do something Australian!"

The air is cold now. My skin feels different in the light breeze. Could I feel this way if I were sober? Could I make this picture look the same? The way the moon picks out the leaves and sends them shimmering. I am happy in the quiet, outside, where I have to talk to no one. I had forgotten how this drug makes it difficult to talk. But here outside, for these few seconds, I love this altered world; the way the colours and sounds have changed, the feeling of the air.

I sleep, deep stoned and restless sleep, and wake in a soft double bed. The sheets are fresh and clean. The rest of the house is sleeping. Frog, or Amy, his girlfriend, have left me breakfast on the side, and coffee. I write a quick note to say thank you and leave the house quietly.

...

Thunderstorms break the first perfect day, of blue and yellow and green, along the Great Ocean Road. I stand with a group of Chinese tourists taking photos of the Twelve Apostles.

"You know, they have to put signs up for this lot," says a voice behind me. "'In Australia we drive on the left.' Trouble is half of 'em can't even speak Australian."

I turn around to look at the angry old man. I'm not sure what to say. I don't think I can speak Australian either, but he doesn't need a reply to carry on.

"At least these lot go home," he says. "Not like them Pakis and Muslims that's taking over."

"Are they taking over?" I ask. "I hadn't noticed."

"Oh yeah," he says, "not like in England, but it's coming. We got friends, had to leave there in the seventies. Getting too much, they said."

"It's funny to lay claim to this country though, isn't it? When it's been inhabited for such a short time by Europeans." Or to any rock or land on earth, I think, but I say no more.

"You know, our English friends can't go back there now. Doesn't feel like home, they say. Ruined, you know. Muslims, Pakis, the lot of 'em."

We look out towards the sea, and I wonder if we are seeing the same thing. The colours, the sound, the light fresh swathes of air that we all breathe in and out; the wind that sweeps its way across the borderless sky. A gust sends the long grass bowing towards the east, and in front of us an old tree stands, its limbs leafless and brittle. Once, I think, it had swayed and leant as the grass does now, its flesh supple and green. Now it doesn't move in the wind, and a snapped limb lies, rotten on the floor.

...

I do not feel excitement as I approach Australian cities. It is not like cities in Asia, where I could wrap myself in luxury for a week, drink until morning, and face the next day unslept, breakfast, lunch and dine in restaurants, on ten pounds a day.

Two days later though, I am looking down at Melbourne from the 37th floor. The city lights shine and I drink the last shot of tequila before sleeping in an armchair. I had only gone to a travel agent to buy a plane ticket, but when I told Briony about my trip she invited me for dumplings, and beer, and karaoke with her friends. It is easy to remember it was worth it, when I wake with a headache and drag myself out of the city.

...

I ride towards the village of Carlstruhe. I am going to stay with the Davies, a family I met only a week ago, on a campsite, and who have invited me to stay. That night they had invited me for dinner in their caravan and there was something open and wonderful about the family.

Now though, I taste last night's tequila on my lips, and my head throbs. I stop in a layby. I want to stop. I'm in no fit state to stay with a family, too shaky. There is a phone box. I could phone and say I can't make it. I said I'd arrive at 5, and now it grows dark, I am hours late already. I look around; a fence, climbable, a field, a huddle of trees. I could sleep here, but I flick on the front light. I am just a few kilometres away.

It is dark when I reach the house, and my hands sting with cold. But the lights glow warm inside, like Christmas. Julian opens the door.

"I'm sorry I'm late," I say.

"Hey, you made it! We were beginning to think you'd changed your plans." He gives me a big hug, and Brenda too, and on the table I see they have already spread out food. Their daughters come and say hello.

"We're very happy you have come to stay with us," says Julian. "Do you want to stay a few days, a week? You can stay as long as you like."

I feel overwhelmed and overjoyed, and welcome.

"So," Brenda asks me. "Do you know where you're going yet?"

"Yeah," I say, somehow again the whole trip seems magic. "I'm going to Alaska. It was too expensive to get to South America and anyway, it'll be winter there soon."

"It's a shame you're not going to South Africa," says Julian. "I mean, we could've fixed you up with loads of people to stay with."

"Yeah, but Julian. Why do think we moved here in the first place?"

The family's move to Australia seems to be just another thing that fills them with happiness.

"It's just safer here." Brenda says. "I remember phoning my dad, the first year we got here, and mentioning that I was going to drive down to Melbourne at night. And he was shocked, 'cos you can't do that in South Africa. It's just better here, with the kids; they'll have their freedom, and we won't have to worry."

"Are there things you miss though?" I ask her.

"Bacon and banana," she says, without hesitation. "The first time we came here, I asked the guy in a café for a bacon and banana sandwich, and he looked at me like I was crazy."

"Bacon and banana?" I look at her like she's crazy.

"You'll see," she smiles. "Hey Julian, can we have a braai tomorrow? We could invite some people round."

The next day, on the way to pick the girls up from school, we stop at Hanging Rock; the land is green now, in this damp, southern corner of Australia. Trees twist through the crags, and below us fields stretch; a rolling pale landscape. Perhaps it is the perfect place; it seems too clean, the air too fresh. It is a place where people should live; farms and livestock scatter the land below.

Jenna's school is an old building; it looks like a university. We drive through the grounds, across a vast flat lawn surrounded by woods.

"It's a struggle," Brenda says. She has noticed my astonished look. "Julian has to work really hard, we both do. But the public schools around here aren't up to much."

"He's an estate agent?"

"Yeah, it's a good job. But it's all commission, so you never know what the next month will be like."

Jenna sees us as she's about to get on the bus. She smiles and walks towards us.

"It must be stressful," I say.

"It's a different kind of stress. We just want the kids to be safe, to live. There was too much fear in South Africa. Bars and gates and high fences everywhere. Since we've been here, we just feel so free. You hear too many things in South Africa. See too many things."

"Hey!" She says to Jenna. "We thought we'd come and pick you up. How was your day?"

"It was good thanks, yeah. How about you guys?"

"Good. Really good." I say. I feel so happy here. I am myself, in these few days. Wholesome. It is a word that makes me shudder; it smacks of falseness. Of hiding things.

But it is wonderful to spend three days with a happy family, with quiet beautiful dreams. I will not remember these conversations or what we eat, or the pale green landscape or maybe anything forever, but I will remember always this feeling; this warm glowing feeling of happiness.

It is dark, and I stand outside with Julian drinking a beer. He has taken a tiny twig and spliced it in two to make a cigarette holder.

"I don't really smoke - just one or two a day," he says. "I should stop, it's too expensive now; 14 dollars a pack."

"Well, if you like it. Two a day won't hurt. That's not a medical opinion."

It is cold up here in the mountains. Though I have been here for three days, and I have forgotten the sting that was in my fingers when I arrived.

"I think people need vices," I say.

"I do. But I'm not sure about everyone. It's like religion. You know we're Christians?"

"Yeah. Well, Brenda mentioned friends from church. So I guessed."

"I think for some people it's easy. But for me; there's something about being good all the time, or the Christian idea of being good, that, I don't know. Maybe you get to a certain point, and you want to go a little bit crazy. It's like a battle within yourself sometimes."

I think about the constant cycles; the dirtying and cleansing. Abstinence I can do, but then I scream against myself, and explode. But maybe this isn't what Julian is talking about. Maybe there are other things behind the words.

"It's different when you have kids," he says. "You lose your old life. You have to do everything for them. Or you would do anything for them."

"I couldn't do it."

"Later maybe. I mean, you get a new life, too."

"Much later."

"You know, I haven't sold a house in a month," he says. "If it was just me, or just me and Brenda it would be okay, but we've got the kids and the school and the house. It adds a lot of pressure." He stubs out the cigarette. "It'll get better," he says. "Something always comes along, you know. These are small problems – not problems at all."

We go back around to the garden. The smell of meat sizzles and crackles. The wood glows bright in the dark, and tiny flames leap out of the cinders. It is the last warm night, with this family, and I will miss them.

When I leave Julian hands me a fifty dollar note.

"Really," I say. "I don't need it. It's kind enough, what you've already done."

"Take it," he says pushing it into my hand. "And if you're in Australia again, come back. We'd love to see you."

I wave goodbye to the family. I round the corner. They have given me the addresses of two friends to stay with on my way towards Sydney. But now I am gone from their lives. Out of sight.

One day, perhaps, I will come back. But if I ever do, years later, I will be scared.

How could I return? It would not be me. And I could not dare to ruin things, to break something that is perfect. Sometimes, perhaps, it is better to leave things as they are. When we come back to places we see that they have changed; the magic has gone, some small thing has been destroyed. It is no longer the place of our childhood, our own romantic past. I leave Carlstruhe, north again, and east. I cannot go back. In all these places I have known only moments; I forget, sometimes, that when I leave, the place will carry on. It is too much to think about, the millions of lives. And in people too, it is only moments I have known. Perhaps, I have made friends; sometimes it seems I have. But some people are too wonderful to meet again. I am scared to see them again, me and them imperfect.

...

The miles slip by. The world changes slowly; grows flat and boggy before the mountains, dry thin grassland turns to moor. Dead trees stand in a river; still and dead, and wet up to their waists. Old bare branches shrink away from the water, as bathers in shock retreat from the cold. I crawl up the mountain slopes and in the golden haze of afternoon slide down them at 40 miles per hour, flying. The wind batters my ears, and brings water to my eyes. To my left, kangaroos skip and jump at my side, run parallel to me, racing, golden now, and the blurred blades of grass swish by, and still they are at my side; two, no three of them. And maybe more behind, but I daren't look; the road twists around a bend. This is moving, I think, this is flying through the world.

...

A lady walks over to me, holding tea and cake.

"I've brought you tea and cake," she says. "We saw you come in, my husband and I, and you look like you could do with it."

I have finished pitching the tent and we look out, over the lake; a fine slice of blue shimmers at its furthest reaches as the afternoon shadows fall.

"Thank you," I say, taking the tea. It is peppermint; its freshness rises up in light clean steam, and the teabag sits in the murky water, growing darker, opaque green. I swill the tea bag round, and lift it out on its string, letting its weight sag, and the water gathers at the bottom to drip, slowly, back into the cup. Normally I would squeeze it with my fingers, draining the last strong flavour of peppermint into the cup, but there is something which stops me; the careful polite manner of the woman, her cardigan or her short grey hair. "It's beautiful here," I say.

"Oh, it is. We love this part of Australia. Have you come far?" she asks me. "You look like you have."

"From England," I say, and I briefly outline my journey across Europe and Asia, to here.

"Oh, that's wonderful," she says. "My husband and I have done quite a lot of travelling too. My name's Anne, by the way."

"Sam."

"Would you like to come over for dinner? I'm sure Derek would love to speak with you."

It is a small campervan; we sit around a table and Anne serves a plate of pasta, tuna and sweetcorn.

"You'll love Alaska," says Derek. "We did, didn't we, love?"

"Oh yes."

"Though I imagine it's changed a little since then. When was it? twenty years ago now?"

"Twenty one, I think. No. 1990 it would have been. Twenty. Do you remember the bears?"

"Oh, yes," he says. "We saw two bears fighting; a mother protecting her cub. Gosh, that really was quite something. Denali National park, it was. And then we drove up through Fairbanks, into the Arctic Circle. What was the name of that place?"

"Oh, I'm not sure."

"Towards Prudhoe Bay," he says. "My memory's not as good as it was. We had driven up, right to the Arctic Circle, and we were camping, and there we were; it was just us. Everything was so wild, incredible landscapes."

"We stick to camping sites now," says Anne. "A bit of comfort."

Derek is from Bournemouth, he tells me. And Anne from Sydney. They met in 1953, when Anne came to England for the Coronation.

"And how was China?" asks Anne. "I expected it's changed a lot since we were there last. We went in the 1980s."

"Do you remember, Anne? How the people crowded round us?"

She smiles. It is a whole world of memories they share together; a rich life full of images and sounds and smells; a fine tapestry of places. And *a* life, it seems; barely two, some shared and wonderful joy.

"You know," says Anne. "We tried once to get into Budapest. It was when the Soviet Union was still very strong."

"And they took your passport."

"Well they turned us away at first, they wouldn't let us in."

"That's right. It was very different in those days, I think; a lot more secrecy. They really didn't trust us, did they?"

"Well," says Anne. "They called us off the train, and took our documents, our passports, and sent us straight back on the train to Austria."

"But the border guard refused to give Anne her passport. Right up until the last moment, when he passed it through an open window as the train left the station."

Anne smiles. "He was just playing with us, I think. They do that even now, I'm sure."

It is night outside, and the night has grown cold. Anne brings out more tea, chamomile.

"You know, the thing about travelling the way you are; you must have had so many ups and downs," she says, pouring the flowery yellow tea, its fragrance delicate now as it glides up the white inside of the mug. "But something always works out."

...

I lie in the tent. My breath billows, freezing in the internal air. The light turns grey, and I hear the first rumbles of traffic in the distance. How far have I walked from the road? These are the same walls; the same yellow light dripping through the canvas. It is cold now. But apart from that I could be anywhere; outside could be anywhere. I sit up in my sleeping bag and as I disturb the tent walls, thin sheets of ice slide off, crash to the ground and break. Into grass? Was there grass outside? I feel the clumps of hard tufts of something, beneath the tent floor. Outside, thin, spindly blades cast their shadow onto the tent, blurry at first, now defined and sharp, with the risen sun. I will wait here until it warms the air outside, melts the ice, and dries the tent.

I take the loaf of bread I bought yesterday for five dollars, when I had walked slowly along the aisles of a tiny shop, picking things up, looking at prices like an old man in a Russian supermarket. I counted the calories and weighed them against their monetary value. Bread was the cheapest thing; sliced in a plastic bag, a little red plastic ribbon holding it closed; a round loaf, expensive looking. But I had lingered for a moment after handing over the $5 note, forgetting there would be no change. Now the bread is frozen –

I prise it apart with my fingers – and I dig into a jar of chocolate spread. It has frozen solid, and my spoon bends against it. I take out a book. I will wait inside the tent until it grows warm. I do not need to move. If my tent is seen now, it is too late; I'm moving on soon anyway.

I have taken to timing things, averages. How long it takes to boil half a litre of water; 8 minutes. How long it takes a millipede to uncoil after being threatened; 47 seconds. I watch ants, carry off my crumbs. If there are crackers and jam on the floor, they ignore the crackers and crowd greedily around the small bobbles of jams like pigs around a trough. If there are only crackers, they take the crackers, lifting huge flakes upon their back and stumbling along the long path, until they reach their nest.

I think of Derek and Anne. I bet there was never a point at which they timed a boiling pot, or attacked millipedes out of boredom, or sat dropping tiny flakes of crackers on the ground to test the ants.

I rouse myself; the grass is still white and brittle with frost, as if it could snap underfoot. The road too, lies under a sheen of ice, and I wind carefully up the mountain to Dead Horse Gap, and carefully down towards Canberra.

...

We leave Canberra, Garrick and I. He is seeing me out of the city. I ride a bike, and he glides beside me on rollerblades, through the strange green centre of the city, the long straight lines and circles; designed organic shapes and space, and too much cleanliness. Where is the city? I wanted to ask yesterday when he and Gerri showed me around the centre, the war museum, and art gallery. Where is the dirt, the traffic, the noise, the dilapidation? I leave, confused about Canberra; apparently I have been to its heart, but I only remember seeing parks.

Garrick met me in the mountains, and invited me to stay. Without hesitation. "Where are you going? Where are you from? Would you like somewhere to stay?" Those three simple questions that I have been asked ever since I left home.

We ride past the war museum, where yesterday we had stood, gazing at the models of planes, and guns, old uniforms and old black and white videos of young men walking, silently, towards their death. The galleries were full of animated voices; men who lament the loss of human life, but seem fascinated by the instruments - the guns, the bombs, the planes, the battle fields and tactics – that brought about this loss.

"Oh no," says Garrick as we approach a lake, quiet yesterday, and see that the roads, and lanes and paths are full of dogs and their owners. "It's the million paw walk! We should have gone another way."

We should have. I have never seen so many dogs in one place. Leads cut across the cycle path, and we move slowly through the barking, yelping frenzy. There are dogs with coats, and dogs with ribbons, and other vile things. Big dogs and tiny dogs and everything in between; there are dogs that seem to hate each other, and pull along their owners, dogs that sit, obedient, and dogs that refuse to move. I look behind me to see Garrick weaving in and out of them. And people look at us in a way which says, "What the hell are you doing here, getting in our way?"

The million paw walk. The idea, as far as I can see, is that thousands of people walk their dog in one place at the same time; I can't remember seeing much that was quite so unfathomably ridiculous, but it is a funny image, I see it myself; a fully loaded bike and a seventy-year-old man on roller skates weaving through thousands of dogs.

We make a detour, and I follow Garrick towards the outskirts of the city. We are picking up speed now, the cycle lane empty, and we must be going at 20 mph when the lane twists above a slope and I brake as I see Garrick tumble over the verge. "Don't worry!" he shouts tumbling over and over again. Below I see a pavement and a busy road. "It's normal," he shouts, though a young girl and her mother have frozen at the bottom, and they stand there, stuck to the floor, watching him tumble towards them. "This is..." I watch him roll, bouncing off the ground, down the steep, grassy slope. "completely normal!" He rolls down toward the road, the skates in the air, his shoulders rolling and bumping, until finally he brings himself to a halt only a couple of feet from where the woman and girl are standing. "This is completely normal!" he says to them, gets up and skates away.

I follow him for few more kilometres and when we reach the road towards Sydney he stops to say goodbye.

"You know, what you're doing," he says. "It's life-changing. I mean, you are a life changing person, even for someone at my age. It makes you think."

The words make me feel embarrassed; I do not know what to say. I am still thinking of him falling down that hill, and all I can think is, *you legend.*

"Thanks for everything," I say, "for your kindness," and I wave, move on, and ride across the final eastern corner of Australia. It has become a wonderful place.

...

On the road I see another bike coming towards me. It is the first time I've come across a bike as heavily loaded as mine. Tarpaulin, plastic bottles, and bags hang off it, and as it comes to a stop a bunch of metal number plates clatter against the back wheel. The guy, Greg, is riding around Australia.

"Do you collect number plates?" he asks, as though it is the most natural thing in the world. As though everyone ought to collect number plates and carry them round Australia with them, rattling away in a see through plastic bag.

"No," I say.

"Oh," he says. And he looks down at the ground, a little disappointed. And surprised, I think. He looks like someone who has told a girl he loves her, only for her to say, "You know I don't, don't you?" And now he looks down, as though he has said, "Yes," he knows, he knew, but now his mouth is dry, and he cannot talk. Like the words that he had thought meant one thing, mean another. Mean nothing. And the words seem to evaporate as their weight leaves them. So that all that is left is the light feeling on skin, when the touch has gone. More like a scratch now. Now he knows that the touch was not a touch, but the strap of a bag. And the words were not what he thought.

"Anyway," he says.

"Anyway," I say. "Have a good trip. Safe cycling!"

...

I sleep in the Royal National park, pushing my bike down an old dirt track, over a felled tree trunk, and away behind some trees. The ground slopes away and the crunch of leaves is dry above the pine needles. It is the same as other parks, except that Sydney to the north is burning into the sky and the underside of a huge cloud is stained a thick, rich yellow and the stars over there are gone. There are planes above; always two or three tiny lights flying in and out of the yellow haze. And often the soaring sound above.

I think of that night, with Emilie, Arnaud and Jan, camped outside Ulaanbaatar, looking down, across at the city. The ground like desert there, and nothing blocking the view as the lights ignited; yellow, silver, mesmeric.

"Well, from here," Arnaud had said, "it looks like a very beautiful city."

I am staring at the end of my ride in Australia. Tomorrow I will ride into the city, and meet Matt and Tweedy, and stay with them in Manly. I will fly from here to Taiwan, to LA, to Anchorage, and the next part of my journey will begin.

From here, I think, Sydney looks like a fire.

Clockwise from top-left: The 90 mile straight – The Davies – Gerry and Garrick, Canberra – Wet camping – Derek and Anne – Going out with Briony's friends, Melbourne – With family in Perth

North America

USA - Alaska

24th May – 7th June, 2010

I look down from the aeroplane window; it is night, or almost night, the sky has blue in it. Below, tips of The Rockies, swathes of white, glow in the penumbra. I cannot feel the speed at which we are flying; the mountains slip by. How miraculous to be flying above them, following the path that I will trace back south. We glide past, roaring.

The plane is half empty. It feels like a night bus. People lie, stretched across the seats, half sleeping. Reading lights pick out magazines, and the plane carries people north for summer work. In 36 hours I have flown across the world and now I am awake; my face glued to the window. It will take three months, for me to reach LA again. The plane flies over the black sea, but there is no true night, still the tinge of darkened blue. As we land it is already light.

At 5.30am I stop at a McDonalds and buy breakfast; a coffee, a McMuffin and a hash brown. It tastes sweet. It feels, for the first time, like something I should be doing.

The streets are wide and the city is full of concrete; new buildings and huge signs for gas stations and cafés and 24-hour supermarkets. There are quarters in my pocket, and nickels and dimes, and they clink together and they clink together as I walk down the sidewalk. I am in America and it never gets dark!

From here the road leads all the way to Panama, to the end of another continent. And from there I will continue, down until the end; to the tip of Argentina.

...

I leave Anchorage. The road goes north before it goes south and I head towards the mountains, and the promised empty space. My bike moves slow under the weight of tins and cans and bags of food.

"Hey buddy" says a guy riding past on a motorbike. "Hey buddy, where you going?"

"Today, I don't know," I say. "But Argentina's the plan."

"You know you're going the wrong way? You wanna be going south."

"Maybe, if I had a boat," I say.

"Well, you caught it right, anyway," he says, "This is about as good as Alaska gets. Don't get no hotter than this. Do you smoke?"

"Sometimes," I say, and he tells me to follow him to his house.

"England, uh." He fills a small bag with weed and hands it to me. "You gotta lot of rules over there, uh?"

"I guess."

"Well that's like the lower 48. Alaska's different, you know? You can pretty much do what you like up here; too damn big to control. It's the winters what's hard, but I'd rather put up with that than deal with all of that stuff down there. You drinking?"

"Now?"

"I mean, you want a drink? You look pretty loaded up there, but I reckon you could fit a couple bottles in somewhere," he opens the fridge and hands me three chilled bottles of beer. "You know, the crazy thing about summer here is you never know when to do what. You might be mowing your lawn or riding to Argentina, the sun keeps pushing you on. Folks get kinda crazy."

I leave, heavier and lighter both. The warm summer sun beats down and water runs from the mountains, breaking winter's ice. Now, well into the night, the sun plays undead in the sky. At 1am, as the sky falls only to a long and lingering dusk, everything is light.

'It's true, I know, I have always needed sleep before. But before there was always dark. And now the dark has gone so too perhaps has the need for sleep. And why should we rest when the sun itself never really sets? And how will we know when it's tomorrow? And when before have I had the chance to ride through the bright, white night, and perhaps the next three nights, or four? And maybe Hume was right. Just because something's never happened before doesn't mean it never will. Maybe it is me. Maybe I will be the first person who doesn't really ever need to sleep. And now the sky is growing lighter again and with it too I am even more awake. And in this newfound state, which must come miraculously from the lack of sleep and from the mountains and the sun and must be connected, too, to the never-ending rotation of my legs, I should and must, surely, carry on.'

An hour later, I drag my things away from the road; exhilaration has given way to weariness. My legs are not immortal, not the never resting sun, and I push my bike off the road, to sleep.

I have not brought rope, cannot hang my food in trees, away from bears, as I should, but I carry it, weary, counting the steps, 100m from my tent, downwind. I rest the plastic bags at the foot of a tree. I leave there too, my toothpaste, soap, anything that smells; I want a bearless night. It is a new fear to sleep to, the thought of being mauled. What footsteps should I listen for? No longer the tread of man.

In the end, it is easier to sleep. Perhaps because there would be no fight. A strange death, a horrible death. But I cannot imagine how it would feel, the ripping of claws through flesh, the breaking of my bones, the teeth. Is this why the chickens did not run? Why they scattered without urgency. Why they dangled pre-emptively lifeless. Or was it because there was no viciousness in the violence, no unnecessary brutality? The blood let to drain slowly to better the quality of the meat. Is it easier to die at the hands of another species, knowing you are becoming food?

...

It gets harder to camp. Fences separate the road from the land beyond and private property signs hang off the wire, promise prosecution. At night - if it is night, this long, dull dusk when the sun slips under the horizon, but still lights up the sky – mosquitos swarm, and sting and pierce my skin. I had forgotten the hell of mosquitos.

I ride along the great sloping road through Denali National Park, and a moose runs by me; noisy, crunching twigs and a huge brown mass flashing through the trees. I follow the road north to Fairbanks before turning south; the easy option, away from the Arctic Circle, and the long forever-day.

It seems, as I ride, that Alaska is somewhere else. Far from this road, beyond the wire fences and private property. It is somewhere in the distance, over the jagged edges of the mountains, beyond those snowy peaks; it is somewhere I won't go. Stupid perhaps, to turn south here. But easier.

...

It is 600 miles to the next supermarket. Between here and Whitehorse, there is barely a village; the odd small hamlet or gas station, but nothing else. I pack my bags with peanuts, pasta, chocolate bars, tins of tuna, bacon and cheese. Fatty, stodgy food full of calories. I am not hungry now, I cannot feel the pain of hunger, but I remember that it hurts.

The road turns to gravel - the tarmac cracked, and bruised by the swelling frozen ground – and RVs drive past, spraying light stones, and dust into my face. It is a new word, RV; it is how people travel to the north it seems; in these buses, these hotels on wheels, towing four wheel drives. I imagine the world slipping by the windows as from an aeroplane. I have learnt these vehicles rarely stop. I see them in the organized camping grounds sometimes, widescreen televisions blazing. They watch me from windows as I stop to fill up my water bottles.

Canada

7th June – 15th July, 2010

I ride the long gap between the border posts, not knowing whether I am in Canada or Alaska. And then, a Canadian border guard stamps my passport, and there is nothing. It is empty. An impossibly empty landscape; the road, a tiny ribbon cutting through it.

Of course, it is not empty; it is full of things untouched; the mountains and the trees, the clean air, the earth pristine. Maybe once the world was like this; roaming beasts, and water, and the land untamed. I stop by a stream and filter water, though perhaps there is no need. It is cold running from the icy north, and clearer than glass. Still, I cannot trust it; I do not scoop the water with my hands, and drench my fingers. Even here, I know the world is tainted, that out in the wilderness there are mines, and logging trucks, and who knows what silent poison lies in the crystal water? But it is as close to a pristine place as I have seen in all my life. The road is empty for an hour at a time, between the passing RVs, and I glide with the wind under a gentle sun, and then fight against a bitter cold breeze and the first spitting rains of a thunderstorm. The weather is changeable here.

Before the storm clouds engulf the sky, and the sun casts crepuscular rays, I see a bear for the first time. It forages on the verge, alone. It is fattening season, I tell myself; a time when the forests are full of berries and the rivers swarm with salmon; cyclists, campers and passers-by, for the moment, are off the menu. I stop at a safe distance and watch. 'How wonderfully like a child I have become,' again, again, after all this time. There is still wonder in moving, rebirth; the way it moves, this bear; big and solid, and the empty world. Like nothing I have ever seen.

I ride into the dusk. Now, further south at 2am, the night has come, a defining point between the days. The sky still glows, but objects in the distance are blurred, and the horizon shortens. My eyes, I realise, ache. The road sweeps along the great flat between the mountains, and a fox runs after me, follows me for miles; stopping as I stop, and running again in a silent game of chase. The world has grown silent, the sky dim, and it is just us for as far as can be seen. And to think that alongside my bike have galloped and trotted, leaped, hopped, slivered and swung, monkeys and foxes, camels and moose. Kangaroos, snakes and bears.

...

The road is pre-determined; a line cut through the wilderness. Long as a country, this road to a shop. A house stands, a hundred miles from its nearest neighbour, but my mind has turned quickly from wonder to arithmetic. Maybe the road is too easy, too flat, too smooth. I do not battle against it, but against the map in my head and the distance to the next town. 'Two cans of Coke. Two Mars Bars. One Snickers. Half a loaf of bread. 200g of cheese. Three tins of tuna. Two packets of pasta meals. Three of rice. 500g of peanuts. Three days to the next village. Or four.' I am eating 5000 calories a day; I do not know if the food adds up; only that my mind is always on eating.

In the afternoon, I meet another cyclist. His name is Karim, from Scotland, and his mind too is set on food.

"7elevens," he says, still dreaming about the States "and McDonalds and Wendys. You know you can just carry different cups around with you and walk in and fill them up for free. What do you eat?"

"Anything. Packets. Shit mostly."

"I know, I just eat all day. I put a packet of nuts in my saddle bag so I can eat as I'm riding, but I don't think it's a very good idea out here, 'cos I look and it's gone. And I'm like 'fuck, I've eaten all my food, and the next shops like six fucking days away.'"

"I started eating bacon at the beginning," I say, "but I don't know. It was splashing and spitting everywhere – I thought I was just marinating myself to smell like bacon for the bears."

"Have you seen many?"

"A few."

"I don't think they're that scary," he says. "I was watching a mother with her cub and I wanted to pick it up and put it on my bike. But there was this Canadian woman and she didn't think it was a good idea. I'd quite like a little bear cub for a pet, though – you could carry it round with you on your bike."

As we say goodbye, Karim tells me about a café, where they let you camp for free.

"You could watch the World Cup game there," he says. "Those guys are cool – they got me pretty wasted though."

We leave each other and say goodbye; two tiny dots on the road, edging north and south. The dot which is me stops at the café.

...

I sit by the campfire, feeling I can take no more, the blunts mix with the hazy smoke and the midnight sun and my mind swims, and tremors.

"Mexico," I say, feeling the effort of the words in my mouth, their awkward shape. "I'm going to Mexico."

"Mexico, hey?" Randy says. "You been down there, and all that stuff, ain't ya Jonny?"

"Oh, I been down there," Jonny says. "You gotta be careful round Mexico."

"When you did the rodeo and all that stuff?" says Randy.

"We was down there, one of the first rodeos I done," says Jonny. "Down by the border," he says, all slurred words. "We was young and stupid at the time, and I just made a shit ton of money, and we was staying in this hotel. In this town down New Mexico way. Well, I knocked my buddy's door and he comes out with this hooker; six-foot-tall, fucking great tits, screaming about going to Mexico."

The sky has darkened now and the yellow flames are bright; they play strange tricks with shadows and the faces of the men in front of me change; their features bending and elongating in the light, and my own stoned mind.

"And all three of us; the hooker too, we gets in the car, driving drunk over the border 'til we get to a bar." He takes the blunt and breathes in deeply, and for a moment there is only the crackling of the fire until he continues.

"Well, we walked in" Jonny says, "and I start throwing money around. Think I bought every god damn Mexican in that bar a drink. And you know what? I barely even know what happened, but somebody didn't want us to be there and the next minute we're tearing out of that bar, and jumping in the car again and this fuckin' gun goes off. Well this hooker she's screaming at us now and my buddy's all like throwing money at her to get her to be quiet, and we drive all the ways back to the border. Trouble is, it's a whole lot easier to get into Mexico than out of it so think I ended up spending every God damn dollar I had on bribing them border guards to get back into the States. But you know what? They're different down there. You gotta be careful."

I feel too high to talk, and finish the last cold dregs of beer, put down the can, and carry myself away from the fire. I walk slowly – my legs don't feel part of me – and, I open the tent door and crawl in. It must be well past midnight, but the tent walls are still translucent and swim with strange light, and the flickering of the fire in the distance. I look at the bag of food on the tent floor. I'll just have a Snickers, I think. And a little cheese. And perhaps a few nuts. I'm so hungry I could eat everything I have. I lie down and look at the light waves the breeze makes above me, the voices now cacophonous and nonsensical in the distance, the gentle whining hum of mosquitos outside. I stop myself from eating anything else, and sleep.

...

On the fifth day in Canada, I see a strange shadow shuffling down the road. I stop and stare down the long straight descent, squinting to make out the shape. Too tall for a bear, but it appears to be four legged. A moose perhaps, though against the trees it seems too small.

I roll down the slope until the shadow turns into the shape of a man pushing a trolley. He inches along the road slowly, or perhaps it is because the place in which we find ourselves is so open and vast that his movements seem minuscule. I stop and ride across the road. An RV rushes past us leaving a warm gust of air in its wake.

"Where have you come from?" I ask. "Where are you going?" It is my turn now, to ask the predictable questions, to feel they are talking to someone doing something incredible, and slightly incomprehensible.

Pierre is from Quebec. He has walked from Vancouver and is heading to Prudhoe Bay.

"But how do you carry enough food?" I ask.

"Well," he says. "Now, I've got this cart. It's mainly food. Before I had a backpack; it was impossible, my back hurt all the time. Up here, it's 3 weeks for me between towns. I love this cart."

I ask Pierre about his journey, his favourite places, highlights, and people he has met. But he talks mainly about his back, and how pushing his trolley, the trolley he loves, his back no longer hurts.

An RV drives past. "They don't understand," he says.

I want to ask him why they should, to say that it is our choice to be out here, riding and walking across the vast emptiness of Northern Canada, that we are here only for ourselves. But I don't. I wish him good luck, and glance back as I ride up the hill. When I reach the top, I stop and look back at him, a tiny black shadow, like a beetle edging his way across Canada. I have never felt so lucky to be riding a bike, to be moving so fast and with such little effort.

...

It is night when I arrive at Fort St John, the first real town since Whitehorse, 850 miles to the north. It blares light into the blackened sky like some neon lit oasis. It is the longest day of the year, but I have travelled so far south that is dark, and the night hides the ugly, square shape of the town, and bright fluorescent signs fill the highway: fast food outlets and supermarkets; Starbucks and ice-cream shops; motels, RV parks and 24-hour diners. It is a dull nothing, nowhere town, but something in me sings with joyful relief. I could stay here, I think, and I'd never have to worry about hunger again.

On the edge of town, I pull into a trailer park. I need a day of rest, and tomorrow I can find somewhere to watch England's last group game. The office is closed, but a woman with short hair, wearing baggy jeans and a hoody, says I can put my tent anywhere.

"Only," she says. "Don't go putting your tent over there by those trailers. They're all a bunch of idiots, hey. Fuckin' drunks is all they are."

The next morning Suzette is sat on a bench by my tent, smoking a cigarette; the empty McDonalds packaging lies strewn across the table. She tells me she's been looking for a job.

"I'm really discouraged, hey," she says. "I been living in this tent for two months now and there ain't nothin'."

"What do you want to do?" I ask.

"Oh, I don't know," she says. "But I'm really discouraged, hey. I don't know how people expect someone to live like this."

I walk into town and look for somewhere to watch the match. A café is open, and I order a black coffee. The guy who works there is Korean.

"Is it possible to watch the England match?"

"Oh! Rooney! Beckham!" he says, and turns on the TV. The noise raises a tired murmur from other diners, who quickly return to staring at their plates, or talking. "They don't understand," says the Korean guy. "They just know hockey."

I sit, watching the game, half regretting that I've cycled 150km every day for the past week just to see it, until he brings me a plate of food, fills up my coffee and doesn't let me pay.

At the supermarket I stock up on food and walk out along the road, across a dull wasteland; a whole field covered in bits of grey concrete, bottles, supermarket trolleys and rubbish; black and empty when I cycled past last night. I stop and drink a beer with some homeless people, trying to hitch a lift south. They drawl old stories at me and lie by the side of the road, cans mounting up. They don't bother raising the cardboard sign now; it is a day for drinking; no-one will pick up this mess, lying sprawled out, and bawling at the road. "Prince George," says the sign. For the first time since Alaska there is more than one road, one option.

Later that evening, Suzette is sat on the bench.

"How was your day?" I ask. "Did you find anything?"

"Oh, I didn't go look in the end," she says. "I'm really discouraged, hey. I just drove into town and went to McDonalds."

"You like that place, uh?"

"Oh, I go there three times a day," she says in a long drawl. "Cheapest place."

"What about cooking? If you haven't got any money, I mean."

"Oh, I don't cook," she says.

The noise of people shouting comes from across the park, as the night sinks in. A man walks past and says hello.

"She still moaning about not getting a job?" the man asks. "There's enough work out there, you know."

As he leaves Suzette turns to me. "He don't know nothing," she says. "He lives in a fuckin' caravan."

We sit for a while in silence, before she says for the third or fourth time now. "I'm really tired, hey. I'm gonna go to bed." And she gets up, and walks to her tent.

...

The towns come now every one or two days, and though I still hide my food, away from my tent, and the odd bear still surprises me, grazing, or crossing the road with its young, I feel I have left the empty north behind. The road rolls still, up and down, past the never-ending pine trees and the distant mountains. But those icy rivers, still melting now in June, are far away from here.

I pass a guy whose shambolic bike is falling apart. He carries with him nothing but food, tarpaulin, a few bits of wood to use as pegs, and cardboard.

"What's the cardboard for?" I ask.

"I use it to write signs on," he says. "If I get a puncture – so cars can stop."

"And it works okay?"

"Well, I have to wait for hours sometimes," he says. "But yeah, it works okay."

I look down at his tyres, worn bare; they sink down into the ground under the meagre weight of food, plastic and cardboard. "Do you need a pump?" I ask.

He pushes the bike down and it bounces on the half-inflated tyres. "I think it's okay like this," he says. "I'd pump them up properly, but the sidewalls are all ripped up and I don't know if it would take the extra pressure."

I leave him bobbling along the tarmac, the bike surely heavy without air in the tyres; the chain rattling. I should have given him oil. I should have given him a Coke, or peanuts, or a ten dollar note. I have grown too used to being the one in need; watching those huge RVs pass, without envy, but knowing I am worse off. All along the road people have given me cups of tea and chocolate and doughnuts, and now, when it comes to my turn to give, I keep my hands out of my pockets. I have climbed the hill and descended, left him miles behind, before I realise my selfishness. When one sleeps in the forest and thinks twice before buying a coffee, it is easy to forget that there are others in greater need.

...

After 2500 miles, the trees come to an end. The road tumbles down into a barren, mountainous desert and a canyon cuts an open gash out of the land. I roll through the wilderness, twisting up and down the contours of the valley; the black line of a train track cuts through tunnels in the sand coloured cliffs.

That night I sleep high above the road, led up the hillside by an overgrown track. It seems country better suited to scorpions and rattlesnakes than bears and moose and bison. I pick Saskatoon berries from the wiry bushes, and the sharp taste bursts in my mouth, sweet and acid sour. The air is dry and as the clear sky fills with stars I look down below at the trucks winding their way south towards Vancouver.

...

I reach the lakes, in the south-western corner of Canada; their surfaces lie like crystal and the whole summer sky swims in their depths. Now the roads teem with traffic, even in the national parks; I hear the hum of cars at night from my campsite, through the darkened shuddering leaves, and when I hear human voices, I do not jump with fright, but lie still in my tent, unseen, and wait for them to pass.

The sea comes, blue and hazy, through the trees. I look, from the industrial town of Squamish, out towards the islands; Gambier Island and Bowen Island, shimmering in the heat. The sun beats down and the thermometers reach thirty-six degrees across British Colombia.

I am about to open my panniers to search for the last remains of peanuts, when a lady comes over, with a sandwich wrapped in tin foil.

"We watched you cycle up that hill," she says. "And we thought you might want this."

I open the packet of beautiful marinated meat with olives and ciabatta bread. It is the best thing I can remember eating.

"You're not vegetarian, are you?" Perhaps there is still some last remains of veganism, some tiny flinch in my features that runs through me, unconscious, at the taste of meat. Or perhaps it's just the joy after eating nothing but packets of powder, nuts, bread and chocolate for weeks on end.

"Not anymore. Not since I started the trip. This is amazing," I say.

"And how long ago was that?"

"About fifteen months," I say; the words make the thing seem laughable.

"Wow," she says. "I'm Catherine. Hey Stephen, Michael – come over here!"

I say hello and we talk a little about the trip.

"So, you're going down to Mexico?" asks Stephen. "How's your Spanish?"

"Terrible," I say. "No – non-existent."

"Well, you've got a little time."

"*Estoy caliente,*" says Catherine, tentatively. "*Estoy?*"

Stephen laughs at her. "*Tener.*" He says. "*Tener calor. Yo tengo calor. Estar caliente* is something else. You've got to be careful about when you say that."

I stare at them blankly. I really do need to start learning Spanish.

"Do you want to come and stay with us in Vancouver?" Catherine asks. "We could show you around. It's a beautiful city."

I tell them that I've made arrangements to stay with a friend of a friend.

"Well, you'll have to come over for dinner then," says Catherine. And after the best sandwich I can remember eating, it is impossible to refuse.

Along the green coast, neat white lines of yachts fill the harbours, nestled in forested inlets, and everything feels clean, and just too perfect.

...

I walk through Vancouver. In the side streets, homeless men push trolleys full of things they've found; the unused remnants of what we throw away; old mirrors and scrap metal, untouched food past its sell by date. People play hockey in the street, in the cold metallic glow, cast by glass-walled buildings. And all these things will be lost; I will not be able to hold on to them. The feeling of the pavement beneath my feet, the feeling in my stomach, the taste of food, and the warm air of a heat wave. Even now, I remember so little of what was said the night before at Catherine and Michael's house. Images flick past, and the gentle conversation; a warm feeling, the garden in the sun, and fragments of phrases. I cannot remember the colour of my bedroom walls at Jayni and Carmello's flat where I am staying, nor the shape of the garden. A brief breeze carries an image through my mind, of the road we walked together down to the sea. And a fragment of a sentence about Jayni's son. "He's moved to America – he wants to make money." And then, what? Nothing. I am losing it already. I remember walking with my cousins round the white harbour and through a park, Stanley park, and the ducks dipping their beaks under water. Or is it just that ducks dip their heads underwater? Did that happen? There were reeds in the lake, and curved paths and the people rollerblading past us. We watched as a woman bought a chilled bottle of water and poured it into her hand for her dog to drink. That, I do remember. But what are these things for, this past - this never-ending stream of images and sounds – when I can barely remember who people are and what they've said, once they leave my side? And who was that other girl with my cousins? What was her name? Already, two days later I have forgotten. A beggar dancing. A homeless man singing through a traffic cone. Was that here, or was it somewhere else? All my life will be forgotten. I am forgetting it now. Too many smells and sounds and conversations. Perhaps later I will look at photos of this trip and feel like I am looking down upon another life. A flower, its orange petal shining with a single dew drop, will only be a flower, not a flower I have seen. Faces and mountains and cities will seem like photos taken by somebody else. Perhaps, there will come a time in my life when I no longer believe I did this. Only repeated stories, twisted over time, will remember themselves to me. And perhaps, one day, I will cease to believe in these. An old man, looking at his memories as though they were somebody else's. I wonder if we only pretend to remember. When I remember nothing of yesterday's conversation, but a feeling. Is it only by telling the story of our lives to ourselves, over and over again that we create something to call memory? Acts, I will not forget. I will not forget that Jon Kikoak, forced me to take a fourth doughnut and filled my bag with smoked moose on the long road in the Yukon. I will not forget that David and Megumi shared their home in Prince George, and that Jayni and Carmelo paid for a new wheel and welcomed me so openly. These and countless other acts, I will not forget. But these are acts, clearly defined by words. They say, this happened and then this happened, and it's objective and true, and cannot be changed. But is this memory? Somehow, the people are barely present in their acts. In acts of kindness or otherwise, people are somewhere in between, in the shadows that memory's light fails to find.

...

I leave White Rock, Vancouver on the 15th of July, seven days after I first knocked on Jayni and Carmelo's door, and grateful and happy for their kindness. Across the body of water, lies the USA. And my nerves rush with the excitement of another country and the impossibility of knowing what will happen next.

I ride slowly toward the border. A queue of traffic has already formed, heading south. I know from the warnings I have been given that this may not be an easy border to cross. The lower 48; the paranoid-post 9-11-security-crazed US. I am likely to be questioned, or searched, or detained for hours, before they let me past. I ride slowly past the cars in line, to the front of the queue, preparing myself for an interrogation.

"Hey!" says the border guard as I pull up to the check point. "How you doin'?"

"I'm good. Thanks."

"Where you goin', buddy?"

"umm... Mexico." I say. Say something simple they had told me; not Argentina, not Panama; just let them know you're going to leave. They don't need to know the whole story.

"Mexico?" he says.

"Yep."

"On a bike?"

"Yep."

"Hey!" He calls to his colleague, scanning my passport, barely looking at the photo. "This guy's going to Mexico! On a bike!" He turns back to me and smiles. "Good luck, buddy. Take care."

Clockwise from top-left: The Yukon, Canada – Bison, The Yukon – David and Megumi – With Jayni and Carmelo, Vancouver – Pierre and his trolley, Canada – With Stephen, Catherine and Michael, Vancouver – A black bear, Canada

USA

15th July – 23rd August, 2010

I say goodbye and thank you to Paul and Rosemary and little Daisy and leave their house, following Seattle's cycle paths out to the sea front and south. It has been a weekend of pubs and concerts and eating good food; walks around Seattle's markets, parks and museums; an easy, lovely weekend, too close to Vancouver. I have been spoiled these last two weeks; the two kind and welcoming homes so close together. The pleasant green parks, coffee shops and second-hand bookshops of central Seattle turn to factories and ports. I have a month to reach Mexico, before my visa runs out, and again I ride through the towns, not knowing where I will sleep, without the luxury of open space that was so abundant in Canada.

Tacoma is a town, south of Seattle, joined to the city by endless industrial buildings and busy roads. It leaps up at me, just as I think I should be reaching some kind of countryside. A grey town in the moments I ride through it, derelict buildings lie empty, their windows smashed, and people fix me with stares. I follow the road out south.

A man wearing nothing but red shorts and white trainers rides a bike in front of me. Tacoma is still around us, its crumbling brick walls and concrete flyovers.

"Hey man!" he shouts, as I pass. "Hey man – where you goin'?"

"Argentina."

We come to a stop. Below the ground is dirty and as I talk to the man, my foot rests in a puddle, stained black and swimming with oil.

"Whoa man, that's intense!" the guy says. "It's awesome, but man you're intense."

He screams the words loud and out of breath, turns and spits out chewing tobacco. It slaps on the floor.

"Man, you are intensive!" he screams. "I get around too, I get around, but not like you, man – you're intense!"

I look at him silently and slightly frightened, thinking no, man – I'm quiet and reserved, man – you're intense. You're really, really intense. He sees a Canadian badge I was given and he starts off again in a fit of excitement.

"You know, man – that's a good idea," he says. "That's a real good idea. I wear one of those too, when I travel. You know, everyone loves a Canadian."

He takes another pinch of chewing tobacco and slots it in the side of his mouth. "You know, man – when I was living in Bulgaria – it's amazing how quickly they found out I was American. I just went into the shop and they were like – 'hey you're the American guy, aren't you?' I couldn't believe it man. I didn't even say nothing. Just walked in there with my shades on, and they knew already. I get around too, man. I get around. But not like you, man – you're intense!"

...

I stop on the road towards Olympia. A huge sign towers above me.

DAVE AND LINDA'S
MOBILE HOMES
THANKS TO JESUS
WE'VE COME THIS FAR

I look at the dirty lot. Caravans stand on breeze blocks. Heavy traffic rushes past. Across the road a car screeches to a halt, the windows are wound down.

"Just shut up!" the woman in the driver's seat shouts. "Just shut the fuck up! You don't know shit."

The passenger door opens, a man gets out and slams the door behind him. "Fuck you!" he shouts through the open window. "Get the fuck outta here!" and the car screeches away.

There's an edge to the town and I clip into pedals and ride away. Thanks Jesus, I think. If it's you that's got us this far.

I ride through the town. What a strange twist in religion, to consider that God in his omniscience is looking after you and your shitty little business while the rest of the world crumbles and slides towards ruin and people live in unfair chaos. Why is he here, taking care of you? Maybe he's too busy making sure people's caravan businesses succeed to be present elsewhere. Once, back out there to the north, under the mountains and the never dying sun, I felt he could be there, but now... What is this religion that thanks Jesus for its cars, and its houses, its plasma TVs?

...

I wake up in Capitol State Forest while the sky is still hazy with night and ride back down to the road. At midday I stop at a McDonalds to wash the forest from my hands, the ingrained dirt and dryness in my skin, to rinse my clothes and hang them on the bike. In the USA, it seems these services in fast food restaurants are small meccas for those wandering - bathrooms, sinks, air-con, soap and Coca-Cola on tap, staffed by people with little regard for their employers' already astronomical margins – when I go back outside a guy with dreadlocks and a beard is stood by his loaded bike.

"You want some of this?" he asks, handing me a giant sized can.

"What is it?"

"Shit, I don't really know," he says. "Four Loko. Some energy alcohol thing – they're trying to get it banned."

The drink is strong and sickly sweet; 12% alcohol and full of taurine and caffeine and some wondrous concoction of artificial flavourings and malt liquor.

I hand the can back. "Thanks. That tastes kind of dangerous. I'm Sam."

"Mario."

We ride out now, towards the sea, taking turns to bear the full brunt of the wind, and racing almost, out towards the west. Mario tells me about his journey so far; from Wyoming, through Montana and Idaho, East Washington and now toward the coast, and Oregon, back home to Long Beach, California. He speaks of the joy of movement and the freedom of cycling, the chance encounters with strangers. And after each recollection, he says, by way almost of punctuation in a voice so full of wonder it seems surprised at itself, "I love people. I just love people!"

We wind through trees on forest roads and catch occasional, brief glimpses of the sea, flashing blue through the green of leaves. Under the overcast sky, tangled ropes and lobster pots lie on crumbling concrete piers, and empty oyster shells pile high against breeze block walls. The afternoon slips happily by. I am not counting the miles, I realise, nor am I troubled about where we will sleep, and our pedals keep turning, south now, along the sea.

"Did you go to Yellowstone?" I ask.

He nods. "That place was cool, man. You know, I hid my bike and my tent in these bushes for three nights and every morning I got up and I was right there in the middle of the park, and all the people were there paying hundreds of dollars for tours and hotels and shit. It was awesome, man."

The sun sinks and we scan the northern shore of the Colombia River for a place to camp: trails and old paths; gaps between the wires and private property.

"It's got to be soon," I say. "Or we're going to hit Astoria."

"Don't worry man – we're not gonna sleep like some homeless dudes tonight!"

Before the bridge, we follow a steep logging track, away from the road. We sprint up the incline, spinning pedals, and as a car passes below we both duck, out of sight. We look now, crouched behind our bikes, down at the empty road.

"It's cool that you get it," says Mario. "The hiding thing, I mean."

We come to a barrier laid across the track; a red and white drop beam with a warning not to pass written across it in big bold letters.

"What do you reckon'?" I ask.

"I don't think anything comes up here – we should be fine."

We ride further into the woods. A long grassy slope leads up to a bare patch of sky.

"Do you want to check up there?" I ask him.

"Yeah, man – wait here with the bikes. I'll go and have a look."

I watch him scramble up the grass bank, looking around for signs of movement, of human presence. The road is barely visible now and the headlamps of a car flicker through the undergrowth.

"It's awesome," Mario shouts, running down the hill. "It's all flat and there's flowers and a circle of trees. It's like this clearing in the woods, it's pretty cool."

We push the bikes up to the clearing. Huge thistles shudder in the breeze and foxgloves hang in fragile cascades, catching the last evening light. We sit down to cook; the gentle roar of our stoves rises above the birdsong and the rustling of the leaves and the occasional drone of an engine from the road, far below.

"I love this life!" Mario says, "I love it – it's all I need. It's all I want! People make life so complicated, you know? They don't realise, that it's just this. This is it, man!"

Now the sky is black. The day has gone. From the first grey light to the last golden dregs of sun and the dim grey dusk, we have been outside.

"Sometimes," I say. "I feel like I never want to go inside a building ever again."

We pour packets of food together to make a strange concoction; Spanish rice, cheese curry and tuna. We are hungry enough for anything to taste amazing.

We wash the plates and pans and Mario lights a pipe in the shape of a cigarette. Smoke coils though the dark, and when I sleep, I do not worry for the forest's nocturnal movements; its rustles and footsteps, its snapping of twigs.

...

The next day we cross the river into Oregon. The road climbs along the coast, under the rare blue sky and the hills slip into the sea like the giant back of something sleeping. We look down at the whitened edges of the waves, breaking across the bay to end their long journeys without ceremony; crashing, dying, exhausted on the sand, swept up again by the sea.

"You wanna try in the next town?" asks Mario.

The great steep slopes we ride along are owned; fenced with warnings to keep out, and we share little will to ride until dark and hide.

"Sure. Could do."

We ride into the town. A banner hangs over the road; Garibaldi Days 23rd – 25th July 2010.

Mario stops at a cherry stand to ask about places to camp.

"There's a campsite, just down the road," says the man, pointing.

"We were kind of just looking for a quiet place to put up a couple of tents," says Mario. "We don't need anything else, you know – just some space."

The man shrugs his shoulders, and we're just about to leave when a guy standing behind us speaks.

"No money, hey boys?" says the man. "I'll see if I can help you out."

He tells us his name is Scott and walks with us into the town. Bunting hangs over the streets, and ribbons sag between traffic cones where a parade has passed.

"Don't worry – they're with me," Scott says as we walk past the campsite office. He takes us to a building, walled off from the rest of the campsite. "We're having a high school reunion here tomorrow, but you guys can put up your tents, or sleep inside, whatever."

We pull our bikes inside and drink cold beer under the warm sun.

"It's a shame you can't come to New Mexico," says Scott. "It's a beautiful state. I live more than 10,000ft above sea level, so it'd be quite a climb."

"I'd love to," I say. "If I had more time. I guess that's the thing with cycling – you see more between the places, but detours are just too far."

"Well anytime you want," he says taking a sip of beer. "You know, you're probably better off crossing at Tijuana than further east. You've gotta be careful though – they're killing people for fun down there at the moment."

It's another warning to add to the many I have heard. "They'll kill you for your trousers," I've been told. "You're crazy to go there now - it's a stupid idea." "Take a flight; San Diego to Costa Rica. It makes sense." "Really, Sam. 10,000 people dead already – you don't need to go to Mexico right now." "For the cartels you're just another gringo – you got money and they don't give a shit."

It is always the next place people warn you about, never the place from which you arrive, unscathed. Ukrainians say Russia is full of criminals. And the Russians tell you to be careful in Mongolia. And the Mongolians say Chinese people aren't to be trusted. I am no longer alarmed by the warnings. But ever since I landed in Alaska, and all through Canada, people have been talking about the drug war; the thousands of murders that are happening every year in Mexico, and the danger at the border.

"You'll be alright," says Scott. "Just get out of the border area fast as you can. For foreigners it's just being in the wrong place at the wrong time."

We drive out towards the beach to watch the sunset. A cold wind blows through the open window and the sand dunes shift before our eyes; brittle grass bends and strains against its force.

"What's this?" asks Mario from the back seat. "An AK?"

"Oh. Yeah," says Scott, and I look behind me to see that Mario has lifted up the corner of a blanket, to find the gun lying on the floor.

"You never know," says Scott as the car bumps along the sandy road to the beach.

And Mario agrees, "You never know."

We stay until the sun drops below the horizon, and the wind howls icy. Still the waves crash white, but the sea becomes lost, its darkened swirling depths now the colour of the sky. Mexico seems very far away.

In the morning we decide to stay. Scott drives us up to the Scout hut and we eat pancakes, bacon and eggs for breakfast, and soon Scott's old school friends arrive.

We watch the parades; kids dressed up and floats, American flags and music. People throw sweets from the trailers and children scramble to grab them from the floor.

"I'm going to the liquor store," says Scott. And we head back to the campsite, with bags of beer, and the barbecue is alight, and more of Scott's friends are there.

Again, there is that warming glow as the beer rushes into me, and the open kindness of everybody there, and the bright yellow sun, and food. We eat barbecued oysters, with shrimps and olives and melted cheese.

"This is amazing," I say to Mario. "These people are amazing. We've just crashed their high school reunion and they've welcomed us in without thinking. They're awesome."

"People *are* awesome," says Mario.

Karen comes into the hall with a bottle of tequila, and pours golden shivers into our glasses. I am already drunk enough; in the warm late slump of the afternoon it's too early for this. I know. Spirits are the end for me. But I have the taste of it already in me. I know I can drink forever this time. Even when all past experience points the other way.

"Arriba! Abajo! Al centro! Pa' dentro!"

And the taste courses through me and sends shivers down my spine. It is the beginning of the end. And the afternoon turns to fragmented moments in a happy haze.

"I'm being British with Sam," shouts Karen. "Top o' the morning to you!" she says, in a perfect cockney accent.

"That's Irish."

"Alright guvnor – calm down!" she shouts, and already I feel myself slipping into what will never be remembered. That familiar point of no return. A kind of death. When I am barely present in myself. A short black hole in the day.

Perhaps I pass out momentarily, or otherwise am lost, but when I feel alive again it is dark and we are walking to a bar. The doorman asks for ID, and I pat my pockets, drunk.

"I must have left it at the campsite," I say. "I didn't think I'd need it."

"This is America, man. People are crazy about drinking rules," says Mario as we go back to the campsite.

When we get back to the bar, the doorman looks at us more doubtfully than before. Or perhaps, the walk has sobered me enough to see his doubt. But I show him my passport and he lets us pass. Mario orders beers, and the room is dark, and I sit for a while in the corner, half-bored and tired-drunk while Mario goes and makes friends. All I see is the flashing of the lights and then noise I barely recognise as karaoke, and people shouting and laughing.

"I'm gonna go on!" shouts Mario.

"What?"

"I'm gonna go sing. You wanna sing?"

"Nah, man." I shout back. "I don't sing. What're ya gonna do?"

Mario looks at me and smiles. "This," he says. And he walks up onto the stage and takes the microphone off the person singing and sings all slurred over the speakers. And then the music stops. There's a wrestle of people. Not a fight. But I see Mario, across the smoke and the flashing lights, his shadow being escorted from the stage. More bodies carry him away. And now there are people, telling me to leave.

"Take your buddy home," they say, and I struggle to my feet, hanging onto the stool.

"I thought he was good." I say back to them. But now they've carried Mario over to me and they point to the door.

"Let's go," I shout at Mario over the music, which must have re-started. But Mario is staying. He walks over to the bar, picks up his drink, and we stand in the corner. For a moment I think it's been forgotten, but then a guy comes over.

"Okay fellas, we called the police and they're on their way."

Mario finishes his bottle and we walk quickly out of the bar, feeling our way, drunk and blinded in the dark, and staggering home under the moon.

...

"You don't remember anything, do you?" asks Scott in the morning.

I shake my head. "We got chucked out?"

He laughs at me. "Yeah. Pretty much. The police called me about 2am to tell me 'my boys' were coming home."

We thank everybody and crawl out of the town, the alcohol seeping out of our bodies, knowing that we will smile whenever we mention the words "Garibaldi Days".

...

When we see Mike pedalling in front of us he looks like those people I have seen ever since I got to the Lower 48. Those people who stand at the intersections of freeways, outside shopping malls, by traffic lights, sitting on sidewalks or on rolled up blankets, clutching heavy plastic bags, or a battered old suitcase, or sitting next to a dog, staring into space, holding out cardboard signs; "JUST LOST JOB..." "JUST LOST HOUSE..." "HOMELESS, HUNGRY..." and waiting, on corners, for a ride to somewhere better.

Some of them seem worldly beggars; the years of hitching rides up and down this coast pronounced in straggling beards and weathered skin. But others seem in shock; the few grabbed possessions in a cardboard box, a neat haircut, clean coat and they sit, suddenly homeless, by the side of the road.

Mike smiles at us as we ride up to him; the happy smile of someone who is moving, who is making himself move. A four-pint bottle of milk and a loaf of bread hang off the handlebars; as he waves, his bike wobbles with the weight.

"Where are you going?" asks Mario.

"Just heading on down south, man. I dunno. I got a couple of things lined up maybe. Just gotta see if it all works out."

"Where you thinking of stopping, today?" Mario asks.

"What's the next town?" he asks. "Smith something."

"Smith River."

"Sounds kinda nice," he says, "maybe they'll have a river." But when we enter the town, our optimism dies.

We stop at a patch of wasteland; dumped rubbish, overgrown grass and electricity wires above. Mike clamps his feet against the back wheel and then slams them on the tarmac to slow down.

"No brakes?" I ask.

"No brakes," he says. "Got wheels though – wheels and pedals. That's the most important."

We pull our bikes around a pile of dirt, and hide behind it. The sound of children's voices reaches us from across the road. We hear cars pull into drive ways – back from work or shopping. And we sit on the long, neglected grass, the sky heavy and damp, slipping from grey to darker grey. A light rain falls on our first night camping in California.

Mike sits eating the plain dry bread and swigging the milk from the bottle. "Wasn't like this in the brochure," he says.

"Yeah," I say. "There should be sun."

"And beaches."

"And girls."

"They lied to us man," he says. "I want my money back!"

I laugh at him as the rain falls, a fine film of droplets on our tents, and clings to the hairs on my arm like dew.

"You know," says Mike, smiling. "I really do want my money back. Some bastard stole most of it coming outta Tacoma. I'd only just started. Now I've gotta 'ply for food stamps in the next town."

"What you gonna do when you get down to Sou Cal?" Mario asks him.

"I want to go to school," he says. "There's a film school down there. I might have a place. Gotta get a job too, mind."

As night falls we sit outside our tents talking. The town grows quiet, and if we peer over the hedge we can see the glow of lights behind drawn curtains.

Mike tells us about getting knocked off his bike in Oregon. "That was cool though, man, 'cos this motel lady – she was real nice – and she let me stay there free while the swelling went down. I mean – it was shitty, but it was cool too, you know?"

We nod. Above us, a fizz of electricity runs through the wires and, in the silence that follows, I feel like I am looking down on a microcosm of a great American migration. I imagine all the other people camped out like this across the states. "I feel like I'm in the Grapes of Wrath," I say to Mario, as we pack the final things into our tents.

"All that's missing is a trash can fire."

...

In Crescent City, Mike stops to apply for food stamps, we say goodbye, and Mario and I pull up at a thrift store. I hand the shop assistant 2 dollars for a pair of shorts and she hands them back to me with a leaflet. The cover depicts a strange cartoon world where clean cut white men wearing polo shirts and beige trousers walk across lush green hills with women wearing long skirts and black and Asian children run around playing with tigers and lions.

"Wouldn't you want to live in a world like that?" the woman asks me.

"I'd worry about the lion," I say.

"But it is only sin which separates us," she says. "When we accept God into our lives we will learn to live as one with the animals, and other people, and when Christ comes back we will be saved."

"Yes, but I don't think the lion would learn not to eat me."

"Maybe forget about the picture for a minute," she says, and offers a confused analogy about counterfeit notes and real ones that I don't quite follow. I look at her puzzled.

"Well, what about when you die? You don't believe there's nothing, do you?"

I shrug my shoulders. I guess this is the price you pay for spending 2 dollars on shorts. "I don't know," I say. "It's probably a lot like it was before you were born."

Mario is waiting outside now. He's packed his bike and he looks through the dusty windowpane to see what's taking so long.

"I'm going to give you a bible," the lady says. "But first, I want you to read something. Just here." She points to a passage on the leaflet she has given me.

It will be very difficult for us to unite, if our own personal beliefs stand in the way. Why don't we neglect and disregard our own personal views, and only accept and obey what is written in the Bible as our guidelines of truth. By this way we will all be united, and that's the will of God.

I'm not sure I want to neglect and disregard my own personal views, but the quickest way to get out of the shop is to take the bible and agree.

I walk outside and hear screaming. A woman in denim shorts shouts at us, "Quick! Call 911! A man's just attacked me and put a knife in my car!"

Mario phones the police. The woman runs out of the yard and shouting comes from inside the house. We ride away. The road stretches long and straight, up towards the redwoods. Mario turns to me. "That place was nasty, man."

Mario rides on ahead. Still, I feel the morning's stiffness in my legs and I climb, slow and steady, happy to be going south, to be leaving the town behind. I breathe in deep as the air grows clean, and a cold damp mist descends.

The sudden squealing of a car comes from behind and I swerve off the road to avoid it. A man leans on the horn, shouts something through the window and I watch as Mario spits on the boot. We keep on pedalling up the road, and the car pulls over; the man gets out, sits on his bonnet and waits for us to pass.

"Do you wanna spit on my car again, motherfucker?" he shouts at Mario. And then at me, "You're taking up the whole road 'cos you're a faggot."

I fail to see the correlation, but we cycle past, with our heads down, as we hear the car door slam again. The engine revs. The wheels spin. But when we look behind the car has made a u-turn, and speeds back down towards Crescent City.

"Do you reckon he's gone to get his friends?" I ask.

Mario doesn't answer me, but he reaches down into his bag and takes out a can of pepper spray. Above us now, the ancient redwoods stand, the very highest branches disappearing in the mist. As we ride deeper into the forest, somewhere far above us, the sky clears to an unseen blue. Blinding golden shafts of light transform the mist to swirling, solid forms. We roll now through the forest, at a crawl, and the forest seems to dance in perpetual silent movement. Our bikes creep along the winding road, like tiny toys now, dwarfed against the giant trunks, and the trees' crowns are lost like mountain peaks. The oldest of these trees have been here for more than 2000 years, long before this country existed. They have survived a European invasion, and forest fires, the industrial revolution, and the rise of the car. And all this, I think as I stare up at their heights, to be able to look down at the ugly grid shaped streets of Crescent City.

The man does not return. With his friends or alone. And we camp again in the forest, in the shadowy swirling mist, below giant trees.

...

Out across the bay, tents nestle under a bridge. We look at them across the grasses, marshy wet and litter strewn, old supermarket trolleys upturned. From a campfire, smoke rises into the low grey sky.

"Under the bridge is where the homeless people sleep – you could try there."

We decide to ignore the advice - cite the cost of our bikes, our wallets and phones, as reasons to find somewhere else, and continue along the road that seems to sink into the marsh, down towards Eureka.

We push our bikes away from the road as it empties, momentarily, of traffic, and we skirt the wire fence. We pitch our tents on a small patch of grass behind a shed. On the other side of the fence wooden pallets pile up and machinery is left standing behind corrugated metal structures. It appears to be some kind of warehouse for farming supplies.

"It's Saturday, right?" asks Mario.

"I think so."

"That's cool – I don't think anyone'll be coming into work tomorrow."

"Let's just hope there isn't a guard."

In the morning we wake early to leave. Smoke still snakes into the sky from the camp across the bay, and we ride into Eureka not knowing what a night with its homeless would have been like.

I'm sitting outside a supermarket, waiting for Mario, when Lola comes up to me. The sickly-sweet smell of old alcohol hangs on her breath. Chemical alcohol. Sweet and putrid, but not as unpleasant as the old rotting fermentation of grapes and grain. It is difficult to guess her age; 25, 35, or 40. But I guess she is younger than she looks.

"You boys on the road, man, hey that's cool," she says drawling, early up and drunk in the morning. She opens a can of alcoholic energy drink, and the metal crunches and cracks and I hear the dying fizz, before she brings it to her lips. "Wish I could get me out on the road," she says, sitting down. "So where you goin'?"

"Argentina."

"Shit, man," she says. "You serious?"

I nod.

"You want some of this?" she asks, and I shake my head. There's something, squeamish and childlike about me that doesn't want to share the can. Something unspoken that repels me for an instant, like sharing a bottle with a tramp; it is a cruel thought, a cruel way to think.

"Are you from Australia?" she asks.

"England."

"Oh. I didn't know from the accent. It sounds kind of similar. My pops went to England, you know, back in the seventies. You should come meet him."

We sit for a while, talking, until Mario comes out with a bag of shopping. "This is Lola," I say.

"Hey Lola."

"You boys smoke?" she asks. "My pops got a load of killer bud, if you want to come over. I got a new puppy too."

We walk with Lola, pushing our bikes round the side of the supermarket, and into a side street. Grass grows over crumbling concrete walls, and the yards are full of old toys and broken glass. We walk past a house with no door; a fridge lies rusting on the ground.

"It's just here," she tells us, pointing to the house next door. And for a moment I catch Mario's eye, raise my eyebrows and see him smile. "You wanna bring those bikes inside."

We lift our bikes over the debris in the yard, and up a step, through the wooden door, hanging off the hinges and peeling, into a darkened hall. We rest our bikes against the wall. Old bottles and cans, scraps of foil and cigarette butts lie on the carpet. We open the door into a room which is a kitchen, living room and bedroom. The sink spews out dirty plates, and the thick smoke hits us; the perpetual gouge-away.

"Pops," shouts Lola over the music. "I brought these two boys back. They're biking down the coast. Take a seat, boys."

Pops sits in an armchair, old, thin and grey haired. He sits in some kind of stupor, running a knife up and down a long stone; the scraping, slicing sound of the slowly sharpening blade. He mumbles something, and lifts his head in a slow, heavy smile, and falls again to sharpening his knife.

Lola hands us a pipe and we sit back in the sofa. The weed is strong, and the room fills again with smoke, pressing against the closed windows, as the sun casts its first light on the dusty panes, and the edges of everything in the room ignite in a brilliant glow.

"Where's Toby?" Lola suddenly pulls herself up in the chair.

"aaannyawoda seena" pops growls slow, and laboured, still sliding the blade slowly up and down.

"Where's my fucking puppy?" she screams, getting to her feet and running outside. "Toby!"

Pops hands us the bag of bud and we refill the pipe, and smoke slowly. Banging and crashing comes from upstairs; chairs are being thrown over, drawers pulled out. Rushed footsteps fall heavy on the staircase, and again Lola is in the room.

"Did you leave the fucking door open?" She screams at pops, and he stares straight, still in front. "Did someone leave that fucking door open?" She collapses onto the chair in front of us and cries. "Oh God, oh fucking God," she cries. "What if he's lost? He dudn't know his way round. Oh God," she sobs, crumpled in the chair. "I've lost my puppy."

I look at Mario. It's time to leave. We've come here by mistake. It's not the time for this; early Sunday morning and miles to do. The front door slams and a tall man in a trench coat half staggers into the room and falls down to floor to sit on a cushion. He takes a swig from a beer can before looking around. He doesn't seem surprised to see us, or to see Lola crying in the chair.

He grins at us, through a rough beard and long greasy black hair. His teeth are so sharp and pointed, blackened and filthy yellow, that I cannot look at his mouth without imagining him biting me. I shake his hand, too stoned, and he laughs a friendly, hissing laugh.

"Have you seen Toby?" Lola asks him.

"Yeah," he says. "Dave's got him. You left him next door when you went to the shop."

Now Lola's sobbing becomes a heaving laugh and she wipes the tears from her eyes and takes the pipe. "Oh, shit man. You're right. You're so fucking right. I forgot. I totally forgot."

The day slips past us. The light of the sun suddenly full upon the window, and the music stays slow, and fills the room. "We should go," I say for the third or fourth time.

Pops lets smoke wind around his face, and it coils into the cloud that fills the room, clings to our clothes and stings my eyes red. "Ooo downa uppin ol ill." He mumbles, barely raising his eyes. "'bout fivin kilome 'n em sou downa weot ol nashnulpark."

We thank Pops for the directions and lift the bikes back out into the bright light, out into the yard, and the air feels fresh and cool against my skin; tired eyes water against the glow.

"It was good to meet you Lola," I say. "Thanks a lot."

She waves from the door, lifting the can to her lips. "You take care boys. Good luck. And sorry I got a bit crazy back there."

...

We ride again up into the redwood forests, and stop to swim in a river. The water is cold and crisp under the stoned Californian light, and we race up the winding climbs that hug the western coast, and the joy and thrill of burning effort in our bodies drives us on, and we dig hard into our pedals, dragging 60kg up the sun-drenched hill, until there is no thought; only the dappled shade that falls from the leaves and flashes across my vision and the sweat that begins to drip and run down my forehead, into my eyes, and my lungs fill and empty over and over; the clean sound of my breathing. I race to keep up with Mario, and as a campervan passes a man looks out the window and smiles and shouts, "I believe in you!" and the van pulls on up the hill and I drive myself into its wake with the new energy his words and smile have given. And at last we reach the top.

We look down at the grey blue sea. Beneath us, as though we too are birds gazing down from greater heights, the vast wingspan of an osprey beats the air, too easy and too slow. Its talons stretch towards the sea and, tightly held in their grip, the still and lifeless body of a fish flies through the air, high above the waves.

Further out to sea, a ship breaks the horizon. A sheet of slate grey cloud, indistinguishable from sky, hangs above it, bends around the curvature of the Earth. Beyond that, now in August, Arctic Terns will be making the journey south. From their breeding grounds in the Arctic they migrate as they migrate each year; flying and gliding over the vast stretch of ocean to Antarctica. The birds fly further than any other species on Earth, from summer in the north to summer in the south each year, so that they not only cover a greater distance than any other animal, but see more sunlight too.

I too have tried to follow the sun around the planet. A journey of four summers. Of long sunlit days. From the northern hemisphere to the southern. Back again, and again.

Though I have not moved as freely as a tern. Though I am clumsy and move heavy, this journey may be the closest I get. To the great, free migrations of the Arctic Tern. The closest I get to terning.

...

To the north of San Francisco, we follow the road around a headland. San Quentin prison sits, across the water, and we follow the road out east, and look out across the bay, before we realise we are lost.

A bike flies past us, and I stare at its hollow frame, strands of carbon fibre forming a cylindrical web. I glance up as Mario chases after the pale man with a short white beard and asks him for directions. I struggle to keep up, and watch them talk for a while, ahead of me.

"Well," I hear Mario say, the breeze carrying his words. "It was nice to meet you Robin Williams."

As the road turns onto a long straight descent, we watch Robin Williams disappear into the distance. Or rather I watch the man whose pale face I had not linked to any film, whose bicycle I had stared at as he passed.

By the time we reach the other side of the Golden Gate Bridge the sky is black and the mist has risen. It clings to the bridge's towers as if it were trying to pull the structure down, dragging it towards the sea.

Our legs fail to carry us up the steep, straight, bursting hills of San Francisco, and we take run ups, sprinting into them until at last we give up and push our bikes the remaining few metres. We ride through the lamp-lit streets - the yellow haze picking out the elegant white lines of masonry and bay windows – until we find ourselves on Haight Street.

"I don't know what we're gonna do," Mario says.

"No-one's got back to you?" I ask. We were hoping to stay with his friends.

He shakes his head. "I'm just gonna go to this liquor store. Watch the bikes."

I stand on the street. The rain falls in a constant drizzle against the colourful shop windows, the tie-dye t-shirts and psychedelic artwork, adverts for pipes, vaporizers and bongs. Mario comes out with two cans of Four-Loko, hands me one, and we look up at the sky wondering what to do.

"We could just ride around the city all night," he says.

"We could," I say. "It'd be great until about 3am and then it would suck, but we could."

We eat peanut butter and bread, and drink from the ice-cold cans, our fingers frozen, and our eyes already fighting against the tiredness of a long day.

We're about to give up, and head out of the city when Zach, Mario's friend, gives him a call. "Awesome, that's sweet. Thanks so much, man. We'll see you in a bit."

We ride, Four-Loko fuelled, through the misty streets, up and down the hills towards Daly City and we arrive at Zach's house just after midnight. His parents are sleeping upstairs and we jump in showers and clean and try to sober up, as we sit talking into the night.

...

Zach and his uncle Edwin ride out of San Francisco with us and we say goodbye and thank you at Pacifica beach. Route 1 takes us down the coast, the Pacific on our right, and we ride across the fertile plains, north of Monterey. The sweet, sugary scent of strawberries fills the air, and Spanish radio blares from pick-up trucks. In the mornings the fields fill with Mexican workers. Whole armies move slowly along the rows of plants, across the vast fields, hands moving quick, in perfect darting motions, and backs bent double to pick the ripened fruit.

In Monterey seals flop in and out of the water on Fisherman's Wharf and waitresses wander round with tiny paper cups offering free samples of clam chowder. We walk the streets quietly and I stop on Cannery Row to look at a statue of John Steinbeck. Though there's no sign of Mack and the boys.

We climb out of Monterey, over the hill and down towards Carmel. Mansions face the ocean, great glass walls reflecting the falling sun, and antique shops and designer boutiques line the cobblestoned streets. Ferraris, Porches, Lamborghinis, Aston Martins and Jaguars fill the small town. It feels like we've taken the wrong road, some private driveway into a world to which we don't belong.

Again, I feel like I am gazing through a thick pane of glass at the world. I haven't felt this sensation for almost a year. There too the road was made of cobblestones. Each one laid by hand, some decades before, and there still, pronouncing the hard labour of days gone by. But just as in China I had watched the old men walk under heavy loads and the goats chiming and the women beating the cows without envy, nor do I here wish to be on the other side of the pane.

"There's no way we're going to find anywhere here," I say to Mario. "This place is crazy."

We ride out of Carmel, find a bridge on the outskirts of town and set up our tents, underneath the concrete arches. The supports are covered in graffiti and as the traffic roars overhead the whole structure shakes and vibrates with noise. Empty spray cans lie on the floor and seem to promise visitors.

"Shall we drink that Jameson's?" asks Mario as the shadows draw long under the bridge.

We take swigs from the bottle; the liquid sends magic shivers around my body, and fears of nocturnal visitors gently ebb away.

"It was a good idea to spend a day's budget on this. If anyone does come to kill us, at least we won't hear them."

...

South then, down to Big Sur. The land falls away under the bridges and my whole body tingles at the vast bare drop, as I imagine falling, down towards the sea, the sand, the rocks, below. Why do we always imagine jumping? When we stand on some great height, and beneath us only an empty expanse of air, why do we imagine ourselves tumbling through it? Why now, do I test the spring in my feet, rise up silently, unseen against the century old wall, and hang over it to watch my falling body crash upon the rocks? I am testing my own free-will, perhaps. I could jump, I have the choice, and I wonder if this is the most human quality of life, that we can choose to end it. Still the shivers run up and down my legs and I know that I could never really do it, that my feet will never fully leave the floor. Just as now I could not turn around and follow the road back north, washed up and down this coast like a piece of driftwood stuck in a wave. I am impelled south. I have the choice, but it would be as easy for me to turn around as to jump off this bridge.

Mario comes screaming joyfully down the hill and we ride on down the Big Sur, the great blue sky above and people looking happy, and gazing out at the sea. As we travel further south it is impossible to imagine that anything bad could happen.

...

Morro Bay, Pismo Beach, Santa Maria. As we leave Mario's friends' place in Goleta, barely slept, it feels like our ride together is coming to an end.

We pass the mansions of Malibu and ride along the sand to Venice Beach. People dance to hip-hop and skate. Tattoo shops and medicinal marijuana stalls sit by burrito stands, bars and restaurants, and we sit down on the grass to watch the crowds and eat.

"I can't believe it's almost over!" says Mario. "I could do this forever. I'd just keep going on and on and on and never stop."

"It's cool hey."

"I've learnt so much, man. I don't even know how to put in into words. It's like, you never need to be bored with life. Ever since I left, the minute I felt things getting ordinary or boring, I'd see something amazing, or meet someone really cool. And people have been amazing. They've made it."

...

It is strange to watch Mario come home, to take keys from his pocket for the first time in three months and unlock the front door as though he were returning from a long day at work. The house is empty and we sit on the sofas in silence.

"Are you alright?" I ask him.

"Yeah," he says smiling. "I'm fine. It's funny you know; it's exactly the same as when I left it, but it seems so unfamiliar."

"I can imagine it's strange."

...

After four days, we say goodbye.

"Thanks," we say. "For everything."

"It's been..." but neither of us knows how to finish the sentence.

"Come to Europe," I say. "Let me know."

We hug and say goodbye and we know that we have shared something that will stay with us forever. An experience that is now part of us. Mario will always be the west coast of the States, for me. My time here, in this place, inseparable from my time with him. A kind and patient person - open and interested in life, excited by life. And for a month the journey has been joyful and fun. There has been no fear and no struggle. And I say goodbye to a friend. A real and wonderful friend.

...

My bike rounds the bend, I glance back, and that's it. I'm on my own. Just like that. My whole experience of the US coast has been an easy, fearless time, but now, alone again, I feel afraid. I cannot put all the many warnings out of my mind. *You're crazy to go there. Really, Sam. 10,000 people dead already – you don't need to go to Mexico right now.*

As much as I try to put the events into perspective, I feel as I ride out of San Diego to the Mexican border more frightened than I ever have before. *They're killing people for fun down there at the moment.* Down there, which when I heard those words seemed far away, is here. I am pushing my bike through the turning metal gates. And handing over my passport. It is the busiest border crossing in the world, and yet there is no queue of traffic waiting to enter Mexico. There are no tourists making the once common passage from San Diego to Tijuana. Though one adventure has only just ended, I feel, as though standing blindfolded over a precipice, the thrill of the next beginning.

Clockwise from top-left: Mario under the redwoods – California Poppy – San Diego – Camping on the Pacific coast, Oregon – A visit from Mario's mum, sister and friend

Clockwise from top-left: Garibaldi days – Sloppy Joes, Slappy Jacks – With Nate in Santa Barbara - Camping under a bridge – Monterrey – An ogre under a bridge, Seattle

Mexico

23rd August – 25th November, 2010

It is like being awoken from a dream to be hurled into life. Some lovely film is removed from my eyes, like an unwanted cataracts' operation. Now all the dirt, each speck of ingrained filth, is clear.

I stare ahead at a Mexican road, following a white line that sometimes falls away in whole chunks of tarmac. To the right of the line and sometimes in its place there is a dirt ditch two foot deep. To the left, two lanes of constant traffic, the blurred uneven road, and the hot noise of engines. In the ditch men pick up plastic bottles and cans and carry them in plastic bags or buckets. And everything is the same colour - their skin, their clothes, the bottles and bags - the red-brown colour of life scraped from a ditch.

I stick to the white line, darting into the lanes of traffic when it falls away. There is enough room, just, for two cars on this road. Each one passes, only inches away, and I stick to the white line, impossibly awake, as the road begins to climb.

I follow the border's fence and San Diego, to the north, lies still, like a toy, or like the fleeting recollection of a dream; a picture that flashes through the consciousness of morning, unwished for, without context or cause, just a strange and vivid image from another made-up world.

My only thought is to leave. To get through the town. Three months of warnings, of being told not to come here, and the still sick feeling of a hangover and the taste of it on my lips send my heart quivering, and my eyes dart around in panic. Tijuana is old and dusty; broken signs and neon lights make it seem like a tacky seaside town in winter. But the heat starts to swell in the ground and there is something livid I am sure; some despicable thing I must escape. I follow the sign for Ensenada through a half-deserted street. A man shouts something at me from under a neon sign; the open door behind him, murky and promising.

I do not stop to put my feet on the ground as I climb. My body trembles in the heat and the dull black feeling of fainting rises in my head, as the city falls away beneath me, its shape squashed up against the fence like a ball of dough pelted in anger against a wall.

The ground tumbles away to the right, as I try to cling to a shoulder which isn't there. The traffic brushes by, wild and fast, and a slow headache comes over me like a black curtain. Still, I cannot stop. Even to reach down for my water bottle seems impossible. I stare straight ahead, scared to wobble into the road, to lose my balance in the heat and be crushed by an oncoming truck. A stupid way to end. A ridiculous, likely death; the likeliest. A common, nonsensical death. Boring and gruesome.

At the top of the hill I find a place to pull off the road and drain a bottle of water. I am still, I realise, glancing around in fear. What do I expect? That here, just two miles across the border, I will be killed, or kidnapped or caught in crossfire in the middle of the day? The truth is yes. I look away from the oncoming traffic, avoiding enquiring glances.

A car passes, screeching fast and so close that I almost come unbalanced in its wake, its rusty red body flying into the distance and over the hill. Five minutes later, the moan of sirens, and two ambulances pass. Fifteen minutes down the road, I reach the wreckage. A single police car is parked in front of two empty crumpled cars. Its lights flash in silence.

I pass slowly, under the heat, following the line of traffic onto the gravel verge, avoiding the metal, strewn across the tarmac. The state of the cars makes it clear people have died. There is no space, in either, for a human form to sit, to survive, uncrushed. It is the same car that had passed me, its rust red frame now contorted in a murderous grin, but the same. Or the same components, now not the same, but twisted, and smashed to pieces, irreversibly. Perhaps it could again be made to return to the same form. The metal frame bent back into straight lines, each smashed window painstakingly joined together, until it became some resemblance of its former self, if broken and useless forever. But the time cannot be turned back, rewound these last twenty minutes, however forcibly, everything that has happened has happened, and now it is too late. Fifteen minutes ago, it could have been changed, but now it cannot. Now it is forever, and I feel like I have watched someone race to their death, in the last five minutes of life. And the feeling is sick. A ridiculous likely death, the likeliest. A common, nonsensical death. Boring and gruesome.

...

In the dying heat of the day, waves lap against Rosarito's dirty shore, dragging out scum, and plastic, and depositing it again on the sand. Children play by the sea, and I ask around for a hotel. It is expensive. Or more expensive than I had imagined. Much more than a day's budget. But it is not the time to bargain; my tired body and head still spin with heat, and the room is cold and dark. Besides, I struggle to string the words 'habitación' and '¿cuánto cuesta?' together – it is hardly haggling vocabulary.

I walk to the nearest taco stand for Quesadillas. Food has become normal size again; no more huge American burritos that fill you up for $4 and I sit in the shade, pleased to have made it through the first day.

...

Baja California is bright and shining. My eyes squint against the sun and I ride into Ensenada. The cool ocean breeze soothes the early afternoon and I give myself a break. It is the last big town, before La Paz in the south. Half a day off won't hurt.

"Hey," a tall American calls down to me from a balcony. It is the cheapest hotel in my guidebook, but seems to have doubled in price in the few months since it was published. "You want a shot of tequila?"

"Sure, I'll come up in a minute."

I roll my bike into the room, lock the door and walk up the stairs. The sunlight is hot against the red dusty tiles.

"Where you riding, man? You want a shot of tequila?"

I don't know which question to answer first. "I'll have a little," I say.

"My name's William," says the man, and goes in for a glass. "This is Sergio," and a younger man comes out of the room, smiles and shakes my hand. Sparkling and golden the spirit cries out not to be gulped and downed, but we knock the glasses back. Sick inducing. Even here, on its native shores the drink bites back, and I realise I've always hated tequila.

"So, where you heading?"

I tell them I'm cycling to Argentina, that I'll take a boat from La Paz over to Mazatlán. And then, I don't know. The coast. The mountains. I haven't decided.

"I've been drinking since morning," William says, explaining why the bottle is empty now, and it's time to go for a wander. "I'm a liberal," he says to me for the third or fourth time since we met, and walks too straight and controlled out of the hotel and into the still bright day. "I've been coming down here for years," he says. "But I'd love to do what you're doing. I've driven it a couple of times, down to Los Cabos. You know from here to

La Paz there's nothing. Like, this is it, man. The end of civilization! You've gotta make the most of it. I'll show you around."

We leave the hotel, and wonder half-drunk around the once clean and touristy streets; the quiet remnants of the tourist trade, not yet fallen into disrepair, but dead, as in winter. In the port, a few white yachts glisten under the sun, but mostly the place is empty and quiet.

"See them hills up there, where those big houses are?" asks William, and I look up. "That's where the drug lords live."

I imagine the stacks of cash, security guards and flashy cars, but the houses seem fairly normal, a far cry from those Malibu mansions, and the cobbled streets of Carmel to the north. If there's money here, it seems well hidden.

I drink in the new words on signs. *Farmacia, Taller, Pescadería.* I mouth them silently to myself. When I'm on my own I mumble the words, testing the sounds and pronouncing things badly. We find a restaurant, where the waiter knows William by name, and order beer and fish tacos. I squeeze lemon onto the battered fish, and spoon green chilli salsas, and salad and smooth guacamole, eating quickly before the bread becomes soggy.

It is growing dark when we reach the strip club and we walk through the garish foyer, into the bar, cavernous and empty and blackened against the dying day outside. Here too William is on first name terms with the staff. Disco lights flash and a girl swings around a pole for almost no-one. We take some stools at the end of a long bar and order three beers that are half the size and twice as expensive as the ones outside. The girl who was dancing around the pole when we came in sees us. Or sees William. And comes running over, in her underwear.

"Willy!" she shouts, and hugs him, kisses him on the cheek. "Are you going to buy me a drink?" Her accent is American, and as she takes her drink, promising to return, Willy explains that she was born in the US, and grew up in California until her family were deported.

"She can't go back?" I ask.

"She probably *could*," he says. "If she really wanted to. Her brother's still there. But she's fucking crazy. You've gotta be at least a little bit crazy to be a whore."

"Whore?"

"Stripper, whore. Not much difference here," and his eyes glance up to two or three black walled rooms hovering above the stage. "This place used to be full of Americans."

"It's early, I guess."

"Wouldn't matter," he says. "Could be the middle of the morning and sunny outside and this place would be full."

I look across the room. No-one but a couple of Americans, sitting hunched over beers at the end of the long bar. The girl comes back, walking in practiced strides and pulls William off the chair. "Willy, I've missed you," she says, and I could swear I hear the sincerity in her voice. If it's a trick I am as duped as anyone could be. "Where've you been?"

She pulls him off the bar stool and starts dancing, her hands all over him. I look down into my beer, the last expensive swills too warm, and I look around, half-drunk, half-lost, at a girl who walks towards me. I'm standing now, and she puts her hand on my shoulder, runs it down my chest and stomach until it comes to rest over my shorts. I'm wearing shorts, I suddenly realise, or rather they suddenly make me feel stupid.

"Do you want to go upstairs?" she asks, her hand still there. There is apparently no reaction, a slight recoil perhaps. A shrinking. She takes my nervous awkwardness for something else.

"Are you gay?" she asks.

"I haven't got any money," I lie and she withdraws her hand. The smile vanishes from her face, and she turns and walks away.

It is night when we leave, though not as cold as night. The alcohol has contrived to make me forget about the morning and I sense the start of adventure. I turn to Sergio and William, not staggering, but walking slow. "Let's find somewhere cheaper," I say. "Maybe without sex."

"There's sex everywhere," says William.

"Okay, well. Just somewhere cheaper."

But time is against the pair who, drunk since morning, seem to sense the end. We stumble now back to the hotel with most of a bottle of tequila and there the night dies.

I wake with the morning light.

…

It is not yet nine, but already the heat has swelled and the tarmac softens. I fill four water bags, and take the road, now quiet and narrow, south out of Ensenada.

Lines of grapevines, chocked by sand and dust, cling to guiding sticks and twine, as though in gentle agony, blistering under the sky. Above the clouds, white and grey, swell and burn away.

I stop at a roadside café and ask for water. My supply is not yet low, but it is a constant niggling fear that I'll run out. I have emptied one of the 4 litre bags already this morning, and I am unsure where the next town will be, or if it will be a town at all. Two villages marked on my map have come and gone, little more than the empty shell of a building, dust and broken glass. Not a well or working tap in sight.

It is noon now, and a group of American surfers sit eating at the table.

"You're riding Baja in August?" one of them calls over to me.

"Uh uh."

"Man, that is fucking crazy," says another one. "You didn't want to wait or something? I mean, it's fucking hot here, man."

"It's not so bad," I say. "Better than rain. Maybe September would have been a better idea, though."

"Yeah, well – I wouldn't do it. October maybe, November. You go out there now, you're gonna fry."

I half-laugh. And say goodbye, duck out of the shaded entrance, walk slow towards my bike. New noon heat sinks into my arms.

Now across the wide, dry valley floor the wind sweeps sand into the air; the earth kicks up into the sky, and a million particles of burning dust ride out, towards the sea. The sun burns a terrible, white hole into the sky, and everything is hot. The wind blows from the east, and it is as if an oven door were being constantly opened in front of me, puffing and blowing its boiling breath at 60 kilometres per hour, into an already suffocating room.

As I climb, I watch the road bobbing up and down through tears; black, wet eyelashes across my watery sight, my eyelids closed, against the sun's glare, and against the sting of sweat, and dripping sunblock. I try to wipe the sweat away, but my wet hand slips. Only the blinding, glistening white of the road and the blurry outline of a shapeless blue sky, swim beneath me, as I gaze at them through a shallow, salty sea.

When the occasional shadow of a cliff falls across the road I collapse into it. For minutes I feel too tired even to reach for water and I lie in the shade, happy simply that the sun is no longer beating down. In deep breaths, I fill my lungs with the dry air, the taste of salt on my tongue. When my breathing quietens and my heart no longer pounds in my chest, I lift the bottle of water and drink all of it. The liquid is hot, like drinking tea.

If there were anywhere to stop and put up a tent along the 9km climb, I would. But cliffs on both sides, and the open barren landscape, make camping impractical at best. Hours later, I reach a small café in a dusty village, exhausted. My arms and hands are covered in white, hard blotches from the sun and the burning wind. I have consumed just over ten litres of water in one day, more than I ever have before. Terrible, terrible Baja. The surfers were right. The day is hot and the night is hot, and everything is horribly dry. I am so sick from heat and hard work that, for the first time in a long time, what I am trying to do seems impossible.

The man working at the café, points to the TV, and points at me.

"*Hoy*," he says, speaking in simple words to make himself understood. "*Cuarenta y siete. Cuarenta y siete grados!*" And he stretches all ten fingers out four times, and then holds up seven, looking at me as if I were an idiot. I probably am, but I'm not sure if he thinks that because I'm struggling to count to 47 with him, or because he saw me ride into the village on a bike in August.

I look down at the white blotches, hard and beginning to itch now in the darkened shade of the café. Tomorrow, I decide, I will leave before dawn.

...

Before I think about what I am doing, the village of San Quintin is behind me. I glance down. The water bags tied around my panniers flap in the breeze and slap down again with a half empty sound. In the bottle fixed to my frame, half a litre of water swills around; golden in the dying sun, and dirty looking, through the sand encrusted plastic. It is now that I should turn back. To fill up on water. Or to look for somewhere to stay. But I stare down at the water bottle, the motion of each leg, up and down, and I glance at the road ahead, hypnotized by movement. 500 metres pass. Then a kilometre. Then two. And I know I will not turn around.

The landscape becomes flat and open. Panic rises in me, at the thought of where I will sleep, but still my legs turn in constant easy movement as if they were stuck in motion.

I turn away from the road, and my bike trundles slowly down a dirt track until the sound of heavy machinery stops me in my tracks. It is a dump. Piles of rubbish lie dried out, under dust. Plastic bags snap against the light breeze and I wheel my bike, quickly out of sight, behind one of the mountains of rubbish. From here I see a truck clawing at the rubbish and lifting it into the air, fine dust blowing from the scoop.

On the other side of the dump there is a patch of wiry vegetation, that too covered in dust, and I see its closely tangled branches; potential shelter for sleep. I pull my bike around the piles, following the marks left by heavy tyres and leaving my own fine lines in the powdery earth. I look up to check I'm not seen.

Slowly I round the final pile, and drag my bike into the bushes. Their wiry thorns scratch blood into my skin, and the sting sends shivers around my burnt arms. I watch the trucks working through thick undergrowth, for some reason wary and silent. I am careful even of my breathing as I roll out the tent and fit the poles together, irrationally scared that a click too loud or a breath too deep would sound over the engines and give my hiding place away. As the night prohibits further labour, I hear the work grind to a halt. A door slams. And then another. Shouting voices grow louder at first, but then fall silent. Another pair of door slams. An engine starts. And I listen to it fade away, back down the track and towards the road to San Quintin.

I lock the bike's wheel to its frame. And sit inside the dimly glowing walls that I haven't seen since I was in the States with Mario. My sleeping bag still holds the warmth of the sun, and I lie out my scratched burnt legs on top of its smooth surface and half-sleep 'til dawn.

...

In the morning a dim light permeates the tent. Not the yellow shafts of sunlight I had expected, and I rouse myself expecting to find the quiet end of night. I unzip the tent door to see that it is already light outside. The wiry branches that surround me are all coated in a fine film of dust and already I hear that work is continuing. There is no sky though. Instead a cold grey mist licks the branches and breathes into the tent. There is a chill coming in from the sea and damp blanket glooming over everything, moisture in the air. I move now, unafraid to be heard, and gather my things quickly. I ride out towards the road to catch the wonderful cold grey day. Something has heard me, I think. Some saving force has heard my thoughts, and has sent this beautiful cold day. I ride still further south, the road now kind.

It does not last long. Soon the sun blazes through the half transparent shroud and, almost immediately it seems, the day is white and blue again. Baja rolls in deep yellow hills and I ride through the day. Legs turn food to miles and sweat dries to scaly patterns on my skin. It does not matter how much water I drink through the day, I hardly piss. I am pissing through my pores, I think. Disgusting. But there is no-one around to see or smell and the hot breeze lifts the moisture away, greedily into the sky. I cross rivers that have not run for years; their sandy banks lifeless and bereft of the marks of water, the signs of flowing currents washed away by wind. If it were not for the signs and the bridges, I would take the deadened beds to be rudimentary tracks, curving their way up into the hills, in rivulets and furrows driven dry into the ground.

My map, I am beginning to believe, has been drawn by cartographers with ambitions to kill cyclists. It is worse than useless. Campgrounds are scattered arbitrarily along the route, but there are none to be found. Villages that promise water, appear first as promising clusters of buildings only to crumble into disrepair, and uselessness. It is not a map, I decide, but a history of places people have decided to leave. It cannot be trusted; would be dangerous to trust.

I am surprised then, when the third promised village of the day turns out to be real. And not only that, but music plays in the dark and gloomy shade of a café. It is in fact the only building in what has been denoted as a village, but it promises food and water. I stagger off the bike and lean it next to a rusty barrel; the door creaks open, heavy on its metal hinges.

The sudden drop in temperature is so welcoming that it takes a few moments to realise that inside it is stifling too. A fan in the corner beats at the hot air, wafting it around the room. A television hums brightly in the corner blurting out words to no-one in particular. A couple of men turn in their chairs, away from cold bottles of beer. "*Buenas tardes!*" they call over to me, and the rest of what they say is lost in the din of the television; though I wouldn't understand it anyway. I am back to smiling over-zealously at people, and nodding and half-laughing at who knows what when someone else does.

I take a seat, ask for a Coca-Cola, and try to make it last as long as possible. I feel it's sugary coldness run done my throat, sip by sip. What I really want to do is down the bottle in one huge rush of joy; by savouring it I am destroying my enjoyment. Frugality is making me miserable; I feel like a grandma sitting with a measly piece of stale cake and a tiny fork in some kind of self-inflicted miserliness. I look down at my sun-blotched arms and the scratches on my dust covered legs and empty the bottle.

The men call over to me. It is incomprehensible. Something with the word *dónde* in it, but it sounds nothing like the phrases in my book.

"*Yo?*" I ask, doubtfully, pointing at myself, and smiling stupidly. The men nod, embroiled now in this ridiculous pantomime. I've forgotten what it's like to speak in monosyllables and gestures.

I piece the words together in my head. *Yo. Soy. De. Inglaterra.* No, the *yo* is unnecessary. "*Soy de Inglategha.*" I say, and they look at me quizzically. "*Inglateggha,*" I say more loudly, but less confidently, struggling with some sound in the back of my throat which I'm sure I shouldn't be making. "*Inglategha?*" I ask, it has become a question now. The men look sorry they tried.

"*Yo,*" the man says, pointing at himself. "*Yo. Mexico. Me-hi-kho. Aquí.*" he says, pointing to the ground. "*Y tu? Dónde?*" He has kindly given up on verbs and other confusing words.

I think again, back to the basic introductory phrases. "*Soy Inglés,*" I say, and at last they understand.

"Aah," they say. "*Inglés. Inglaterrrra! Rrrrrr! Rrrrr!*" they say, the tips of their tongues vibrating against their teeth. "*rrrrrrrrrrrrrr!*"

Again, the man asks me something with the word *dónde* in it; this time he spins round his arms like pedals, and points at the helmet resting on the chair.

"*Voy a Argentina,*" I say, and the men look at each other perplexed.

"*En bici?*" he asks. "*En serio?*"

"*En serio,*" I say, mimicking the words with uncertainty. "*A Argentina. En bici. En serio.*"

The men seem unsure. Don't I know that I'm halfway down a peninsular, leading only to the sea? I take out a world map, determined to show that I'm not a complete idiot, or perhaps prove beyond doubt that I am. I show them the line I have drawn across Europe, Asia and Australia; from Alaska and down to the border at Tijuana. I haven't drawn anything for the last few days. Trying to denote progress on a world map is demoralizing.

The man places his finger on the tip of the Baja peninsula. "And from here?" he says. Or words to that effect. "From here to the mainland, how?"

"*Desde allí,*" I say. "*En, er, en borca.*" I look up to see puzzlement drawn across the men's faces. They are talking to a fool. By boat, I think. From here by boat. "*En barco,*" I say, trying to recover. "*Desde allí, en barco. A Mazatlán.*"

Through a series of awkward exchanges, they invite me to camp in the yard behind the café. They are friendly and bring me water, point to the best place to pitch a tent, and watch curiously as I hammer the pegs into the hard ground with a rock. They give up on the excruciatingly slow and limited form of communication, and leave me to rest. It is the only building for 30 miles, and I sit in the yard as the sun falls. Though the flower beds are full of cacti, it is as pretty as a garden, the deep reds of impossible flowers are in bloom and a bench sits under a tree.

Across the road, soldiers stand by a truck, guns slung over shoulders. They stand smoking cigarettes and talking loudly. A makeshift checkpoint and their presence is the only thing to suggest that Mexico is still in the middle of a drugs war. For now, this quiet road and the shaded yard could be the only things that exist. I lie down, and sleep almost immediately.

...

I do not have to look to see whether the road is clear. In Baja California I hear the motors long before they pass. Still, I glance back to check that there is no-one around, no car in the distance, or silent passer-by. This has always been the rule; camp out of sight of the road, don't let anybody see you dart into the forest, or under the bridge, or into the desert. My mind wavers on the brink of paranoia when the time comes to sleep. Every passing car may be following me; tracking my every move. I no longer worry about an angry Dutch man, but other outlandish thoughts take root and flourish inside my mind. The tales of kidnappings have not left me unaffected, but even the everyday, every-night, worries of grim opportunity lie underscoring my feelings. I no longer have company; I guess that is the problem. With Mario, every stealth camp was a carefree adventure, without any other consequence than a potential telling off. I pull my bike from the road.

The desert looks like something that a child has drawn. Alien. I watch the hard ground for scorpions and weave my bike around the spikes and thorns of cacti. I know that some of the spines that appear livid and dangerous are in fact all show, almost soft when I brush past them. Others that appear inane are sharper than needles, puncturing skin and tyres at only the slightest touch. I know that some of the plants are okay, and that others are bad, but I have not learned which ones so I do my best to avoid them all as I look for a place to camp. The sudden psssting sound of air coming from the back tyre tells me I have failed.

I sit down carefully. The area is flat enough for a tent. Plants, three feet high, sit like spiny bottles all around. Others, their flowers deep red balls of fluff lie scattered across the valley. And other cacti stand so high that I wouldn't believe they were real. I set up the tent quickly, roll the sleeping bag out. Remove the wheel from the bike, and the perpetrating thorns from the inner tube. I patch the rubber, sanding down a rough little square and holding down the patch to ensure that it sticks. I pump the tire quickly; the noisy air surging in, and making a satisfying breathy sound which finishes with a high pitched 'p' sound, and I pump until the tyre is hard to the touch, and beads of sweat drip from my forehead.

I stop. Something is wrong. Some unnerving presence around me causes me to freeze. I look around and see nothing. Only that the hill is now not brown and yellow, but golden. And the cacti bend into strange shapes in the shadows, bristly and warped and then as though they are melting. It takes a while to realise that what has unnerved me is silence.

I do not think I ever knew silence before coming to the desert. I have to admit that I can't remember the silence in the Gobi being so complete; maybe the swelling skies and thunder and wind did not permit it. Strange that now I can barely go back there. How my memory works only in flashes and false starts; impossible to time travel even in my head, to transport myself to some even recent time and walk through it as I had, with the same weight of time. Why can I only flit through it, catching bright pictures, and sounds, like flicking through a photo book, or stuck in a poorly edited montage? Perhaps there had been silence; perhaps it went unnoticed there. Certainly though, there has been nothing like it since.

The silence is full and saturating. The sound of nothing moving. No leaves rustling. No wind. No cars, or voices, or radios, not the distant constant drone of far off noise, or the constant humming activity of creatures and tiny beasts. Not even the sound of breathing. As I write, the pen's scratch is the loudest noise. Me. I am the loudest thing here. Occasionally a bird calls, though it silences itself immediately, as though the move to sing was too brash, too bold. As though it realises it has broken something very delicate, and wonderful.

It is true that every hour or so a distant engine ruptures the quiet and reminds me of the world, but there are intervals of very many minutes when there is nothing. When my ears ring, and the world is full of something far beyond quiet. When every movement I make and every breath I take is amplified and huge. And across the golden valley full of strange silhouettes, it seems possible to hear grains of sand dropping to the floor, the scuttle of tiny legs across the ground, the sliding body of a snake, or the beating of insects' wings. I open the small plastic bottle I filled with Tequila in Ensenada and take a swig. It is still hot from the day's sun, and the taste sends shivers through my body. I look across the valley. It may be the most beautiful place in which I've ever camped.

...

Again, my wheels roll south. A condor flies overhead. And so high that its shadow is vast and fuzzy as it sweeps across the road, a wingspan of two lanes. It circles me once. Twice. And again, the predatory shadow is so huge that I am mouse or marmot, and I look up with the expectant terror of prey. But the sun is playing tricks. The circles are being made over something else, and I continue riding south; a victim only of scale.

...

I look at my map in anger. My throat is still painful and hoarse from shouting and cursing. I will not make the 110 miles to Guerrero Negro today. It may have been possible, but a snapped chain and a problem with the front shifter jamming against the chain rings, mean that now it is too far. The chain I fixed in minutes, though the latter problems have taken the best part of two hours to resolve, and still the bike clunks and moans painfully. I curse myself for being inept at these things after so long on the road.

It is not until I am sitting with the sea beneath me to the south that my annoyance and frustration is forgotten. I stare over miles of desert and look down towards the road. I have spent an hour or more riding and pushing my bike up this huge hill, skidding and stumbling in the red brown earth and the loose stones. And though the road has refused to disappear, the world again is empty.

I am in shock still at Baja. I did not expect this stunning, magical beauty. This freedom. I sit a while outside my tent, drinking tequila, watching the stars and waiting for the moon to rise. I cannot remember a sky like it. Clear, warm, sparkling night. The rock I am sitting on holds all the heat of the day, and will cling to it till morning. I take a tiny pink flower from a thorny branch and squeeze it without thinking. It excretes a perfect white cream, smells of scented soap.

...

The track leads down to the beach; the gentle rolling bump of gravel and stones gives way to sand and I push my bike to a shelter, and collapse into the shade of its palm roof.

It is still so hot under the palms that my whole body leaks over itself. Red, blotched white skin, still burning. But now under the shade I am comfortable. More comfortable. The water still swills warm in my plastic bottles. Yes, like tea. Like warm tasteless tea. Or maybe the taste of dirt. But this beach, even under the desert heat, is the kindest place I have been for days. Beneath my feet, the sand warms but does not burn. This is where I will sleep.

A man comes over. A brown pot belly and an open, friendly face. "*Dormir?*" he says. "*Quieres dormir?*"

"*Sí,*" I want to say. "*quiero dormir, hasta que la tierra me trague, y no me sienta más, y todo este gran dolor al que me enfrento se desaparezca, y la profunda añoranza, que inunda mi cuerpo, se derrita como mantequilla en la arena.*" But I do not have the words, so I just say yes, I would like to sleep.

"*Veinte pesos*" he says. And I take it from this that he has built the shelter, and that he will keep me safe.

Night falls. The sky grows black like resin and the cover of cloud muffles even the glinting of the sea. In the tent the air is still close, and the surfaces of my skin clam together; the clinging dirt and sweat of my thighs rub and the sand scratches warm and sticky on my arms until the heat and the closeness become suffocating. I pull myself outside where the air is cooler, but not cool enough.

I shuffle now, blindly across the sand, towards the sound of the sea. The crashing of tiny waves, if I could see, would be tussled and white under the night. But there is no light for them to reflect, and the whites of the waves are nothing. Are black, if I am to put a colour on it.

Now the sand is damp, and cool. And soon tiny waves roll over my toes and I sink in, submerge myself. And then there is magic. The water ignites. In tiny phosphorescent shimmers beneath the surface I bring the sea to life. My limbs cause the tiny organisms to erupt in great fireworks all around me, and I see in the darkness that the sea is alive, and that everything is alive, and always was. Even when I thought it invisible and dead.

I play with the sea now. And what at first had startled me becomes a toy, a beautiful, shimmering, stingless toy, and for the first time I am cool, and free.

As I look up to the sky, I feel the first warm raindrops of the night. And those too send the phosphorescent lights shimmering across the bay: each tiny droplet ignites a rippling physical reaction and the whole sea dances with light. Soon the rain falls heavy and the sky crashes into bright thunder and the world is seen again in second bursts, in sheet lightning. I wade out of the sea towards the tent, visible now in the dark, and frightening shadows fall across the beach. I sleep, face down and wet; sand caked upon my feet, and spattered up my legs.

...

In the morning, pelicans dive across the bay; their huge bills spill over with fish, squirming for a moment then dead, or still as dead. They group together and come to rest, perched on the fishing boats, though it is a firmer stance than a perch; rooted like soldiers looking over the sea. If I had more food and nowhere to go, I could stay here for a long time.

I trundle back along the track, the sun already burning and the ground a recently ignited filament, and I remember coming the other way; the first welcome glimpse of Playa Santispac, through eyes stinging with sweat and the relief that always comes with the end of a tiring day. Now I do not feel the relief. Nor, as I glance back towards the beach, do I feel the sting of yesterday's sweat in my eyes, nor yesterday's tiredness in my legs. And for a moment it feels that I am looking at another person. Perhaps, I think, that's all memory really is. And if I find it so hard to feel what I felt only yesterday, what of my memories of a year ago? Are we so different now, so changed from what we were before, that when we remember past events it is not ourselves which we inhabit, but our current, fleeting self? We are not one person I think, looking out across the sea, the sky now calm and clear, drained of all its thunder. We are not one person, but each of us, many hundreds of thousands, renewed and altered, rejuvenated, disfigured or thrashed around with each passing event. And what of those constants, that we call character? Well, perhaps I am losing those. Without any surrounding constancy to hold me to myself, perhaps I am tumbling through my many selves all at once. But then I look at the sea and I feel the tingling light all around me; those tiny bacteria that my movement turned to light, and the whole deep beauty of which, as yet, I have spoken to no one, and I feel that it is in me. That it will always be in me. That with every passing moment, I am not changing, but simply becoming fuller. I do not, for now, worry that this whole trip might fill me more quickly. I do not consider even the possibility of a finite capacity to hold these things within me. That I could so quickly become closed to all things new. Like Tarkovsky's tree; strength and rigidity, the precursors to death.

A pelican takes flight, and I turn around, back towards the road.

...

In La Paz I meet backpackers, stay in a hostel and spend three days eating fish tacos, drinking beer and smoking cigarettes until I realise I am spending too much money, and rotting. I take the ferry across to the mainland, to Mazatlán.

The city is split into two halves. An old ramshackle town, with crumbling plazas and shady trees and a new sprawling expanse along the beach. I find somewhere cheap to stay in the old town and walk aimlessly around. I follow the beach to where multi-story hotels crowd against the shore. It is a dull place, built for people who like the sun, but want to live in Disney Land, and everywhere there is the strange dead feeling of an ugly seaside town out of season, and a sad sense that there'll never be another summer, that the tourists will stay away.

As night falls in the old town, the streets fill with music and life. Mexico is celebrating 200 years of independence, or 200 years since the *Grito de Dolores*. I sit on a bench and watch passers-by, and a man sits down next to me. His eyes water with sparkling, drunken tears; a shimmering glaze in front of deep brown eyes. If he blinks I feel sure that the tears will fall steadily down his face, and he will appear to passers-by as though silently, happily crying. But I never see him blink. He has a thick, black beard; his skin is rough beyond his years, dry and worn out by the sun. His clothes are torn, and the lines of his calloused hands are exaggerated with the ingrained dirt that clings to them. He has the look of an unhealthy man, only, when he smiles, he reveals perfect white teeth and his drunk-kind eyes sparkle as he holds out a plastic bottle of *Mezcal*.

I take the bottle, flip open the plastic lid with my thumb, and take a sip of the liquid, warmed by the tropical night. Its warmth runs down my throat and lightly burns. The man's hands move slowly toward the sky, back and forth, his palms up turned; drink more. The *Mezcal* makes my body shudder and a smile spreads wide under the man's thick black beard as I thank him and he takes the bottle back.

Later, a couple stumbles past; or perhaps it is the man who is stumbling, the woman holding him up, for when he frees himself from her grasp to stagger towards me, she stands perfectly straight and rolls her eyes. The man, in his fifties perhaps, or sixties, has pissed himself. There is something in his posture that says he is aware of this, but he stands unashamedly in front of me, one trouser leg soaked. The woman is younger, slightly, with dyed-black hair, and though her inebriation manifests itself in subtler ways, there is a sway in her walk as she comes to pull him away.

I am surprised when he speaks English and introduces himself as George, in a drunk, American accent.

"This is my wife," he says, collapsing onto the bench. "I hate my fucking wife."

The lady, whose name I don't catch makes it clear that she is not his wife and makes to leave, an almost empty bottle of vodka in her hand.

"Yes, yes, yes!" George screams. "She's my wife, and I fucking hate my wife." The lady, rolls her eyes again, walks away and shouts something that I don't understand.

When she is gone, George turns to me, half blubbering through a grin, "I love my wife," he says.

I spend the next half an hour sat next to George as he shouts obscenities at passers-by. "*Puta, pinche, pendeje!*" he screams, but no one reacts. His glazed eyes follow the path of pretty young girls, staring after them, so I feel forced to hang my head, to distance myself from this man, whose pissed-soaked trouser leg is almost touching my thigh. Then just as they turn away he sticks out his tongue and pulls a face of disgust. "*¡Qué fea es!* She's so ugly. *¡Qué fea!*"

...

The next day I cycle in the tropics for the first time since Indonesia. The heavy air and waxy green plants, crashing brown waters of streams, and the languid movements of people carrying woven baskets, remind me of Laos or Sumatera.

When I arrive in Acaponeta though, all thoughts of Asia disappear. An old church catches the last light of the sun and children run around joyously tormenting the pigeons. They clap explosions of wings into the air and run among the small pecking heads as soon as the scattered crumbs entice them. The children squeal, delighted with their newfound abilities, which allow them to control nature, and make it dance in terror.

Old men sit on benches under trees. Some hold cigarettes, and let curling waves of smoke lick the air. Others sit with arms tightly folded against vice. People sit on high stalls at taco stands, pouring salsa, and sprinkling coriander over the small round disks of tortillas, drinking *horchata* or Coca-Cola.

The last clouds turn to shades of purple, light greens and yellow in the sky. Electric lampposts glow and the parents begin their efforts to tear their children from the birds. I too, grow tired of watching, and walk away along cobbled, peaceful streets, back to a cheap hotel.

...

Now there is life along the roads. Not that solitary empty desert, where it was only me, nor the confined life of the United States; those organised roads and houses where everything lay in its place. The sky is heavy; the clouds hang low, air close. Plants rise from the soggy earth; a mess of clinging roots and the constant scurrying of life: the humming of flies and mosquitos and bees; the constant tread of beetles, ants, and termites; the flutter of butterflies and deeper in the undergrowth the slithering and scuttling of things unseen.

I stop by the side of the road, and a woman ladles ice cold *horchata* into a clear plastic bag, ties its ends around a straw, and hands it to me over a wooden table. What would life have been like here before ice? Before refrigeration? Before the road and its constant stream of trucks and cars flowing from the coast up into the mountains? The movements of the people then, more sluggish still; a slower, harder life. But, how quickly we adapt; to need what before we never had, to take for granted all that makes our lives comfortable, and to rot somehow, into the slow and easy languishment afforded.

The road climbs and my legs feel heavy. The humid air breathes moisture in until it can take no more and black clouds crack with thunder. I find shelter from the rain, under the outcropping roof of a taco stand and sit down. Three *tacos de carnitas* lie in front of me on a paper plate, the glistening fat of pork spoils into the bread and coils up in wet delicious steam. A whole bubbling cauldron of the meat simmers on the ground and I spoon a thin green chilli sauce, onions, tomato and coriander over the meat, and lift it to my mouth, trying in vain to stop the contents escaping and trickling down my hand. It is food I could eat every day until it killed me; food I could kill the pig for, the best thing I've eaten since *buffalo rendang*. I feel myself fall into simple greedy happiness as I wait for the rain to die down.

...

Under the light shadows of high and wispy clouds, neat rows of agave plants shift in tone, from deep green to turquoise and sea green hues; their turgid outstretched arms, static in the breeze. For miles around, the plants fill the gentle mountain slopes of Jalisco, as the agave for all the world's Tequila lies pristine and ordered, growing slow. The road rolls above the quiet fields, and then a field appears, torn and ripped apart.

A *jimador* holds a *coa*. The instrument, hoe like, has a handle as tall as the man who takes it in his grip. The man's white shirt, open at his chest, sticks, wet, to his back, even under the cool, high sky, as he hacks violently, time and time again, at the ripe agave. The outer leaves of the plant lie scattered around his work - torn and fractured like dismembered limbs. The man's actions appear desperate. Around him, where the hearts of other plants have been torn from the ground, craters appear, as if small shells had exploded, rupturing the soil. Again, he strikes the plant. Sweat flies. He thrusts again. And a new limb is torn away. The harvesting looks like a murder.

I cycle on, past the fields, towards Tequila.

...

I leave the town's historic centre and follow a long line of tacky stalls and ugly buildings to a dirty motel I can afford.

It is dirtier than I first thought so I go outside. I sit, in what could be described as a courtyard, but is really a neglected patch of concrete and overgrown grass, my head lost in the pages of Mishima's *Spring Snow*. I look up from the beautiful serenity of Japan to a woman and her painted red lips. Her belly is exposed, as she toys with the waist line of her hot pants, her finger slowly coiling inside and pulling the fabric down until a line of paler skin is visible. She looks at me longer than women who are not whores look. Her eyelashes slowly close in a way that says she knows men well enough not to be coy, knows that all men are the same, have the same shallow desires, and the ones that find themselves in this motel are not ruled by their heads.

She stands for a while longer before talking to me, slightly swaying it seems, her hips at eye level, forcing me to strain my neck to look up at her eyes.

"*De dónde eres?*" she asks. The conversation begins as any other might before, after about 45 seconds of banality, she realises I have exhausted all my Spanish. Whatever she is saying now, I do not understand, and faced only with my shrugging shoulders and a lost apologetic look she gives up. Perhaps there is something about the way I am, the way I recoil and shift uncomfortably, that dissuades her from explaining herself with more adamant and universal gestures. As she walks away, another girl calls to her and they laugh at something I feel sure is me.

From among the rooms opposite, a door opens and a man walks out towards the street, his head hung slightly towards the ground. A few minutes later a girl emerges and rests against the doorway looking out, a cigarette hanging from her lips. It will be a long and restless night, it seems, of unseen comings and goings, of clattering head boards against paper thin walls.

...

The next day I leave Tequila. The road winds once again through the fields of blue succulents, silently awaiting the *jimadors* and death. Here, in the mountains, the air is clean. I feel good, I realise – healthy. The world slips by, not effortlessly, but with greater ease than before. And butterflies flit, light, in the breeze. Bright white wings against light blue sky, and the deep green of passing fields.

Beneath, along the road, lizards dart and scatter, in sun-fuelled panic. Grasshoppers flick themselves from the peril of my turning wheels to the long green grass, or from peril to greater peril, further into the road. Occasionally, the green-blue-silver-black-gold-metallic shimmer of a beetle's back catches the sun, as it attempts a journey, surely doomed to fail. The bodies of grasshoppers lie; dried, or half-dried-gooey-wet, internal organs spilled. And then another huge white butterfly dips in front of my eyes, dancing as if the petals of a flower had been brought to life.

For a moment the butterfly dances at my side. Another joins it then and their bodies entwine, coiling and tumbling as if for a moment it were only them. As if they had forgotten their smallness and all the world around; they tumble through space, tightly clasped together. I leave them behind as a tail wind catches my bike and lifts me forward, across the open flat of the road, fast towards Guadalajara and into the path of a reversing truck.

I shout some wordless noise and slam my hands tight against the brakes. The truck's brakes hiss and there is a dead moment - a second, no longer than a second, where I think nothing. I realise I will hit the truck, that it is now inevitable, and I think nothing. There is a moment of empty sickness, but I could not tell you where; if in my stomach, or spreading up my throat, or perhaps it is my heart stopping. Or not stopping, but simply that the time between each heavy beat drags on, as if for a moment I am unsure whether the next one will come, and it is this that has created the sick empty feeling. But still I do not think anything, only perhaps a rushed and inarticulate version of this: I am going to hit the truck; my face will hit the truck, my feet are stuck in my pedals: what will happen to my feet?

And then I am standing. My feet on the ground, knocked out of the pedals by the force of the collision. And everything static. Beneath me the front wheel is jammed under the truck; the bike held upright, squashed against the ground. For a moment I feel nothing, only that the empty feeling is still there, but the sickness has gone. My face tingles with a strange numb sensation, and I stand over my bike, unsure of what to do.

A man looks around out of the front window, and I raise my hand. The doors of the truck open and four men get out, ask if I'm okay.

"*Sí,*" I say "*Sí, muy bien. Estoy muy bien, y usted?*" I ask the driver stupidly, as if he'd just had *his* face driven into by a truck. He smiles apologetically, but doesn't respond.

I smile, dumbly at the men as the tingling feeling turns to a dull thudding pain. I feel like I've just been punched in the face by something very big and metal, but all I can feel is an overwhelming sense of relief that I'm not dead, and a kind of shock that I managed to head butt a rusty metal truck, without acquiring any injury.

I step over the bike, still upright, its wheel stuck fast under the weight of the truck. The thought of the bike being broken doesn't even cross my mind as the men lift the back of the truck, until the bike is freed. I roll it away; the wheel straight, without even a puncture. It is only this, I realise, that broke the collision, the horizontal fall. If the truck were two centimetres higher, it would have been my head and not the wheel that felt the full force of the impact. I look down at the wheel, perhaps the only thing between me and a broken neck. But I feel okay. The wheel turns, the brakes work. I say thank you to the men and make to leave.

One of the men says something in Spanish with the word hospital in it.

"No, no." I say, shaking my head, and waving the idea away. "*Siento muy bien. No necesito.*" I say, trying in terrible Spanish to convince them that I feel fine.

"*Sí, qué necesitas,*" the man says, pointing to my chin.

"*Es poquito,*" I say. "*Nada,*" and I touch my chin to further illustrate that it is really nothing at all, but what I feel is not my chin but a strange wet and gooey mess of open cartilage and my hand comes away covered in blood.

"Okay," I say. Perhaps a hospital is not such a bad idea.

They put my bike on the back of their truck and I sit in the front with the driver who introduces himself as José. He offers me *elotes*; corn on the cob, wrapped still in their leaves and steaming hot. I say no and thank him. I do not know how to say that I have never felt less like eating in all my life. Perhaps it is the new motion of the truck, or the fact that I have slumped into a seat and suddenly find myself still, but I realise that I'm shaking and, under the heat of the Mexican sun, I feel cold.

"*Como te llamas?*"

"*Me llamo Sam. Samuel.*"

José seems pleased with my name. "Samwell!" he repeats, smiling. It is a biblical name.

"*Cristiano?*" he asks me.

I look up and see the icons hanging from the rear-view mirror. "*Sí,*" I say, in a half-hearted lie, not feeling up to discussing agnosticism, "*Cristiano.*"

It is the right answer and he turns to me smiling, "*Católico?*"

"No," I say without thinking and stare out the window at the road rolling by.

We arrive after only a couple of minutes. It was the perfect place apparently to cycle into a truck (or to be driven into by a truck, I no longer care); right on the edge of a town. I cover my chin with my hands as we enter the waiting room, José explains what happened, and they usher me into a private room. The doctor or nurse, I'm not sure which, asks me lots of questions I can't understand, and I realise that it must be hard for them to work out whether I'm showing signs of concussion, or if I just appear stupid and confused because I can hardly understand a word they are saying.

Every so often I recognise a word. *Cabeza* - head. "*Mi cabeza está bien*" *Dolor* - pain. "*No tengo dolor.*" "*Puedo ver*" I can see. "*No otro dolor*" I say, guessing then at the things they might ask me. This would have been much more difficult a month ago.

The doctor or nurse administers a local anaesthetic to my already numb chin, and holds something like alcohol under my nose, as I begin to faint and my grammatically incorrect chatter, attempting to convince them that I'm fine, comes to an abrupt halt. The black curtain that has drawn across my sight clears and I look at the room for the first time clearly; the dizzying waves and trembling gone.

Standing in the corner, a fat girl of about twenty watches as my chin is stitched back together. When I entered I had taken her for an assistant perhaps, but, as my face is being mended, it seems that her only role is to make shocked, slightly disgusted faces, occasional sounds portraying queasiness, and to give a general impression that she is finding the whole scene far too much to take. Perhaps it is simply a week of work experience that will lead her to decide that the medical profession is not the one for her.

In less than half an hour I am ready to leave. José pays for the treatment. And a ridiculous and quite unnecessary bandage is wrapped around my head. The effect is apparently so comic that José, the nurse-doctor, and the girl who did nothing useful at all, decide that we must all have a photo together. I take the camera out the bag though, to see it has been crushed by the accident and no longer works. Still, a broken camera and a cut chin is not the worst I could have come away with, and I happily say goodbye and thank you to everyone who helped, and to some people who didn't, as I leave toward Guadalajara.

...

I ride now, my eyes fixed in a continuous stare ahead, so that when the city erupts from the ground, my eyes sting with the constant wind, and my neck aches, craned in unflinching concentration. As the road swells from two lanes, to three, to four, I turn off, seeking a quieter route to the centre over a train line and down a backstreet. The crumbling walls of tiny houses crowd the tracks and small children run and giggle, clambering over the rails.

An androgynous doll dangles upside down from a girl's hand. She climbs over the track and the doll's head smacks against the metal, twice, both rails, like something forgotten. Each time though, the blue unblinking eyes still stare, expression unchanged, at the swaying upside down world, and pouts at it with peeling red lips. The eyes gaze blankly at the small concrete blocks, dangling right angles into the sky, as the sizzling crackle of dough on burning oil snaps. Smoke seeps down into the sky, before melting into it and the scene sways uncertainly; stones, metal, concrete, hanging above the sun.

An older girl calls the children to eat, and they turn, straight away, and run. A red ball bobbles over the stones, Barbie's head smashes against the metal for the fourth time, and they run towards the sound of sizzling fat.

I lift my bike across the railway, on the fringes of Mexico's second largest city, thinking about planning permission; about the bribes to keep away bulldozers, tiny perhaps, but too expensive, immobilizing. I wonder what it must be like to have a functioning train track instead of a back yard.

I ride back onto the main road, crammed now with new German cars and old buses, coughing black fumes. At the traffic lights, adolescent boys in dirty t-shirts too big for them, and faces too old for them, squirt soapy water onto windscreens and wipe glass that was already clean. Women in long skirts walk between the cars selling sweets, crisps and cigarettes, unhurried and slow. They walk, knowing the exact amount of time they have before the lights turn green.

In front of the waiting traffic, a young man in a dusty top hat and a black magician's cloak stands, holding a black box. He holds it upside down, displays the empty interior, and the next moment pulls out a small dirty-white rabbit. The rabbit is sleeping; bored by the trick, repeated all day and every day, at every red light, in the choking fumes, and as the magician walks down the lines of cars, in the hope of a couple of pesos, the sleeping rabbit lends a decidedly anticlimactic ending to the performance, and the windows stay closed.

...

Night fallen, I wander.

I walk the long pedestrian shopping streets and the smaller side streets and the alleyways, the streets bustling over and the foreboding silent streets that warn you away as the darkness quickens. I am walking along a busy street, the pavement in front of me full, when a murmur comes from the people in front and they cross the road, leaving the pavement bare. About three or four metres in front of me, a homeless man lies on his back, his trousers around his ankles and a dirty blanket thrown over him. His hand moves rhythmically up and down under the blanket, and through half closed eyes, he looks up at the sky; past the orange haze of the streetlamp above. He is smiling; a huge wide shameless grin and I turn and follow the crowds across the street toward the main plaza.

...

A man with a fixed-wheel bike stops and asks if he can sit next to me and for the next two hours he sits at my side greeting every passer-by, smiling a smile so warm and open it unnerves almost everyone to whom it is directed. But still he calls after them "*Buenas noches, qué la pasen muy bien!*" with nothing but openness and warmth in his words. And in those times where it is just us he talks in long and animated spiels, forgetting I don't understand.

At times it feels like I am following him and I nod enthusiastically, perhaps at my own interpretation of what I'm being told, and I smile and offer a small reply; which he treats always as apt and at times, miraculously insightful, and the conversation, if you can call this fumbling, frenzied barrage of words and simple gestures a conversation, rolls on.

At times, I have to tell him I am lost, and I turn to him, apologise.

"*Lo siento,*" I say. "*No te entiendo.*"

He smiles just the same, "*No importa,*" he says with a voice that seems to transcend words. "*Da igual. Nada de lo que digo es importante. Lo que importa es la vida.*" And on and on he somehow talks, life and joy pouring out of him, tireless and open. "*Me gusta la vida,*" he says, over and over again.

He turns to me and smiles, "*Y a ti? Qué te gusta?*"

I sit, quietly pensive, slowly forming the words that clank together awkwardly, like puzzle pieces that don't quite fit.

"*Me gusta...*" I say. I like. Travel. To travel. "*Me gusta viajar.*"

"*Por qué?*" he asks.

"*Porque... porque es como nacer otra vez...*" And somehow with broken words and stitches that threaten to burst every time I smile, I tell him that I love to travel because when you see something you've never seen before, you feel like a child. Suddenly life is new, everything becomes full of wonder, as though you have just been born. And, miraculously, I think he understands.

...

I spend a week in Guadalajara, waiting for my chin to heal, and take the road south east out of the city until the buildings disintegrate and Mexico is green again. Ocotalan, La Barca, Ecuandereo, Zamora, Zacapu, Iratzio. The road reaches Morelia.

...

I pay sixty pesos for a room that lies crumbling into a courtyard and I walk along the side street towards the main plaza. Café doors hang open and I glance at a couple eating; hunched quietly over a plate of tacos, the bright green of salsa against the chequered red and white of the plastic table cloth.

When I reach Morelia's cathedral the sun is setting on the ancient streets, and for a few wonderful minutes the city glows golden. The central square fills with families and people selling helium balloons and candyfloss. The cafés fill with people drinking coffee and beer, tables spill out onto the streets. As the sky grows dark the cathedral shines, now not with sun, but electric light, and an orchestra starts to play.

I stand for a moment in the sound of violins and the reverberations of cellos, and it is here that I meet Adan. Or he meets me; to practice his English, he says. He is my age, perhaps a little older. He wears the jacket and trousers and shoes of an older man, but I cannot decide whether they make him look older or younger than he really is. We walk around the central streets, full of people and life and still the swooning noise of the orchestra rises in crescendos and ebbs away as we walk in and out of its reach.

"It is the celebration of Morelo's birthday," Adan tells me as we find a seat outside a café and order a beer. I don't know who Morelo is. I don't know anything about Latin American history, only that I imagine it as the long drawn out sacking of one and a half continents. I should ask, but I feel embarrassed; there is a sense that I should know already so I nod my head stupidly and let the conversation carry on.

It is getting late when we arrive at the small door of a club; a tiny sign says *Limbo*, in black and red letters, and there is part of me that knows I should probably go home. Nothing good ever happens with me and alcohol and darkened clubs with stupid names like Limbo. Though maybe there is no good name for a club, I think, as we step through the door.

The room is dark and smoky and we take some wooden steps up to a mezzanine and look over what looks like a small pub. A waitress comes over and Adan orders beers that cost twice as much as anywhere else and we sit half comfortable, half drunk. Adan takes off his jacket to reveal that his shirt is embossed with a giant Union Jack. I try to stop myself from laughing, but barely succeed.

"What?" he asks.

"Nothing," I say. "It's a good shirt," realising that for lack of inventiveness I've had to tell him I was laughing at it.

A few people shuffle around the stage, placing drinks carefully behind amps, before the band start playing something which I take to be Cumbia, but am told is not.

I look down to see people dancing, their movements beautiful and thoughtless. They move like liquid, I think. They move, I think, they dance, in the way that I might breathe, with the same amount of thought, the same level of comfort. It seems so unthinking and beautiful, and yet from here just a gentle shuffling, and the whole floor beneath me moves in time; they have been dancing like this since they were born, I think, and I know I should never, never try. I look to Adan, and he asks if I'm having a good time. I nod and smile over the music.

A group of girls sits beneath us, on stools around a small round table. I keep catching their eye as I look around the room. Each time I glance at their table one or two of the girls are looking up. And soon it becomes like a game; each time our eyes cross the girls laugh to each other, or at me.

As the bar fills, waitresses stop coming round the tables and I walk down the stairs to the bar. I pass the table and two of the girls smile at me, and I smile back and as I carry the bottles of beer back up to where we are sitting, cold condensation wet on my hands, the two girls say hello and I say hello back, walking quickly past them. Now we are stuck. As I go back to Adan the girls keep glancing up, until soon they are waving us down.

"They're just silly girls," says Adan, over the music. And for a while I sink back into the chair, light another cigarette, and try to avoid looking down, until our beers are almost empty.

"I'll go," says Adan.

I watch him walk to the bar, and the girls stop him, and he talks for a minute or two, before walking up the stairs towards me. He seems reluctant to convey their message.

"Do you want to go down?" he asks.

"Can do. It's up to you," I say. "It might be nice."

He motions for me to come and I stand up.

"One thing," he says. "I told them, I'm your friend from England. They think I'm from London."

I look at him, slightly perplexed, and follow him down the stairs.

It turns out that one of the girls speaks better English than him, but still, he keeps up his charade for the whole night; the girl wincing every time he says, *the people is,* or that *he wants that we understand.* The other girls complement him on his remarkable Spanish and he takes the complement with grace, not seeing that a scattering of eyes and tiny looks, criss-crossing across the table, has found him out, and the girls are laughing at him.

It is late. The girls give up trying to teach me to dance. I am a hopeless case, a lost cause, and if anything, practice has made it worse. Adan, though, dances quite wonderfully. Especially for an Englishman.

We sit down, and the girl at my side leans into me and I feel her hand, soft against mine and she reaches over and rests her other hand on my knee. I don't know what we are talking about; I catch the odd word over the music, too loud now for conversation, and she smiles and shrugs her shoulders to say she can't hear anything either.

The volume of the music has turned the bar into one of those places which are not for me. It is not that I rely on words, for I have little more to say than anyone else and always say it badly. But my awkwardness manifests itself more clearly in my body language. These are places for confident, well-dressed people who can dance and laugh freely; there is something primordial in the way that you can barely talk and that to attract someone else you must rely on something beyond or before words, some part of you that is not expressed in language. I feel a gentle touch on my thigh now, and incautious now with the night's long drinking I lean over to her.

"Do you want to leave?" I ask above the music, so loud that for a moment I worry that everyone will hear.

"What?"

I am not sure whether she is shocked or genuinely hasn't heard, but next time I lean over I change what I am saying. "I'd like to see you again."

"I'd like to see you again too," she says, and before we leave the bar, I hand her a piece of paper with my email address written on it.

Outside it is black and cold; the warmth of inside is still on her skin as I kiss her cheek and we say goodnight and she says she'll write to me. A tipsy, easy feeling of lightness fills me as we walk away from each other, and I force myself not to look back.

...

The next day I check my email, three times. Each time, I feel the same slight disappointment, the same flutter of nerves followed by a light empty feeling, and I try to think of ways to use the 15 minutes of internet that I have left. I check the football scores; Sheffield Wednesday have lost again. I start writing an email to a friend and delete all of it so that I am left with just her name and the word Hi. Then even the word hi seems stupid so I give up, pay and leave. I should just forget about it. How many phone numbers given out in bars are ever called? I guess, I don't know; I cannot remember ever giving one to anyone before.

The streets of Morelia are beautiful; stone walls and leafy streets; small bronze statues and plazas. I wander through a university building, open to the public, and into a quiet courtyard; a fountain burbles in the centre, and a door stands ajar; the aching lull of a cello floats out of the room. I stop, looking stupidly at plants I don't know the name of, and sit down on a bench. For a moment I forget that I'm waiting for something.

Later, I take a seat in the corner of the café with the red and white table cloths and order eight tacos. I take a book out, and fold it open at my side; flit between Mexico and Mishima. I like eating alone. I like sitting and watching; eating at my own pace, not having to worry about conversation, but I always need something next to me; a book, a map. Something to show that I am not truly on my own, that I have company, or am occupied at least.

I walk the long way round to my hotel. There are people milling around the cathedral still, but the orchestra has gone, and the cafés sit half-empty. I go into one last internet café; there is nothing. Just an email from the foreign office service I subscribed to; something about mudslides in Guatemala or Panama. I don't read it. Perhaps, I should think about leaving.

...

The next day there is an email.

I'm Lucía, she says. *We met in Limbo.* As if I would forget.

It is true, though. We never really know what the person next to us is thinking. That a moment that changed our lives, that we replay, over and over again, a moment that we fill with meaning could, for the person next to us, mean nothing. That it could be not the foot, the loving foot that is resting against our back, in some secret message of love, but the strap of a bag. Of a dull, insentient object.

I look at the email in front of me. *We met in Limbo. I want to see you again.*

I write back. *Okay. I'd like to see you again, too. I don't mind what or where.*

Las Tarascas, she says. *At 19hrs*. At 19hrs; it feels like a spy rendezvous.

Okay, at 19hrs, I reply, not 7 o'clock, *I'll see you tomorrow*.

...

Las Tarascas is a fountain, or a roundabout depending on how you look at it, but for me it is a fountain.

I sit for a moment on the cold stone wall, white water cascading, from one high pool to a gathering basin below. In the centre of the fountain, three women kneel outwards, holding a giant wreath of vegetables and grains above their heads, an offering, it seems, to the gods.

I look at my watch. Ten past seven. Quarter past. How long do I wait? Maybe this is normal in Mexico. Maybe I was crazy to get here on time. I'll wait until half-past, and then I'll go back to the hotel and forget about it, carry on tomorrow. I can't stop looking at my watch. It seems sometimes an eternity that I will myself not to look and when I do the second hand is still ticking round the same slow minute. At seven twenty five, there is part of me that is happy she will not come, relieved. I've never been good at these things; it will save me the embarrassment. I scan the streets around the fountain. It is not possible, is it, that I haven't recognised her? I cannot conjure her face in my mind the way I can with faces I know, but I wasn't so drunk. For the next five minutes I see her, momentarily, in the features of half the girls around the fountain, only to realise I am mistaken. Seven twenty nine. Seven thirty. One more minute? No. I pick myself off the wall, and cross the road, glancing back to check that she's not there. She's not.

I walk, slow and aimless, until I pass an internet café, and linger outside for a moment. Seven forty five. I'll let her know at least that I turned up.

I sit down, and open my email. The computer winds slowly, as though powered with whirring cogs. There is nothing but more advice from the foreign office.

Hey Lucía,
Guess maybe you changed your mind... don't worry.
If you haven't and you're just running late, I'll be in the internet cafe down the road from Las Tarascas, maybe until 20.10 ish....
Either way, hope everything goes well for you. It was fun to meet you on Friday.
Take care
Sam x

I wait, ready to waste another half hour on the internet. I leave my email open, though I don't expect a reply; an excuse tomorrow, perhaps. But ten minutes later she writes back.

please!!!!!!!!!!!!!!!!!!!!!!!! wait for me?
i was in la calzada. and i never sow u
i thought u were the one who changed your mind

The minutes are shorter now, and when she arrives she is prettier than I remember, or than I'd let myself remember. I feel each awkward movement of my body and everything seems unnatural, like I have forgotten how to walk and I think about how close I am walking to her, too close, or too far away and I feel how horribly sober we are and how everything seems tense, as if the world could shatter at any moment. The feeling is unpleasant I decide, like that sick feeling before an exam, or speaking in public. It would have been better to go home, I think. Not to put myself through this. Ourselves. My nervousness is so apparent, I think, that it will be a terrible night for both of us. Somehow we manage to fill the silence, but even as I listen and try to talk, I don't know how.

"Are you hungry?" she asks.

"Are you?"

We walk along the Calzada Fray Antonio de San Miguel. Around us couples walk comfortably in each other's arms, laughing under the green cover of the trees and the gentle light of old street lamps. Along the pedestrian lane a long stone bench runs and more couples sit together holding hands and talking. I fall into silence.

There are candles in the restaurant, and the table we sit at is tucked away in a tiny room. We order beers, I order a quesadilla and she orders pizza. And I sit there, trying not to peel back the label on the beer, but my efforts fail and soon I find myself sliding the label around over the cold surface of the bottle and I feel the strange gooey sensation of glue and condensation on my fingers, and I put the bottle down.

We sit eating food which should be eaten with our hands with knives and forks. We order more beer, sit and talk, and somehow with each word it becomes easier, and I slowly find myself finding out more about her; that she plays the piano, and that her parents are divorced, that she has an older brother and sister. She is twenty-one; her Italian is better than her English. I feel slightly stupid talking to her; I don't play anything and the words of languages I've learnt are all but forgotten, and hardly worth remembering. She laughs at something I say, or maybe it is the other way around, and then our hands are on the table, fingers brushing slightly together, gently tangling, and for a while it seems that neither of us knows what to do, how the hands should disentangle, and something about it has made us fall into the silence again, and we are stuck for what to say. Finally, a waitress comes and our hands fall away naturally and we order one more beer.

She doesn't let me pay and we split the bill. *I'll drive you back to your hotel*, she says, and I don't ask her about the beer and if it's okay to drive, and I get in, and we drive through the streets so different now from the front seat of her car.

"Do you want to do the changes?" Lucía asks.

"The changes?"

"On the car," she says, and she points to the gearstick.

"I can't drive," I say, and she says it doesn't matter and I put my hand on the gearstick and she puts her hand over mine. I feel the clunking of metal underneath, and the streets and the lights of cars rush by.

We are outside my hotel. The car motor is still running, hazard lights on, and we say goodbye, not quite knowing what to do. I close the door, and wave stupidly, and walk away, thinking, that's it, I'll never see you again. I watch the red lights of her car slowly disappear. And I open the door to the hotel and walk up slowly to my room. I lie down on the bed, looking up to the ceiling for an hour before turning the light off and staring at the blurry dark space, where the ceiling was, until at last I close my eyes.

...

In the morning, I decide to leave.

And then I decide I cannot.

One more day, I'll wander round the leafy streets on my own. I am not sure if last night went well or not; I was too nervous. Maybe I lack the confidence to make girls feel comfortable. I don't know. A picture of the night comes back. Sitting in the passenger seat, and looking at her, and saying thank you, or something stupid, my whole body frozen. And not knowing whether to kiss her, or hug her in the car, and the engine turning over, and then the headlights of the car behind. And in the end, I do nothing. I get out of the car and I say goodbye, and no matter how many times I play the scene over, it will not change.

I walk into a café and drink coffee and *arepas* and I flick through my book which never makes me feel awkward and never asks for anything, and I walk aimlessly around the city again and again. Until I decide to check my email, without hope this time.

don't go tomorrow!!!!!
I like you
my classes finish at 14 hrs.
if you stay let me know

...

We meet at the fountain, at three o'clock, and seven hours vanish. Time doesn't seem real, and we talk and all the awkwardness of yesterday is gone and when we walk down the calzada I am no longer looking at other couples when she takes my hand. We sit at a cheap café and the light drains from the sky and now the beautiful warm Morelia light seems perfect, and everything sparkles, and in her eyes the whole world seems to shine. And after about three hours, she tells me she has a boyfriend.

I am bored, she says. And when she talks about him I feel nothing. I am nodding and saying words, but it is not really me. I guess I don't know her. It is impossible to be hurt in three days, I think; but I am thinking about me, not him. And somehow we talk for two more hours, and when she drops me home I don't even think about kissing her, and I know this time, as I watch her drive away, that I will truly never see her again. I am happy though, lying on the bed. There is no doubt as there was the night before, and I play over the gentle night again and there is no bitterness, only joy.

When there is a knock on my door, I feel so sure that the sound must be coming from next door, that I do not get up until the knock comes a second time.

She is standing there, even though I'd watched her drive away. There is a tiny silence, and then when I am sure she has not come back to return something I've left in the car, I ask if she wants to come in.

"I don't want to come in," she says. "I just want to kiss you."

The words are still turning around in my mind when I realise I have been sitting on the edge of the bed for minutes without doing anything, and the door is still open, and I'm on my own. If she had stayed there any longer, I think, she would have stayed forever. And I think about J M Coetzee, and *Disgrace*, about every experience being enriching. And I feel no guilt about borrowing her for a while.

...

The next day I leave early. The road rises out of Morelia and into the mountains; I wind slowly under a rich canopy of trees, until the city lies beneath me. I cannot say, even to myself, what it is, that I am feeling.

I am on my way to *Nevado de Toluca*. At 4,680m it will be the highest I have ever climbed. Maybe, I think, the ties you have grow weaker, the higher above these ties you rise. Though, from what I know already, from the desperate feelings of loneliness I felt at the beginning of this trip, I imagine the opposite will be true; that, with each metre, the yearning will increase for all that lies below.

...

I climb 10km out of Zitacuaro, and stop at a café. There is a long wooden table with two benches running along it on either side, four young girls, perhaps twenty, perhaps not quite twenty, and no sign of food or refreshments. For a moment I stand in the doorway and one of the girls, with a distractingly low-cut top, says something I don't understand with the word *coger* and then something else with the word *chingar* and then seeing my puzzlement, says clearly and in a way that makes the other girls laugh, "*Sexo, quieres sexo?*"

"*Quiero un café*," I say, "*o una Coca-Cola*"

We don't have coffee, the girl says, or Coca-Cola. Water? I nod, and she brings a glass of water and places it on the table in front of me. It is hard to say whether the girls are relieved they don't have to sleep with me, but it is clear that my presence amuses them. I drink the water slower than I should, wondering whether it came from a bottle, or if it was boiled, or if it's going to make me ill, and the girls talk to me, trying to make me understand things I am incapable of understanding. They look through the pictures on my camera, at the towering cacti of Baja California as though it were another world. Then, they reach The States and pass around a picture of the harbour in San Diego; the sun shining, the masts of yachts like a bare winter forest in front of the pristine city. They get bored before arriving to the fields of strawberries outside Monterrey and the armies of Mexican workers bent double under the sun.

Eventually I finish the water and the same girl asks me if I want more. I shake my head, say thank you, and leave.

...

The road rises steadily out of Toluca and I feel the excitement of cycling higher than I ever have before; some paradoxical phenomena that even as the sun climbs higher in the sky, and I climb closer towards it, the air grows colder. Then, the first hazy glimpse of the mountain comes, the peak like dark grey smoke, or like the shadow of a mountain against the sky.

The dirt track turns to bare rock cut into the ground and trees dissipate to leave a barren scrub of hardy grass. A park warden's truck stops, and the men wave me over.

"It's too dangerous," they say.

"A storm?" I ask.

"Cold," they say, speaking as simply as they can after seeing how long it took for me to come up with the word *tormenta*.

"Cold is okay. I have lots of things for cold," and I point at my panniers.

"You should sleep further down," they say, pointing back down towards the trees.

"There's no storm?" I say. "No bad weather?"

"No," they say. "But up there it's dangerous. It's dangerous because you're on your own," and they repeat the word, just to make sure that I realise: alone, *solo*.

"Okay," I say. I don't have the Spanish to reason with them and I make as if to turn the bike around and I slowly follow them down the mountain. The metres that were so difficult to climb slip by with frustrating ease before the truck rounds the corner and I turn back and climb towards the summit.

...

It turns out I am not alone. I reach the *refugio*, a short walk from the crater and see that a group of friends from Xalapa have hired the bare concrete rooms, austere beds and the rudimentary kitchen and filled the building with noise, the smell of food and laughter. They are all wrapped up in thick coats and hat and scarves. *Frioleros*, I think for a second, before the heat from my burning limbs and the effort of the climb evaporates into the air and I find myself scrambling over to my bike and rummaging around for warmer clothes.

I find a flat patch of land behind the shelter to pitch a tent. The summit above is enshrouded with a thick and icy cloud and the sunlight that reaches us is fleeting and thin. It is not like real sun; so bright and clear and yet almost heatless on my skin. Like an English winter sun, I think and turn, remembering it's October and that somewhere far away it's autumn.

I spend what is left of the afternoon talking with the people from Xalapa. They do not let me open the miserable packets of nuts I have carried up the mountain and, as I eat their wonderful food, I feel somehow part of their extended family. I feel such warmth from their stories and generosity that I barely notice the cold as I walk after nightfall to sleep in my tent; the sky clear now; the lights of Toluca, a strange florescent puddle down below.

...

I reach the summit of the mountain as the sun rises. Still, to the west, stars hang in the sky, and the first solid rays of light fall over a blanket of cloud; punctured here and there by jagged, rocky peaks, like soft white cloth torn and caught on a thorn bush, impaled and flapping in the wind.

Somewhere below me, under the cloud, Mexico DF is waking up. I have chosen to avoid the capital; the thought of riding through a city six times the size of Guadalajara fills me with dread, for the traffic, nothing else. I have planned a route that will skirt around the city, through the mountains, to the south. I sit on a rock and watch the world that seems now only to be these jutting outcrops of rock, three kilometres high, and the sky itself above, an ever deepening blue.

...

When I check my emails there is a message from Lucía. *If you're not too far, on Monday,* it says, *I could come and see you. I could take a bus. If you want.*

The message is three days old. Above there is a newer one, from today. *Hi Sam, I guess you don't want to. Sorry. I don't want to be annoying. Have fun cycling to Argentina. xo.*

I write back to say I want to, and that I'm sorry for responding late, and that tomorrow, Monday, I will be in Taxco, and that if she still wants to and if she can, I would love to see her there.

I wait, sat at a computer while teenagers around me play online games, for an hour. There is no response. I eat. I read, and just before the internet café closes, I check again. Nothing.

In the morning there is a message. *I don't know Taxco*, it says, *but let's say the cathedral. I'll be there in the morning, I'll wait for you there.*

...

The ride to Taxco is shorter than it would be if no-one were waiting for me. I stop only for water and ride the last steep climbs with a slow puncture, the weight of the heavy load and gravity pulling against my pedals, so that when I see her I am breathless.

We walk through the narrow streets of Taxco, along narrow pavements, and a taxi, a white Beetle from some decade last century, rushes by, its tyres clattering and slapping against the cobblestones, and we breathe into the walls, rising up on tip-toes to let it past, pulling the bike in, against the wall.

"These small towns," Lucía turns to me, "so *dan*gerous!" She says the first syllable like the name, Dan. "So *dan*gerous," she says again, shaking her head.

I feel the eyes of the hotel staff boring into me as I fumble around for my passport. I smile as I pass it over and they smile back in the polite and distant way that hotel staff do, but I see the exchanged glances, the speculation, and the judgement. And as we walk away I feel eyes at our backs, pinning down roles and circumstance.

It is a pleasant hotel; plant pots line the stairs, and a small fountain gurgles in a courtyard, behind panes of stained glass. The room, when we enter is white, yet somehow warm, cream, with a dark wooden floor, and a double bed in the middle.

There is distance between us now, as we stand in the room, alone with what we are doing. As I stand there, I do not think about how different this must be for her; that this is no longer a chance meeting with some foreign boy in a bar, but rather the riding for hours on a bus and the renting of a hotel room in full premeditated sobriety. I do not feel what she must be feeling, I think of no one else. There is no one in this country of 120 million people that I know. Only, perhaps, this girl who is standing in front of me. And yet, I do not know what she is thinking. I can barely guess at how she feels, and as I look for a moment in her direction, I wander if she is thinking about Fabian, whether regret has already crept into her mind, as doubt's companion. Perhaps she has come too far now, and there is no turning back. Perhaps for both of us now, there is no turning back as we stand in this hotel room, maybe everything from here is inevitable; we have made our choice, and it seems I could no more turn away from it, than hurl myself off a cliff. I do not know if it is guilt she is feeling as she looks to me and smiles, but I know that it is betrayal. And I am not just complicit in the betrayal, but the catalyst for it, the perpetrator of it, its instigator. And this when we are only standing, slightly awkwardly, looking across at each other, knowing that it is too late to go back.

"I hope you don't mind," she says. "I thought..." and I don't say anything.

"You'll want a shower," she says, and I nod. "I'll wait for you downstairs."

...

We climb the steep streets of Taxco, shops selling silver jewellery and empty bars. We take a path that climbs high, up above the town, to a statue of Jesus. And now Taxco appears as two hills, evenly covered in pretty whitewashed buildings; a bell tower rises from its highest point, like an illustration from a children's story book.

Words fill the silences between us, but the ease with which we spoke last time, when everything was free and light and inconsequential, has been replaced with a nervous air of expectation.

Tourists mill around us, taking photos and leaning over the stone wall gazing over at the town for long measured periods of time. There is that mood, like the mood of a museum, where people become suddenly slower and softer in their gaze; that air of meditated, slow perspicacity, when suddenly everyday things take on the value of art. Across the viewpoint, people's eyes linger on each other, glancing away when their eyes meet, but knowing that in this mood they are part of the display. I wonder what we look like. Stood here, looking over the town, close but not touching. I wonder if they see the nerves, the conscious effort in our bodies, the tiny meanings in each movement; everything so unbearably electric and sober. I am wondering whether it's just me, when she turns to me. *Let's get a beer,* she says.

...

It is night when we walk back through the hotel doors, the kind of drunk where everything is alight; that ephemeral part of tipsiness before everything becomes heavy. We walk quietly up the stairs, like teenagers sneaking into their parents' home, her hand now holding mine, and something tells me that I have to be careful; that when she told me earlier in the bar "I can't stay tomorrow," and I thought she said *can,* that she *could,* that she *can* stay tomorrow, I know that my heart had leapt too wildly with happiness, and I know as we walk up the stairs, and as she takes out the key, that that kind of happiness is dangerous, and cannot lead to anything good.

...

For a moment the light in the room is brighter than before, more unforgiving. Accusing.

We both lie, looking up.

I don't want to go, she says, *but I have to.*

Maybe our time will seem longer if we don't go to sleep, she says, and we talk into the night, and slowly, it becomes easy again, like before.

I do not know who falls asleep first, but when I open my eyes, hers are right in front of mine, our noses almost touching, and it is light outside.

...

We sit at the bus stop, waiting to say goodbye. I feel the numbness of an almost sleepless night in everything. Words feel disconnected, alien, and difficult to say. And there is sadness too.

It seems there is sadness between us, but perhaps we can never really know what another person is thinking, what the same words mean to another person, the same touch. Whilst it is sadness that I am feeling, it is not inconceivable that she is waiting anxiously for the bus to arrive, that she is berating herself, regretfully, for getting on the bus, for meeting me at the fountain.

I think that the sadness is between us, that it is not just something I have conjured from the silence, but I cannot be sure. It is easy to mistake the strap of a bag for a foot, for love.

As the bus comes, she turns and kisses me. "Write to me," she says.

I watch the bus go, her face dark behind the tinted windows, and I turn and walk away, not quite knowing what I am thinking, but with a strange sensation that I am back on my own, that this is how it's always been, but somehow now, being on my own is different. *Write to me.* What the fuck does that mean?

...

I ride through the mountains to the south of Mexico City. Miacatlán, Xochitepec, Cuernavaca, Yautepec, Cuatla. It is hard cycling. In the distance the smoke pale peak of Popocatépetl rises, snow clinging to its shadowed face.

...

I stop in Hueyapan for food and water and sit by the side of the road opposite a small, single storey brick building; half-dwelling, half-shop. Its wooden beams stretch over the outer wall, and air flows between these and the overhanging roof. A pile of sombreros, neatly stacked, sits on a small wooden stool, and brightly coloured ponchos, blankets and bags hang on the wall.

A few minutes later a woman dressed in bright pink, her dark grey hair wrapped up in intricate plaits, brings out a tiny wooden stool.

"*Ponte aquí,*" she says "So you're more comfortable."

I sit, facing across the road now, to where moments ago I was sitting, and Elvia goes inside to make coffee.

She comes out with two small cups; the coffee is black and sweet, like syrup, or tar. The sun shines from behind us in the south, so we huddle in the light shadow of the awnings, out of the bright white mountain sun. It seems barely possible that only kilometres away there is snow.

"*Eres Estadounidense?*" Elvia asks.

"*Inglés.*"

"Ah," she says. "I have never been to England. I lived in America for a year. Boston, 1966."

I ask her what it was like.

"It was different," she says. "There, in The United States, they finish the buildings. Here," she points to the houses crowding the road. "I liked Boston. I worked in a hotel. But it wasn't Mexico. I had to come back. I wanted to."

Any English she once had has abandoned her in the forty four years since she left the USA. We speak in my bad Spanish and gestures, and she is patient with me; I feel I am improving slowly, but conversing with me must be testing. She asks if I want to stay, to eat, to sleep. There is a room that I can sleep in, she says. Her son's old room. And I gratefully wheel the bike inside, and lean it against the bare wall. She must be seventy, at least, I think. But there is something childlike in her: the way she looks with gentle curiosity as we talk; the way her eyes sparkle.

No one buys anything from her shop. A few neighbours pass by and enquire about my presence in quiet voices. I understand only snatches of their conversations. The same, over-rehearsed phrases I am used to repeating, explaining where I'm from and where I'm going.

As it grows dark Elvia begins to cook, in a small kitchen, which I never enter. I sit in the lamp lit gloom, reading until Elvia comes in with an enormous plate of food; steaming hot potatoes, mounds of white rice, spaghetti, cut into little pieces, and a dollop of mayonnaise.

Later, her son, Adan, comes round to say hello, and we drink mint tea. She shows me old black and white photos of the hotel staff in Boston. She points to herself in the front row. Her face is almost the same. She begins to tell a story, and I try to follow her though really my reactions are led by her tone, more than her words. Adan looks at me and smiles apologetically, and interrupts her.

"*No creo que te entienda,*" he says. I don't think he understands.

Elvia waves a hand slowly away, as though it is not necessary for me to understand, that it is enough simply to tell the story. Or perhaps she is telling it to herself, as much as to me, and there is joy enough in that.

...

We are sitting in the car, the sun cascading in through the open windows, and we have barely left the bus stop in Morelia, when Lucía turns to me and says, "We've broken up. Fabian and me."

Perhaps I should say something, but I don't. I wait in the silence for her to continue. Perhaps I should feel guilt. Or at least panic. Perhaps I should wonder at myself. How I could be responsible for this? If this has happened then it's serious, isn't it? We've done something serious, we've broken something. But I feel almost nothing. Calmness, perhaps. I feel calm. And I wonder if that's because this is what I wanted, and now somehow it means something; that the sadness was between us, was shared, and not imagined. I look over at her; she looks beautiful and tired.

"I told him about you," she says. "I couldn't not tell him about you. I was too culpable. Too guilty. So I told him. And he was really angry. But then he told me everything," as she says this I want to laugh at her words. I wonder if she has thought about them before, if they were conceived of as she waited for my bus. We could be rehearsing for a telenovela. Only the performances are too stilted.

I wait for her to tell me the everything that he told her, and for the first time, wonder if I was right to come here, to leave my bike in Puebla and see her one more time. The words, *You are getting yourself into something*, cross my mind, but they're immediately followed with *Good. I'm glad. I'm happy.*

"He has been seeing someone else," she says. "Him too. In another city. But him, he's even worse than me. For two years. He has been with her for two years, more than half the time we have been together, and he never told me."

Still I don't say anything. What could I say? I touch her hand and she takes mine and they clasp together, moving the gears through the city.

"I told you it wasn't right, didn't I?" she says. "When I told you about him the first time. I told you something was wrong."

"You told me you were bored."

"Yeah," she says. "Bored. Bored and fucking stupid!"

I look out the window at the city rolling past when the car lurches and my hand moves quickly under hers, and I'm thrown forward in my seat.

The car in front crawls along in the middle of the road and Lucía leans on the horn, "*Oye, viejito, no mames wey!*"

...

We lie on the bed. Sunlight shines through the window, and the curtains billow in and out of the hotel room, swelling huge as they fill like cotton lungs, to be sucked out again. It is like we are part of one huge breath, one thing, my breathing and hers, and the huge outside; in and out, the curtains dance, billowing like sails and taut again, and with the wind, the breath of outside, we too breathe together.

It has become easy. We have learnt to be together, our bodies fold, unthinking now, and envelop into the other. Outside, the singing of birds fills the plaza, and though it must have always been there, it is only now that I notice that the sound has filtered softly into the room with the light.

But still, I know that the world is not this room, not this place. Though I do not think of this, the huge great unknown continent of South America lies untraced, and unlike a map, to the south. I have started this journey now, and it is impossible for me to stop, until I reach the southernmost reaches of Argentina, the end of my journey. Something that once seemed so unnatural and forced is now inevitable, and I know that I shall follow the plot of my original design, that even with this new much kinder world within my arms, I will turn away, like a character over whom I possess no authority. Whose movements are dictated by something else, pupeteered by my original will, but stronger than me.

...

When I wake in the morning there is a hand around my shoulder; fingers fine and gentle. When I lift them between my calloused ugly hands I am amazed by their softness. And not only that, but that they are a part of someone else, and yet so close to me that they could be a further part of myself. It is hard to know if they are sleeping hands; they fall soft and pliable and move between my fingers without resistance, but it seems they are not unconscious. I let the hand go and it comes to rest, silently against my skin.

...

I return once more to Morelia, leaving my bike in Oaxaca, and sitting those long hours on a bus, as it winds its way through the mountain roads, bumps uncomfortably over potholes, and grinds to sudden halts. *Campesinos* hold out pineapple and chilli in clear plastic bags, or *tamales* wrapped in leaves, and pass them through the windows, in exchange for a few small notes.

This time, we know it is the last time and we make promises. I will come back, I say. I can finish the rest of my journey in six months, less perhaps, and then I will come straight back. I will find a job teaching English, and those streets that will always be the sunlit golden streets of stone and quiet plazas, will be my home. And she will wait, she says. It is only six months. It is not a long time. She has her studies, and her friends, and she will wait for my return.

As we say these things, her face becomes the face that I will remember, and carry with me, and conjure in my recollections; so open, so honest; her eyes wet with unshed tears, and I know that this is shared. We are still two people as we say these things, but I no longer doubt the similitude of our feelings, no longer doubt that what I feel, she feels too. And as I take the bus away from her, she says she will see me soon. *Well, kind of soon.*

...

In Oaxaca people carve sand sculptures in the square; skulls and skeletons, their temporary bones adorned with temporary flowers. Over the grainy surfaces, the sculptors sieve powdered paint, until the central plaza of the city is a strange and glowing sandpit of deathly shapes.

I go to the cemetery with some backpackers and we pass around a bottle of Mezcal, golden and half sweet, with a bite more vicious than Tequila's. I tip the bottle upside down, desperately I realise, so that it glugs down with such force that I feel its vibrations knock back through the glass. I feel sick, I pass the bottle, tears coming to my eyes. Stop, I tell myself. Go slow. There is no need to seek oblivion. Now the sick feeling is gone, I feel more comfortable in the company of these people, who seem so able instantly to laugh, and tell jokes. The night around us is shining, quiet, and we follow the crowds to the cemetery.

Candles flicker in the darkness, resting on every gravestone and marking the earthen paths between the tombs. The candlelight glows steady over flower petals, red and yellow wreathes. Families sit around, talking into the night, drinking from flasks, and unwrapping picnics. And the talk is gentle and quiet, but very far from sad, as all the world sits in the light of tiny flames, and below them their mothers and their fathers and their uncles, aunts and all the long deceased lie under the ground, and the still quiet chatter goes on until morning, a night spent with the dead.

The picture is enough to sway me from further drinking, and we walk, close to silence, through the cemetery drenched in light. As the first tinge of drunkenness fades from my body, I feel myself grow intoxicated with a strange and melancholic happiness. I walk, for minutes lost on my own, and though I understand almost nothing that is around me, it feels that death is somehow different here, that it is not the same thing as it is in England; it is gentler somehow, warmer, and closer.

...

I pack my things; the routine automatic now, the order of things, the way they slide into each other, the weighting of the panniers.

I leave Oaxaca, towards Puerto Escondido. The road hugs a wide valley and falls away in great chunks, taken by past floods. A jagged desert fills the stifling heat of the valley; its light is yellow and bright, but to its details I am blind. For the days since Morelia, my thoughts have been consumed; I have bored backpackers talking about a girl they don't know, and at each opportunity I write to her. Now, it seems that I am leaving her, and though I know that I will come back, the time that we will be apart seems greater than the distance of a continent. She writes to me, telling me about her day at the university, and her friends' relationships, and things about her family, and I tell her about the things that I have seen and the people I have met, and we tell each other of our feelings and it seems they are the same feelings, and we say that we are waiting, and that we'll see each other soon, but that we'll talk even sooner, and then I leave the *locutorio* and ride again, until I find another.

...

I scream at the mountains. It is not the gentle winding down to the coast that I had expected. The road shoots up unforgivingly only to drop again. Even the shadows of palms, and other trees, are black and burning. It is hot today, and the cycling is hard. I can be blind, but I still know that.

...

I reach the town of Puerto Escondido two days later; backpackers and surfers fill the hostels, cafés and bars, I pay too much to stay in a twelve-bed dorm and spend the night playing some kind of drinking pool game, before going down to the beach with a bottle of tequila.

It is the cold that wakes me and I realise before I open my eyes that the hardness of the floor is not a bed, but concrete. When my eyelids separate, each clinging to the other, I see the sky is the deep cold blue of dawn, neither stars nor sun, and that I am curled somewhere between a wall and a hedge. I feel my face, to see if I'm still there; the last thing I remember was standing on the rocks, and someone taking a photo. There is a face above me. A woman, whose haggard face bears down upon me, is telling me in English that I shouldn't sleep here. I want to tell her that it's probably too late, but make do with checking my pockets as I scramble to my feet. Everything is still there, but I sway, still drunk, and lean against the wall.

"You don't know where y'are, do ya?" she says.

I hang my head and brush away the tiny stones that have implanted themselves in my cheek before looking up. "Mexico?"

She looks at me a moment. "You wanna come with me? We got some hella good 'shrooms."

We walk along the shore, which I barely recognise from the night before, until we get to her caravan. She is thirty, she tells me – though I would have been less surprised if she'd said fifty. A man comes out from the caravan, sells me some magic mushrooms, and tells me that he thinks he is Jesus. It takes an hour to realise he is not joking, and I long for my bed and sleep. I am not good on my own.

...

I leave Puerto Escondido; its scent, the stench of cigarettes and spilt tequila, and the mulching texture of mushrooms still etched into my brain.

The next days are better. I camp on the beach at Zipolite, lying in a hammock, drinking beer and reading, and swimming in the sea, the days stretched out and long. I watch the sun cast itself across the sky, from one side of the bay to the other. It would have been better just to come here, I think. To be here, quiet and restful, with the sea, under the warm shade of the trees. But no amount of will can change the past.

My dad will arrive in Costa Rica for Christmas, and December is already drawing close. After two days on the beach, I pull my things together, roll up the tent and leave. Barra de la Cruz, Salina Cruz. The world grows ugly now, away from the coast. Long flat stretches of road fall away in front of me. A wind comes in from the south; its stronger gusts throw me across the road and twice sweep me off the tarmac.

It is a hot and dull time. I count the kilometres and taste some kind of bitter, fine dust that has blown in upon the wind, until I reach Salina Cruz, a strange seaside town, full of arcades, and empty hotels and a disconcerting mixture of shiny tackiness and neglect. It reminds me of English seaside towns. But maybe this says more about me than the place. I walk the streets until I find a *locutorio* and sit in front of a computer.

I read the email from Lucía twice.

like I told you, i forgave Fabi, we have been talking about our whole situation. we went back to the source.... and looking back we discoverd that both of us stopped nursering our relationship and basically we made the same mistakes... we'd like to start over again. i know it's too fast... but actually we are getting engaged..

maybe. i am stupid..... but i realized that... i want to be with him... we had problems... and sometimes i felt like.. love was gone!!!.. we have always had a very special connection.... and now after all these situations... i feel like.... I love him

i'm very sorry if i caused you troubles... i felt very confused about all, including you!!!! because you have been so nice to me... and understanding... i really wish you can forgive me and we can keep our friendship... and in touch.....

por favor perdonameeeee!!!!!!!!!!!!!!

...

We write again. For the next few hours. I say she has done nothing wrong, that I will remember her with fondness. We agree to keep in contact, though as I write I doubt we will. And at last she sends me a message to which I don't reply. I read it once more, before the computer times out.

...

yes.... she writes *i'll bother you ...... sometimes.....*
love ..... lucía XXXXXX

...

Strange, that these words will always be there. This exchange, each reply, each measured and unmeasured word. That they will always be there, the way they were written at the time, the same feelings perceptible within them, unchanged, unwithered. They will be in any place at any time, behind only a password and a click, along with everything else. Every job application, every bank statement, every correspondence, personal or otherwise, and somehow immortal; long after my death they will be there, undecayed, for there is nothing to decay.

The words I read now will not be kept, like a letter, in a box, in some corner of a room, or in a drawer, or a cupboard, treasured, or cherished in secret. With a letter, each time, the passing of time is noticed; the paper becomes more crinkled, yellowed, imperceptibly thinner, smoother where it has been thumbed, the ink more faded. Though for years it will be there, and though its very existence, its apparent permanence, owes itself to the importance placed upon it, it will, each time, be changed. A letter is a moment in time; more than a photo, it is the photographed itself, for its life continues after the name is signed and the envelope is sealed; it wilts, and thins and ages. And each time it is taken out to be read, it is another letter; there is more distance between the writing and the reading of it. And though the distance may provoke in the reader more heightened or dimmer feeling, it is a distance which is visible in the letter itself.

But the words that I am reading now will always be the same. If in some years, I choose to scroll down the long stagnant inbox of my email, and open something posted from a half-forgotten time, the words will be there just the same as they are now, unaltered and bright upon the screen. As though they could have been written yesterday, or as if I were receiving them for the first time once again. Though, the feeling, I hope will be different. The distance, though not visible in the slow decay of the page, will be there in the reader, in me.

...

I give up on my search for a map of Central America and sit on a bench in the main square of Tapachula, close to the Guatemalan border. I sit, half-reading, half-watching-passers-by. It is another plaza, with trees, and fountains and people selling balloons and street food; *horchata, tacos* and *churros*.

A man comes over, stops in front of me and asks me where I'm from. His name is Juan Jose. He is from Guatemala and he switches to good English upon finding out where I'm from.

"Fifteen years ago, I caught a bus from Guatemala to the USA," Juan Jose tells me. "I paid the driver $350 to hide me and he took me over the border to California. I spent eight years there, working as a janitor."

"And," I ask. "How was it?"

"I liked it for the time," he says. "California has really good time."

"Weather?"

"Sorry, weather," he smiles. "If you don't use it, language goes. Now I don't use it so much. I work as a driver on the *colectivo* buses."

I ask him about the journey to the States, about his family, about his decision to come home, but he talks mostly about his duties as a janitor; strange monotonous details to recall after seven years. About brushing, and mending shelves, and hanging doors. He talks about cleaning and being in charge of keeping the field cut. And he talks about locking up at night and opening in the morning. I sit there for twenty minutes listening to the daily routines of a janitor. There is something hypnotic about the rhythm of his words, like the steady turning over of daily tasks, comforting and safe, and perhaps after all this time more memorable than paying coyotes to be smuggled across the border. Are these the stories he will tell his children of America? Will they too, want to go?

I tell Juan Jose where I am going and mention that I haven't found a map yet. He takes a piece of paper and draws me what he says are directions. A line goes, from a circle which he labels Tapachula, right, to a circle that he labels Guatemala. He follows the same trajectory to his town, Zacapa, before turning down the page linking four more circles; El Salvador, Honduras, Nicaragua and Costa Rica. It is almost worse than useless, but I thank him as though without it, I'd be lost.

...

The next day I cross the border. I have been in Mexico for three months. It feels like longer.

Left: Baja California **Right:** Día de los Muertos, Puebla

Clockwise from top-left: Baja California - Playa Santispac – Sunset, Baja California – Volcán Toluca – Elvia and Adam – Taxco – Refugio, Volcán Toluca – Near playa Santispac

Guatemala

25th November – 28th November, 2010

Guatemala feels like a country that has been squeezed together; pushed into the lowlands by the central volcanoes and pressed together by its borders on either side like a belt which doesn't quite fit. The roads are full of cars, and bikes and people walking, and a constant busy noise. To my left a volcano's peak is obscured by factory smoke. Everything feels unfamiliar; the number plates and the signs and the wooden stalls by the roadside.

I reach the first town, Coatepeque. A market has taken over the streets and I get off my bike, push through the throngs of people and the clamouring noise. Faces turn towards me as I look around in search of somewhere to sleep. There are no stalls. No tables, or chairs. But women sit, their hair in tight black plaits, by woven baskets full of vegetables and beans and things I can't identify. I feel people brush past me and I reach down into my pocket to check the small wad of Quetzals I changed at the border is still there. It is, though I have only a vague idea of its worth; I feel like I will leave this country before I get a hold on it. To the left a dirty sign, hanging over a concrete doorway, reads *hospedaje*. I push my way through the crowds, saying sorry to everyone and smiling apologetically, pay what seems a ridiculously small amount, even for the bare concrete room to which I'm shown, and crash exhausted on the bed. Metal springs dig, lovingly into my bones, and the noise still burbles in the street below.

Sweat drips down my neck, tickles and dries in my hair, runs, and soaks into the bedsheets, not damp, but wet now, into the mattress to mix with the sweat and other excretions of many other hundreds. Perhaps that is the difference between expensive hotels and hotels that cost less that a bunch of bananas and a plate of rice; the way your predecessors are disguised. The more expensive the room, the more it seems that it has only ever been you; the linen taut and fresh and clean, the absence of hair, of stains. In cheap hotels, the beds feel warm from bodies still. The smell of others' sleep, of others' sweat and sex, still dimly perceived, if not there truly then there in spirit, like the lingering of a hundred ghosts, stagnant in the tropical heat, and writhing on the concrete floor. Doors slam, and outside it is suddenly night. I turn on the bare light bulb that flickers above me, swinging with the thud of footsteps on the ceiling.

For some reason, boredom perhaps or the tickling heat, I take a razor and shave the hair off two sides of my head, leaving a line, a rough mohican, down the middle. It is a mistake I feel, even as I'm doing it, but once the first hair falls away, to reveal the white unsuntouched skin it is too late, and I look at myself in the dirty, mottled mirror of the bathroom, with light regret. I take a bucket and spool a cold stream of water over myself and the singular clump of hair remaining falls dark and wet over my face, and I do not look like me.

...

The next day, I stop at midday. I drag my bike into the shade of a wooden roof, standing on four pillars. The sizzling of barbequed meat sputters out its fat in small explosions and bursts on hot charcoal. It is hot today, like every day in the low-lying tropics; the sun a constant nagging bore. A jealous and fearful lover, it loosens its grip only in the few small hours of the morning, between four and six, before waking again, and raging. I order churrasco, which is the only thing there is to order and the girl talks to me about the colour of my eyes, avoiding, or not noticing my ridiculous haircut. It is strange what draws attention, inquisitive glances, or hidden stares. Sometimes I know it must be the colour of my skin, or an overloaded bike, clothes bought in another country, or a paperback book. Sometimes I realise that it must just be my movements, the ingrained gestures that I make before I even speak, so hard to shake and so betraying of my foreignness, that catch the eye and call for second glances like a dancer, out of sync on stage.

I eat, hungry but slow. Each moment under the cooler shade runs by faster than the turning of pedals in the constant heat of the sun. I pay for the food and Coca-Cola, and say goodbye. I still have most of the money I changed at the border; steak, beans, rice and Coca-Cola for less than three dollars. I am rich with my fifteen dollars a day. Perhaps that is why the girl mentioned my eyes and not my haircut.

The road winds on, flat, until I reach Cotzumalguapa, the name of the town like two languages squashed together, refusing to entwine, to give in to the other, stubbornly holding their ground.

I ask, as always, for a cheap hotel, the cheapest hotel. Even with my newfound wealth there are habits which don't die easily. I am pointed up the street to an *hospedaje*; it costs less than my midday meal to stay, and is worth less. The walls and floor are bare wet concrete, and a worrying open gutter runs around the square of rooms, which sit facing each other. There is the smell of sweat and wet dirt, of cheap, strong tobacco smoke and tired men. Often cheap hotels are full of whores, but I don't think the men here could afford a whore between them. They are workers, it seems. *Campesinos.* I do not know what they do, but I imagine they do it for next to nothing and are not paying 25 quetzals a night to stay here. They look at me as I push my bike around the courtyard, as I push my toy, I suppose. They look at me tiredly, without interest and without unkindness. I wouldn't blame them if they robbed me, but they do not. Later, a man, my neighbour, offers me a cigarette as I am sitting on a concrete step, my feet on the floor and dirty water running along the gutter beneath. I take it and he asks if I like reading, pointing to my book. He passes me a lighter and the smoke rises, bitter in my mouth, and welcome. He has been here for four weeks, and he has made his tiny room a simple home; a photograph, a candle and a few things stuck on the concrete walls. He is from a nearby village, he says. He is working, but I do not understand what it is that he is doing, and he does not seem concerned enough that I understand to explain it in simpler terms. Just working, he says, and we sit quietly for a while, the tobacco's scent invading the rooms behind.

Before we go to bed, he asks if I have a fan with me, and he points at the one he has bought, whirring the hot and stagnant air around his room. I shake my head and he laughs at me.

"*Pues, ya verá,*" he says, "*le va a costar mucho pegar un ojo esta noche.*" And he is right, I do not manage to sleep until the jealous sun loosens its grip at about four thirty am.

El Salvador

28th November – 1st December, 2010

A day later, I cross the border into El Salvador. Already, it seems these small Central American countries will pass by before I get to know them or feel comfortable; two or three days cycling along a busy road, eating fried bread and cheese, two or three cheap hotels, a couple of small conversations, and the country will be gone. Perhaps, I will cycle across a country without even talking to anyone.

I still do not have a map. I stop early in Sonsonate to look for one, but the search again is fruitless. None of the shops are open, nor the internet cafés. Though the streets hum with people and dirt and the stench of things rotting, and outside the closed and shuttered shops, market stalls stand. I look hopefully at the stalls, but there is nothing that isn't plastic and, for what I can make out, useless. I go back to my room. Without a map, tomorrow, I will have to follow the road to San Salvador.

...

The run into the city is the same. Pot-holed roads, busy and fast, sliding down the mountainsides, and the plastic signs of Burger King and McDonalds, like toy flags stuck into any patch of land in which there are rich, successful, fat people.

Three lanes of traffic at a complete standstill. Shards of light, solid and swirling, black and silver fumes. Police blow whistles, and horns rupture further the restless unquiet, as though in an effort to disperse the vehicles with noise alone.

By the time I have weaved through the cars, to the centre of San Salvador, it is three o´clock. A stagnant, sticky hour, the sun´s heat reaching its climax. At three o'clock street-vendors can gauge whether they have enough money in their pockets, and, with the knowledge that there are less than three hours to change fortunes, the noise becomes a bawling; a cacophony of products and prices, screamed into the hot and seething air.

A bus with a flat tyre blocks the last remaining lane, the cause of the gridlock. The rest of the road has been invaded by people trying to make money.

Clothes stalls. Christmas decoration stalls. Fruit and vegetable stalls. Meat and fish. People carry their wares on shoulders yelling into the crowds. Dresses $3!! Brooms $1.25!! Old ladies sit in front of baskets of bread, waving plastic bags, tied to sticks, to keep away the flies. Young girls sit in front of open bags of chicken´s feet, and heads, and other limbs, doing nothing about the flies taking meagre bites from the warm, wet flesh and defecating on it.

Bootleg CDs and DVDs, porn magazines and cooking magazines, TV times and crossword puzzles. Fake Puma, Nike and Quiksilver. Men with missing limbs, and women with babies strapped to their breasts, with hands outstretched, and eyes that turn. Pleading. Desperate. Gone.

The sound of sizzling oil comes from somewhere. The sound is indistinguishable from that of running, inconstantly trickling water, but the scent of *pupusas* frying, and the melting cheese within them, rises sweet and strong, amongst the pungent smell of rotting meat and discarded fish bones lying on the floor, and the acrid sweet-sick smell of ripened fruit, decomposing in the sun.

Whole rows of stalls selling nothing but coconuts, nothing but tomatoes, or cucumbers. And Barcelona football shirts are everywhere. In downtown San Salvador it seems that about 10% of the population wear Barcelona shirts. In the crowded throbbing streets, it would appear as if match day had arrived, and the stadium were drawing close, if only there were some consensus in direction amongst the blue and burgundy stripes.

Boys in T-shirts, black with dirty oil, crawl out from under the bus. Huge metal wrenches are passed in sweating urgency as horns sound their disapproval. On the other side of the bus, the street is empty of vehicles, full of people, and I glance down side streets, hoping to catch a glimpse of a hotel or *hospedaje*.

'*Feliz Noche*,' says the sign. Happy Night. Without even the plural to suggest that one might return. Certainly, the iron-barred gate, and the heavy padlock do not look happy. Nor the razor wire, spiralling around the roof. Nor, when the padlock is unlocked and the gate squealed open, is there a happy face to greet me. The proprietor, if that is what he is, has the face of a nasty, underfed rodent, thick black whiskers, glaring eyes, a twisted unmovable scowl. He folds his arms against a dirty, stained vest, that used to be white, and tilts his chin back to look at me.

He pauses for such a long time when I ask him how much it is per night, that I am left in the silence wondering whether he is simply not used to calculating the cost for a whole night, or if he's slowly trying to work out how much money he can squeeze out of me. Both, perhaps. $10. I'm too tired to argue.

I have to be out by 8am. This must be a peak time for the establishment I realise, and I smile at the sense that makes as he shows me to my room.

The walls in the bathroom don't reach the ceiling, and negotiations from next door filter through the gaps. I can't understand what the man is asking for, only that it's going to cost him $3.50 extra. Everything I can imagine makes the room seem even more expensive than it did before, and I leave to find some food before they stop talking.

In the dusk, her face is painted, an unwell white. So shudders run, to think that what it hides could appear worse, more startling and desperate, more unwell, than the mask itself - shining almost, glowing and sick, against darker surrounds - and out of it, stare those cold brown eyes.

Hands cling now to my hand, and my arm, cold in the heat of everything else. But moist, as though waking in cold nightmarish sweat. Though the eyes stare, not feverish, but business like, with something in them that may be approaching cruelty, so that when the proposition comes, not in the teasing, coquettish language of a whore, but in her other language, in that simple need to be understood - "*para llevar*" she says, with the eyes still cold and staring, and the hands gripping tighter still, "to take away" she says - so that when the proposition comes, the subsequent refusal owes nothing to a distanced consideration of morality, but, rather, to an instinctive biological repulsion and the need to tear myself away.

On the streets around my hotel, people lie on cardboard boxes. A man, face down, half on the road, half on the pavement, lets a thick string of dribble fall, from grey lips to the floor. A scream echoes then, around the darkened streets and brakes squeal in the distance. Footsteps patter. Stop. Run. And I walk, head hung to the floor.

Men stagger past me and faces lose their features in the slowly surrendering dusk. I reach the hotel. The metal gate clanks open. The bolt slides across, and the shadow of razor wire shudders on the wall. 8am, I think, is not too soon.

…

In the morning the city has changed. I leave, before things steeped in colour shine, in the grey light, when the air is cool, long before the obligatory 8am. People make their way to work, stalls are closed. A few *Pupuserías,* sell fried dough, stuffed with beans and cheese. No prostitutes ply their trade on the street and the men passed out on the pavements have gone. It even seems, though I cannot be sure, that some of the rubbish has been cleared away.

I ride until the noise has gone and the sky glints silver off the lakes. Heat sears, and the mountains breathe, their backs thick green. Though there is no quiet, here on the busy road, I imagine the other sounds on the mountainsides; the sounds of birds and insects, the croaking and hissing of reptiles, the rustle of leaves and the deep wet soggy mulch of the ground. There is a whole country here that I am rushing through, that I will not see, that I will not give a chance. By the time the sun goes down I am in San Miguel, in the east of the country, just sixty kilometres from the Honduran border.

...

I can make out from what was sold to me as a map, but is really just an outline of Central American countries for children, that I will pass through only the southern part of Honduras, before entering Nicaragua, rounding, or sneaking across, the underside of the country poised like a bent knee, its half Nicaraguan patella jutting out into the Caribbean. Nothing more is distinguishable. No cities, no roads, no trace of mountains, or hills.

Honduras

1st December – 3rd December, 2010

The road in Honduras is almost empty. A few wooden houses dot the green landscape and people slouch into hammocks; dead, heavy weights in the stifling shade. Occasionally a bicycle passes, a man waves, or children walk with sticks and other found things. They laugh and shout after me, until again the road is quiet. I feel happy to be in this forgotten corner of the world.

I stop to piss by the side of the deserted road. I lean my bike against a pole and walk towards a small cliff, think nothing of the rustling in the vegetation. It is the echo of my footsteps perhaps, in the long dry grass, the tiny scurry of small and frightened animals. I glance back at the empty road, and undo my zip to piss against the dry and crumbling wall, but stop. A snake slides between the blades below, smooth and silent past my frozen feet. The snake slithers up the cliff in front of me, yellow and dark brown stripes running down its body, glimmering and shifting like a mirage with the contractions of its body and I stand there, unable to piss and unable to do up my fly. The snake's head reaches eye level, and this is the moment it will strike, I think, at the jugular, though I know nothing about snakes, and the head has moved higher, and I stare straight ahead, not daring to look up, until at last its tail follows the trail of the head and with a flick it is gone from my field of vision. Still, I stare straight ahead, until I'm sure it must have gone, and without looking up, walk back to my bike, checking each step now, before placing my foot and flattening the grass.

I cycle along the quiet road until I reach Nacaome. The town is peaceful in the heavy shade of evening. Five cafés in the centre all sell fried chicken and share enough customers for just one café between them. I choose one, without thinking, and sit down to eat the same thing that is being eaten in all the other cafés in town, before walking back to a leafy, cheap *hospedaje*.

I talk and smoke cigarettes with the owners until midnight. It is a slow and limited conversation, full of long silences and small, sweet cups of coffee, but it is welcome, and it makes me happy. The bells of a church ring in the background and the streets of San Salvador seem very far away.

...

The next day I wake early and eat breakfast before eight; a fried salty egg, beans, cheese, fried chicken in batter, fried bananas and tortillas. I leave sleepy Nacaome as the air grows warm again. A family crosses a bridge into town, piled on a single, rickety bicycle. A small naked girl stands up in the basket, clinging onto the sides, while her mother sits across the rusty frame. The father's legs rotate slowly and awkwardly around his wife and over the back wheel the elder daughter sits and waves.

...

A wall of mountains rises unexpectedly between me and Nicaragua, and though they appear as an impenetrable wall, I hope against logic that the road will cut through a deep unseen valley, or a tunnel. Thirty kilometres later though I am still climbing and I curse the cigarettes and coffee of the night before and I feel my body rattle, my breathing laboured. After all this time, why is it still hard? My body is no more what I want it to be than before I left. The pedals turn with no less effort. Fat gathers above my hips. My thighs ache most nights. Sometimes there are shooting pains in my knees. It is no real suffering. No suffering at all. They are happy, pleasing twinges, dull and welcome pains. But they note my limitations. They remind me that my potential is finite. And that inhibits dreams.

As I reach 1000 metres the air seems just as hot as in the shallow rolling hills below. I look across the valley; from the brittle dry grass and steep slopes across an empty landscape to the pale pastel blues of distant hills. With the sun hanging almost always above, I cannot work out which way is north. The twists and turns of the road have disoriented me and, with no map, I do not know whether what I am gazing upon are the hills and distant mountains of Honduras or Nicaragua.

Nicaragua

3rd December – 12th December, 2010

Perhaps it is easier to like a country when the ground falls down towards it, when the hills tumble effortlessly onto its open plains and volcanoes lie, smoky grey and sleeping on the horizon.

I cycle across the north-western corner of Nicaragua, until I reach León. Whitewashed colonial buildings stand scuffed, with blackened edges, worn old walls, charmingly crumbling into the streets. And a street market fills the cobbled streets with colour.

I pull my bike into a hostel. For the first time since Mexico, I've found somewhere I want to rest.

...

Sun lit shafts of dust swirl into the room and light glows in cracks around the heavy door. Mosquitos fly, slow and heavy with my blood, and I open my eyes to their whine and a half-empty bottle of £2 rum, lying on a concrete floor. I seek revenge for the night, but it is over zealous, cruel. Beyond an eye for an eye. I squash and squelch and tear the mosquitos into red blotches on my hot wet skin. I scrunch their black bodies, roll them into tiny black and squidgy balls. I hold their legs and tear their wings.

I take a bucket of cold water, though I know it must be the same temperature as everything else in this room; the temperature of blood it seems. Always, hot and cloying and draining the body of liquid and horrible for a hangover. Perhaps it is the heat that draws out cruelty. I look over the mess covering my room and at the bike I have to ride.

Later, under the midday sun, a horse lies, dead. On one side, smooth, bare ribs stick out towards the sky. The shrivelled black heads of vultures jostle for meat. Wings flare up and two pairs of talons grapple and scratch. There is half a horse left, but already, reason to fight. The horse's head turns away, nonchalant, as though uninterested by the score of vultures feasting on its flesh.

Behind the vultures, green grass glistens, wet, and in the distance the faded silhouette of a volcano dims the sky. I stop for lunch at a wooden shack, a single stove connected to a gas canister. Chicken, rice and beans.

The fields dissolve into the dust and noise of a city; the market places and three-lane streets, new glass buildings and shining cars. A public park lies covered in make-shift shelters; corrugated iron sheets, branches of trees and black plastic bags stretched taut. The structures are packed so tightly that there is barely enough room to walk between them. There are no doors built into the shelters nearest to the road, but inhabitants of the settlement come and go, through the gaps in plastic-bag walls. It is difficult to see the size of this make-shift shanty town. Nor is the age of the community clear; it lacks those establishing materials, bricks and cement, but these materials are expensive. It may have been erected yesterday, only the paths are worn to mud between the shelters and the rubbish seems to have become a part of the ground. It is too vast, also, to have grown recently. Rusty corrugated iron seems to be the greatest investment on display, worth sadly more than the time it has taken to construct the camp. All those hours and days of time that is worth no money; their time, their skills worth so much less than mine; free almost. I wonder how long the settlement will be allowed to stay as two children of about five or six years old run past an old man sat smoking in a doorway, which has no door.

I cycle through Managua, the capital city of Nicaragua, home to a third of the country's population, in less than 2 hours. The dust and noise dissolve into fields once again.

Now shadows lengthen, fade and disappear. Only a faint glow remains above the western horizon and on the outskirts of Masaya, I stop and ask a man at the side of the road for directions. He replies in an American accent, and tells me to follow him to his home.

There is a stable outside Bisma's house. Two horses chewing straw. Dogs in the yard. Machinery everywhere. Three trucks are parked together and outside the gate another pulls up. The working day comes to an end.

"That," he says, pointing at one of the trucks, "is the one I drove from LA. That's where it started and now I have five."

He tells me that he spent five years working in the States. With the money he managed to save he bought a truck and started a transportation business. He is the first person I have met who has brought something other than stories back from the US.

The drivers get out of the trucks. Cold beers appear from inside, and we sit outside on rocking chairs. Bisma hands me a cigarette and the next few hours are spent chain smoking, talking and drinking beer.

"*Vete a por más cerveza,*" he says to his friend, handing him a roll of notes. "*Y algo pa' fumar, más cigarrillos también.*"

A few minutes later his friend returns with more cigarettes and beer, and it is late before the cycle ends.

The thick black night of the tropics closes in and I feel the happy weight of the beer; not drunk, but not sober enough to worry about how much Bisma has drunk as we get into his car. If the thought does cross my mind, then I do not mention it; it is a display of ingratitude to question someone's sobriety and ability to drive a car. I would rather not be rude. And for a moment I wonder about how many of those people killed in the passenger seat of a car hesitate, before getting in, only to keep silent, preferring to take the risk of dying than that of upsetting a friend or a host or a stranger, and lost besides in their own untroubled tipsiness. The worry, if it is there at all, does not trouble me as the road rolls underneath us, shining under the headlights, and the darkness is broken here and there with the lights of a house, until a few minutes later we reach the town.

We pull up and are welcomed into Jose's house, full of people and noise; music and happy talking and the smells of barbequed pork, sizzling and spitting on the *parrilla*. Jose welcomes me into his house as if I were a friend, his eyes shining through his glasses, and as we step inside Bisma turns to me. "This is Nicaragua."

We sit drinking golden rum, and eating crispy, salty plantains, and pork and lightly spiced rice. It is the town's festival, and we sit in a room at midnight, full of people, music blaring now from the street as well as inside, that constant moving music, which no one can hear with sadness and children drop their bikes outside and run in to drink juice and eat plantain crisps, and run out again to play. There is such a closeness between the people, and an openness towards me, towards a stranger, and generosity, and it reminds me briefly as Jose fills my glass with rum, of the deep sincere hospitality of Russia, or Ukraine.

We are the last to leave, full and drunk; the streets are quiet, and the darkness cool.

"Come back tomorrow, stay for a few days," says José, showing us out.

"I can't," I tell him. "I'm meeting my dad in Costa Rica." It's a conversation we had only an hour or so ago.

"Ahh, Costa Rica. Tell your dad to come here. He would be very welcome."

Costa Rica

12th December 2010 – 11th January 2011

I cycle out to the expensive hotel near the airport and wait in the lobby. The sofa is soft and expensive. I don't lean back on it, but sit on the edge, half-reading. I hug my dad when I see him. It has been almost comfortable to hug him since I moved out and the infrequency of our meetings calls for it. I feel that neither of us wants to hug, but it is less awkward than saying that, so I hug him briefly, knowing that we won't have to do it again for another three weeks when he leaves. I ask him how he is and he asks me how I am and I am a son again. I am on holiday with my dad.

We take a small aeroplane to the outskirts of Corcovado National park and stay in a lodge in the shade of the forest. We sit in the evening drinking coffee or wine and sharing a meal, and take excursions into the park during the day, or walk, guided, through the forest at night, the light of an expertly held torch picking out vivid green snakes, and tiny frogs. My dad is the same. He talks about his work. There is more that he doesn't say than he does. I love him. He loves me. But there is something that will stop us from saying that. It is not something we say. I'm proud of you, he might say. I really appreciate everything you've done for me, I might say. These words are okay. If, one time, he says it, he will say *we*, your mother and I, *we* love you. The I is there, it is in the we, but I would not want him to say it, and so he doesn't.

Though the sky threatens rain, I take one of the kayaks up the stream which runs into the sea, round a sand bank, and disappears into the forest, engorged twice a day by the tide.

The patter of rain begins; dimples and small splashes on the thick brown water. From the stream, I can hear the crashing of waves. A grey bank of clouds on the horizon, above the sea. The glow of a burning sun, barely perceptible through a grey and tearful mist.

Mangroves dip moist hands, unseen, beneath the murky depths. Barnacles cling to them. Sometimes I feel their scratch on the underside of the kayak. Along the branches hermit crabs scurry. Beady black eyes like demented puppets stare out of the shells. Far away, a howler monkey calls.

The rain falls, heavier now, and the ruptured water sings. Tiny explosions on the surface at first, and then full soaking sheets, gushing from all sides. A heron takes flight. To shelter.

I am as wet as I think you can get, so I carry on; past the gentle curves and banks of sand, the full and bustling trees.

The darkened sky flashes, a sheet of electric blue. And then, not a crack of thunder far away, but a noise that swallows me, a sky that's full of sound.

Then. As the raindrops lose their force, and thin strands of sunlight find water to make shine, something happens. I see something I have never seen before. Perhaps will never see again. But I know exactly what it is. It is a Basilisk. A Jesus Christ lizard.

I saw a picture of one once in a National Geographic. I remember the fragile drops of water, caught like frozen glass in the air. And the feet stretched wide, lightly catching the river's surface, muscles taut and a body bursting with speed, even in the motionless shot. A blurry green background, and each successive step, miraculously made.

In real life you don't see any of these things. Just a very fast lizard running across a stream, quite impossibly, before your eyes. No individual movement discernible from the next. A blur. And yet, the flash across my sight is there, and will be there, I know, forever.

...

I say goodbye to my dad. He pays for an extra night in the hotel for me, which costs what I would usually spend in twelve days, and pays for breakfast which costs what I would usually spend in two, and as he flies away something leaves me too. Grounding, perhaps. A link to myself. Something which makes me me and keeps me myself. Perhaps, we are only who we are because of those constant people, reminding us, letting us know we have to meet their expectations. Too strange, not to know a man. Too strange, for a man to be quiet one day, and loud and boisterous the next, melancholic and serious, then light and uncaring. We need to know who we are, so that other people can place us; can say 'him – he is like this – if you do that, that is what he'll do'. And as my dad flies away, that is what is gone, not just my dad, but an anchor. Maybe I am wrong. Maybe you are only yourself when you are alone; much less constant, kaleidoscopic in character; darker and unsafe, bereft of moorings and swept out of the harbour, to the wild and twisting sea.

I sleep uncomfortable broken sleep on the too soft bed in the too clean quilts; the air outside too hot and inside too cold. I watch international television and don't read. In the morning I can't eat the breakfast as I would like; the hour too early, and my stomach unslept. The pastries and fruit and coffee and fruit juice and sausages and bacon and eggs are there and I know that in two or three days' time I will be dreaming of them, but now it goes almost to waste. I wrap two pastries in a paper napkin and load my bike for the first time in weeks, and cycle out as the warm air soaks into my skin.

...

Now, left only with what man has made, Costa Rica becomes dull. Golf courses, gated resorts, restaurants that look like they've been taken off the set of a sterile TV movie; a retirement village for the USA, a place for people to die in the warm. My bike still moves towards Panama, though my legs turn, apathetic. I ride past gates which say things like *Exclusive Wellness Retirement Community* or *Exclusive Golf and Ocean Community*, and for a moment I am angry, and then I am tired again. The last night in Costa Rica I stop in Ciudad Neily, put my tent up at a hostel and wake up under a table in the bar.

Panama

11th January – 23rd January, 2011

"Don't go down there," the man says. "There are bad people that way." He waves his arms. "*Por allí, mejor que no, eh! Que hay mucha mala gente.*"

The man looks drenched in *mala gente*. He looks like *mala gente* have brushed against his skin like sandpaper and got in behind his eyes. Something about the way he looks at me says he has been here forever. He seems beyond kindness. He seems to be stopping me from going down the street, because it is easier, because this way I won't be killed or robbed by the *mala gente*, and that is easier. A woman comes across to join him in his argument and points back toward the centre of Panama City. *Turistas*, she says pointing – that's where the tourists go, not here. And I say thank you, turn my bike around, and look for a hostel.

...

I find a boat leaving for Cartagena in five days and go to take out 100 dollars from a cash machine to pay for the deposit. Outside it is hot and dirty. So many clothes shops, and stalls, and people everywhere, and children wandering directionless. So much poverty and so much unnecessary shit for sale; useless, plastic things which will break with one use, or two. I feel the wad of notes in my pocket nervously, and I know I shouldn't, but I go into a bar. I order a beer; it is cold and tastes strong, and I order another; pay a dollar for each, and leave. The next bar is dirtier; a swinging wooden door and a curtain, and as I enter everyone at the bar looks up for a moment, looks down. There is a television showing hard-core pornography behind the bar, and the women are conspicuous for their small number and the way they are dressed. For the way they drink slowly from tiny bottles of beer latched onto men and the way they laugh unnaturally. Two beers ago I would have left, but I am sat here now, full of courage, and I put it down to fateful experience and get another beer. The man beside me strikes up conversation, and we talk until we are on the other side of three more beers, and he invites me to a long shot of rum that the barman brings over, and this is the moment I should leave. But my mortality has left me, with all my fear. And time swims so comfortably and happy in this dirty, grimy bar, with its cheap dirt beer, and ejaculating penises on the walls, and old whores. I finish the rum, the bite of it catching in my throat, and get another beer, for myself and my passing friend. And when the girl comes over we get her a drink, which is twice as much as ours and half the size, and the man gestures to the back room, but I shake my head, and we stay at the bar, until, when I leave I am staggering, and the night has come. In the dark, the faces have changed, but if they are the faces of *mala gente* I do not see them. Already, I am not inside myself; and I do not know if there is another bar or two, but when I am awake again it is in the dark and unlit corner of a street, and there is no-one around. My pockets have been cut open, the money removed. I feel around though to find my bank card is still there, and my limbs intact; good, kind, merciful thieves. I look down, and I wonder if I pissed myself before or after I was robbed. Or perhaps robbed is too strong a word – before they took what was lying there gifted on the street, in a dangerous city, and didn't take all that was gifted. I can't remember a thing, but I know I have been lucky. And I think of my stupid self, drifting on the sea, and my father and my mother, to keep me to myself, and I tell myself, staggering back cold, through the end of night, that the next continent will be different and soon I will be changed.

...

I take the boat and stop at the San Blas Islands. The archipelago barely rises above the sea, the islands crammed to the edge with wooden huts and tangled ropes, boats and rubbish, children's joyful cries. I watch as a small boy swims up to a bird, bobbing on the water. The boy, beneath the surface, takes it in one swoop; a hunter, he swims with it back to the island and holds it by the tips of the wings and lets it hang, alive. The boy smiles a big white smile and we say goodbye and leave to another island.

South America

Colombia

23rd January – 17th March 2011

When dawn wakes us on the fifth day, the boat is resting in the harbour at Cartagena. I uncover my bike, take off the plastic sheet, and again load the panniers as the weight sinks onto the wooden planks below and they give into the water. I roll the bike onto solid land. From here, it is land until Tierra del Fuego, until the end of my journey. I push my bike into town.

...

The rolling hills of northern Colombia lean into the sun. Heat rises from the ground, beats down from the sky and buffaloes wallow in mud to their shoulders. Cows huddle around the trunks of trees, the intermittent shadows of leaves dappled on their hides.

I haven't cycled for almost two weeks, and I haven't learnt and I haven't changed, and drinking too much and sleeping too little haven't helped. Several times I stop, climbing out of the city, slumping into the hot shade. I hang over my bike, and my vision blackens in a faint. My eyes are wide open, but everything is black. I shake myself from the faint and drink water. I know that with time I will feel better, but I wonder when this will change; this dull cycle of dirtying myself in cities until I feel broken and tired and lost, and the days after; the distance, and leaving, and feeling more myself. Still I know, that the first taste will remind me of oblivion, not every time, but sometimes, and I will forget myself and seek it, and maybe one day I will not return.

Small wooden shacks line the dusty roadside, counters piled high with fruit: oranges and pineapples; passion fruit, guavas and tree tomatoes. Cafés serve an abundance of food better suited to the frigid climate of the highlands than the low-lying tropics: mountains of rice; beans and potatoes; slabs of meat and legs of chicken; deep fried empanadas and deep-fried bread. Hot steam and hot smoke under the hot roofs rise, and all I feel is ill for now, for the long day's climb.

I am tired when I reach San Juan Nepomuceno. Too tired to ask coherently about a place to sleep, and much too tired to pronounce the town's name. A man leads me though, to a *residencia*, and its crumbling concrete walls. I thank him, and he nods – cheap, I had said, *barato,* mumbling through my tiredness, and that he has understood.

An iguana swaggers slowly across the yard. Hens scratch in the dust and dried leaves, leading a trail of young. And humming birds hover; blurred wings against the sky, and a falling sun. Inside a moth beats itself against a dirty white wall, and does so until it dies, exhausted, on the floor. I lie down happy. It is comforting to see senselessness in the animal kingdom; it makes me feel less stupid.

...

I rise and leave early the next morning.

The mountainsides grow cool; trees stand soaked in tears, and a drizzle falls slowly, onto the ground below. The sky is that thick mist which keeps everything enshrouded and keeps you guessing at the sun. For hours, it could be dawn; the day one timeless moment, the sky hidden.

As the road climbs higher young boys on BMXs, or old mountain bikes with rusty gears, fly past, clinging to the backs of trucks.

The mist closes further in, and the far-off peaks turn grey and disappear. The glow of the sun falls dull, and then glows not at all, at the bottom of a misty sea.

For the next few hours I climb through clouds as though half-blind; a grey-white blanket, spread thickly all around. The edges of the road, just two metres away, disappear from view.

Small villages announce their presence by sound alone; the monotonous beats of reggaeton fill the wet air and children cry and laugh, unseen. Mothers call to them, "*Ven aqui,*" through the noisy, grey mist "Come!"

As I ride invisibly by, I catch glimpses of unseen gossip. It is like I'm riding blindly through an ocean, and the words are all in snippets and not in my language, and I keep riding past, unseen, as if I were never there; an unseen ghost slipping through these lives.

"*Casi siempre, me dijo, siempre,*" says a woman. "Almost always, he told me. Always."

"Well I saw her," says another voice. *"Pues yo la vi. El otro dia. Bailando."*

"Nooo!" comes the reply, and the long drawn out 'o' sound follows me up the mountain.

Later, in another village, an argument reaches my ears; a woman's voice hard and strained, *"Me molesta señora, me molesta."*

Another woman's voice snaps back, *"Sí, pero dos veces ya! Dos!"* and I imagine two fingers being held up to emphasize the point, *two times already,* but I do not see them.

"Ya, señora. Que se vaya usted de aqui." Leave. Get out of here. Go.

Invisibly, I climb, through the grey and noisy mist.

The sound of something crashing falls quickly through wet leaves. Fast and heavy. A sound to make you jump. Then, the small black outlines of children appear. The youngest might be four, the eldest eight, perhaps. They hold catapults and stones.

I climb slowly towards them. The eldest toys with the elastic, and laughs at the terror in my eyes. He hasn't even turned the thing towards me and already he's won the fight. I haven't been this scared of an eight-year-old since I was eight. The other boys laugh, say something about a gringo that I do not understand, and catapult stones into the trees.

I watch the clouds break apart and the deep green Andes appear. Teasing and misty, the foothills slink out of the ground and rise above the clouds. It is the beginning of the longest mountain range in the world, and I am here. The long steep climbs, each difficult turn and the burning in my legs tell me I'm here. There is happiness in this effort. And with each hard rotation of the pedals I feel better and the bike moves further south.

...

The next day I sit in Santa Rosa de Osos, in a plaza, trying to send a message home. All the bars around here have that expensive looking lighting; strips of colour and silver and black, like the world won't stop until all the grimy, nasty places where old men forget about their wives have disappeared and we're all sitting in lounge bars listening to ambient jazz on a CD that comes with the logo of a coffee chain on the cover. I sit on a bench, half reading, half watching the blinking green lights of my satellite tracker, half looking around. A man comes to a stop in front of me; dribble falling from his mouth, piss soaked jeans, flies undone, mumbling and offering a cigarette, which he pulls from his pocket. I refuse. He rocks back and forward, so unsteady that for a moment I am tempted to push him lightly to see if he will fall. He leans over towards me now, the dribble a thick and stinking pendulum, and I don't want to get its wetness on me, and I don't want to be brushed with those warm wet jeans so I grab my things and walk off. It is a pathetic, saddening sight from the other side and as I turn around to see him slump into the bench, I tell myself that I will not be that man. And what surprises me is that I have to.

...

Medellin comes slowly into sight, the warning of it reaching up into the mountains; traffic and more noise, a widening road. And then it appears, filling the valley floor; the grubbier, corrugated iron reaches of it splash up the mountainsides like exploded shrapnel.

I spend one week in the city, and I am not that man. I meet backpackers at the hostel and we take the metro around the city and visit museums, and watch a football match. We take the cable car up and out of the city until the air is cold, and the city is hidden below, and then we go out to the bars.

...

It is 5am and tomorrow I have said that I will leave Medellin. Or today. This morning.

A Colombian girl I have been talking to gives me her number as she says goodbye and gets in a taxi with her friends. I know I will never call; she's too scarily beautiful for me to talk to sober, and besides I'm leaving tomorrow, no – today, in four hours, three.

The next bus back towards the hostel is at 7.30am – I don't have enough money for a taxi, and the square is almost empty. I'm here, I think, as I begin to walk. I'm here on the other side of the night, conscious of myself and my surroundings, not too drunk, and I start to walk. Even the boys selling chewing gum, cigarettes and cocaine have disappeared.

I walk down the steps and towards the main road that cuts through the city. It is still warm, but the sky starts to spit light rain in the dark and it swirls sparkling and hazy in the streetlamps. It is about three kilometres to the hostel, and the sky that I thought was getting lighter in the east has turned to black again. I walk, following a dirt path that runs along the road, behind a gnarled wire fence. The mud becomes slippery with the rain. It is only me and I start to wonder if this was really a good idea. Even in the day the city has an edge. Bridges cradle crack addicts in their every corner; blood shot eyes dart, and slack jawed mouths blow out thick white smoke as people pass. I had never heard of Pablo Escobar before I came here, but there is something here in the air like ghosts. Or maybe it's in the faces. The faces which say they have nothing to lose; faces that even in the daytime, on a crowded street, send my heart racing.

I am about halfway back, the sky still black, when I see a man crouched up ahead. He is a silhouette only now, about 200 metres away. I look behind. Just me, and a strange kind of mist that tumbles in with the drizzling rain. I keep walking. I wonder if it would be better if I were drunk, really drunk, then there wouldn't be this fear and this racing of my heart. My pace has slowed, and yet my heart pounds in my chest so that it takes up both sides and my body begins to ache, as if I were nearing the summit of a mountain.

The man hasn't moved, and I am closer. 100 metres away. I check my pockets. A hostel key. A few crumpled notes. Enough for the bus, not enough for a taxi. That's it. I left my wallet at the hostel. That's good, I think. And then in the same instant, maybe that's not good. What if it's not enough? What if he doesn't believe me about the wallet?

I'm 50 metres away, and I'm thinking that I should have stayed at the square, even as it emptied of beautiful girls, and people going out, and even as the last bar closed. I think back to when everyone said they were leaving and I said I'd stay and talk with the Colombian girls; not drunk, not drunk enough to hope for anything more than talk, but wanting to stay. And then walking. And all the many choices and all the twists and turns and everything I have ever done, by accident or on purpose, has brought me here, where at the very best, I think, I'm going to be mugged.

I glance back again, there is no-one. The road is empty too. Not that a passing car would help in the dark, early morning, two silhouettes doing whatever our two silhouettes will be doing in a few moments. Or whatever the one, the active, will be doing to the other.

20 metres away. I know I have no fight. It is not in me. I freeze. I wonder even if I will be able to run. What if he has a gun? No use running, if he has a gun.

10 metres now. I can see he is holding a pipe. I can see that he sees me. And as he looks up I see something in his eyes. 2 metres. Kindness.

"Hola," I say, for we're on our own, and we're both looking at each other and it would be stranger not to.

"Hola," he says "¿cómo está? ¿Pa dónde va?"

I point up the road. I can't remember the name of the area where I'm staying. "Por allí, no me acuerdo como se llamaba la zona."

The drizzle has shrunk so small it has ceased to fall. Instead it encircles us and tumults upwards as floating mist, silver and yellow in the light.

"I thought you might rob me," I say, struggling with the r, it comes out throaty and uncomfortable, nothing close to how it's supposed to sound. "Pensaba que me robaría," I say, "but then I saw you." I search for the word for kind, thinking maybe I'm not as sober as I thought. "Usted tiene ojos bondadosos."

"Pues sí," he says, slowly. He takes a baggy and tips some of the white powder into his pipe, and draws on it deeply as he holds the lighter and the white turns to red cinder. He is high, but he speaks slowly and clearly and makes me understand. "I don't know about kind, but I don't steal. I've never stolen. I've got a family, you know. A house. But like this, when I'm like this, they don't want me.

"Tengo una hija," he says. Not sad or happy, just distant. "Tengo una hija. Pero así, así no puedo."

When I leave the man, the sky is a little lighter and headlights fly past through the mist. I look at my watch. I hadn't thought about him stealing my watch. 6am. There's no way I'm leaving today.

...

I follow the same road, south out of the city, a day later. The sky is clear and no-one is sitting on the bank, behind the twisted wire fence. I do not know why I expected to see him, still there, as though his life stood still, merely a prop to my life.

It is too hard to think of all the millions of lives carrying on at the same time. It is hard to think of life all at once; all the visions and thoughts, the accumulative whirring of our consciousness; each day, seven billion days. Each minute, billions of minutes. And I think of all the people that I've met, and their lives. The boys in the Gobi desert, a year and a half older. Dima now, in Alzamai. And I picture Gerna, still looking out from his *dacha* at the flat landscape outside Talovaya, sat on the bench under the tree. Will he be there? And Svetlana and Oksana, and Victor and Igor, Ivan, Ren Hong Chang and Mad Dog Song. I stop before it becomes too much because every thought leads on to another person, and I, just a passing prop in their lives, crisscrossing.

...

I look across the road - now, under construction, only churned up mud - at a wooden door; the worn-out letters of the word *hospedaje*. I am here by mistake. I often feel this way in small towns, but this time I really don't want to be here. It is the wrong town. The wrong turn. I've gone the wrong way.

When the town of Supia came into view it should have been another town, the road I should have taken, 15 kilometres behind me.

It is too late to turn around though and I stand looking across the debris at the uninviting walls, and the closed door of the place I will spend the night. There is something about the place which says you have to be desperate and I stand for a moment, immobile.

A man passes and I ask him about other places to stay.

"You don't want to stay there. You'll be robbed!" he says. And he motions for me to follow. "There's another place," he says. *"Ven conmigo."*

His name is Humberto and he walks me up the road to a hotel where I won't be robbed, and arranges to meet me later.

The road tumbles down a hill in cobblestones and we walk around the plaza, now in evening shadow. We stop to talk to friends of his that we bump into. I hang back, and smile and don't say anything, like a child whose parents are talking with friends. I catch words, not the whole meaning of things, and remember that there was a time like this in my own language, when I couldn't understand the whole, and the conversations of adults seemed magical and out of reach. I wonder if learning this language properly will make the magic disappear, just as adults' conversations lost their mystery.

A group of ladies sit on stools around a shop front, eating from paper plates. When they see Humberto, his kind drawn out face and square smile under a baseball cap, they call him over. He introduces me, and tells me it's the birthday of one of the ladies, and after offering our congratulations we sit down to eat.

"I'm twenty-one," she tells me, in mock confidentiality, and the ensuing laughter proves that the joke travels well, not just across international boundaries, but through decades as well.

At Humberto's house we eat again, the dining room open to the cool night air, and I talk with his family; his wife and two daughters. Catalina, the youngest daughter gives me her email address, and tries to explain why it says Cata la lata in it, because lata is can, I say, why are you a can? But it's a pain, as well, she says, a nuisance, like *dar lata* so Cata la lata. But you're not a pain, I want to say, but don't.

An hour or two later, perhaps tiring of saying everything slowly for my benefit, or sensing that we have very nearly exhausted my vocabulary, Humberto stands up. "Let's go and see Brent," he says "and Marta and her parents. *Brent es Canadiense – es ciclista también."*

We walk down past the main square and turn left, back down the road, past the public swimming pool, almost to the end of the village, and take a left, up a short track to a large wooden house with a veranda sat in a beautiful, quiet garden of blossoming trees. Brent and Marta are there, and they meet us with the openness and warmth of old friends so that it is hard to remember I do not know them. We sit indoors and talk. Twenty-three years ago Brent cycled from Canada to Peru. He had met Humberto in the same way I had; an irreparable puncture, rather than a misguided sense of direction, leading him to Supia, and Humberto had taken him to the same hotel by the plaza to which he has taken me. Brent and Marta met, moved to Canada.

"And now we're here," says Marta, bringing the story to where we are now, so that sitting here, the four of us, becomes a small part of the story too.

Marta tells me that they're living with Marta's parents and when Don Humberto and Doña Muriela arrive, they invite me to stay. They are quiet, kind people. And some part of their nature seems to emanate from them, filling the house like deep soft breathing, flooding out into the garden and the flowers and the trees so that everything seems a part of them.

The house has wooden beams, white walls and high ceilings. Antique clocks hang on the walls, ticking and unticking. Some chime on the hour, and others rotate their hands in silence. Some mechanisms require winding and one is operated by a long rope and two weights - one falling slowly to the floor. There are clocks on tables and clocks standing on the floor. Beautiful, wooden antique clocks, - more clocks than I have ever seen in a house before. One thing is noticeable though; the hands point to each other, or to the sky or floor, at almost as many different angles as there are clocks. Just two, I see, are in accordance, and I feel quite comfortable to be in the house of someone who has such a fascination with clocks, but an apparent disinterest in timekeeping.

...

The next afternoon we go for a walk. A muddy path cuts through the sugar cane, growing above our heads, and a light rain falls from a light grey sky.

Small buildings sit on the hillsides; bamboo skeletons, stuffed with dry sugar cane. Steam escapes from the nearest, and we follow a path towards the sound of voices. "They're making panela," Marta says. "Do you know panela?"

We walk inside the bamboo building, padded soft and warm. A man feeds a fire with dried cane, and in huge metal bowls a golden liquid bubbles and shines, caramel and hot. A furious boiling steam fills the room and the man ladles hot liquid into the cauldron-like bowls. A weak and hazy sunlight shines through the bamboo walls, and the tiny frothy bubbles glow silver now and blinding. On a table, the pressed round cakes of sugar lie in neat rows; deep brown on the white paper, and as we leave the man stops us and gives us a clear plastic bag full of warm and crumbling *panela*.

Back outside, Marta tells me that they used to wrap the crumbs of *panela* in banana leaves when they were children. We pass the bag around and I feel the sugar dissolve warm into my mouth and we follow the track back down through the sugar cane towards the village.

...

That night we go out. We start drinking rum, and we talk in the plaza. Then creme de ron. Then aguardiente. And then I wake up in a bed I've never seen before.

Fuck fuck fuck fuck fuck fuck fuck. Again. Not again. Why have I done it again? The last thing I remember is the ice-cold taste and the aniseed sting of aguardiente, its sugary, sticky sweetness, and laughing, and taking photos, and drunk untroubled talking, and faces which had names for an instant and then the names were gone and new faces had appeared – and all smiling and happy, and then, and then... there's nothing. I could have died and I would not know, the night lost in a black empty nothing. And the worst thing – that I was there, but was not there. So perhaps I wasn't myself, my body usurped, and I worry about what I might have done. I will never get back those few lost hours, them and so many others, when I am there, but not there, standing, or the shell of me standing, but already lost. But why have I done it again? Why here? With the warmth and the kindness of these people?

I am lying in a different bed. It is not the bed I had been shown by Don Humberto. I look around to check I am on my own. The room is empty. I get up.

When I open the door, I think that perhaps I have been kidnapped by the mafia. The brightness of the day glints off perfectly polished black and white tiles. A stone statue stands in the hall, and everything else that my haggard gaze finds seems to be made of glass or marble. I feel my head spin and I stand there, on my own, trying not to fall, scared to touch anything.

I click the door behind me and a uniformed maid appears. She seems unsurprised at my hungover state. And much less surprised at me in general than I am at her. I manage a "*Buenos dias*", but nothing more. What do you say to a maid you have never met in a house you have no memory of entering?

The girl leads me to a glass table, and sits me down, brings me coffee and fruit. I want to ask something, but I have no idea what. Instead I look, still half drunk, but in a generally questioning and puzzled way towards her, as she places a silver pot of sugar in front of me.

"*Salió*" she says. He left. Or she left. No. I don´t think so. He. But I have no idea who. The maid goes out.

I sit there slowly sipping the syrupy black coffee, and eating small pieces of fruit that I half want, until the maid comes back and asks if I want anything else. I smile and say no, thank you. Who are you? I want to say. Where am I? What have I done? Was it a bad thing? Why am I here? But I sit, stuck to the table, and looking at the silver bowls, and the polished marble floor, and wait.

A man comes back a little while later, and reintroduces himself as Diego. He laughs at me and fills me in on the previous evening. He is kind I think, and though he tells me it is not the same as remembering. He laughs at me again, and restores me to the house of Don Humberto and Doña Muriela.

I spend the rest of my time in Supia, conscious, awake and remembering; surrounded by warmth and kindness. We spend a day by the swimming pool with Diego´s friends and family and when we go out again, I drink much less. We ride out, Norely, Marta and Brent, to *Las Piedras* on motorbikes, and sit on the huge boulders under the waterfalls, eating tamales. I ride on the back of Norely`s motorbike to do an interview with telesupia. And we sit in the house full of clocks eating the lovely meals that Doña Muriela makes and spend the evenings on the veranda, drinking coffee, and talking with new friends as the sky grows dark.

It is hard to leave Supia, to roll the 15km back down the hill, to correct one of the most wonderful mistakes I can ever remember making.

...

Pereira. Salento. Armenia. Buga. Cali. Santander. Piendamo. The days have become short. I ride slow, my legs ache with the effort. And I know that it can't just be the hills that kick up and the heat which presses me down, but the drive has somehow left me. The days' rides have shrunk to pitiful, inching distances. I ride for twenty miles and stop. For twenty-five. And worse, I feel exhausted.

...

I reach Popayán four days before my birthday and meet Alex at the hostel. We go for a beer, and the beer becomes two, and three, and the talk with strangers becomes easy, and then the bar is closing and we wonder back too soon, along the darkened streets of Popayán, and everything is quiet and we strike on an idea.

We wave down a passing taxi, open the back door and climb in, without mentioning a place, with the drunken impression that taxi drivers are the all-knowing amoral messengers and carriers of the city, and we know that if we want the night to continue that we're in the right place. I'm not drunk enough though, to just come out with it, and I stammer and splutter over the stupid words. *"No quiero ofenderle, señor,"* I say. What I want to say is that I know your country is much more than this and that I'm just a stupid drunk gringo, but I don't. I say, "I don't want to offend you, *señor*, but I was wondering, we were wondering. *Nos preguntábamos.* If you knew. If you could take us," fuck, just fucking say it, *"donde comprar coca."*

The driver says nothing. True to the drunken expectations I have of all taxi drivers, he doesn't react or seem to pass judgement. He nods almost imperceptibly and takes a left, through the darkened city, and the old white buildings disappear as we drive out of the centre, and I glance at Alex in the back seat, and perhaps he's thinking the same. That we could be going anywhere, and after what we've just asked for, it might not be anywhere good.

About ten minutes later the driver takes another turn through some gates and we approach what looks like a club; the taxi stops outside the door, and we pay the driver and get out. Two security guards step aside and usher us in, without questions and without asking for any money. We walk through a corridor, carpeted towards the double doors and the noise of music, and lights. And the doors fling open.

No one turns. No one cares we are there. All eyes turned to flesh, olive, smooth and young. Maybe it's the lights, but it seems like magazine flesh; flawless and unreal. And I look, but cannot look for long. Something stops me from staring, perhaps it is the company, so the scene just turns to flashes, and the flashes to images that burn on the retina like the sun, and will haunt the next few wakeful days, and jilt and stutter in their brightness like holograms, tilted back and forth. We walk through the asses, and brown nipples and tits, and fake white smiles, and laughs, and round brown buttocks and a haze of smoke, and a girl walks past in high heels and knickers and the white flash of eyes follows me for a minute, until I wonder if it's me that's following her, and untangle my gaze, and in all the corners the nakedness of flesh, and glitzy, stringy sparkly strappy things and nothing is real. I walk past a man, huge and draped in a young girl, or a girl my age, like he's playing some too-obvious part as an extra in a gangster film, and then I am at the bar and I'm buying beers, and a bag of white powder, which is so cheap I get three more and still there is change from the not much money that I have. I walk back to Alex, the plastic bags, all four, rubbing together in my pocket. And I am like an excited school boy as I come back and sit at his side.

"4,000 pesos."

"Do we need to hide it?" he asks.

And I shrug, "Maybe. I don't know."

"Or can we just do it here?"

Maybe, I think. I mean, I just bought it at the bar like the two beers - there can't be those kinds of rules. But we take it to the bathroom, roll up notes, and my body surges, and everything is sharp and even the music, just noise and clatter before, becomes full and wonderful inside my head, and this is not like coke I've had before. And I look at Alex, and his words come crystal clear, like each note and every other sound is a kaleidoscope of noise, and my head feels pumped and full of blood, and a thick, full feeling settles down into me, and why do I feel comfortable in this strip club? Like the boss of it. And I rise up and out and beyond it, and fill my lungs with the air and smoke and sweat, but they're not my lungs, but the bursting crackling flaming lungs of a... of a... We go into the toilet and do another line. And it surges us further than the first. So that when the police come in I barely move.

I hear Alex next to me, over the music, though he can only be speaking in a whisper. "Do you think we're okay?"

And I nod, or I think I nod, but something about me is static. The police walk through the room, and through the flesh, the sweat and the bodies, that surely now I think of it, must be riddled and unclean under the magazine sheer of it all, excreting, stinging, moist and stinking or symptomless disease, but the music doesn't stop, and we don't move. There are six of them stood there, and something fluorescent on their uniforms and their guns and the black boots makes them impossible to miss. Like reality thrown into a dream.

"It's the best place we could be," I say, but I don't know. And if it weren't for the coke, I'd be freaking out, and sweating, and my heartbeat racing, but maybe all of those things are happening, but somehow I'm calm. "I don't reckon anything could happen to us here," I say. I make up. I guess. And the police go. And we do another line. And then outside, the smoke from cigarettes courses into my crackling lungs and my eyes feel heavy, and my whole face tingles with the cold night and burns, and as morning comes, we take a taxi back to the hostel, still with two full bags, and the images are burnt, and don't leave, but don't hold together either so they seem unreal, and two days later I am still awake, on my own, each line not levelling me out, but bringing me right back to the first time, and I lie under the covers of my bed, headphones sending music deep into my head, until at last I know it is enough, and I throw half a bag away, and decide that tomorrow I will leave.

...

There are birds singing outside, before the first light. Perhaps they have grown too impatient to live and are calling for morning. Like it's their job to trigger the turning of the earth, or wake up God to paint light. The bird song sounds like broken glass. Jingling. My hearing's still fucked. No. Not fucked. Sharper. I don't know if I've slept. Most of the night I've just been lying here with my eyes closed, feeling how my body feels heavy, and waiting to feel normal again.

But now, the birds are like knives sharpening. I open my eyes. My face feels white. I put my things together, and leave Popayán as the sun comes up. I climb up and out of the city, and though I feel half unalive, I am grateful for the cold morning air on my face, and the slope slips by, and the days and nights of a racing heart seem to have made the climbing easier. And again, I am cleansing myself after the city.

...

South of Popayán, Colombia turns to the vast stretched mountains of the Andes and the stark and blistering sun. I feel happier as I climb and my body burns with the effort; below the world shrinks until it is toy size, and the road winds around, and around and up to the bare heights that chill and feel frosty at night, and slides down into the valleys where the sun makes the green leaves steam, and the air is sticky and hot. Four days later I ride into Pasto.

I leave the hostel and walk around, looking for something to do. At 9pm the sky is black and under it the grey and empty streets feel post-apocalyptic. Piles of rubbish, and a ghostly quiet; all dogs, drunk beggars and not much else.

On Monday night, it seems that everything is closed. Shops and restaurants shuttered and little hope of anything to eat. I walk around for an hour, until eventually I find a shop; its dim lights cast a miserable yellow puddle onto the street, and a darkened face behind metal bars eyes me with suspicion.

"*¿Qué?*"

"*Comida,*" I say again. "*¿Algo para comer?* Or a place to eat? If you know."

The face leaves the barred windows to rummage around what can barely be described as a shop, and I wait there in the pool of light, like a spotlit gringo waiting to be mugged. The street shuffles and groans in the dark. The man comes back with something that looks like white bread, and dusty lukewarm beer. I hand him a few crinkled notes through the metal bars and walk quickly through the blackened streets, clutching the plastic bag.

The next morning, I go for a walk. The air is fresh, and the sun glints off glass and metal window frames onto the crowded streets. I walk aimlessly about the city and stop to eat empanadas with salsa that tastes of water and drink coffee, which is black, but tastes only of sugar.

The multi-coloured dome of a church catches my eye, winking between the white walls and the blue sky, and I turn a corner towards it.

I stop. There is angry shouting. Two men stand on a truck, piled high with metal poles, and two others shout at them from across the street. I linger on the corner, held as much by a school yard fascination as the fact that other passers-by are waiting too. Not daring to walk down the street, but not walking away either, unwilling to miss a fight. Already a small crowd has gathered on the corner, the voices rise again, each layered on top of the other, until for a moment there is silence.

Then two of the men start running. From behind the truck another man walks, his arm outstretched, holding a gun. And now the small gathered crowd moves as one, turns and runs.

I run too, but I am not made for this scene. I am wearing flip flops, I realise, that don't quite fit, and my toe grips the little plastic stringy thing, and I am holding a plastic carrier bag, so that instead of diving or sprinting away from a gunfight as you might imagine yourself doing, I just kind of slowly and incompetently skip, trying not to let my flip flops fall off. And I follow a woman and her baby through a door, into an open shop, and step inside as a shot is fired.

The sharp boom fills the air. Just one. Real guns don't sound as real as movie guns. We stand; there are four of us in the shop, five if you count the baby, and we look at each other and no-one speaks, and we wait for more shots to be fired, but nothing happens. A little while later we leave, and I walk away from the shop and the church, and back through the crowded streets. The air still fresh, and cold, like mountains.

...

There is a drizzling rain as I leave Pasto. The road climbs, the sky bears down, and my legs keep turning. Tiny crystal dew drops that cling to my hairs turn to slush on my skin, a slippery mixture of rain water and sweat. Before the road falls down the valley towards the river again, the sun breaks through like a hand cleaning a misty window.

I stop at a cafe, and sit in the shade. The sun has grown hot again, and I sit eating the terrible chicken that this part of Colombia is full of, and half read.

The waitress comes over and asks if I like the food and I lie. She has a pretty face, a chipped white tooth and a German surname. She asks me the usual questions, and tells me the usual things, and smiles and laughs nervously and then she says something I don't understand and I stupidly say 'yes' instead of 'I don't understand.'

"*¿Sí?*" she says, and though she seems surprised and yes is obviously the wrong answer. I am too slow to realise and I'm talking again.

"*Sí,*" I say. And somehow, even though I have no idea what I'm saying yes too, the sound that comes out of my mouth seems more decisive than ever.

She looks at me for a moment, walks away, and doesn't talk to me again.

As I leave the café and head south, I am still wondering what it is she could have asked me. 'Yes' is always the right answer. Who asks something they want you to say 'no' to? I console the pangs of embarrassment with the comfort that I never have to see her again and the fact that by tomorrow an international border will lie between us.

Clockwise from top-left: With Bisma, Nicaragua – San Blas Islands – Norely, Don Humberto and Doña Muriela –Brent, Marta and Humberto – San Blas Islands – My Dad, Costa Rica – Telesupia – with Humberto's family, Supia

Ecuador

17th March – 16th April, 2011

Not much changes crossing the border. Or the changes are too subtle, or I am too ignorant to notice them straight away. At lunchtime I stop at a restaurant, pay $2.50 for *almuerzo*, and watch as the waiter weaves and squeezes his way through a sea of obesity. It seems that every wooden chair in the restaurant is straining under an enormous weight, and I gaze around at folds of fatty necks, and brown slumping rolls tumbling out from under t-shirts and heads that seem to melt into bodies. It looks like some kind of tragic convention. The waiter reaches my table and puts enough food for four people in front of me. Two steaks, two eggs, chips and a mountain of rice. In all my time in the States I never saw anyone eat this much. Perhaps, I think, sawing through the crispy fat of the first steak, I should just choose restaurants based on the number of morbidly enormous people eating in them.

...

In Otavalo I meet an Austrian couple, and they invite me to their hostel to drink rum. Their names are Marra and Roland and they have matching tattoos that are brightly coloured. They have known each other for three months and they tell me about how they are going to buy some horses and ride across Ecuador before going back to Austria and getting married.

"And then," Marra says, "I'm going to join the army."

"Really? You don't seem like," I struggle for the words, in the way that you do when you've just met someone and you don't want to upset them. "It doesn't seem like something you'd do."

"She's a pacifist," says Roland, agreeing with me, I think.

"But I need it," she says. "Well, I need the structure. Or something. Like discipline, I don't know. Anyway, I can't just be taking drugs all the time."

Roland pours the last of the rum and the last of the mixer into our plastic cups, and though it was just going to be a drink or two and a quiet night, we go out. The streets are deserted and black, but the sound of music leads us to a bar.

Inside the heat of people and music hits me like warm breath, and I go to the bar and come back, the necks of three cold bottles clutched in curled fingers. Joyful light drunkenness fills everyone, and I feel happy in the company of Marra and Roland, and the crowded bar, and we shout over the music, and find a table in the corner. I stare, lost for a moment, into the dark wood; something about it reminds me of home, and I'm surprised that this remembrance stings with no longing or nostalgia, and comes with only with a vague and distant sense of something unreal. I look up to see Marra slam three shot glasses onto the table and the sound of the glass against the varnished wood clinks against the music.

We stay until the money in my pocket has gone and its value is unclear. We stagger into the street and I stop at my hostel, to get more cash, on the way to somewhere else.

I climb the three flights of stairs to my room, breathless with cigarettes and drunkenness, and when I come downstairs with fifteen dollars in my pocket I find the door has been locked. I look at my watch, squinting with one eye shut and make out the time - 02:14. Too early, I think, not time to sleep, as the glow of the numbers blurs.

No one is around, so I walk out into the courtyard and stand in the cold, black air. I stare up at the wall and the roof three storeys above, and trace a route over the building.

In the yellow haze, I follow a line with my eyes up a drain and onto a corrugated roof, and again up another drain and onto the roof above. From there, three storeys up, I figure, there'll be a way onto the street, and I'll be out again, in another bar, and so I begin to climb the drainpipe.

My legs push against the cold stone of the wall and I pull myself up, and reach out for the gutter. It feels flimsy and plastic and there's a cold wet mulch in it. Again, I push myself up and this time drag myself on to the corrugated metal roof. I am lying on it flat, my face against its cold, rough surface, and I hear my breathing in the quiet. I look again up the wall and as I push myself up, I hear a crack before I feel myself fall and land on the concrete floor. The drainpipe hangs from the roof, and I see the lights turn on in the room where the owners stay.

When the door opens I am on my feet and running up the stairs. I hear the steps closing in on me as I race into the room and jump into bed. I hide under the covers, breathing hard. The door of the dormitory creaks open and I lie rigid, trying to hold my breath, less like someone sleeping than a statue in spasm. And even though I'm still drunk, I feel guilt creeping in and already sense the dread of morning.

The next day I wake, apologise to the owners, and offer to pay for the damage. They refuse. It was a broken, rotten roof, they say. You were an idiot for trying to climb it. I say sorry again, and decide that I have to stop drinking.

...

A cock fight is not the place for a hangover, and it is not the place to begin a new era of sobriety, but it is where I go. I sit in the room full of smoking and shouting and wretch inducing *aguardiente*.

I am not horrified by the cruelty because I don't understand enough to see it. I watch as two men cradle birds and tease them, bringing them close together. Then there is silence for a moment and the birds scrap and scrape and kick and peck at each other, but it is too small, or maybe too fast, to see the suffering of the birds, and then the fight is over and one of the men holds a limp bird in his arms. He buries his head in the bird's plumage, his mouth pressed to its body, and the bird dies. I feel nothing. And I wonder if some part of me is lost. And I leave.

I decide to go back to the hostel. I long for undrunk sleep. The night is black already and the rich yellow light of the streetlamps swims in the puddles like oil.

A girl crosses the road towards me and I look up to see her smiling. "I'm Kelly Estrella," she says. "Would you like to come for a drink?"

The hand Kelly holds out to me is small and delicate; she wears the intricate gold necklaces, the high collared white and turquoise blouse and long black skirt worn by most indigenous women in this part of Ecuador. I don't want to do anything but sleep, but I am agreeing already, because I can't do otherwise, and because Kelly looks at me with wide eyes and because it's so strange, the way she came up to me, that I am not thinking.

I look over the road to where an old woman has stopped and is watching us. She too wears traditional, indigenous clothing though her hands are hidden, wrapped in a thick woollen blanket, against the evening's chill.

"My name is Sam," I say. And as we reach the pavement, the old woman walks along beside us, without saying a word.

"This is my mother," says Kelly Estrella, and I wonder if that's her real name and decide that it probably isn't. "She's coming with us to the juice bar."

We walk, a strange looking triplet through the empty streets of Otavalo, where, at this time yesterday, poles and tarpaulin had lain scattered on the floor and unsold goods were packed into trucks or vans, or carried away in baskets.

The juice bar is a brightly lit room, fluorescent and unforgiving, as though the proprietors have decided that this will be a place where people see themselves, unhidden by smoke, dim lighting and a drunken glaze. I sit on a plastic chair at a plastic table; myself on one side, the mother and daughter on the other. The whirring then of an electric blender, juicing fruit. *Maracuya. Tomate de Árbol.* And *mango.*

"*Sí, tenemos mangos,*" I am saying, "*y maracuyas.* But the fruit in England isn't as good as it is here."

I feel half sick in the supermarket lighting, talking about passion fruits, and trying to get through this small talk and not knowing why I am here. I wonder if they can see how wretched I feel.

Between Kelly, who is twenty-three, and the lady wrapped in the blanket, there seems a missing generation. It is like these women do all their aging at once. I catch myself thinking that if I married this girl, I would wake one day to a woman with all of life's emotion drawn upon her face in deep worn lines, like a myriad of photos, each placed on top of the other, tracing every expression from grief and fear and sadness, to joy, amusement and hope. And I would look at her face and I would know that some of those lines were because of me. *Is she really your mother?* I want to ask, but don't.

We sip the juice through plastic straws and the conversation rotates around what my Spanish can manage.

Every Sunday, Kelly tells me, she and her mother come into town to speak with her older siblings, studying in Germany. It is the happy killing of a prejudice to learn that two people from a small indigenous village are studying in universities half way across the world. And as Kelly tells me about helping her mother to make clothes and her studies and the last sweet drops of crushed iced and passion fruit juice disappear, I am happy. She pays for the drinks despite my asking her not to and we go outside to wait for their taxi. Still the yellow oil swims in black water.

"Would you like to come for a walk, to the waterfall, with us tomorrow?" she asks, and I tell them, sadly, that I have to leave.

I say goodbye, I say thank you, and as the taxi door slams the way car doors always slam with that heavy hollow thud that sounds the same everywhere, I turn and walk away.

...

The first glimpse of Quito comes as the mist parts and the rain lightens, and the green of mountains and trees gives way to the white and grey buildings piling up the valley walls. The city lies, squashed between two mountain sides, a long and thin constricted sprawl. I have the address of Gonzalo and Silvia, friends of a friend of a friend. They live in Cumbayá, on the outskirts of the city, and I climb towards it, away from the valley floor. I leave the busy wide avenues and the glass and concrete buildings of banks and offices which snake through the modern centre of the city and up through piled up squatting neighbourhoods, where everything looks like it hasn't been painted or washed for years and then a kilometre or so further from the city, I am standing over my bike checking my map and the address, and looking nervously at a gate and a security guard's cabin.

The guard comes out and smiles, "*¿Le puedo ayudar con algo, señor?*"

I am not used to being called *señor*. I look down, embarrassed, at my clothes and offer him the scrap of soggy paper with an address written on it.

The guard opens the gate, and points me down a tree lined road. I roll past huge houses, and high walls and polished wooden gates, or gates of intricate wrought iron and hanging baskets and perfectly trimmed hedges and glimpses of pristinely kept gardens. It feels unearthly; like a street picked out of a film and placed here. I roll down the empty road until I come to the house.

A man in a uniform comes to the door. His name is Luis. Everyone is out, he says, but he smiles and helps me wheel the bike through the garden.

"*Su dormitorio será esa,*" he says. "On the other side of the garden. You can sleep there."

I nod and smile, barely taking in the words. I look around at the garden. I feel slightly disoriented; everything appears like it is not from here: the manicured hedges and the quaint cobbled paths that crisscross the lawn; the ornate turns of lampposts; ferns and thick leaved plants and pine trees; creeping roses and ivy that tumults over the gabled windows.

Luis shows me to my room, which is in a separate building to the main house, and mirrors its white walls and black wooden beams.

"Gonzalo is watching his grandchildren play tennis," says Luis. "He'll be back later." We put my things inside and he says he will take me to meet the girls in the house.

Sofia is nineteen and too beautiful to look at without it hurting. She is living with Gonzalo and Silvia while she studies. Her friend, Lily, and I stand in the kitchen and we talk nervously while Sofia gets me a glass of water.

In the evening, Silvia and Gonzalo arrive and they welcome me warmly into their home. We sit at a long wooden table in the dining room and eat beautiful tamales and drink coffee poured in a concentrated liquid into hot milk, and I try to speak and follow the conversation. I struggle, though despite speaking excellent English, Gonzalo lets me try and I look to him for help, only when I am lost.

After dinner Silvia brings out a terrible green liquor which she pours into a crystal glass. I notice Sofia shudder at the sight of it, and Silvia says something and everybody laughs. I decide not to mention my new dry spell, and thinking that a taste won't hurt, reach gingerly for the glass.

"*Es de un lago,*" Sofia says. At first, I think she's joking, but after its taste ignites my body and I grimace, I wouldn't be surprised if it was from a puddle.

I can't hide my disgust, and to demonstrate its strength, Gonzalo lights the tiny dregs, and they ignite with a roar.

...

The next morning Gonzalo drives me into Quito. The traffic twists down into the city, flies through tunnels and we make a swift descent. I catch a glimpse of Cotapaxi, its distant snowy peak. The road slices through the cliff once more and when we emerge from the lamp-lit tunnel we are in the city.

Gonzalo drops me in the modern business district, where he has a meeting, and I walk through the long snaking city of Quito, until I reach its heart. The whitewashed walls of old colonial buildings blend into the white cloud sky, and uncertain shadows dance in the intricate corniced edges of museums and churches. I walk into La Basilica de Quito, the sound of my footsteps becomes louder, and I take in the smell of stone and darkness and that echoing cold feeling that seems to be the same in religious buildings everywhere, like they spray them with old church smell. Or maybe it is only a Christian smell, this cold dankness. I gaze up at the many depictions of Jesus in the windows, his Hollywood torso, and the flimsy white hands of his disciples, until I feel like I have spent enough time staring quietly at things to warrant having come inside.

I walk around the cobbled streets; hill tops bubble up out of the city covered in old buildings and the winding alleys flatten out and flow into plazas. It is a beautiful city. I walk, stop for coffee and walk again.

I see a woman walk out the doors of the central bank. She wears high heeled boots and tight trousers, and an expensive looking purple poncho. I glance at her again, because it is hard not to, and walk away.

On the next street I see her again. Only now when I glance I meet her gaze and she talks to me in English. "Hey," she says. "I know this seems strange, but you remind me of my friend in Miami."

I don't know what to say. It's not a question and it's not a statement I can have an opinion on, and I look for a moment thinking about the fact that designer ponchos must exist, and hoping that she'll say something that's easier to respond to.

She doesn't so I say something like "oh."

"So, what are you doing here? Where are you staying?"

I answer both of the questions, and I'm surprised that she seems disappointed that I'm staying in Cumbayá. I don't really know why this woman is talking to me, and I become suddenly aware that I am carrying a plastic bag with all my things in it. I guess at her age; late twenties perhaps, or early thirties; older than me.

"Oh," she says. "I live in El Centro." I don't know if it's feigned disappointment, but I'm terrified that this beautiful woman in expensive clothes seems to want to see me again.

"How long are you here for?" she asks.

"I'm leaving tomorrow," I lie.

For a few minutes the conversation lingers on, until at last she seems to stop it with her eyes fixed on mine.

"I'm never going to see you again, am I?"

Perhaps, I think as I walk away, with a mixture of relief and something else. No, probably, I think, she is crazy.

...

When I get home that evening Silvia is entertaining friends and the sound of women's laughter comes from the dining room. Joanna, the maid is in the kitchen. Silvia calls me in as I walk through the front door and I say hello to room full of elegant middle-aged ladies and gold necklaces, before hurrying out.

Later, as we are eating, Silvia catches my eyes following Sofia out the room, and she smiles at me, "*Guapa, ¿no?*" in a voice too loud for Sofia not to hear, and she laughs at my silence, and answers her own question. "*Sí, guapísima.*"

It is a warm and welcoming home. And when I say goodbye to Gonzalo, Silvia, Luis, Joanna and Sofia, it is with a familiar happy sadness. I roll again, down the road which seems like somewhere else, wave to the security guard as he lifts the gate, and ride back into Ecuador, and south.

...

I wake early and walk through the town of Latacunga, looking for breakfast; grey rain and unsmiling people. I find a restaurant with its door hanging open and two men and a woman sit, apparently waiting for customers.

"*Buenos días,*" I say.

"*Buenas.*"

I find a chair in the empty room and sit down.

After five minutes I decide that you must have to order at the counter, and I get up.

"*¿Puedo pedir algo?*" I ask, and the man stares at me from under a baseball cap and says nothing.

"Is there anything to eat?"

"*No,*" the man says.

"*Nada?*"

"*Nada.*"

"No breakfast?" I ask. "Or coffee?"

"Nothing," the man says. "*No hay nada.*"

I leave, stopping myself from saying thank you and without asking them what they were all doing sat around in an apparently open restaurant, and look for a way to get to the mountain.

...

The next day I make it to the National Park. Wisps of silver grey cloud slide across Cotapaxi's face, and a monotone grey hangs above. Just a degree south of the equator the snow falls horizontally and breaks into stinging hail. Then the air turns cold and dry, and the clouds part; teasing glimpses of the world below, and a crown of blue rests above the peak, until the hail falls again.

When I return from the mountain, Sunday drunks lay scattered around town. Working men lie face down, or curled up on the pavements, wrapped in dirty coats and alcohol. The smell of rancid fruit from the morning's market; meat and fish left in the sun too long; and rubbish on the floor.

...

I follow the grey dirt road out of Baños and wind through the barren ashy landscape and jagged rocks, within spitting distance of Tungurahua. The smell of fat and corn and cheese stops me and I watch as a woman flips tortillas on a heated slab of rock.

As I approach Riobamba the sky closes in, threatening and dark. I stop at a café. A woman, full of smiles, comes out and waves me inside.

"What do you want to eat?" she asks.

"What is there?"

"Fish," she says

"Only fish?"

"Only fish."

"Then fish," I say, and sit down.

The fish that comes on a plate with rice and raw onions and chips is less fish than a fried bag of skin wrapping an inedible, entangled ball bones, and the odd dry flake of grey flesh. I push the wet skin around the plate and eat the rice and chips, wondering how much money she will charge me.

She seems delighted as I hand her the dollar she asks for. Perhaps most customers don't pay.

...

Every day in Ecuador, I wake with the hope that it will not rain, and every day it does.

The rain comes as a thin, grey mist, barely perceptible; tiny droplets, clinging to eyelashes like frozen pearls.

The rain comes from dark grey clouds in a dark blue sky; fleeting, with assured heaviness – a beginning and an end.

The rain comes slowly; lightly, but unending in a cold grey day.

The rain comes as hail; small frozen stones, thrown down for an hour at a time, stinging skin red.

The rain comes as the day's heat swells, each drop fat and heavy the sky full of water, like standing under a million shower heads, the water frozen cold.

...

Cuenca. Oña. Saraguro. I ride down the back of the sierra until I reach Loja, where I have arranged to stay with Sofia's parents.

Two Swiss ladies are staying at the house and we take a jeep together down muddy, rocky tracks for hours to the hidden and forgotten countryside to see some of the projects their foundation has helped to fund.

We stop at three tiny hamlets and are brought *choclo y queso* three times; the warm corn on the cob and the huge blocks of white cheese grow more daunting each time.

We visit a school, where the foundation has funded a new roof, and watch as the children dance and mime to recordings of pop songs. We sit in on village meetings as heated discussions break out about missed appointments, broken promises and I'm not sure what else. And then we take the jeep back down the tracks again. And the villages, which are only twenty or thirty kilometres away, but hours in a car, lie hidden once again, behind the mountains.

I realise as I sit in the jeep, rolling now along the tarmac into Loja, that I am tracing only a line around the world, that I am seeing so little, or leaving so much unseen, and the unending fathomless size of the world rears up inside of me. The next day, I leave to trace the line ever further south.

...

I arrive in Catacocha in a downpour. Water runs down the sloping streets; as fast as a river and ankle deep. Clothes stick, cold and tight to my skin and I shiver.

...

The next day, as I ready to leave, the sky is blue and the streets no longer run as streams, but crack under the morning sun.

I meet a man named Freddy, and he asks me if I like Catacocha.

"I like it when it's sunny," I answer, and he recites me these lines:

Si algo hermoso Dios creó
en este suelo
y bajo este cielo
eso es mi lindo Catacocha

"That's very nice," I say. "Who wrote it?"

"I did," he says.

"Ah, you're a poet."

"Yes. I just need to write it down, but I'm too busy. No time for walking," he says, walking, being, what poets do. And he says again, *"No me da tiempo caminar. Es que estoy siempre ocupado."*

"In a couple of years," he continues, "I'm going to have lots of money," and I laugh, thinking he is joking.

"No, no," he says. "People like to read poems, these writers are very rich."

I ask him who he likes to read.

"Lord Byron," he answers immediately. "And this other one, from Guayaquil... ah, *cómo se llamaba?* I can´t remember his name."

I ask him to write the poem down as a memory of Catacocha, and as he takes the piece of paper his phone rings. "You see," he says, pointing furiously at the phone. *"Lo ves? Muy, muy ocupado."* He puts the phone to his ear and shouts as though not trusting the phone's ability to carry sound, "Hello. No, no. I'm too busy today. I´m in Loja."

A young boy, who has been sitting on the steps behind me, throughout our conversation, looks at me with a shake of the head and smiles.

It is Friday, and realising as I do so, that I am betraying that undesirable attitude of adults who believe that, for at least five days a week, children should be hidden from view in an institution somewhere, I ask him why he isn´t at school.

"We don´t have classes until Monday," he says.

"Oh, cool." I say, trying to make up for the stupidity of my first question. "What are you going to do today?"

"Es que no lo sé," he says. "I don't know. It´s going to rain at 3."

I look at my watch. It is 9am.

Clockwise from top-left: Gonzalo and Silvia's house, Cumbayá, Quito – Cotapaxi, Ecuador – Mountains in northern Ecuador – Leaving Baños.

Peru

16th April – 3rd July, 2011

I cross the border into Peru, and the world changes. Everyone shouts *Hola* and *Buenos días* as I pass. Smiles and stares follow me down the road, with the echo of the words, and the earth grows hot. The road drops, flat and dry, and I race towards the desert, the ground slipping away beneath me, and after all this time in the mountains it feels good to be making progress.

Everything feels more intense than in Ecuador and Colombia. Dirtier and less organised. Sandy, old crumbling desert towns, with no banks or cash machines, full of rickety shacks. The food tastes good and spicy and the rice is freshly cooked, and I keep turning, marvelling at the flatness of the earth and the ease with which my pedals turn, and I'm moving again.

I find a concrete hotel, where I stay but don't sleep. Late loud sex echoes and screams around the building all night and the whine of mosquitos keeps me up.

In the morning I sit outside my room reading. An old woman shuffles along until she stops right next to me and stares at my feet.

"Are you okay?" she asks.

"I am."

"Do they hurt?" she says, pointing at my feet and I shake my head.

"Are you ill?" she asks. "Are you cold?"

"I'm fine," I say. But she looks at me doubtfully, like she's looking at someone who is doomed to prematurely die, and walks away, shaking her head and muttering.

I look at my feet, in flip flops for the first time since I skipped away from the sound of a gun, and I understand her concern; they are whiter than feet should be.

...

The long flat stretch of desert road lies before me, 200km until the next major town. Dust, scrub, sand and hot blue sky. Half-built walls, the same colour as the sand on which they stand, lie abandoned, stunted in their growth as if the time spent laying the foundations was enough to convince the prospective inhabitants that this really was no place to spend their lives.

Others though, are hardier. Or less wise. Donkeys and people share the scarcity of shade, and rows of completed houses lie in grids, there being nothing in the landscape to hinder man's dull tendency toward the uniformity of squares, nor anything around to inspire other forms. Nor, on the face of it, anything to sustain any kind of life at all.

I sit, in the small dark shadow of a bush, eating bread and jam. Next to me stands a house made of sticks, and everything is dusty and dirty and worn out by sun and wind.

From a concrete-box church across the road comes the calm voice of a man, distorted only slightly by the speakers used to sermonise those unwilling or unable to attend in person.

"*Gracias señor por la luz y el sol. Gracias señor por este nuevo día.* Thank you lord for the light and the sun. Thank you lord for this new day."

The voice sounds so content and sincere that I sit in amazement wondering how this man could still be grateful for these things, living here, in the hot desert dust. It is 8am and already I am sick of all three of these, God's gifts.

I clip back into pedals and ride the long hot day into the desert. And the day after that. And the day after that. Until I reach the city.

...

Chiclayo burns under the sun. A huge market sprawls across an open expanse of concrete, and grey buildings, tangled wires and the roaring traffic make the whole place seem like it was built without the time to think of beauty.

I walk, Western and conspicuous and followed by eyes. And the whole place seems on heat. I find my eyes trapped in other eyes and it feels strange and uncomfortable and good. I walk the streets for no reason. There is nothing to see. Ugly buildings and beautiful girls. Or are they beautiful? Maybe it is just the way they look. Straight at me, unashamed and full of sex. Like they are talking without talking. Obscene words, and it can't be just me, it is not my own imaginings. And the whole city heaves and strains against itself under the heat of the dying sun. Stairways lead to places unknown, open doors and dark rooms. And I walk until the market begins to empty and the shadows draw out long towards the east. The streets begin to grow cold. And I'm still not drinking. And I still won't drink. And where would I go on my own? If I went, there would be trouble. I go back to the hostel, and force myself to sleep.

...

I follow the road along the desert coast, the town full of dirt and stink. Something seems to be rotting. And the people slouch and sit and wait for the sun to blow the rot dry and the wind to carry away the stink.

The road passes abandoned towns, and I wonder why anyone would think to live here, and how long it will take for the town, already shells and ruins, to turn to dust and desert again.

I ride into the wind, long hot no fun hours. Pacasmayo. Trujillo. And as I approach Chimbote, entering the town of Santa, I am stopped by the police.

"*Me deja sus documentos, por favor.*"

I lift my t-shirt and take out my passport. The policeman flicks through it, not getting to the photograph page, and staring, slightly puzzled, at the stamps with strange Chinese characters or Cyrillic script. Policeman who stop me on the road always seem lost when they ask to see my passport, but they never let on that they don't know what they're doing. He hands it back to me with a feigned satisfaction.

"Where are you going?"

"Today," I say, trying to remember the name, "*a Chimbote.*"

The policeman looks at me, concerned. "*Muy mala idea,*" he says. Very bad idea. "*Chimbote es muy peligroso.*"

"Dangerous? Why?" I am used to people telling me that the next town is dangerous, or the next country, always the next, never the last, but I have never been told this by a policeman and the uniform adds gravity to what he is saying.

"*Pues ya verá,*" he says. "*Allí, hay mucha mala gente, muchos ladrones, muchos... bueno, de todo.*"

I look at him, and ask what I should do. And the policeman eyes me seriously. "If I were you, I'd stay here for the night. Then tomorrow morning you can leave early. You'll have passed Chimbote by midday."

He points me in the direction of a hotel he says is cheap and I thank him for the information. There is a question though, that I keep to myself. Why, if there are so many thieves and bad people in Chimbote, are he and his colleagues here checking people's papers and not there doing something about it? I bump down the potholed road, thinking it a good thing not to have asked, and come to the glass door of the hotel.

There are three types of hotel in Peru. One with pictures of Jesus and Angels and quotations from the Bible on the walls. One, with naked pictures of Pamela Anderson, and other topless girls with permed blonde hair on the walls. And one with nothing on the walls, holes in the ceiling, no light bulbs, soggy mattresses, mosquitos and old men drinking all the little money they've got.

This is the second type of hotel. The girl at the desk speaks to me from behind a pane of glass, and calculates the price by multiplying the 2 hour slots together and then offering a discount. I ask about the bike. She looks at me for a moment, says she really doesn't care what I take up to the room and turns away.

...

I leave early, ride through Chimbote and follow the desert road, the Pacific Ocean on my right, until I reach the banks of the river Casma. Barren desert soil erupts in lush greens; rows of orange trees and grape vines run away from the water's edge, and brightly coloured flowers line the hedges.

I climb the road for 47 hot miles until a truck stops me and a man tells me it is impossible to pass further ahead; the road is blocked by a landslide. It's being cleared, he says, but will not be passable until the morning.

I cycle slowly into the next hamlet to the usual whispers, calls and shouts of *gringo* and I slow to look for a kind face, a face that smiles, and come to a stop by a small hut. A woman sits outside.

"I'm sorry," I say. "I want to ask you, if I can, if it would be possible to camp here. Or if you know somewhere I can camp."

She looks at me for a moment, turning my stumbling words into sense, and then speaks. "Here." she says, pointing, "There. Anywhere."

I pick *there*, and she tells me that *there* would be a bad place because there's pig shit everywhere, and that *here* would be better, so I say that *here* would be fine.

The lady's name is María. An older lady, who I take to be María's mother, sits beside her on the concrete step. They watch me as I put up my tent outside their home.

"Where's he from?" the old lady asks María.

"Where are you from?" María asks me.

"England," I say.

"England, he says."

"How old is he?" asks the old lady.

"How old are you?" María asks me.

"I'm 25."

"He's 25"

"What's his..."

"Why don't you ask him yourself?"

And from that point on the questions are asked directly, from one person to another. A crowd has gathered to watch me hammer in the pegs. Children hang at the corners of walls, staring; I don't know if they are more interested in me or the tent.

María invites me inside, and we sit in her house. Bare dirt walls and a dusty floor. Wicker furniture, a television, calendars with garish depictions of Jesus, a broken scanner, and shelves of clothes María has bought in Lima to sell here, in Chacchan. A line of bottles. Pepsi. Fanta. Inka-Kola. Brown cardboard boxes. A steady stream of visitors reveal that this is the village department store.

María asks me about England. About how much money people make. I find myself understating salaries and hourly rates and trying to emphasise how expensive everything is, but still a look of disbelief creeps across her face.

"There´s nothing to do here," she says. "People can only work in the fields. I just sell these things. Almost all the young people leave. *Casi todos se han ido.*"

Soon María´s husband, Marcos, comes home. From the television set a dubbed Baywatch momentarily fills the room, before videos of traditional Peruvian music. Harps, panpipes and fat men in white suits.

At intervals of no more than twenty minutes children poke their heads round the open door, eyes resting on me momentarily, as they forget the task they have been sent for.

"Errmm,,,¡véndame!"

"¿Qué?"

"Coca."

And Marcos gets up, walks to one of the cardboard boxes, takes out a small bag of coca leaves and the children give him 1 nuevo sol and run giggling out the door.

One family stays the whole evening. Two children try on new clothes and get excited about new shoes or a pink cardigan. The father sits, visibly wincing at each new item taken from the shelves, and speaks with Marcos, falling, unconsciously it seems, from Quechua to Spanish and back again.

I sleep well in my tent outside as the village falls quiet, and I wake with the pigs, the dogs, the donkeys and cows. The villagers also up, rising before dawn.

In a tiny room, in a separate hut away from the house, María cooks breakfast. Smoke fills the air, and billows in the strong shafts of morning light. Flies buzz, incessantly in the smoke and hover over red buckets of water. From under the mud-walled stove, two guinea pigs come out and forage on the floor, unaware that since birth they have been destined for the fire above.

María hands me a bowl of soup; potato, pasta, garlic and herbs swim in a broth that tastes of the wood smoke from the stove.

I thank Marcos and María and promise I will send them the photos I have taken of their family, but as I look at the address Marcos has given me, I feel doubtful they will ever arrive. It contains no numbers, nor the name of a house, so that when I post it just 50 miles away, in Huaraz, it seems to read like this.

Please send to Marcus Sanchez
Who lives near Pariacota
In a house made of mud and straw
With some pigs and a dog outside of it.

Sender: Sam Gambier, Huaraz.

...

I leave my bike in the city and go for a walk in the mountains of Huascaran National Park.

Now, I move slow. I stop for beetles to crawl and heave themselves across vast and tiny landscapes. I love the way they grip rocks and seem always to go straight, over boulders, and sticks, and anything else that gets in the way. I love their defiance; the plated metallic shields which cover their bodies and shine gold-blue-greens in the sun. I love that they keep climbing and trudging on even as you watch. That they seem always to be going somewhere, so uncaring of the eyes that look down, that they do not scurry or hide. I love that they are almost always alone.

Now, I move slow. I watch the long unending streams of ants, the lines that carry food, and sticks and leaves. I watch the way they tear apart other insects, larger than themselves, long dead. I watch the unceasing march, the long drawn out single-file of ants, the way they struggle to lift a crumb, and work together. I watch as they carry their dead; an ant carrying an ant. And I don't know to where or why.

Now, I move slow. I stop for the trickling or the burbling of a stream, the flash of movement in the undergrowth. There is time to look up at the wild blue sky and feel the changes in the wind, and watch as the clouds engulf the nearest peaks. I clamber over boulders, and follow the stream, and the green, wet squelch of the ground. Light mottled specks of algae grow purple and green, where the water is still and stagnant, and the sky and mountain peaks shine inconstantly on its surface.

A flock of sheep chimes across the valley floor; the deep broken clangs of cracked bells and unmelodic baas, and the jingling, happy notes of bells intact. A shepherd sits. And though I first see him as I approach the open meadow from below and I glance at him now and then as I follow the stream along the flat valley floor, and look down at the man once more as the path kicks up and winds towards the mountain pass, all he does is sit. Around us, the mountain slopes are green and trees seem not to struggle, but flourish in an easy, effortless existence. Further up, within sight now, are the jagged, rocky peaks, snow covered and frozen. The slate grey rock is visible only where the face is too sheer, and the cliff too inhospitable even for snow.

I walk for four more days, over passes and down the twisting rocky paths to the lush and living valleys. The days are long from sunrise to the vanishing light of dusk.

In Llanganuco I find the minibus that will take me back to Huaraz. There are bags and sacks of grain to be taken to the city. There are baskets of vegetables and cages with chickens. There is also a pig. But the sow is at the side of the road and squealing, and the squealing becomes a scream and it sounds like vocal chords tearing, and the scream sparks panic and the other pig kicks out and pulls against the rope tied around its neck. Then the mini bus begins to rock back and forth and I realise that one of the sacks is a pig, and that it's struggling to break free.

They have the pig on its back now, and three men fight to hold it down. A boot presses down on its neck, against the sand and the gravel in the road, and now they have the four legs tied together and they are tightening the knot. And still the pig is screaming as they throw a sack over its head, and it thrashes as the men lift it onto the bus, and the bus sags with the extra heavy weight. I step into the bus and sit in the corner, the pig rolling and thrashing on the floor, and as the doors are closed the sow is screaming still.

The bus crawls slowly out of the village. And the road is gravel and rock. The mountain plummets down. Streams lie so far below us that the white of the water seems unreal, painted and moving in unnatural ways. And the houses and cars so tiny that it is like looking from the window of a plane.

The bus jolts as it twists round yet another hairpin bend and the sack smacks against the floor, the bus rocks and we come to a halt. Two men get out to tighten the ropes, tying the animals fast to the roof, and the brakes are left to cool. We continue our descent, until finally the rivers move as rivers and the road becomes smooth.

...

Once more I leave the city to climb into the mountains. Further, this time, into the punctured sky.

We camp on a rocky outcrop on the edges of the snow, pristine and untouched like shining egg white. Under the peak of Vallunaraju the night is sleepless; a constant tossing and turning in the dark, and we listen to the weather and wait.

At 3am we are up. We sip steaming tea, but don't eat. The world just the sphere of torch light, and all it catches, the steam of tea and breath, and faces braced against the cold. Beyond this light, the darkness is empty and silent. We walk to the snow line, clip crampons over our boots and tie into the ropes, walk slow and steady towards the summit. I follow the footprints, a narrow path trodden into the snow and in the dark it is a never ending trudging, a blind conveyer belt rolling steadily upwards, through the moonless night.

The hours stretch and lengthen and each footstep is harder, and the air colder and drier to breathe. I am happy when the blackened sky betrays the first blue light of morning. Where before there was only a pitch-black darkness, now crevices drop away, feet from where we are stood. Stalactites like pins drop from overhanging snow. We walk on, faces numb and the world blue, white and cold. At last the peak is in sight.

My head begins to ache, and the cold creeps into our bodies as we stand, at 5688 metres, looking down at the mountains below, and across at even higher peaks. The sun's rays cast their cold light onto the summit and we look to each other; the snow slips from blue to golden yellow to white, and we are ready to go down.

...

Still, as I leave the town of Huaraz and follow the road over the ragged back of the Andes and down towards Lima and the coast, I feel the dim remembrance of a dull headache, the cold ache of teeth and the sting of an icy wind. It is no more though than the memory of pain, and the conjured pictures of frozen walls and the cold sun and the world below delight me still, and the insignificant effort is forgotten. Already I am dreaming about the next mountain I will climb.

From Conococha the road tumbles down, twisting through a series of hairpin bends. From the snow that dusted the village and the bare stubbly grass, the road plummets, until I feel the warmth of the sun in my hands, and trees begin to grow, and I feel less pity for the livestock led to graze. It is easy going down, when the road runs smooth and effortless. With each new turn of the pedals the air feels heavier and thicker, and I close in on the sea.

And then the earth turns barren again. And filthy.

Around me the desert is grey, and the air stinks like death, maggoty and dry. I stop on the crest of a hill. The whip of sand, caught up by wind, sprays into my face, and I duck against it, chew the stench around my mouth, and spit.

I look down at the slate grey desert and the slate grey sea. Lineless at the shore, like watching the world through a gauze, and the sky grey and hazy too. No cliffs, no birds, no crashing of waves, nor glints of rippling sunlight on the surface of the sea. So I watch, unsure of what I am watching; the dull and motionless ocean or another dead desert plain.

Then, towards the south, the darkened shapes of rocks strike out of something dusty or swampy-looking, and in the shallow water the whites of waves, break lightly over rocky, jagged edges. From this distance though, the white looks grey. It is the sea, I think, the sea. A grim and dismal sea.

Miles later, the rocks and the crashing of waves appear more clearly: as an abandoned house; the crumbling or half-built walls of out buildings; lifeless, skeletal shrubs, black and hawthorn-sharp, and on their branches the whites of waves; old carrier bags and nappies, blowing in the desert wind.

The ocean stretches away before me, a flat expanse of litter-strewn sand. And beyond that somewhere the real ocean, dull grey and litter strewn too. When I get to the town, it is worse.

The town smells of days-old fish, and the carcasses of dogs. I roll my bike down streets of sand and rubbish and broken glass, the smell of piss and shit. And the dry air whips up again and the sting of sand slashes against walls of mud and sticks.

Elections are coming in Peru and slogans are scrawled across the walls in orange and white letters. *KEIKO: siempre con la gente.* Always with the people, the one and stinking people, here between the desert and the dirt grey sea, stretched out for pointless, dirty miles, filling the gaps between the corrugated iron and thin wooden walls, like insects clinging to shelter and living in the cracks of a desert plain. The people in the town have calloused hands and down-trodden stares, and seem unhappy and tired. Too much work for too little money, or too little work for nothing at all. Another campaign poster flaps in the wind. *Oportunidades para todos.* Though what kind of opportunities it does not say. And the wind throws sand at the poster, and the stink of shit and fish and piss and days-old death starts to stick, and soon the poster will rip, and fall into the sand.

...

I ride back into the desert; the traffic swells.

There is a sense of something simmering.

Lima is over the hill.

Already it is spilling over the sides in grids of huts; their painted walls squat in the sand and cling to the hillsides. Words carved into the slopes above promise that Christ lives. *Cristo Vive!* it says in stone or bare rock, hanging above the sprawling masses. The road widens and courses through the slums. My heart quickens, not only with the rush of traffic, but because still somehow, despite it all, I think I love the city. I hug the edge of the road and swerve between the potholes and the traffic behind, squinting at the flying dust and the clamouring noise, and I lend the city song. A simmering, buzzing, energetic, boiling – still I love the city. And I race towards the centre, to the shining core, through the crumbling mess, and a horn seers through the air, and I pull my bike out of the way, off the edge of the road, onto the sand, the broken glass, and shards of metal, and, the bike dips heavy, and under the noise of engines and horns, the familiar hiss of a puncture.

I pull my bike to rest against a concrete wall, and look around. Two boys roll a threadbare tyre back and forth to each other, and a man, polished brown skin, dusty and clinging to the shapes of his bones, slumps into the shade of the wall, holding the neck of a bottle in a plastic bag.

I take the panniers off my bike, turn it upside down, and search for the hiss of air, under the noise. The man stirs, looks at me through drunk eyes, and turns away again. My hands rush in panic, but I don't work quicker, only more hurriedly, and I fumble as I pull on the tyre lever. I look around and see that people have stopped to watch what I am doing, and stare from windows and corners, and there is something like dread that tells me I shouldn't be here. I try not to look around, and concentrate on the wheel. The same simple tasks now hard; I pump up the inner tube and hold it to my ear, though over the traffic I can hear nothing. I move it around until I feel the exhaled pin of air on my lips, and clean around the puncture, press down on the patch until it holds. And all the time I'm thinking, this is the wrong place, and I'm here and rich and white, and I've just laid all my possessions on the ground and taken the wheel off my bike so that I cannot ride away, and I know I cannot fight. It is a bad place to stop.

A car pulls up. My things still lie scattered around, and I pull the tyre back over the wheel, and it's ready to inflate.

"*Aquí no, eh!*" a man shouts from the car window, and I look up.

"*¿Qué?*"

"*No deberías estar aquí, en este barrio,*" he says. "You shouldn't be here."

I half listen, trying to ready the bike. "*Aquí te van a robar,*" he says before driving off without offering a solution. They're going to rob you, he says, and finally the wheel is on, and the patch is holding. Though maybe they were just waiting for me to fix the bike and load it with my possessions before they take it from me. I look up, a man is walking towards me. He carries a wrench, and stands too close.

It occurs to me that I might lose the bike. The bike that has carried me, that I have pushed, all these many miles. The bike I have screamed at and cursed. The bike I have not loved. I glance at the milometer: 31,119 miles. Together. The bike I don't want to let go. I still don't have a name for it. If I gave it a name, I would call it Tern, but I do not. I look at the bike, between the man and me. Cold metal and wheels. A chain. Dead material things. Something too expensive to lose. But not only that. Now, not only that. We are almost there. It would be a shame not to make it together.

"*¿De dónde eres?*" he asks.

"*De Inglaterra,*" I say.

"*¿Y a dónde vas?*"

"*A Argentina.*"

"*¿Argentina? ¿En bici?*"

I nod. He holds the wrench by his side and smiles.

"*Pues, suerte,*" he says. "*Qué tengas un buen viaje.*" Good luck, he says. Have a good trip.

...

I stay with friends of friends in San Isidro, in the centre of Lima. They live in one of the many glass and steel buildings with underground parking on pretty tree-lined streets. In most places in the world it would be a very pleasant place, but here it seems opulent and luxurious, like a wonderful other world.

They take me to the seafront, and we eat in wonderful restaurants, and they welcome me as if they know me, and I warn myself not to take such kindness for granted.

Steve goes to work in the day, and Lupe and I take taxis around Lima to shopping malls, or the historic centre.

The car stops at traffic lights and we look down at a six or seven-year-old girl, sat on a traffic island, four lanes of cars on each side. A single extracted sheet of a newspaper rests on her head to protect her from the spit, cigarette butts, bottles and cans that fly from the windows of cars.

The girl's mother, we assume, is one of the women walking between the vehicles selling chewing gum and tissues. Part-time workers, given the restrictions of red and green lights, but twelve hours spent still, in the fumes and the noise, and maybe never days off. Children cry and sell sweets and run around the cars in bare feet. I catch myself wondering whether the tears are real, and apologise to God in case he is there and can read my thoughts. But every traffic light is the same; a tear stained, miserable theatre.

We are close enough to the girl to see that she is doing her maths homework. I wonder if other kids from her school are sat, on different traffic islands in the dirt and fumes, waiting for their parents to make enough money for dinner. And I watch the girl as she sits with a pencil, drawing out sums. It will be a thing if she gets out of here with that, I think. Quite a thing. Quite an impossible, wonderful thing.

We look sad out the window.

"*Pobrecita.*" we say. Poor thing. Said in sincere tones and heartfelt tones; all those tones that make us human.

The light turns green. The car drives on.

...

Three days later I leave Lima. The city crumbles quickly from the organised centre, into a chaotic poverty that doesn't know when to stop. Still in the desert, where Lima should have ended, the huts cluster in waves, like nests, or dens, or burrows.

Then the city is gone and there is only the desert, the road and the breeze coming in off the Pacific Ocean. The sea rolls by, and I keep it, always to my right, and it's the last long stretch towards the end I think, the world slipping quickly by. If I kept up at this pace I could reach Tierra del Fuego in a couple of months, I think. And then I remember the route I am planning. Up into the mountains to Ayacucho and Cuzco, and towards the *altiplano*.

...

Along the river Pisco, grapes and cotton fill the banks; dry crops – the grapes dusty looking and the cotton caught on darkened twigs and blowing in the breeze. The cotton pickers throw the too light crop into huge squares of material and pull the corners together, tie them to make sacks. I watch as they collapse into their day's work, placed like beanbags on the dusty road, and wait for a truck or a bus to carry them home, or to summon the strength to return by foot.

The road climbs slow and steady along the wide river banks. I pass a sign for Pámpano. The village sits above the river, too small I think, to offer an *hospedaje*, and I continue climbing as the sun slips down behind me and the shadows climb up the mountainsides.

I turn off the road and bump down a rocky dirt track to the river banks. Just rocks, no space for a tent. But a stubbly grassy growth on the sandy earth convinces me that even if the river floods, the water won't reach this far.

Across the river there is a hut. A man has seen me. It is too late to continue, the sky grey with dusk, so I wave. He waves back. Murderers don't wave.

I lay out the sleeping bag on the ground and lock the bike's wheels together. I read until the light fades; still the sun's heat in the sand and rocks; sand fly bites cover my legs in swollen white bumps. Stars appear, the night sky clear, and I lie down to sleep, staring up as the air grows cool.

A dog starts to bark and does not stop. Angry voices. Torch lights shine from the banks across the river, and still the dog barks. Sand flies hop in the sand, bite at my wrists.

I watch the torches move along the banks opposite and pick out the broken water of the river and the twisted limb of a tree carried along by its current. The torches stop and search for me, and a voice shouts something angry, which I cannot understand over the noise of the river and the dogs. Then the torches disappear, and for two hours I lie in my sleeping bag, staring up at the stars, and waiting.

The torches come from behind me then. I get out of the sleeping bag and move into the light, shining my own torch on my face and the lights stop in the darkness.

"*Es un turista,*" the voices say. "*Sólo un turista.* We thought you were a thief."

"I'm sorry," I say. "I'm not a thief. I'm sorry to disturb you. I just wanted to sleep."

"*No pasa nada,*" one of the men says. "It's just that sometimes we get thieves. *Por eso...*" he says, explaining why they've come across the river.

The men wave over the children who had stayed back, in case I really was a robber, and the chubby, smiling face of a boy gets caught in the torch light.

"*Está durmiendo en el suelo, no más,*" he says to his father, half laughing. "He's just sleeping on the floor." He moves his light from my face to the bags, the bike and back. "*¿A dónde vas?*"

"I'm going to Argentina," I say. "But not now. Tomorrow. Now, I'm sleeping."

We wish each other goodnight and I apologise again, and the search party returns. I watch the torches bob away, floating in the night, in the shape of steps, until again they reach the other side of the river, and the lights go off.

The dogs bark, and still the torches shine out across the river, flies still bite in the dying warmth of the sand, and I don´t sleep, but wait until dawn to leave.

...

I pick up my bike and continue as the last vanishing sparkle of the stars fades into the sky.

I stop in Huaytara to eat. The café is a concrete room, thick with dust and grime, and the kitchen a single wok and stove behind a curtain. The *lomo saltado* tastes like old dead dog, fried to death and disguised under half a bottle of soy sauce. As I chew over the meat, peppers and onions, my mouth dry with salt, I look over at the cook. I'm eating and swallowing because I'm hungry, but part of me knows I shouldn't.

I leave the café and a woman asks where I'm going.

"*Ayacucho,*" I say. "*Voy por Abra Apacheta.*" At 4746m it will be the highest point I have reached on a bike.

The woman looks at me doubtfully; my tired sleepless eyes, and the blotches on my skin. Maybe she can see that the dead-rat-rotten-dog-saltado is already making me sick.

"*Te vas a morir en frío,*" she says flatly and walks off. I think about her words as I get back on the bike. I'm going to die. I say. *Me voy a morir. En frio. En frio?* In cold. Not of cold. In cold. I'm going to die in cold.

Above Huaytara, the road twists and climbs. And I ride at 4 miles an hour for 8 hours. Trees stop growing; just a harsh and barren grass, and alpacas, and the descending herds of cows, escaping the evening´s chill.

I am tired from no sleep, but I feel okay. As the world grows higher and colder my body burns with effort. Road workers tell me it will be too cold to camp, but I climb, further still, until the bleak black crest of a hill seems to flatten out above, and I drag my bike off the road, try to pull it out of sight.

I am dragging the bike still when the sun's heat vanishes, and its yellow light leaps from the thin blades of grass to the frosty shadowy sky, and rests for a moment on the undersides of clouds, and up again, leaving everything a cold light grey.

The crest is not a crest, but a never-ending slope, and the road is still visible below. Now the wind is biting and stings my fingers, and I realise I am exhausted. My bike gets caught in a ditch, and I scream, half crying with the pain in my fingers, and as the tears come, I begin to feel ill. The frozen wind picks up, and I pull at my bike and scream, *you shitting cunt, you dirty fucking dirty fucking twat, you shitting fucking twat,* and the words are enough and I pull the bike free. I hold my hands in my armpits, give up on finding a hidden place to camp, and begin to set up a tent, on the frozen rocky slope above the road.

I have climbed too fast, I realise. From sea level to 4500m in one and a half days, with no sleep, and a frozen wind. For a moment, as I push the last peg into the hard ground, I stare shivering in thoughtlessness. Just get everything in the tent and sleep. Tomorrow will be better.

I lie down inside the tent, but I have forgotten how to sleep. The wind beats and flaps at the walls and slowly the feeling returns to my fingers, and stings. I am thinking of the tiny shifting blades of grass outside, and the ever-moving wind, and I don't know why, because all I want is sleep. But I'm trapped in a circle and I can't get out, because the wind is blowing the clouds and the clouds swell and burst and the rain falls and falls, and slips and sinks and drops in tiny droplets into streams and rushes in rivers and down to the sea, and I don't know why I'm thinking about this, because all I want is sleep, and my mind is just tumbling in circles, and the water rushes, and the sun and the wind sprays and carries the salty water and again I'm in the fucking clouds with the wind and it's always moving and I just want to think of something straight, in a straight line, with a beginning and an end so I can think it and go to sleep, but now the water and the drops and the rain are falling again into the trees, and I can't stop. And somehow now I am outside myself, and I feel separate from my limbs. Just put my legs to sleep, I think, and the legs sleep, and I feel them dead and heavy. And my arms, I think, and then they too, go dead. And this is how you sleep, I think. But my mind races with impossible useless nothings. And I close my eyes too tight. Outside the full bright moon illuminates the sky, as light as dawn or dusk, and I turn and close my eyes, and still no sleep.

Twice in the long and windy night I wake, elated to have slept, and twice I look at my watch to see no more than twenty minutes have passed. I lie then with my eyes open, with no hope left for sleep and watch as the walls grow grey and yellow with the early rising sun.

...

I am awake. Though I feel worse than the day before, and the thought of eating makes me gag. The light is golden now, but not yet warm and I unzip the tent to find that the bicycle wheel is flat and the tyre worn bare.

I pull the old tyre away from the rim of the wheel and set about mounting the new one. It should take no more than five minutes, but I have forgotten what to do. There is a part of my brain that feels empty, like a disc, or some memory has been removed, and the words corrupted file flash across my mind. For two hours I try to fix the tyre, and for two hours the press conference scene from *Notting Hill* repeats itself in my head. From "And you are?" "Writing an article about how London hotels treat disabled guests," to the word "indefinitely" and the flashing of cameras, and back again, for two whole hours as if the part of my brain which knows how to mount a tyre has been replaced by the script of a romantic comedy. I sink into the ground and lie, gazing up at the sky until I remember what to do.

I am so breathless I cannot stand up. My brain feels dull, and tired, and stupid, and for whole minutes at a time I forget who I am and what I'm doing.

I crawl around on the floor taking down my tent. The sunlight grows warmer, and I tell myself that when I've taken down my tent I will lie on the floor to sleep. But the exercise is futile. I've forgotten what to do.

I ride the whole day. Or I ride in bursts, watching the metres tick over on the speedometer, 200 more metres then I'll stop. 100 more metres then I'll stop. 50 more. 10 more. And I drop my bike and lie on the ground by the side of the road. Not a single car has passed all day.

I will myself to get up. Another half mile. And another. And another. Until I have dragged myself twelve small miles across the mountain plain, and that's enough. There is a pile of gravel next to the road and I pull the bike behind it and crawl along the ground, gasping for air and unable to stand up. It takes two hours to put up the tent and another to put the panniers inside, rolling them along the ground because I don't have the strength to lift them and I collapse into the ground outside.

For the first time in 60 hours, I sleep blissful, exhausted sleep and half an hour later I wake and crawl to my tent and sleep for half an hour again.

I wake to the pangs of food poisoning, drag myself out of the tent and crawl as far away as I can before shitting water.

Back in my tent, I realise again that I have forgotten how to sleep. And now at intervals of twenty minutes, I rush outside the tent. It is dark outside, the stars and the moon hidden behind clouds. Sleet falls sideways as I shit water and piss and vomit at the same time, and every time I shake uncontrollably in the freezing night. And in the morning, I am empty. The contents of my stomach and bowels and bladder lie, in frozen, scattered puddles, around the tent.

I have nothing left. I reach the pass and look at the sign. 4746msnm. I want to go down. I want the road to roll back to oxygen, and I want to scream at the woman who fed me the poisonous food, and I want to cry. But the road runs straight. And I ride another twelve miles, three miles above the sea, until at last I reach a village, and lie outside a lady's hut in the afternoon heat.

After two hours she comes out. "Are you okay? Are you just resting, or do you feel bad?"

"Feel bad." I say. "But okay. Just resting."

She tells me that in the next village there is a place to stay. I thank her and close my eyes.

When I open them again there are three boys, no more than five years old, stood around, with a mobile phone.

"We want a photo," they say. "We want a photo with the sleeping gringo. *Ponte allí*," they say pointing to the bench. I look up and shake my head.

"*No puedo hablar*," I say, and close my eyes.

The boys are laughing and playing with my bike. I don't care. *Mira el gringo cansado*, they say. Look at the tired gringo.

"Where has he come from?" one of them asks.

"*Los Estados Unidos*," says the other boy.

"The United States doesn't exist," says the boy.

"*Sí, sí existe*," the other boy argues, "I have seen it on the tele."

The next time I open my eyes they have gone. I ride another 6 miles to the next village.

The *hospedaje* costs $3. It is a dry mud box with no windows, a corrugated plastic roof, a candle on a plywood shelf, and it appears as some sort of paradise. I take Loperamide again for the diarrhoea and co-dydramol to sleep though that's not really what it's for. The next day, I eat for the first time in two and a half days and at last the road begins to descend. I roll. And roll. And, eight days after leaving Lima, Ayacucho comes into view, beautiful and small, the way cities are when seen from above. But even as the town becomes ugly and dusty and real, I have never been so happy nor so relieved to arrive anywhere in my life.

Already though, I am forgetting. The word suffering seems too much.

...

In Ayacucho, the days drag on. I am waiting for another tyre to be sent from Lima, but I walk around the city, until my walking each day becomes an unconscious circling, a tracking of the same route, like I've used up all my curiosity in getting here. I walk under the arches of the plazas, in the shadows, and out of the historic centre, to where the city grows suddenly dirty, and back again. I am waiting for the tyre, but I am still shitting out the contents of my stomach before I can take real sustenance from anything I eat, and I spend the days reading and watching TV and walking identical walks. On the 7th day, I meet two students in a café and they invite me to play football. They mention something about Wayne Rooney, and tell me to meet them the next day. I spend the morning of the 8th breathless, tired, and lost on a football pitch. It is like being in dreams I have, where I order my limbs to move but they do not respond. They take me off and do not mention Wayne Rooney again.

It is good to rest without guilt. I wait for the package to come, half glad that it hasn't belittled my journey over the mountains by getting here too soon. On the 10th day the package arrives. I fix the tyre. And stronger, but not strong, I leave Ayacucho.

...

On the ridge of a mountain, as I reach sixty kilometres for the day, I pull my bike behind a pile of gravel and pitch the tent. No one is around, the city far below, and I watch as the bare mountain colour drains into the sky. I go inside to sleep.

I catch those tired minutes and hours of sleep that are not quite sleep. Or perhaps it is the sleep of our ancestors, when predators roamed; those minutes of darkness and rest and dreams, but always an open ear, a readiness to wake. It is sleep, but not sleep. Not the sleep you get behind closed doors, safe from the world, wrapped up in blankets and duvets, with nothing to wake you, but an alarm or a dream. It is a half-sleep, kept restless by imaginings. It is sleep where heartbeats sound like footsteps, and birdsong like the sharpening of knives, and the wind like someone screaming, and the distant yelps of animals like a hunting party growing near. It is a battle always, between sleep and wakefulness. And even though I know, it is better to sleep, that were true danger to come, there would be little I could do, the sleep that I fall into is always connected to the world outside. So that when a blast of light disturbs my dream, I am not surprised to find the light still there when I awake.

Three further explosions sound, like the crack of gunfire, and the sky above bursts in light through the tent walls. A flare gun. The sound of men's voices and running passes the tent, and then a sudden quiet.

"*Hola,*" I say into the light outside.

Nothing is said. Perhaps, the footsteps were further away than I thought. I look at my watch. 11.44. 11.45. Still there is light outside, and I climb out of the sleeping bag and quietly unzip the tent. The flare still hangs in the air, but dimming now, the light it casts is dull and the bodies of the voices are nowhere to be seen. I wait for the darkness to grow, and return to sleep, that is not quite sleep.

...

On the road to Cusco I meet thirteen cyclists in eight days. From the States and Japan and Switzerland, Germany and France, they have almost all started in Ushuaia, five months before, and all are heading north; some to Colombia or Ecuador, and others up to Mexico and the USA, and a couple all the way to Alaska. We exchange stories, we talk about the road and cycling things and food and sleeping and people, and no-one, not one person, asks the other why. Why is everywhere, in everything, so evident and yet impossible to describe. It is. It just is. And now maybe we are all at the stage where the why has been forgotten.

Sometimes we eat raw sugar cane from the side of the road, or share some nuts, or a map we've used. Sometimes the conversation is awkward and slow, or stilted and hard, and sometimes it's fun and easy. Sometimes we stop and talk for five minutes, and sometimes for an hour. But we always stop. And wish each other luck. And each time, as I ride away, the bike feels a little lighter.

The road to Cusco is long and dusty, full of rocks and stones. The earth beneath my wheels falls away at times, washed away by the flooding river, and carried downstream in chunks of concrete and sand. The air is hot. Eyes blinded, full of dust every time a bus passes, I stop and curse the route. I pick clumps of dried dirt, like sleep, from the corners of my eyes, and again begin to crawl towards the city.

Some days I stop after four or five hours and only a few slow miles. I am tired still. But short days make me happy. They give me time for doing things which aren't cycling. Sitting. Eating. Talking. Drinking. Reading. Nothing. And these things are good.

A few days later I reach Cusco. I climb the last slow climb of the day, over the final lip of the hill, until the city spreads out beneath me, and the street lights ignite in flickering chains, like sparks or embers across black coal. Above, a bruised and purple moon hangs huge and bursting in the sky.

...

I walk to Machu Picchu on the Salkantay route with a group of backpackers. Horses carry our bags and when we arrive at each camp our guides cook our meals. It is easy and carefree and, for these five days, I will enjoy it. Strange not to be thinking, as the afternoon sky spits rain and dark closes in, about where I will sleep, strange not to panic or curse. The path leads up through misty mountain passes and turquoise lakes, down again into the valleys and tropical heat.

On the fourth day we camp in a village and I get drunk for the first time since I fell through the roof in Ecuador. I wake alone in the tent. I remember nothing, but for the next two days, Catalonian backpackers that I do not recognise come up to me smiling and shouting *"Hey, Sam ¿qué pasa? ¿qué tal, hombre?"* like they expect to talk to someone far more confident than me. Far more fun. I do not know what I did and no one tells me. Nothing bad, they say. Nothing bad.

Across the road from our campsite a cow staggers and collapses onto a slab of concrete, its legs buckled. I do not realise it is being killed, until I follow the stream of red liquid back to an open gash in its throat. It kicks out at the air, lying now on its side, and waits to die. Two men hose away the blood and it swirls down the drain and flows along the gutter, soaking into the ground. Already, one of the hooves lies on the floor and the men set about skinning the animal. Knives are sharpened against hard stone, and incisions are made, expertly, and it strikes me that each animal must be more or less the same as I watch the skin being pulled and sliced away, the animal still warm. The men work quickly and the skin is pulled from the animal as neatly as a chef might shell a prawn or peel an orange, each specimen following the same predictable pattern. The cow is on its back now, four legs facing up towards the sky, two hoofless. The gash becomes a gaping hole, and already, the beast resembles meat; the way the fissures of white tissue stretch across the darker flesh. The animal must still be warm, yet I can see it hanging in the market.

We walk the last two days up to Machu Picchu. It is as it is in all the pictures, and we walk around the postcard for a day with that strange feeling of seeing something you have seen before.

...

I leave Cusco with Gerard, who has cycled from Ecuador after working for a few months in Cuenca.

Now the crescent moon is a thin and shining gash in the sunlit sky. And the roads are flat and blissfully smooth for the first time in hundreds of kilometres. It feels good to be moving again, to have company, to be heading further south.

We ride into a village. Across from the only *hostal*, a lady sells bread. The owner is not there. He will come back later, the lady says.

"Do you know when he will arrive?" Gerard asks.

"No está," the lady says. *"Más tarde."*

"Yes," says Gerard. "but do you know what time, more or less?"

"He's not here," she says again. And then, as though explaining something to a very stupid child, *"más tarde."*

...

The next day we follow a dirt track, along the lines of fences. Llamas and alpacas of varying species fill the fields, bathed in a frozen sun. Single storey buildings, dirt white, sit around concrete yards, the years of neglect visibly hanging from the roofs and collecting in dirty, forgotten corners. The sign from the road said The South American Camel Research Centre, but what appears before us is a ghost village of strange rectangular buildings; the most obvious thing to be surmised from any research being carried out, is that at altitudes where these animals thrive, people do not.

We ride another kilometre along the track until we see steam rising from the ground. Striped yellow red patterns run smooth in the earth and a pouring torrent of water swims, bubbling and hot. We spend the afternoon soaking and half swimming in thermal baths; at 4200m, the cold air all around. As the sun slips slowly up the mountainsides, we pitch our tents and sleep.

...

I am awoken by the hopeful light of morning, filtering through the tent walls. I watch my breath swirl above me and wonder that it does not fall, frozen to the floor, but clouds and disappears. The light glows, and then grows grey again.

Outside Gerard is awake. "It´s snowing!" he says, his voice cracked.

I undo the zip to see a white and hand-numbing snow fall from a bleak sky. We make tea, and eat cold pasta, pack wet tents, and get ready to leave.

The warm mineral water heats the earth, and steam melts the snowflakes, instantaneously to tears. I watch as the water sinks into the ground, carried to the pools below.

The llamas watch us leave. They have snow on their heads and backs, the way that roofs collect snow.

...

The road continues to climb towards the pass, and the snow falls ever thicker, drives like sleet. As we stop to drink water and rest for a moment, we see a German couple we met at the hostel in Cusco riding up behind us. Alexander and Sabina are riding from the coast in Peru to the Bolivian jungle. Gerard puts their age at 67. We haven't asked them, but as they reach us, their bikes loaded, dressed head to toe in waterproof clothing, at

4300m, they do not even seem out of breath. Alexander has told me about their last trip, kayaking around Greenland, and has touched on other adventures. He has a wonderful habit of interjecting his own speech with positive remarks, whenever he realises what he has said might be perceived as a complaint.

"No water," he says, describing the place they stayed the night before, "no electricity, and dirty. They had no blankets on the bed. But qvuite comfortable!"

We talk about the weather as we pack the water into panniers. I daren't complain.

"Qvuite comfortable, ummm?" he says. "One degree outside. Yes, yes. Very good."

I am putting on my gloves as we wave goodbye.

"Maybe we'll see you along the way," says Sabina, and we watch them ride off up, towards the pass. I am staggered at their fitness.

...

At the pass the weather breaks. The shreds of white dissipate and give way to a light blue sky and we roll down the long descent, speeding along the tarmacked roads, towards Bolivia. The mud walls of cob huts dot the flatter landscape and children trudge after their animals.

Gerard turns and says something I don't hear.

"Flying?" I call after him.

"No," he says. "Life. Life at this altitude must be hard."

"Oh, life. Yes. Really."

"Those children," he says. "And the burn marks on their cheeks."

Yes, those children. And the burn marks on their cheeks from the cold, raw sun. And those babies wrapped up against the cold, bare faces to the wind. And those children with their small flocks of sheep, and sticks and whips and cows. And cold mud huts. And those children with their children. Those children with old hands, old cheeks, old squinting eyes. And those children with their children. Life at this altitude must be hard.

A vulture cuts black circles into the sky. And we too swoop, past the cob-walled huts and the glimpses of lives, as the road flattens out onto the *altiplano*, and towards Lake Titicaca.

...

Strange now that the sun is behind us as we ride, and that we chase our shadows through the day, and that east and west have been turned upside down. If I were from a different time, I think, a time without maps, or compasses, or space crafts, satellites or missions to Mars, I feel sure I would take nothing from the fact that the position of the sun and stars has changed. How many years of watching would it take to be sure that summer follows spring, that the snow will melt and the days grow long? The sunlight glances, now blinding, off the huge expanse of water to our left. We follow its shores the whole morning until it's time to eat and we stop at a fork in the road.

"Is there a restaurant along the road?" asks Gerard a man standing there. "Or do we have to go through the village?"

"On the road there is nothing," the man says. "You'll have to go through the village."

"Okay, thanks." says Gerard. "Really, there's nothing on the road?"

"There's a restaurant."

"On this road?"

"Yes."

"And in the village?"

"Nothing. In the village there is nothing."

...

We ride on now, through dirty Peruvian cities. Juliaca, Puno, nothing to do, so we keep riding. The lake is huge; sometimes ugly and full of the stagnant stench of old fish, something rotten and dead, and sometimes the lake is beautiful - the smell of nothing but air or ice, the smell of grass or trees. Still the nights are cold, and the sun blinding and stark through the days. We stop for fried fish, rice and miserable shrivelled little black things they call potatoes, before reaching the town of Juli.

In Peru, it seems, people do not afford themselves the luxury of finishing buildings. I have been told that finished homes are taxed more than buildings under construction, and for this reason the rigid metal poles to protect walls from collapse remain uncut, or plastic tarpaulin stretches over facades and remains that way for years. The whole place seems tortured between the freezing nights and the burning days, and people slump into the shadows, like they are waiting for something to happen, without hope that anything actually will.

We stay in a miserable hotel; the woman looks at us with beady eyes and watches everything we do. She stands outside the bathroom while Gerard is washing and tells him off for wasting water. She hangs outside the door, tutting and looking at a clock.

"I'll have to charge you more," she says, and we give up bargaining and go out for a drink.

The cold bites now. The sky is black. We follow noise to a bar, the monotonous droning *dumde dum dum, dum de dum dum* beats of *reggaeton*. We take off our coats and drink beer, until we are invited over to join a group of teenagers. Gerard glances back at our coats, and a boy takes him by the shoulder and shouts into his ear, "*Qué no se preocupe, que aquí no pasa nada.*" Don't worry, he says. We stand in a circle passing around a single plastic cup of rum and coke. Each person takes a sip, and passes it to the left, and I curse the idea. I hate these stupid drinking games that get in the way of drinking, and I look around and Gerard's coat has gone.

A stupid drunken rage fills me, and for a moment the thought of fighting crosses my mind. Gerard looks to warn me as the boy comes over. There are people who do not want us there, he says. It's best to go. We walk back angry, but resigned to the loss, the black night, colder now and ice in the air, and just as we reach the hotel we here footsteps running behind us. I turn, wondering whether we can run or will have to fight. Or how many of them there'll be.

It is the boy from the bar. Gerard's coat in his arms.

"Sorry," he says as he holds it out to us. "Small towns," he says, and smiles.

Top-left: Making *panela*, Ecuador **Top-right:** outside a village meeting, Ecuador. **Bottom-left:** Desert road, Peru. **Bottom right:** El Desierto de Sechura

Clockwise from top-left: María's house, Chacchan - Parque Naciaonal Huascarán-climbing Vallunaraju – Outskirts of Lima – Machu Picchu – outside the campsite – Vallunaraju - Parque Naciaonal Huascarán

Bolivia

3rd July – 12th August, 2011

The next day we cross the Bolivian border and ride for four more days until La Paz lies before us, the highest capital city in the world, spreading out over a great deep basin. Snowy mountain summits strike into the sky, and we slide down into the city as our journey together comes to an end.

...

I look across the table at the English girl I met at a hostel in Cusco, and again in Copacabana on the shores of Lake Titicaca. At the girl I am drinking with.

"So you want to come with me?" I ask, bringing the glass to my lips. We are sat outside, the traffic heaves through the Bolivian capital and the air is thin. I want her to say yes, but I don't know if she will.

"I'd love to," she says.

We walk around La Paz looking for a bike and planning our journey through the country, south to Salar de Uyuni. There's a whole street of bike shops. This seems to be the Bolivian way; a street of electrical shops, a street of fruit shops, a street of butchers. I don't know if it was an idea, or if it has just evolved this way, and I don't know if it works, but we look in all the bike shops and find nothing. There is not one bike which costs more than £30, and not one that looks like it would last more than a day on the rough Bolivian roads.

We ask around the adventure tourism shops, but no-one will rent us a bike for a week long trip. After a whole day's search, we give up and book bus tickets to Sucre. I leave my bike in La Paz.

...

A week later I walk with her to the bus station and we say goodbye. I walk back to the hostel on my own, missing her company even as the bus is climbing out of Bolivia's capital.

It is hard to leave La Paz. I drag myself up the 9 mile climb, onto the plateau, to El Alto. I walk for two hours through the street markets looking for alcohol for my stove and when I find it, it does not ignite. I while away hours watching youtube videos in a cheap internet café. I should be sending emails. I should be writing the blog. But I do nothing. Tomorrow, will be easier, I tell myself; tomorrows often are.

In the morning, I eat a huge pile of *ispi*; fried fish and sweet boiled maize. For the first time in weeks I am on my own. Just the road. Just me, and the sky. So much more is left. Still the road unfurls, and the horizon slowly changes, and this I've never seen before, and this, and this, and this.

I stop in Sica Sica. I use the new stove I have made out of two beer cans, and people stop to look, to talk. Two young boys ask me questions; the children here so old. They are like children with an adult sadness. I offer them tea, and they decline, out of politeness it seems. As night falls, I go to lie down; a familiar yet much missed tiredness in my body, my muscles and bones. And sleep comes more easily than it has for a while and I wake with the rising sun.

...

Oruro is the last city for days. I load up on chocolate, instant soup and noodles. Still, after all this time, I underestimate the amount I eat. Even as I squeeze everything into panniers I know in a few days I will be cursing myself for not buying more.

I eat in the market stalls; warm potatoes and tripe soup that I struggle to swallow and *chicharrones* which are the most delicious thing I have found in this country, salty and crispy hot.

As I stock up on the last few things, I notice a man looking straight at me. His eyes bloodshot, I watch as he clambers to his feet and falls flat again on his face. For a moment he stays there, face down on the dirt floor, but again, he picks himself up. He is the tallest man I have seen in Bolivia, and as he staggers over towards me I look up towards his face in terror. I step back. His staggering becomes a toppling, and his toppling a run, and the run a dive as he crashes head first into the market stand, and the whole stall shakes and packets fall onto the floor, and the giant is on the floor again, looking up at the sky through drunk-blind eyes. I walk away. I have never seen people as drunk as I have in Bolivia. Four kilometres above sea level and 96 percent proof, even in Russia they didn't drink that stuff.

...

I ride south until the road becomes a corrugated track and my bones shake and rattle with the constant battering. I ride as the road turns to deep soft sand and my wheels sink, and I am forced to push. I spit and curse as my tyres puncture and at the constant pumpumpum of the track and after hours I have to fight back the tears. I can cry, if I have to. If I miss people and home. But tears of frustration are stupid. It is better to scream.

Another puncture pierces my tyre as night begins to fall so I pull off the track, and pitch up a tent. There is nowhere to hide on the *altiplano*, but nor is there anyone around. The nights are too cold for violence I tell myself, and crawl inside the sleeping bag.

I am awoken by a dream that my teeth are falling apart. It's a recurring dream. Nothing much happens. The time scale is unclear. I see myself as though in a mirror, inside white walls. It always starts as a chip in one of my front teeth. Nothing causes the chip. It is more like my teeth are crumbling by themselves. Then I notice more chipped teeth. Some teeth are broken in half. The front ones by now are no more than small triangular spikes. I never feel the pieces of teeth inside my mouth, but I feel them break away. Sometimes shoots of blood spray from the fractured teeth. I am always annoyed in the dream that my teeth are falling apart.

I wake up. I bring my hand to my mouth. My teeth are intact.

It is 2.43am. Outside it is minus 15°C. And inside it is minus 15°C because the zips don't work on my tent. The frozen midnight breeze swirls around me, invisible in the night, like a cold unwanted ghost. I think I am having this dream because almost everything I own is breaking; it is camping equipment, and people are supposed to go camping for 2 or 3 weeks, not 28 months.

In the morning I swear, half laughing, half actually angry, at the cold and useless sun, and the bottled blocks of ice, at the leaking mattress and rusty pans, panniers full of holes and ripped open tyres, and at the spaces left by lost things.

I jump, because jumping warms you up and I'm too cold to do something useful. I sing songs loud, well, bellow and shout, because around me there is nothing and nobody, and I can see all around for miles. And in the cold, bright light of morning, singing, screaming and jumping, I realise I am happy. And not just that, but excited too, about where I am, and where I'm going next, and it's a very simple joy.

Hours later, a man rides past on a rusty bicycle, herding one hundred llamas. Exactly, he tells me. We complain about the cold, and he asks if we can swap bikes, and I tell him, no. I tell him that in England with all those llamas he'd be a rich man, and he tells me that in Bolivia with all those llamas he isn't.

I watch the herd of llamas disappear, pack my things and leave without eating or drinking, the bottles still solid ice.

...

Around the corner, as promised by the deafening brass, the drunken horde stumbles and dances. Gigantic women made of pork fat, and young stick thin boys; ancient men and women full of wrinkles and hardened skin; men with shining, round faces, huge bellies and dirty shirts and women in bowler hats all cling to each other in some wonderful drunken oblivion.

One of the pork-fat-ladies tears from the crowd, half-dances to the music, and waves a plastic bottle in the air; the last remaining contents swilling around, lime green, with the movements of her arm. Others behind her wave glass bottles; those too, half empty, the glistening golden dregs of 5pm.

A sober plaza watches the parade. The melody is simple and repetitive, but the band are struggling. Round, sweaty faces, and staggering feet. The pork-fat-lady is drawn back in, stumbling and backwards, drunken joy shining on her face.

What is remarkable is that the crowd of all ages, shapes and sizes has become one thing - one gloriously drunken being that has forgotten how to dance, its many legs keeping vaguely to a beat, its hands waving bottles of all kinds, and its many faces beaming, as the afternoon grows cold.

The same sequence of notes stumbles slowly up the street and I go back into the cafe and carry on talking to Alexis.

"Every day?" I ask.

"Every day this week."

"What's it for?" I ask.

"It's a festival for... for..." she doesn't know. "We have so many festivals in Salinas." Alexis asks around the cafe. Nobody seems very sure.

A middle-aged man, sat alone, offers a vague answer. "It's a festival for a saint."

"It's a religious festival? Are you sure?" I don't know why I'm surprised, but I am. The only God the parade seems suitable for is Bacchus.

Alexis wants to go to Paris. She wants to go there more than anywhere else in the world. She likes the way they talk.

"How do you say *te amo* in French?" she asks.

"*Je t'aime*, I think," I say "but maybe that's more like *te quiero*." and the words stick out and hang loud in the room. People glance round to look at the gringo who just said *I love you* to a 17-year-old girl he's just met, and drunks make obscene gestures, laughing behind her back.

A perfectly timed crescendo outside fills the cafe; the wail of trumpets drowns out words, and the attention falls away from us to the band outside.

Alexis wants to go to Paris, but doesn't have any money. And I have that thousandth conversation - the one that goes, it's much harder for you than us, and I'm sorry I was born in Europe, but if you really want to, and you really try, it's possible.

"Yes," she says. "It's my dream to go. I'll try." There is silence. "Where do you go tomorrow?"

"The *salar*. It's beautiful, right?"

"I don't know."

"You've never been?"

"No."

"But you live here. Why not? It's supposed to be one of the most incredible places in the world."

"I don't have any money," she says, looking straight at me.

"It's 10km away. You can walk. I'm cycling there tomorrow. You don't need any money." And she doesn't say anything and I begin to doubt that she will ever go to Paris at all.

As I fall asleep later, tireless trumpets, tubas and trombones sound. Still the bottles fly in the air, now in the frozen black of night, and shouts filter through the window from the street.

In the morning, I wake to the same tune. Outside, a man already falling about alone is directed again towards the gathering hordes, and as he joins them I see that the drunken being is alive again, and haggard.

...

I ride my bike out of town, down the well-worn track towards Jiriri and Tahua, until the great white flat of the Salar de Uyuni stretches before me, and I roll onto the salt.

I ride what I think is directly south. The water starts spraying away from the tyres like riding through a puddle, and I cast off; it is like leaving dry land and I look back along the shimmering wake I've left in the water, like the slithering slime of a slug, back towards the shore.

The water is knee-deep now. I ride above the salt, through a body of water that has swallowed the sky and reflects it perfectly back, the symmetrical backs of mountains far away to the south.

I ride on, and with each pedal I submerge my foot in the freezing water. I try not to think about the damage it is doing to my bike, or my panniers, full of holes. I wonder if my books will survive.

At last the water gives way, and the salt flat becomes almost dry. I watch as the water drains through my panniers like a sieve, and still forty miles later I have no idea where I am. On the blank white plain all relation to size has gone, and I ride towards the horizon, in what I hope is a straight line, towards the town of Uyuni. As the sun sinks though, I am lost on the salt. All around me is only white, and tiny mountains far away. In the cold white dusk, not knowing where I am, I pitch a broken tent and sleep.

...

To the south of Uyuni, the road worsens still, and the long slow days on the washboard surface leave my wrists aching and weak. Villages lie half-empty. There is nothing to be gained, it seems, from the road and the passing trade, so the villagers turn their back on the world, and sit, huddled and cold. I ask around for a restaurant or a café and the people stare at me like I've just asked for caviar and champagne to be brought to me on a platter. There's a shop, they say, in that building over there, and I pedal away over the bumpy road and peer in at the dark room through an open door.

"*El pan está duro por el frío,*" the woman says miserably. The bread's hard because it's cold. But already I see the green mottling of mould creeping into the crusts. I put it down, and smile apologetically. "*Qué más hay?*" I ask and she hands me a dusty packet of old biscuits and two tiny chocolate bars for children.

"*Quince,*" the woman says, and I pay, wondering how much it should really cost, and leave.

Outside a man is standing, hovering over my bike and when he sees me, he begins to walk over.

"Pzzfk," he says. It sounds like pzzfk. With his eyes glazed and shining, and white frothy saliva collecting in the corners of his mouth. "Pzzfk," he says again, his eyes stare through me.

"*Pzzfk?*" I ask. "*Qué es eso?*"

"*Pzz... pzzfeeto,*" he says, his hand held out.

I ask him what it's for. To get more drunk? And he smiles, almost toothless, and his eyes close, and he gathers himself and nods, once. His head hangs staring at the ground. He looks up, I shake my head, and he stays there, fixed, with a smile.

I gather my things, put the stale biscuits and the chocolate in a plastic carrier bag, and leave the village behind. Women sit outside huts, staring at a sandy, washboard road, at deserted buildings and broken glass. They throw stones at dogs to teach them something, shout at children, hit goats with sticks, and sit, waiting for the men to come home. And the men drink the 96% alcohol that I use as fuel for my stove. And the villages are dead and empty, or dying. And the countryside has moved to the city.

...

The road drops down steep climbs and up again, and the bike rattles, a constant hammering, and I wonder that it has not fallen apart. A puncture hisses, for the third or fourth time today, and I stop. I have no energy to be angry. I throw the panniers on the floor, turn the bike upside down and set about releasing the inner tube. It's a break from the jarring of the road, I think, but a joyless break. Everything is covered in sand and dust from the road. I hook the last pannier onto my bike and bob away, with each light blow thinking the tyre will burst. A silhouette comes over the crest of the hill. A woman pushing a loaded bike.

"It's a pretty awful road," she says.

"Is it bad for a long way?"

"More than a day. I think," and she looks down at the milometer on her bike, "about 124km."

"About 124?"

"Well, it's really bad, yeah. I've been counting. What about the next village?"

"I think about 25 kilometres."

"And there's a shop?"

"There's something," I say.

"Aah," she says. "Bolivia. Nothing ever works."

We talk about the dirty hotels and the empty promises of hot water, and the dirt floored shops and their empty shelves, and the constant sitting and waiting; that cold, high stagnation everywhere. Even the money tears and crumbles, like worn out scraps of paper.

"It's beautiful, though," she says. "It's very, very beautiful. A strange beauty, you know."

I agree, and we say goodbye and wish each other luck. I follow the track, carved into the cliff, hanging above a landscape dotted with cacti, and red blue hills. Deep canyons cut through the sandy earth, and spiralling turrets of rock shoot out from the ground, and I follow the corrugated track all the way to Tupiza, as it turns into a road, and Argentina grows near.

Clockwise from top-left: La Paz, Bolivia – Lake Titicaca – Hot springs, Peru – Salaar de Uyuni – Tupiza, Bolivia – Abandoned villages, Bolivian altiplano– Sabina and Alexander – Gerard, Abra la Raya

Argentina

12th August – 8th October, 2011

There are no searches at the border, and no questions; the border guards smile politely, stamp my passport and give me a three month visa. I have waited in line for no more than ten minutes. Such efficiency is unnerving, and I wait for a moment at the window, to be handed a form, or for someone else to come out, but they do not.

"¿Ya está?" I ask.

"Ya está. Bienvenido a Argentina."

I roll past the guards. Funny, I think, how I no longer flinch at the sight of guns like I used to. I ride into the border town of La Quiaca, and not much changes; there is a little less rubbish, the buildings a little neater, but not much else. Perhaps, at 3500m above sea level, not much can change.

I stop for a moment in front of a sign. *Ruta Nacional 40 - Ushuaia 5080km.* It is the first sign for Ushuaia. The first sign for the end.

The road runs straight out of town, and the sky is the same deep blue Andean sky, and the same *altiplano* stretches on. There are sign posts on the road for the first time in months, and fences run on both sides, and cars pass, the light hum of new engines; VWs, Chevrolets and Fords and behind the glint of windscreens, European faces. Outside though, the faces are still the same round faces of Bolivia and Peru; soft features, brown skin and high, sunburnt cheeks. This part of Argentina used to belong to Bolivia and, in a way, it does so still. As night falls I pull off the road, and drag my bike through a break in the fence, and down to the wide river valley.

...

The next day, the Altiplano comes to an end and the mountain falls away in jagged rocks. My bike should fly down the long fast descent, but a wind is raging below, and I fight against it, even when the road is steep. I wonder if it's true, about the wind in Patagonia being worse than anywhere else, and I hope that it is not. Still the road descends, down and down until I can feel the heat from the sun again, warm and hazy through the thicker air, and the road flattens out. I cross the Tropic of Capricorn. I have been in the tropics for more than 11 months, almost a year to go not so far. I have moved like an insect caught in honey.

North of Salta, the road winds through hills and shady woods, past lakes, and along streams. The city is pleasant and organized. Expensive looking cafés and arches surround the plazas, and on the polished stone walls I see a poster for a cinema festival. It seems like another world; beautiful to look at, but too expensive to touch.

I ride south to the city's campsite, take the wrong turning over a bridge and the city falls to pieces. A toothless drunk with scars across his cheeks and a dirty t-shirt, stained the colour of dried blood, staggers towards me and I ride away. There are houses with no windows and no doors. I ride past an overgrown yard; broken concrete and broken glass. Two men start arguing and a woman screams, drunk and frightened screaming, and two children run inside.

A man on a scooter slows and looks straight at me. "*Afuera,*" he says. "Get out."

I ride on. I'm trying to leave, but I don't know if I'm riding towards a dead end or whether it's going to get worse. Already it would be difficult to turn around. An old car stops, the door opens and a man steps out. This is the part, I think, where they take all my stuff, and watch me walk out of this place with no money and no bike. If they watch me walk out. If it is not worse. What a funny way for it to end; a wrong turn over a bridge. But then any way is a funny way, I suppose. A ridiculous, silly way.

"*Aquí, no puedes estar,*" says the man. You can't be here.

"*Ya me di cuenta,*" I say. I realised. "I'm just lost. Sorry. *Lo siento.*"

"*No,*" he says, "*Lo siento, no,*" and I wonder if this is when he says, not sorry, but your money and your passport and your bike. But he just says, follow me. He gets back in the car, and I follow it out as it jumps through red lights and I feel that I'm being followed by unwelcome stares the whole way, until at last we are out on the main road and the car horn hoots and I wave relieved, and search again for the campsite.

...

A hot and sandy wind blows through Quebrada de las Conchas, so that the best part of the day is stopping. The wind has blown against the landscape until, now, there is nothing left; only the deep blue sky and the red rocky earth; clouds, grass, trees and plants, carried far away. Even the red earth seems to be disappearing; worn bare and hollow under overhangs, where the wind batters and eats it away.

...

The road climbs towards 3000m, leaving Amaicha del Valle and the warm red earth around Cafayate to the north. The mountainsides are covered with stubborn scrubby brush and hundreds of cacti, like giant hands pointing fat fingers to the sky.

The road climbs further still. A shimmering of ice and dusty snow clings to the floor and the sun is lost in a thick and freezing mist. Even with the effort of climbing and extra layers I am cold. White icicles hang from bare tree branches, and tiny blades of grass are white and frozen still.

At the summit, a vicious wind stings my face, and fingers. Granite boulders stand backed into the gusts of burning wind, bare on one side, their sheltered faces scattered with ice and snow, carved like crystals by the relentless wind, and at last I begin the descent. The cold has seeped into my hands now, and my fingers sting, even under thick gloves. My toes grow numb and then burn like they've been set on cold fire. The road descends and the wind bites hard. The pain becomes hard to bear and as I ride down the mountain, into the wind, a dry and tearless sobbing catches in my throat. For an hour and a half, I am caught between trying to cry and screaming in anger and pain at the freezing wind, and at last the town comes into view and the pain becomes a tingling pins and needles, and I search for food, a place to sleep and warmth.

...

Further south, I walk the green streets of Catamarca. The central plaza is shady, and the people smile politely and say hello, and some ask me where I'm from and what I'm doing. School girls play near the fountain, and teenagers shout and laugh and push each other, boisterous and noisy in a town with not that much to do. There was a time when I might have called its pleasantness boring. But now, there is something quite wonderful about sitting on a bench, around trees in a square, speckled with the shadows of leaves, and the burble of passing conversation and laughter.

I go to buy ice-cream. It is another new Argentinian joy; rich, delicious ice-cream that I can afford. The girl in the shop is too pretty and I stumble over the words.

"*Una cucaracha,*" I say. She stifles a laugh.

"*Quieres una cucaracha?*" she asks.

"*No, no,*" I say. "*Perdón.*" I am still too slow for humour in this language. "*Un cucurucho.*" A cone, not a cockroach.

The girl asks me what I'm doing here and when I tell her she looks at me for a moment.

"*Qué lindo!*" she says, and turns to the other girl. "He's riding around the world."

The girl comes over and asks me simple questions with wide eyes. Sometimes I forget that what I'm doing is a surprise to other people. And the girl's surprise makes her prettier, and her prettiness makes me awkward and shy, and I bring the conversation back to the ordering of ice-cream so I can leave, even though I want to stay.

"*Y la bici?*" she asks as I walk out the shop.

"*En el camping.*"

"*Ah,*" she says, and I wonder if she mistrusts what I have told her, and she looks up again and smiles. "*Pues, que te vaya bien.*"

"*Igualmente,*" I say, and turn around.

At the campsite I talk with a family, as people light kindling beneath *parrillas*, and smoke rises and snaps in sparks before the charcoal ignites and glows red.

The woman looks at me. "*¿No tienes miedo?*" she asks. You're not afraid?

"I was scared at the start," I say. "But I'm not now." And as say those simple words it seems somehow to be the whole story. The beginning, middle and the end.

I tell them about the kindnesses of all the strangers I have known, and that in almost every single country I have been taken in to people's homes, and welcomed and given shelter and food. I tell them that it's been the same all around the world. That I have learnt not to be afraid. Though at times of course, I feel something like fear, it doesn't do any good.

"The most dangerous thing is the traffic," I say. "People are good."

Before they go, the woman turns to me and wishes me good luck.

"*Y, no confíes en nadie,*" she says kindly. Don't trust anyone.

I want to stop her, and say no. That is exactly not what I was saying. Yes, trust people, I want to say. And strangers. You haven't understood. People are good, is what I said. But I am not the news; not as convincing or relentless as the papers, I am just one boy. If all else is telling you not to trust, then I guess that's what you'll do.

In the morning I make a small detour to the shady plaza, for the ice-cream I tell myself. The girl is not there.

...

The road is perfect and smooth. An effortless movement, more like sailing than cycling, carries me through the sunny day on an immense and blustering wave. I feel the wind's hands upon my back and I am pushed along the great flat road at fifty kilometres an hour, not even the ticklish touch of air resistance on my face.

I am in love with Argentina, with its small and wonderful things. With the bread that is fresh, not chewy and stale, and the cheese that tastes of cheese. With the olive oil on shop shelves, and with the apples that are not powdery deceptive lies, but crisp and juicy. With the meat that melts and wine that doesn't make you grimace and shudder at its scent.

Everything is good. Glossy, shining supermarkets, shelves piled high with food. Clear cold drinkable tap water and strong hot showers. Signposts, cleanliness, order and receipts. Queues and politeness. Everything is good. And the wind keeps pushing at my back. The sun glints off windscreens, hands wave, horns sound and carry me easily south. I am flying, I think, and I've almost cycled round the world. Just a few thousand kilometres and I'll be there. And it's easy, so easy. What a wonderful, easy end.

Then there is a change. The wind flails and twists around until it is there in front of me, its cold breath fierce like a wall, whipping up sand. The wind robs happiness with a relentless unkindness, and empties me of everything.

I hate Argentina, and all of its terrible things. Its food is expensive and the bustling, raucous street markets have disappeared, to be replaced by cold impersonal fluorescent lights, and loyalty cards, and car parks, and queues. Its billboards are everywhere saying stupid things. And everything closes for four idiotic hours in the middle of the day. And the countryside is a monotonous desert full of sand and nasty plants and barbed wire fences, and wild camping is a nightmare. And traffic jams and roundabouts and ring roads.

The wind sweeps me off the road, over and over, and I can't lift my bike against it. I'm on my knees and screaming, furious angry words, that tumble lost behind me, and the wind here doesn't listen, even when you scream.

The wind keeps pushing and holding me down, and like a leaf, like a play thing, like a plastic bag, I'm thrown all over the road. The sun that glints off windscreens laughs, and the hands that wave and horns that sound smack only of schadenfreude, and I am fighting slowly south. I'm tired of this. This stupid idea. I only want it to end. I picture the map in my mind; how the long curling foot of the Andes stretches down towards Antarctica. My stupid, stupid idea.

...

The roads are long again and the landscape has become a flat never-ending nothingness.

I pull my bike off the road at dusk; a day or two north of Cordoba. I am convinced this must be one of the very worst places on earth; desolate, barren, full of flies and nasty plants. I drag my bike away from the road, dodging cacti, until I find a slight dip in the plain; enough to obscure the tent from the road, but not to hide it completely. I wait for the sky to turn black, and crawl inside; angry snatches of wind rip down the walls. I do not worry about being seen during the night. People have sensibly decided not to live here.

It is Sunday when I reach Cordoba. The city of one million people seems pointless. Nothing happening, quiet and dull, no markets or street food. I walk into a McDonalds, the only place open that seems affordable, and walk straight back out again when I see the prices. With ten pounds a day, I am no longer rich.

...

I ride west towards Mendoza, on the Ruta 40 again. I ride from nowhere to nowhere; from one barren landscape, where I pitch a tent, to another. Sometimes I ride all day into a constant wind and after 10 hours riding I have made 45 miles. Making miles, I think. Counting down. Wishing away. It is too early to be thinking like this, but the wind drives on, and it takes all my strength to ride into it. Slow as climbing mountains. The wind makes crooked the plants and gnarls the trees, so that everything is stunted, and I go to sleep with the battering of it still in my ears

I reach the northern edge of Patagonia and pitch my tent in sight of Volcán Tromen. It is one more milestone. One more border. And the world is beautiful again. I am happy, I realise, but ready for the end. I am so close, but still I know there are 2,000 miles to go. Just 2,000 miles. Only, 2,000 miles. But 2,000 miles. A month, perhaps.

The wind begins whistling, and the plants shiver and shake in their eternal torment. I hammer the pegs in and weigh the tent down with my bike and the panniers, but the guide ropes won't stick, the ground too loose and sandy, full of rocks. I tie the ropes around stones to anchor it, and as they seem to hold, I climb in to sleep.

All night I am aware that there is nothing between me and the great howling wind but two thin sheets of material. I imagine being tossed up in the sky, like a kite, as the fabric snaps taut and waves rush down the tent walls. I cover my ears against the deafening noise. It feels like all the power of the sky has come together and is blowing straight at me. I sleep in snatches before being woken by the wind again, and in the pitch-black night I feel beneath for solid ground.

I do not know if I am awoken by the faint light of dawn, or the sudden silence and stillness of the air, but when I open my eyes it is morning and, for a brief moment, it seems the wind has died.

I rush, preparing to leave; fold and roll and stuff and pack until everything is ready. But now the wind is alive and coming from the east. The tent wall is bearing down on me and I run outside quickly to get the tent down. The wind whips and a guide rope pulls a stone loose. The wind digs a vicious dip into the tent and two tent poles bend, and snap. I release the last pole, before that snaps too, and try to gather everything together. I stuff the tent, unzipped, into a rucksack, and I stand, holding the two snapped poles, shards of angry metal, and scream into the wind.

I roll the bike back to the road, blind to any beauty I may have seen before. The wind blows all day. I lean into it with all my weight, but still it sweeps me across the road, and takes my wheels from beneath me. Again and again, I am pushed off the road, and I fall down on the rocky hard shoulder. Two hours later, I reach a village, and patch the tent poles with the last of my repairs. If another one breaks, I will not have a tent. Will not have shelter.

I leave the village and still the wind is there. Howling and tireless. Pummelling. Emptying. I hate it. There is not a human on this planet, not a thing on Earth, that I hate as much as this wind. What did I do to it? I wonder. What the fuck did I do? It is a hateful, hateful thing. And my legs turn slow and hard. And I have no energy to scream, and I just turn my legs, resigned, and my mouth is locked in silence. I'm empty. If I make a noise, I feel sure that I will cry. I ride another 6 hours into wind. Another thirty miles. At this rate, I calculate, it will take me another three months to reach Ushuaia.

...

South I ride still and with each pedal I am closer, with each rotation of the wheels. But I put so much into pushing and get so little back. The dry wind drives on, cold from the south, and the roads stretch on without end. Corrugated dirt tracks go on for miles and even when the tarmac runs smooth, it is a joyless tunnel of wind and my bike swerves dangerously, barely under control. I ride from nowhere to nowhere. One night, as I turn straight into the wind after hours of riding, I do not pitch the tent. I am too tired and I fear that it would be whipped out of my hands, and carried away in gusts. I pull the bike behind a pile of dirt and hide from the road. The sand whips hard and stings my face and the sky has become a timeless grey; not dusk nor dawn nor day, but grim and sunless. I build a barricade with my bike and bags, and roll the sleeping bag out behind it. I listen to the sand ringing and shattering on the bags like tiny shards of glass and listen to the wind howl all around me and I bury myself in the sleeping bag and hope for the wind to die. Please, I hear myself say to no-one, and realise I am praying.

...

At some point in all the falling off the road, and the battering of the wind, my camera has been broken. Now I look at the lakes around Bariloche and the wooden beamed buildings, like some kind of theme park version of Switzerland, just to look. I will have to remember this myself, I think. What I do not realise is that I will remember everything at some point in my life. That I will be walking to work and a picture of a pile of logs will enter my mind, or a layby, or a distant corner of a forest, or the burbling of a stream, or a recollected scent or a familiar sound, and, at first, I will not be able to place them. And I will think, is that me? Is it from my life? These strange fragments of the world that I must carry at all times, that must always be there, the whole of what I've seen, and smelt and heard, and touched. And though I will not be able to beckon life and memory and make it appear, it will always be there; the whole of what I am.

Clockwise from top left: Crossing the Tropic of Capricorn – A broken tent – A silver mine, Potosí – A cold pass, Argentina

Chile

8th October – 14th October, 2011

I cross the border into Chile and the rains begin; the sky a constant mist, and falling drizzle, or a torrential wall of water.

The road slips through the mountains, along river banks, inlets and lakes; the obscure damp border between the land and the sea. For the few brief moments of light, when the snagged shreds of blue appear fleetingly in the sky, it is beautiful. But the sky soon closes in, and the world becomes only a suffocating haze. Thick undergrowth bears in upon the road; it is jungle-like, but cold. The thick green leaves creak under the water, and all around the earth is mud and swamp, the sound of sodden branches falling. And the road is a thin gravel line, unsurfaced but smooth, and the sand and tiny stones crunch under my tyres. I roll further south, slow but constant.

As night falls, I pull my bike from the road and into the vegetation. I follow tracks or paths to clearings, or roll my bike through the long, wet grass and over fallen branches, hear the dull uncrunching collapse of their rotten bodies as my weight crushes them further into the ground. I find a piece of flat ground, soft, but not yet swamp, and I begin to pitch the tent. Around me, soggy bark, and bearded moss drip wet, drenched in silver droplets.

After six days camping and not a dry day, everything is wet. The walls are damp and smell of rain and mould, and my sleeping bag is cold and sticky with old rain and sweat, and possibly crawling things. My clothes are wet, my panniers are wet, and the books wrapped in plastic bags have shrivelled up their backs, complaining of damp and mildew and neglect. My fingers and toes are wrinkled, as though I live in a bath.

After a month of no rain in Argentina, the dry air had traced dusty, spider-webbed marks all over my skin. Now, in a cold wet Chile, I feel like I'm becoming an amphibian. Only that I feel less comfortable in this cold, wet tent than a toad might.

...

The next day I reach Villa Mañihuales and I walk into a shop. Its wooden walls, and half-empty shelves remind me of the small desolate villages of the Bolivian altiplano, only that everything here is three or four times more expensive. I have the details of someone to stay with, but the paper is soggy and the ink has run so that the address can no longer be seen.

"This may be a strange question," I say. "But, I'm looking for the ummm.... the cyclist hunter?"

"Aah! Jorge. Sí sí, claro. El cazador de ciclistas! La casa de ciclistas!" The shopkeeper draws me a map on the soggy piece of paper and I arrive at the house on a bicycle laden with soaking, dripping wet things.

When the door opens I don't say anything. I have not called or written, but Jorge smiles a real smile, hugs me and tells me that I'm the first cyclist of the year. His wife Diana and daughter Nickole come to greet me. "Come in, bring your bike. This is the kitchen, there's a shower and hot water - you can wash and dry your clothes. This room's used as a church, but not until the weekend. Help yourself to cake. Do you want a cup of tea? This is your house - you mustn't pay anything. We're happy to have you here."

And in such warmth, I make myself at home in Jorge's house, flicking through the pages of messages left by the many cyclists who have stayed here over the years.

...

I leave *La casa de ciclistas* with dry clothes on my back and in my panniers for the first time in a week. The road traces a thin grey line between the mountains and the sea. Farm houses sit on hillsides, behind wooden fences and the rumble of a distant tractor sputters through the trees. I drag my bike back into the forest and camp on the misty shore of a lake; fallen trees slink into the water, and round pebbles lie on the ground, coated in moss. The shadow of the far shore disappears and again the sky closes in. This southern corner of Chile would be a beautiful place, if I could see it.

Argentina

14th October – 8th November, 2011

I cross the border further south. The rain stops and the green of Chile disappears, replaced by a barren dirt brown. The steep mountain slopes and luscious valleys are left behind as the earth stretches out into the long open flats around the Ruta 40. Beauty vanishes, and the wind again is born.

...

I ride for whole days along unbroken wire fences. Two days, three days at a time. Sometimes the wind carries me, bumping unstably along the corrugated roads, or gliding along rare tarmac. More often though it sweeps me from side to side or claws away at me the way an ocean wind eats away at a cliff until its overhangs collapse into the sea. I wonder if I am getting smaller, worn away by the wind; my parts and fragments lost, and tumbling.

I spend days looking out at the world through the fences. They are so constant, the length of small countries, that it seems they have burned sad lines across my retinas. The wind kicks up the sand from the road in a constant bluster, a wind full of rage, striking against the fences. Is it too much to think that the world is angry?

At night I climb down from the road and sleep under it, in the drainage tunnels. It is easier than pitching a tent in the wind, and without lifting my bike and all my panniers over the wire fences, I am left with no other option. The silence of the night is broken only once or twice, by the rumbling engine of a lorry overhead. I listen in the dark as the sound, loud enough to wake me, fades away to silence.

...

The road is long and straight. Grey gravel, and the slow up down up down of the wheels. I ride for hours, my arms shaking into the corrugated road, and my eyes tired and stoned and dull; not a grimace or a smile, just the long gravel road running below.

There is a scraping in the pedals that will not go away. It is a new sound, and I have come to dread new sounds that I cannot explain or fix. There is no town for hundreds of kilometres, and in twelve hours on the road I might see three or four cars. The days are plagued by winds, or plagued by punctures and other mechanical failures, and I turn the pedals blindly from first to last light. Just get it done, I think. It is a new thought. A miserable thought. The opposite of what I am doing, but slowly as the wind grows and everything seems grey it is there; a constant nagging as the gravel rolls underneath and the scraping becomes a horrible wrenching wail with every turn of the pedals. Just get it done. Get it done. Get it done.

...

Progress is slower than I thought. I look at the map and at my food in anger at myself, overcome by a sudden sense of fear. The next village is miles away, much more than a day. And I have half a packet of crackers, an old tiny pot of disgusting pâté and a stupid bottle of balsamic vinegar. What the fucking hell was I thinking, buying balsamic vinegar?

I ride now slow and empty, and I wonder whether, if I go slowly, I can ride without consuming energy. The wind eats away at me. I want to collapse or cry. But I try to subdue the bitter rage I feel at the place – anger uses up food. I sleep under the road without eating. I am still 100km from the next village; I will need that food tomorrow.

I ride through what is almost a desert. But it is not the desert I see; rather a stream of rich, colourful food rolls in front of my eyes; garlic bread and soup, and garlic bread again, and risotto, and food I haven't eaten for years, and I ride, trying not to think of food, and thinking only of food. And a girl. There is a girl, with dark hair. A kind smile. I do not know the girl. And I glimpse her only in fleeting moments. In flashes. Eyes. Lips. The light touch of a hand. And the warmth of home. The warmth and softness of a bed. And white sheets. The green hills of home. A walk along the beach. Waves crashing on a Cornish shore. A cup of tea, wood coloured; translucent mahogany and white china. A cat and a fire. My family. My brother. My mum. My dad. I hear the laughter of friends and see smiles around a table. And then food again. Shared. Warm, rich food. Spoonfuls of chili and rice, and a crisp salad, and crusty bread. The pedals screech and I feel them grow stiff, and hard to turn. Though perhaps I can simply push no longer, and I stop, and eat the food, shaking. The last crumbs of crackers I eat soaked in balsamic vinegar. The acid taste on my lips reminds me for the next few hours I have eaten everything I have.

...

At Tres Lagos the road becomes a road; a kind ribbon of tarmac. I buy more food than I need from the village shop, stuffing it into my mouth, faster than I can swallow. My pedals have seized up so much that I can no longer turn them, and I push the bike, walking up the hills and rolling down them, until at last, 40 miles from El Calafate, I wave down a pick-up truck to take me to the town. There was a point in this journey when the compromise would have upset or angered me, but as we reach the town, I only feel relief.

...

I leave El Calafate with a new bottom bracket. The wailing sound has gone and the pedals turn with ease. I look down and touch the cold frame of my bike for a moment. It is the same bike I left with two years and seven months ago. Almost the same. New wheels, and pedals, and chains, but its core is the same. I have never taken so much from an inanimate object before, nor given so much either. We are almost there, I think. We have almost carried each other around the world. I have to remind myself that only one of us cares.

I think of seeing my brother, in Buenos Aires, when this is over. When this is done. When I have finished. Even though I am almost there, what I imagine is a different person. Not the me now, but the future me who has cycled around the world. I still don't know who that person will be, but I hope that my brother will be the same. The thought of seeing him helps me fight into the wind, and keeps me going.

...

The next sign I see for Ushuaia says 600km. Then 300km. 200km. 150km. And then it is there, over the final mountain, the final climb, the final descent. The end in sight. The end.

...

That night I go out to drink. To celebrate. I buy a pint of Guinness for £4, and sit down at the table of some backpackers. Three German girls are opening a bottle of wine that isn't the first, or the second, or most probably the third.

"You know the most beautiful place I've ever been?" the girl is saying. "New England in fall. It's just the colours – they're sooo... beautiful. Like red and brown and orange, and you know, beautiful. Have you ever been to the States?"

I nod. "Not the east though."

"You have to go! You've never really travelled until you've been to New York. It's *amazing*." She lets the long 'a' sound linger and waits for me to ask her about New York. I am tired.

"Do you know what there is to do here?" she asks. "We went on a boat trip earlier, but it was kind of boring, you know. It's like, it's cool 'cos it's the southernmost point and you've gotta say you've done it, but Ushuaia – it's kind of boring. We're gonna get flights to Buenos Aires in a couple of days. I *love* Buenos Aires. Have you been?"

"No."

"You've *never been* to Buenos Aires? What are you *doing* here?"

"I'm just cycling."

"Oh. You should go to Buenos Aires – it's *really* cool."

I put the empty pint glass down on the table, say goodbye and walk outside. Even now at night, the sky is tinged with blue. The air bites, a light breeze stings my face. And I look out, over the water at the never-ending world, and I realise that perhaps all I was ever doing was looking for a story. I am at the end, and I don't know if I have found one.

United Kingdom

My parents are waiting for us at the airport. It is the first time we have been together for almost three years. Since the evening we sat at the port in Plymouth, waiting for the ferry. The sky dark then, the first night of spring. My dad had bought take-away pizza and we sat on the harbour walls. I pulled at the stringy cheese, feeling guilty after eight years of veganism. I didn't know what to say. They didn't know what to say. So for a little while we sat in silence, before it was time to say goodbye. It was a time when words just wouldn't fit. When they couldn't really say anything. When everything was unknown. So, for minutes at a time, we just sat. It was the scariest thing I had ever done. And it was worse for them. As I think of it, it seems that everything was different then, but I can't explain why.

I do not cycle home, from London to Cornwall. Perhaps I should, but I am tired of cycling. Besides, I've done it before. The first trip I made by bicycle. I was 19, cycling home from university on a mountain bike from Halfords, without a pump, a map or oil. Just a cheap bike, a backpack and a couple of addresses of friends I knew along the way.

I was trying to impress a girl then. I don't know what I was thinking. It hadn't worked, of course. Going for long bike rides doesn't impress girls. Or if it does, it's not the kind of impressed which makes them fall in love with you.

I did find something, though. That I loved. That didn't need to love me back.

I loved the way my bike rolled out of London, along the green banks of the Thames, and the feeling that I wasn't going to turn around. I loved the excitement at every turn, and every new village and town. I loved the way the world felt, how I began to understand the distance between each place. The way, I didn't have to wait to get anywhere, that I was somehow always there. I loved every conversation, and every person I met, and the feeling of crossing the Tamar, of turning a five-hour journey into a journey of five days.

So, the next year, I rode a little further, from Land's End to John O Groats, and the next, a little further, from London to Rome, until at last I was sitting in my room, cross-legged on my bed, poring over an atlas - tracing the lines of roads, spreading from Europe to the east. Imagining camels, bullets and my death.

Acknowledgments

I am deeply indebted to everyone who was part of this journey. Those who provided shelter, food, company and kindness are too numerous to be held in these pages, but I would like to extend my sincere thanks to each of you. Thanks especially to Jeremy, Ivan, Igor, Yulas, Yulya, Oksana, Lesy and Lena, Sasha, Olena and her family in Poltava, Gerna, Victor, Gerna and Svetlana, Dima and Olga, Mikhail and Anatole, Anton, Alex and Sasha, Mad Dog Song, Tiggy and Martin and everyone in Kuala Lumpur, Ichenck and friends, Desy, Guntur, Fitsariati and Fany, Alastair and Andi, Debbie and everyone in Perth, Frog and Amy, Briony, The Davies family, Garrick and Gerry, Derek and Anne, Matt in Manly, David and Megumi, Catherine, Stephen and Michael, Jayni and Carmelo, Paul and Rosemary, Scott and everyone in Garibaldi, Zach and his family in San Francisco, Nate in Santa Barbara, Mario and his family, Elvia and David, Bisma and Jose, Humberto's family, Norely, Marta, Brent, Don Humberto and Doña Muriela, Gonzalo and Silvia, Iván and Vera, Steve and Lupe, Marcos and Maria.

Thanks to those I travelled with. Jan, Emilie, Arnaud, Ren Hong Chang, John, Mook, Boonlert, my mum, my dad, Mario, Sophie, Gerard and my brother, Joe.

The journey raised money for Shelterbox and the fantastic work they do. Thank you to everyone who donated so generously and worked so hard to fundraise. Special thanks to the Allen family at the Deli in the Square and St Aubyn Arms, Andrew Body, Mervyn Hall, The Ingleheart Singers, Crowan Church, Crowan School and Camborne School.

Thank you to all of those who helped and gave support from home. To Jo and Shey, to Jez with fondest memories and Pam. Thanks to my wonderful friend, John for bringing the wheel to Thailand. Thanks to Dave in Ulaanbaatar, to The Rotary Club, Shelterbox, and Clowance Estate.

I give my thanks to Lynne, Gill, Michelle and Phil, for their feedback and guidance on this book, but lay on them no responsibility for its shortcomings.

My love and thanks to Charlotte, for living for years, not just with me, but with an unfinished manuscript, even after working all summer so I could write.

Lastly, to my parents. Thank you for your untiring love and support. For all that you have done. This book is dedicated to you.

Printed in Great Britain
by Amazon